Journal of the American Revolution

JOURNAL

OF THE

AMERICAN REVOLUTION

ANNUAL VOLUME 2022

WESTHOLME
Yardley

Westholme Publishing, LLC
904 Edgewood Road
Yardley, Pennsylvania 19067
Visit our Web site at www.westholmepublishing.com

ISBN: 978–1–59416–385–2

Printed in the United States of America.

CONTENTS

EDITOR'S INTRODUCTION

For the second year in a row, the online content of *Journal of the American Revolution* has been strongly influenced by current events, reminding us of patterns in history and the importance of viewing current events in a broad context. And as it always does, this annual volume contains a selection of articles from the online publication, many of which resonate strongly with recent events in the United States and around the world.

The shortcomings of the Electoral College system for deciding presidential elections were recognized at the time the system was instituted, but so were the shortcomings of every viable alternative. Impeachment was included in the United States Constitution as a safeguard against abuses by certain elected officials, and officials have been impeached since the nation's earliest days. Techniques for reducing the impact of deadly diseases—in this case, inoculation for smallpox—have always been accompanied by controversy. The United States has always had a diverse population, but the roles and contributions of Native Americans, African Americans, and women of all backgrounds are largely understated when the complexity of past eras is summarized as a few major events driven by a few senior leaders. And of course, history includes the actions, interactions, and experiences of countless individuals, each leading their own complex life, making decisions without knowing what the future would bring. This is the present, and it was also the past.

The point is not to arrive at a simple conclusion, such as "history repeats itself," but to recognize that knowledge of historical events is crucial in keeping current events in perspective. The questions of today may have been asked before. The institutions and mores of today came about through debate, conflict, compromise, and reason. The severity of today's events has been seen before. History helps us learn from the past in order to face the present in a rationale, informed manner.

Massachusettensis and Novanglus: The Last Great Debate Priot to War

JAMES M. SMITH

When John Adams returned to Massachusetts after the session of the First Continental Congress, he was surprised to find that there was growing opposition to the radicals and the work of the Congress. It was led by a man who identified himself as "Massachusettensis." On December 12, 1774 Massachusettensis published the first of a series of articles in which he decided to take the American "patriots," as he says they styled themselves, head on. His pamphlets were very readable and persuasive. There were seventeen letters in all, each published about a week or ten days apart. When Adams heard about the articles and the influence they were having on the population in Massachusetts, he wrote a reply under the name of "Novanglus." In the last few articles written by Massachusettensis, the author replied to Adams and in the last article evaluated the work of the First Continental Congress. In these two men the two sides had a final argument in which issues were discussed and analyzed prior to fighting actually breaking out. After that it was too late for any more discussions of this sort.

History books often acknowledge the articles of Massachusettensis but only refer to them to allow a fuller discussion of the articles written by Adams under the name of Novanglus, thus allowing a further defense of the patriot's point of view. If, as Adams feared, Massachusettensis was persuasive enough to have a serious impact on the people of Massachusetts, to the extent that the position of the radicals was feeling threatened, then what Massachusettensis had to say needs to be understood.[1] In the preface to the 1776 publication of the Massachuset-

---

1. The letters were originally printed as separate broadsheets with the first appearing on December 12, 1774 and the last on April 3, 1775. In 1776 they were combined into a single publication in London. That is the publication used for this discussion.

tensis letters in London, the editor explained that the word "Tory" had a very different meaning in America from the understanding of the word in England. In America a Tory was "a friend to the supremacy of the British Constitution over all the Empire. A Whig is an asserter of colonial independence, or, what is just the same, one who supports the idea of legislation, distinct and divided from British legislation, in all the several provinces." These are the meanings that Massachusettensis used throughout his letters.[2]

In the first four letters the author related the history of the resistance movement in Massachusetts. He referred to the muzzling of the press, the intimidation of people who tried to speak out in favor of the government, the burning and destruction of property, and the physical abuse some endured through tarring and feathering. The radicals "cut the bands of society asunder," and he asked the question, "is not civil government dissolved?" "We feel the effects of anarchy . . . mutual confidence, affection and tranquility, those sweeteners of human life, are succeeded by distrust, hatred, and wild uproar; the useful arts of agriculture and commerce are neglected for caballing, mobbing this or that other man, suspected of thinking different from the prevailing sentiment of the times."[3] He went on to point out how the Whigs at first said that it was OK to pay external taxes set by parliament, but not internal taxes, then it was permissible to pay taxes that regulated trade, and finally wound up saying that no taxes or laws passed by parliament had any validity in British America at all, yet somehow they kept telling everyone that Americans were "loyal subjects of the king" and "entitled to the rights of the English constitution." Finally, he said, the Whigs, as everyone knew, asserted total independence, yet pretended that it was not so.

Letter Five, written on January 9, 1775, is arguably Massachusettensis' best letter. He outlined the complaint that Americans had against parliament and then analyzed it thoroughly and came to some sobering conclusions as to why the Whigs were in error. He said, "I intend to consider the acts of the British government which are held up as the principal grievances and inquire whether Great Britain is chargeable with injustice in any one of them; but must first ask your attention

2. Massachutensis, *A Series of Letters Containing a Faithful State of Many Important and Striking Facts, Which Laid the Foundation of the Present Troubles in the Province of Massachusetts Bay, Interspersed with Animadversions and Reflections, Originally Addressed to the PEOPLE of that Province and Worthy of eh Considerations of THE TRUE PATRIOTS of this country, by a person of Honor upon the spot* (Boston; reprinted London: J. Mathews, 1776), VI, files.libertyfund.org/1332/0951_bk.pdf.
3. Ibid., 3.

to parliament. I suspect many of our politicians are wrong in their first principle, in denying that the authority of parliament extends to the colonies." Massachusettensis started with an outline of the three kinds of government then known in history. He said each had their own kinds of problems buried within. The first kind of government was "monarchy"—government of the one and subject to becoming a tyranny. The second was an "aristocracy"—government of the few and subject to faction and usurpation. The third was "democracy"—government of the many and subject to degenerate into violence, tumult and anarchy. However, "a government formed upon these three principles [together] in due proportion, is best calculated to answer the ends of government, and to endure, *such a government is the British Constitution*."[4] He went on to say, "The distributions of power are so just and the proportions so exact, as at once to support and control each other. An Englishman glories in being subject to and protected by such a government. The colonies are part of the British Empire."

With the revolution of 1688, the monarchy was finally made subservient to Parliament. With that, the concept of "King in Parliament" became the guiding principle of English law. The king ruled through Parliament. This meant that American Whigs who kept petitioning for the king to reign in Parliament and have Parliament rescind the laws they had passed with regard to the American colonies, were asking of the king that which he was forbidden to do by law. Massachuttensis tried to make it clear that Americans were also covered by such a perfect form of government. He went on to make the most important points that Loyalists held, the center points to their whole position, that is, the supremacy of Parliament coupled with the fact that, for them, as well as for the people of Great Britain, the British Empire was a single state, not a collection of states. A colony was simply an extension of England. Massachusettensis started by saying:

> Two supreme or independent authorities cannot exist in the same state. It would be the height of political absurdity . . . If then we are a part of the British Empire, we must be subject to the supreme power of the state, which is vested in the estates of parliament, notwithstanding each of the colonies have legislatures and executive powers of their own, delegated or granted to them for the purposes of regulating their own internal police, which are subordinate and must necessarily be subject, to the checks, control and regulation of the supreme authority. This doctrine is not new; but the denial of it is . . .

4. Emphasis added.

The principle argument against the authority of parliament, is this; the Americans are entitled to all the privileges of an Englishman; it is the privilege of an Englishman to be exempt from all laws that he does not consent to in person, or by representative; the Americans are not represented in parliament, and therefore we are exempt from acts of parliament, or in other words not subject to its authority . . . If the colonies are not subject to the authority of parliament, Great Britain and the colonies must be distinct states, as completely as Britain and Hanover are now. The colonies in that case will owe no allegiance to the imperial crown . . . as the title to the crown is derived from an act of parliament . . . Where shall we find the British constitution that we all agree we are entitled to? We shall seek in vain in our provincial assemblies. The houses of representatives or burgesses have not all the powers of the House of Commons . . . they have no more than what is expressly granted by their several charters . . . Thus, the supposition of our being independent states, or exempt from the authority of parliament, destroys the very idea of our having a British constitution.

On January 16, 1775, Massachusettensis published his sixth letter. He began by saying that, had someone fifteen years prior to 1774 denied that the British colonies were a part of the British Empire and subject to the authority of Parliament, "he would have been called a fool or a madman." In this letter he showed that the right to tax the colonies and the supremacy of Parliament were fully consistent with the charters of the various colonies.

It is curious indeed to trace the denial . . . to the supreme authority of the state. When the stamp act was made, the authority of parliament to impose internal taxes was denied, but the right to impose external taxes ones . . . was admitted. When the act was made, imposing duties on tea & etc., a new distinction was set up; that the parliament had a duty to lay duties upon merchandise for the purposes of regulating trade, but not for the purpose of raising revenue . . .

Having got thus far safe, it was only taking one step more to extricate ourselves entirely from their fangs, and become independent states: That our patriots most heroically resolved upon, and flatly denied that parliament had a right to make any laws whatever, that should be binding on the colonies. There is no possible medium between absolute independence and subjugation to the authority of parliament . . .

My dear countrymen, it is of the last importance that we settle this point clearly in our minds . . . to deny the supreme authority of the state is high misdemeanor, to say no worse of it; to oppose it by force is an overt act of treason . . . [The colonies] as they have been severally annexed to the crown . . . became a part of the empire, and subject to the authority of parliament, whether they send members to parliament or not, and whether they have legislative powers of their own or not ...

Our charter, like all other American charters, is under the great seal of England: the grants are made by the king ... It is apparent, the king acted in his royal capacity, as King of England, which necessarily supposes the territory granted, to be a part of the English dominions, beholden to the crown of England.

The above paragraph is important. What Massachuttensis was saying is that the land in North America was English *before* there was a colony in Virginia, Massachusetts or Plymouth. It was English by right of discovery.[5]

Massachusettensis then pointed out that the charter of Massachusetts stipulated that the colony "may pass such laws as are necessary, *but only* to the extent that such laws and ordinances be not contrary or are repugnant to the laws and statutes of this our realm of England."

He then pointed out that the king granted people of Massachusetts to be

free and quit from all taxes, subsidies and customs in New England for the space of seven years and from all taxes for and impositions for the space of twenty-one years in the other, plainly indicates that, after this expiration, this province would be liable to taxes then. Now I would ask, by what authority those taxes were not to be imposed? ... It must ... be by the king or parliament: it could not be by the king alone, for as king of England ... he has no such power, exclusive of the lords and commons; consequently, it must have been by the parliament.

5. This issue of the right of European kings claiming land in the western hemisphere has been an issue that Native Americans have had to live with ever since Columbus set foot on an island in the Caribbean centuries ago. As long ago as 1640 a Pilgrim settler in Massachusetts made the argument to the authorities in Plymouth and Boston that the lands in America did not belong to the King of England, but rightly belonged to the people that had been living in America long before Europeans even knew of its existence. The king, he said, had no right to grant settlements on lands belonging to other people. What he got for his troubles was banishment and a threat of arrest to be sent back to England in chains. Instead, he fled to the woods in the middle of winter and found refuge among the various tribes of Native Americans. Then he was granted a tract of land where he and any who would join him could live in peace on land that was not in any of the organized European colonies. That area of land we now call Rhode Island. It is the only colony that was founded on free grant by the Native Americans themselves, and not an English King. Later, to keep the other colonies from claiming the land themselves, Parliament and later King Charles II granted a Royal Charter to Rhode Island, thus forcing Massachusetts and Connecticut to keep their hands off. The Pilgrim settler was Roger Williams. He is one of ten Reformation leaders to have a statue in his honor at the Wall of Reformation in Geneva, Switzerland.

Quoting a part of the Massachusetts charter one more time:

Let us consider the clause in connection with other parts of the charter.
It is a rule of law . . . to consider each part of an instrument, so as the
whole may hang together, and be consistent within itself. If we suppose
to exempt us from the authority of parliament, we must throw away all
the rest of the charter, for every other part indicates the contrary, the
inhabitants of the American colonies do in fact enjoy all the liberties
and immunities of natural born subjects. We are entitled to no greater
privileges than those, that are born within the realm; and they can enjoy
no other than we do, thus, it is evident that this clause amounts to no
more than the Royal assurance that we are a part of the British empire,
not aliens, but natural born subjects, and, as such, bound to obey the
supreme power of the state, and entitled to protection from it.

In his seventh letter published on January 23, 1775 he went over the
history of the arguments used by the people he styled "patriots" and
showed how they originally agreed with much of what he had said and
how they changed their position time and time again, thus constantly
trying to back Britain into a corner. "The powers of legislation [in the
colonies] are confined to local or provincial purposes . . . by the words,
so long as the same be not repugnant or contrary to the laws of this our realm:
but . . . it is impossible to reconcile them to the idea of an independent
state, as it is to reconcile the disability to omnipotence."

Massachusettensis then referred to a pamphlet published by James
Otis. Otis was a hero of John Adams and had, in Adams' own words,
been the spark that lit the resistance movement in New England and
especially in Adams' breast.

A pamphlet published in 1764, by a Boston gentleman, who was then
the oracle of the Whigs, and whose profound knowledge in the law and
constitution is equaled but by few . . . says 'I . . . lay it down as one of
our first principles from whence I intend to deduce the civil rights of
the British colonies, that all of them are subject to, and dependent on
Great Britain, and the parliament has undoubted power and lawful authority to make acts for the general good, that, by naming them, shall
and ought to be equally binding, as upon the subjects of Great Britain
within the realm. Is there the least difference, as the consent of the
colonists whether taxes and impositions are laid on their trade and other
property by the crown alone, or by parliament? As it is agreed on all
hands, the crown alone cannot impose them, we should be justifiable
in refusing to pay them; but we must and ought to yield obedience to
an act of parliament, though erroneous, till repealed.

Massachusettensis then quoted from the writings of John Dickinson of Pennsylvania,

> The Pennsylvania Farmer [John Dickinson], who took the lead in explaining away the right of parliament to raise a revenue in America ... tells us that 'he who considers these provinces as states distinct from the British Empire has very slender notions of justice or their interests; we are but parts of a whole, and therefor there must exist a connection in due order. This power is lodged in parliament; and we are as much dependent on Great Britain as a perfectly free people could ever be on another ...
>
> Thus our wretched situation is but the natural consequence of denying the authority of parliament and forcibly opposing its acts.

About this time John Adams returned to Massachusetts from the Continental Congress in Philadelphia. He was astounded to learn that the people of Massachusetts were being influenced by the writings of a Tory and that the articles were having a negative impact as far as the Whigs, or Patriots as they styled themselves, were concerned.

The Massachusettensis pamphlets were written by a man named Daniel Leonard (1740-1829). He graduated from Harvard in 1760 and was elected to the House of Representatives. He became an attorney and was acquainted with John Adams. As the Whigs under the direction of Samuel Adams and James Otis became increasingly vocal and even violent in 1773 and 1774, he became much more active in the political debate on the Tory side. He decided, late in 1774, to take up the pen and try to stem the tide of the Whigs, whom he saw clearly as leaning towards independence.[6]

Adams wrote his replies under the name of "Novanglus," Latin for "New England."[7] He began by asserting that the plan to "enslave" America came not from people in London, but rather from people in America. Adams was principally speaking of Sir Francis Bernard, the royal governor of Massachusetts and his successor, Thomas Hutchinson. Adams, throughout his life, was under the delusion that Hutchinson was the primary author of all the troubles bringing about the revolution.

Adams, in referring to Massachusettensis, wrote:

> This, ill-fated and unsuccessful, though persevering writer, still hopes to change your sentiments and conduct ... to convince you that the system of colonial administration which has been pursued for these ten

6. *Encyclopedia of World Biography*, vol. 6 (New York: McGraw-Hill, 1973), 437.
7. All of the following quotes from Novanglus will be taken from *The Political Writings of John Adams.*

or twelve years past was a wise, righteous, and humane plan; that Sir Francis Bernard and Mr. Hutchinson . . . are your friends.

I, on my part, may perhaps . . . show the wicked policy of the Tories [have presented] the design of enslaving the country.

He went on to assert one of the issues most hotly debated in the First Continental Congress, the idea of natural law. The debate over natural law, and the rights derived under natural law, were setting a foundation of the Whig cause on a fixed principle *outside of English Common Law*, and thus completely separating American rights from anything having to do with British law. He began by saying:

[Liberty] has been placed in the nature of man by God; and if it is the manifest design of the prince to annul the contract [between himself and the people] on his part, [this] will annul it on the part of the people . . . [and there is] a settled plan to deprive the people of all the benefits and blessings, and end the contract, to subvert the fundamentals of the constitution, to deprive them of all share in making and executing laws, (this) will justify a revolution.

In letter two he continued by taking on the Tories and their alleged "evil ways." He wrote, "I have heretofore stated my intention of pursuing the Tories through all their dark intrigues, and to show the rise and progress of their schemes for enslaving this country." In his argument against the Tories, he made the point that Americans were already paying taxes to Britain because the colonies could only trade with Britain, and accept a lower price than they might have at other markets. The difference, he said, "is a tax to Britain."

The end of the French and Indian War created, as far as government officials in London were concerned, a whole new dynamic different than when the colonies were established. Great Britain had a new and larger empire, and had created a huge financial debt in obtaining that empire. Because of this, Royal Governor Bernard, right after the conclusion of the French and Indian War, wrote to London in 1764 suggesting a new way of thinking about governing the empire. He said, in effect, that because of the greatly expanded empire, there was going to have to be a new way of governing the empire. It had grown too big to be ruled in a hap-hazard fashion. "Benign neglect" simply was not going to work anymore. Therefor he suggested that new regulations may need to be considered, but this new way of governing the empire might upset some people in the colonies. Therefore he suggested a "go slow" approach and that governmental officials "reason with them [those who would oppose the new measures] at liesure," in order to give them time to come around and be more receptive.

Adams saw this document as a dark and sinister plot to overthrow the rights of Americans and accused those whom Massachusettensis defended with nothing less than the total political destruction of the colonies of North America. For Adams, the issues were clear as black and white. The two positions as expounded by Massachusettensis and Novanglus cannot be seen in any way but stark contrast. For Adams, "There are but two kinds of men in the world, free men and slaves. The very definition of a free man is one who is bound by no laws to which he has not consented. Americans would have no way of giving their consent to the acts of parliament; therefor they would not be free men . . . What would be your condition under such an absolute subjection to parliament? You would not only be slaves, but the most abject sort of slaves to the worst of masters."

In subsequent letters Adams took Massachusettensis on with respect to his arguments on the nature of British law and government, and revealed that he felt British law had absolutely no authority over America. In doing so he completely separated the government of Great Britain from the governments of the colonies and also separated the role of the king from that of Parliament, ignoring the Glorious Revolution of 1688 in which the authority of the king was merged into that of Parliament.

> I would ask, "by what law the parliament has authority over America?" By the law of nature, it has none; by the common law of England, it has none; for the common law, and the authority of parliament found on it, (that authority was) never extended beyond the four seas; by the statutes . . . it has none . . .
>
> This language, "the imperial crown of Great Britain" is not a style of the common law, but of court sycophants.

Adams conceded Massachusettensis' assertion that American Whigs claimed that:

> The colonies owe no allegiance to any imperial crown, provided such a crown involves in it a House of Lords, a house of Commons . . . indeed we owe no allegiance to any crown at all. We owe allegiance to the person of the king, not his crown, to his natural, not his political, capacity . . . If . . . he appears king of Massachusetts, king of Rhode Island, of Connecticut, & etc., this is no absurdity at all; I wish he would be graciously pleased to assume them.

Here we see that Adams, like other American Whigs, completely resisted the results of the Glorious revolution of 1688 in which the power of the king was subsumed into Parliament. Adams would contend that the empire existed only in its allegiance to the king in person, stripped of any connections with the Crown of England. He went on to develop that distinction. Where Massachusettensis stated that there needs to be

> "Some superintending power, to draw together all the various do-minions, in case of war, and in the case of trade" [Adams replied] in fact and experience it has not been found so. [When] the proprietary colonies . . . did not come in so early to the assistance of the general cause of the last war as they ought, and perhaps one of them not at all . . . the inconveniences were small in comparison of the absolute ruin of the liberties which must follow the submission to parliament . . . But admitting the proposition . . . will it follow that parliament, as now con-stituted has a right to assume the supreme jurisdiction? By no means!

Adams talked of a union of the colonies with the mother country, but set some conditions. He completely failed to mention the plan pro-posed in the First Continental Congress by Joseph Galloway, but rather he presupposed conditions that obviously were unworkable. "A union of the colonies might be projected, if America has three millions, and the whole empire twelve millions, she ought to send a quarter part of all members to the house of commons, and . . . the haughty members for Great Britain must humble themselves, one session in four, to cross the Atlantic, and hold the parliament in America."

Adams failed to mention that no American ever proposed any plan of union or representation to Great Britain and in the one case where such a possibility was suggested in the congress, the plan was quashed and erased from the books. Adams was not interested in compromise, only in Britain conceding to America on all points. He continued:

> When Massachusettensis asks, "if Americans are not subject to British law, then can they claim the benefits of the English constitution, as the Whigs are always claiming?" [Adams answers] If we enjoy, and are entitled to more liberty than the British constitution allows, where is the harm? Or if we enjoy the British constitution in greater purity and perfection than they do in England, as is really the case, whose fault is that? Not ours.
>
> That a representation in parliament is impractical, we all agree, but the consequence is, that we must have a representation in our supreme legislature here. This was the consequence that was drawn by kings . . . . more than a century ago . . . and it must be the general sense again soon, or Great Britain will lose her colonies.

Here one may wonder if Adams was not contradicting himself. Ear-lier he had completely separated America from Great Britain by stating that Americans owed allegiance to King George III *only in his person, and not as king of Great Britain.* And he repeatedly said there was no connection between America and the British Parliament. How, then, could Great Britain "lose" any colonies that she did not have? But he continued with a discussion of British common law:

> By common law, I mean that system of customs, written and unwritten, which was known and in force in England in the time of King Richard I. This continued to be the case to the reign(s) of Elizabeth and King James I. In that time all the laws of England were confined to the realm, and within the four seas. There was no provision made in this law for governing colonies beyond the Atlantic, or beyond the four seas, by authority of parliament? No, nor for kings to grant charters to subjects in foreign countries.[8]

Adams continued this theme of the power of kings and their charters. As a result, he forced a conclusion that can only be interpreted as leading to independence. "When a subject left the kingdom by the king's permission, and if the nation did not remonstrate against it . . . he carries with him, as a man, all the rights of nature . . . his allegiance bound him to the king, and (that allegiance) entitled him to [the king's] protection. But how? Not in France or America . . . he had a right to protection and the liberties England *upon his return there,*[9] not otherwise." Adams was saying that Americans were only entitled to the king's protection and the liberties outlined in the English common law when they were physically in Great Britain. By living in America, they were outside British law. He went on to explain how he felt Americans derived their rights.

> How then do we New England men derive our laws? I say, not from parliament, nor from common law, but from the law of nature, and with the compact made with [the] king in our charters . . . Our ancestors, when they emigrated, having obtained permission from the king to come here, and never being commanded to return to the realm had a right to have erected . . . a perfect democracy, or any other form of government they saw fit. They, indeed while they lived, could not have taken arms against the king of England, without violating their allegiance, but their children would not have been born within the king's

---

8. It is interesting that in addition to referring to monarchs that existed before 1688, he ignored any British law or political history since the Glorious Revolution. In addition, he said that the charters could not be used to connect America to Great Britain as they had no force in British law.

9. Emphasis added.

allegiance, would not have been natural subjects, and consequently not entitled to protection, nor bound to the king.

Adams made, in the last few paragraphs, any issue of taxation by Parliament moot. Despite all the talk to the contrary up to this point, Adams was saying that in the winter of 1774-1775 the American colonies were independent and sovereign states. They might have offered King George personal allegiance, if he would accept it, but if not, there was no other legal bond between America and Great Britain.

Massachusettensis responded to Novanglus in his sixteenth letter published on March 27, 1775. In this letter he took on the First Continental Congress. In his seventeenth and last letter he replied directly to Novanglus. In the issue responding to the First Continental Congress, he began by saying:

> Our patriots claim, that humble petitions from the representatives of the people have been frequently treated with contempt. This is as virulent a libel upon his majesty's government as falsehood and ingenuity combined could fabricate . . . Instead of being decent remonstrance's against real grievances, or prayers for their removal, they were insidious attempts to wrest from the crown, or the supreme legislature, their inherent, inalienable prerogatives or rights . . .
>
> Even when Great Britain has relaxed her measures, or appeared to recede from her claims, instead of manifestations of gratitude, our politicians have risen in their demands, and sometimes to . . . a degree of insolence . . .
>
> None but idiots or madmen could suppose such measures (as passed by the congress) had a tendency to restore "union and harmony between Great Britain and the colonies." Nay, the very demands of the congress evince that was not their intention . . .
>
> The delegates call themselves . . . "his majesty's most faithful subjects". . . Yet . . . disown him in the capacity in which he granted the provincial charters; disclaim the authority of the king in parliament; and undertake to enact and execute laws, without any authority derived from the crown. This is dissolving all connection between the colonies and the crown.

In his last letter to the people, published on April 3, 1775, just a few days before the battles at Lexington and Concord, Massachusettensis took on Adams's writings in Novanglus. He opened by asserting Locke's principle that the will of the people is expressed through the voice of the majority and that the minority have no authority to change the government on their own, and used that premise as a paradigm for America.

Novanglus has accused me of traducing the people of this province. I deny the charge. Popular demagogues always call themselves the people, and when their own measures are censured, they cry out, the people, the people are abused and insulted. The terms Whig and Tory have been adopted according to the arbitrary use of them in this province, but they rather ought to be reversed; an American Tory is a supporter of our excellent constitution, and an American Whig is a subverter of it.

Novanglus abuses me for saying that the Whigs aim at independence ... by separating us from the king as well as parliament ... Novanelus tries to hide the inconsistences of his hypothesis ... Surely, he is not to learn that arguments drawn from obsolete maxims raked out of the ruins of the feudal system, or from the principles of obsolete monarchy, will not conclude the present constitution of government.[10]

This letter ended the debate. Within two weeks shooting started and men were dying. The time for talking was over. This was the last chance Tories and Loyalists would have a voice in America. "Before independence was declared it was necessary to resolve the conflict between Patriots and Tories. This was by identification and ultimate suppression of the Tory voice, wherever, and whenever possible,"[11] and, one might add, by any means possible.

10. Here Massachusettensis makes a great point. However, the idea that the empire was a whole and America a part of that whole was a premise that Adams and the radicals could not agree to. Had Massachusettensis restricted his comments to the possibility that the Whigs, as the Patriots called themselves, represented less than the whole of America, then perhaps his argument would have had a greater impact, but that effort, tried by Joseph Galloway in the first Continental Congress, was completely rejected by the radicals.
11. H. James Henderson, *Party Politics in the Continental Congress* (New York: McGraw-Hill Book Company, 1974), 4.

Wampum Belts to Canada: Stockbridge Indian Ambassador's Dangerous 1775 Peace Mission

ttt MARK R. ANDERSON ttt

In early May 1775, with the Revolutionary War not even one month old, western Massachusetts Patriot leaders and their Stockbridge Indian neighbors developed a plan to use diplomacy to neutralize a looming danger in the north. Stockbridge ambassadors would take a peace message from their community to the New England colonists' traditional Native enemies in Canada. The Indian delegation's resultant mission promoted this objective but also inadvertently sparked a diplomatic incident that further helped the American cause.

The primary target for this outreach was the Mohawk village-nation of Kahnawake (historically spelled in variations of "Caughnawaga"), west of Montreal. Kahnawake was the central council fire of the Seven Nations Indian confederation, composed of Catholic mission villages in the St. Lawrence valley. For almost one hundred years, warriors from these villages had episodically raided New England and New York frontier communities, often as part of the British-French colonial wars—killing settlers, taking captives and plunder, and devastating entire villages. They were a legendary terror for the colonists. While Kahnawake and other Seven Nations Indians villages considered themselves to be independent, sovereign enclaves within the British Province of Quebec, they generally kept good relations and frequently allied with their Canadian neighbors' imperial government. So, with Revolutionary War hostilities commencing, northern colonies believed new frontier attacks could be imminent if these Indians allied themselves with the king.

American Patriots had their own Indian partners to turn to, the foremost of which were a composite people identified at the time as the

Muhheconneock—Mohicans/Mahicans, Wappingers, and Housatonics. Those Indians' largest settlement was in the western Massachusetts town of Stockbridge, a community founded in the 1730s as a multi-tribal Protestant Indian mission. In the French and Indian War, many Stockbridge Indian men had demonstrated marked commitment to their colonial neighbors by fighting on the British side, most famously in Rogers' Rangers. After that war, settlers quickly encroached on Stockbridge, displacing many original Native inhabitants. By 1774, the town had become a hybrid community, dominated by Massachusetts colonists who outnumbered the 200 remaining "praying Indians" five-to-one.[1]

Despite the settlers' impositions, the Stockbridge Muhheconneocks remained strong allies to their American neighbors. On April 1, 1775, even before hostilities commenced at Lexington and Concord, they proclaimed a "firm and steady attachment to the [Patriot] cause." Muhheconneock captains led warrior detachments in the local minute men and informed the Massachusetts Provincial Council that "the natives of Stockbridge, are ready and willing to take up the Hatchet in the cause of liberty and their country."[2]

The Stockbridge Muhheconneocks also offered to apply their substantial diplomatic influence with diverse Indian nations including the Haudenosaunee (Iroquois) Six Nations confederacy, the Ohio Valley Shawnees, and the Seven Nations of Canada. With the situation ripe for war in early April, Muhheconneock Capt. Solomon Uhhaunauwaunmut visited Six Nations Mohawk chiefs to "know how they stand," and if needed, to offer persuasive pro-Patriot messages. By May 9, he returned with largely encouraging news—at least according to the chiefs he met, the Iroquois Six Nations were not inclined to fight alongside the British and viewed the Americans favorably.[3]

1. Letter from Thomas Cushing, August n.d., 1776, i78, r93, v5 p57-58, M247 Papers of the Continental Congress, National Archives and Records Administration (NARA). Colin G. Calloway, *The American Revolution in Indian Country* (Cambridge: Cambridge University Press, 1995), 90-91. The spelling "Muhheconneock" is taken from Stockbridge-Munsee Band of Mohican Indians, "Our History," www.mohican.com/origin-early-history. See also Patrick Frazier, *The Mohicans of Stockbridge* (Lincoln: University of Nebraska Press, 1992) and David J. Silverman, *Red Brethren: The Brothertown and Stockbridge Indians and the Problem of Race in Early America* (Ithaca, NY: Cornell University Press, 2010).
2. April 1, 1775, Massachusetts Provincial Congress, and same to Johoiakin Mtohskin, April 1, 1775, Peter Force, ed. *American Archives.* 4th [*AA4*] and 5th [*AA5*] Series (Washington, DC: M. St. Clair Clarke and Peter Force, 1837–53), *AA4* 1: 1347.
3. Speech delivered by Capt. Solomon Uhhaunauwaunmut for Massachusetts Provincial Congress, April 11, 1775, *AA4* 2: 315-16; Petition and Memorial of John Sergeant, Missionary to the Mohekunnuk Tribe of Indians at Stockbridge, (read November 27, 1776),

Just days later, the people of Stockbridge got wind of plans to take British-held Fort Ticonderoga at the south end of Lake Champlain. Muhheconneock Indians and their colonial neighbors were concerned that the Kahnawakes in Canada might be alarmed by this armed Patriot intrusion into the periphery of their home region. Stockbridge leaders, including Timothy Edwards (soon to be a Massachusetts congressman and Continental Indian Department commissioner) and village missionary John Sergeant, Jr., worked with Stockbridge chiefs to send ambassadors north to "find out the temper of the Canada Indians," and use their influence to sway the Kahnawakes and Seven Nations confederates into neutrality.[4]

The Stockbridge chiefs composed a speech that opened with a traditional invocation to council and then described the new war from their perspective: "One Morning I got up, I heard from Boston that the Regulars came out against our People, and there was a great deal of Blood shed," and "Very soon after this I heard from Boston again, that our People sent some Men up North to Ticonderoga to take Possession of them Forts." In figurative language, they explained that their white "Brother" only seized Ticonderoga and Crown Point to "guard himself against his Enemies"; the Kahnawakes need not fear attack and were reassured that the Americans had "no evil design against you." The Muhheconneocks' speech then suggested that they and the Seven Nations people should "sit down, and smoak our Pipes, under the Shade of our great Tree and have our Ears open and see [watch] our Brethren fight" and advised "let us keep our Convenant Strong[,] do not let any one break that which we made at the End of the War, that we never would fight against one another again." Captain Abraham Nimham and two other unidentified Stockbridge Indians were selected to travel to the Kahnawake council fire to deliver this speech with the requisite wampum belts for a formal diplomatic overture.[5]

AA5 3: 868-69; A Gentleman at Pittsfield to an Officer in Cambridge, May 9, 1775, *AA4* 3:546; Letter from Thomas Cushing, August n.d., 1776, i78, r93, v5 p57-58, M247, NARA. There was no clear political consensus in the Mohawk nation or Haudenosaunee confederation in 1775 or at any point in the war.

4. Petition and Memorial of John Sergeant, (read November 27, 1776), *AA5* 3: 868-69; Elisha Phelps to the Connecticut General Assembly, May 16, 1775, *Collections of the Connecticut Historical Society* 1 (1860): 176; Stockbridge Indians to the Caghnawagas, May 13, 1775, James Sullivan, ed., *Minutes of the Albany Committee of Correspondence, 1775-1778*, volume 1 (Albany: University of the State of New York, 1923), 129-30.

5. Stockbridge Indians to the Caghnawagas, May 13, 1775, Sullivan, *Minutes of the Albany Committee*, 1: 129-30.

Before Nimham and his compatriots reached Fort Ticonderoga, on or before May 20, they learned that the post and nearby Crown Point had been taken by Ethan Allen and his Green Mountain Boys, various Connecticut and western Massachusetts men, and nominal co-commander Col. Benedict Arnold. Allen and Arnold proved unable to get along, so after arrival the Stockbridges conferred separately with the two Patriot leaders. They first talked with Arnold, who encouraged their peace mission. He wrote Nimham a letter of introduction to Canadian Patriot leader Thomas Walker, saying "any Assistance and Advice you are kind enough to give him will be gratefully acknowledged." Arnold also arranged for Patriot interpreter Winthrop Hoit to join the Stockbridge travelers. Hoit was a valuable borderlands agent, a repatriated Kahnawake captive who had been adopted into the community for four years during the French and Indian War and was conversant in Mohawk. Hoit had also visited the village just a few weeks earlier in a pre-hostilities intelligence-gathering trip.[6]

Four days later, they conferred with Ethan Allen at Crown Point. Taking advantage of the Stockbridge ambassadors' trip into Canada, Allen wrote a letter for them to deliver to what he called "the four Tribes": Seven Nations confederacy members in Kahnawake, Kanesatake, and Odanak (St. Francis), and somewhat arbitrarily, he included the Oswegatchies, a small community with only ill-defined confederacy ties. Allen's letter recounted British fault in starting the war and detailed recent American military successes. The Green Mountain Boys leader also shared his desire that the Indians in Canada would "not fight for King George against your friends in America." To this point, his letter conformed with the Stockbridges' mission objectives and other Continental leaders' strategic intent. Trouble came from what followed.[7]

Allen then boasted, "I was always a friend to Indians, and have hunted with them many times, and know how to shoot and ambush like Indians, and am a great hunter," and declared "I want to have your war-

6. Benedict Arnold to Thomas Walker, May 20, 1775, fol. 148, Colonial Office [CO] 42/34, Library and Archives Canada; Arnold to Jonathan Trumbull, June 13, 1775, *AA4* 2: 977; "Benedict Arnold's Regimental Memorandum Book," *Pennsylvania Magazine of History and Biography* 8 (1884): 371-72; Ethan Allen to New York Congress, June 2, 1775, *AA4* 2: 892; John Brown to Committee of Correspondence in Boston, March 29, 1775, *AA4* 2: 244; David W. Hoyt, *Hoyt Family: A Genealogical History of John Hoyt of Salisbury . . .* (Boston: C. Benjamin Richardson, 1857), 51.

7. Allen to Assembly of Connecticut, May 26, 1775, *AA4* 2: 713; Allen to "The Councillers at Koianawago [sic] pr. Favor of Capt. Nimham, CO 42/34 fol. 149-50 [also *AA4* 2: 714].

riours come and see me, and help me fight the King's Regular Troops."
The rest of this plea is oft quoted: "You know they stand all along close
together, rank and file, and my men fight so as Indians do, and I want
your warriors to join with me and my warriors, like brothers, and
ambush the Regulars." In return, he promised "money, blankets, tom-
ahawks, knives, paint, and any thing that there is in the army." His invitation for the Canada Indians to take up arms on the American side
was a wholesale break from the Stockbridges' mission for simple Kahnawake neutrality.[8]

Historians have frequently misinterpreted Allen's letter as evidence
that *he* launched the Stockbridges' outreach to Canada, and that the principal objective therefore was to recruit Indian warrior allies. Instead,
Allen appears to have taken advantage of his position as the last American leader meeting with the Muhheconneock delegation to promote his
own agenda—hoping to gather Indian allies for an invasion of Canada
that he soon began pitching in earnest to Patriot leaders. It is not even
clear whether Nimham and his fellow ambassadors actually knew what
Allen's letter said. Regardless, they agreed to carry it into Canada.[9]

Four Kahnawakes visiting Crown Point at the time offered to serve
as guides, and in the next day or two they cruised north on Lake Champlain with the Stockbridges and Winthrop Hoit, entering Canada on the
Richelieu River. The Indian escorts planned to land at Fort St. Johns,
the first settlement on the other side of the border, where their Stockbridge guests could rest while they sent to Kahnawake for horses to
ease the last thirty miles of the party's journey. Fort St. Johns, however,
had only been recently reinforced by scores of British regular soldiers
and Canadian Loyalists after Arnold, and then Allen, separately raided
the post on May 18. Interpreter Winthrop Hoit thought that stopping at
the fort was a bad idea, "fearful of being taken prisoner," so the party
dropped him ashore upriver from the post, and he ventured through the
woods to Kahnawake on his own. Then, just as Hoit predicted, the entire complexion of the diplomatic mission changed in a flash at Fort
St. Johns.[10]

8. Allen to "The Councillers at Koianawago pr. Favor of Capt. Nimham, CO 42/34 fol.
149-50 [also *AA4* 2: 714].
9. Allen to Assembly of Connecticut, May 26, 1775, *AA4* 2: 713; Allen to Continental Congress, May 29, 1775, *AA4* 2: 733; Allen to New York Congress, June 2, 1775, *AA4* 2: 892;
Allen to the Massachusetts Congress, June 9, 1775, *AA4* 2: 939; Barnabas Deane to Silas
Deane, June 1, 1775, "Correspondence of Silas Deane," *Collections of the Connecticut
Historical Society* 2 (1870): 248.
10. Abraham Nimham's Relation, July 5, 1775, Sullivan, *Minutes of the Albany Committee*,
1: 131; June 5, 1775, "Arnold's Regimental Memorandum Book," 371-72.

The Fort St. Johns garrison was on high alert with frequent reports of rebel American scouts probing the provincial border. So, when the Stockbridge strangers arrived, British regulars detained them long enough to inspect their packs, discovering the wampum, and more importantly, the telltale correspondence from Arnold and Allen. The redcoats justifiably interpreted the latter document as evidence that the Muhheconneocks came to Canada with hostile intent. The soldiers released the Indians for the moment and waited to act on their discovery.[11]

That evening, while the Stockbridges sojourned, British soldiers "decoyed" them "to the Waterside when they bound them tight with Cords laid them in the Battoe on their backs tied their Legs to the Top of the Battoe, leaving them in that Condition all Night." At dawn's light, the redcoats expeditiously and roughly transported the three Indian ambassadors a dozen miles down the Richelieu River to the more secure British post at Fort Chambly. There, Abraham Nimham successfully begged to be taken to Montreal, where authorities could straighten out the situation—presumably with the expectation that he and his companions would be released as Indian ambassadors, who were traditionally given free passage under Native protocols, even if coming from enemy nations.[12]

As Abraham Nimham recounted, when soldiers delivered the Stockbridge ambassadors to Montreal, the "Commanding Officer ordered them untied and gave them refreshment"—seemingly a positive sign. However, British officers privately held a court martial to weigh the evidence and judge the Stockbridge ambassadors, allegedly determining that the Indians should be hanged, since they had been "sent to engage the Indians to fall upon the regulars." These were tense days in Canada, and Gov. Guy Carleton and his military officers were realistically concerned about rebel American spies, incursions, and even a potential invasion.[13]

Unfortunately for the historical record, Nimham did not identify the "commanding officer" by name. Carleton (who was also the commanding general in Canada) had recently moved his headquarters to Montreal but given his consistently delicate handling of the Seven Nations and other Indians, it seems unlikely that he would have been directly involved in the court martial and insults that followed. The "command-

11. Nimham's Relation, July 5, 1775, Sullivan, *Minutes of the Albany Committee,* 1: 131.
12. Ibid.
13. Ibid.; Extract of a Letter from a Gentleman at Stockbridge to a Gentleman of the Congress, June 22, 1775, *Pennsylvania Ledger* (Philadelphia), July 1, 1775 [also *AA4* 2: 1060-61].

ing officer" in Nimham's account was probably Lieut. Col. Dudley Templer, the senior field officer at Montreal; yet it also seems peculiar that if Carleton truly was in the city that day, that he would have been completely oblivious and uninvolved in the incident—perhaps he was away.

While the British court martial took place, Kahnawake leaders got word of the Stockbridge ambassadors' abduction and rushed the ten miles downriver from their village to Montreal. About twenty Kahnawake "Chiefs and Warriors" arrived, first seeking to comfort the distraught Muhheconneocks who had since been warned that their lives were at risk. A sachem—one of Kahnawake village's hereditary clan leaders—told Nimham, "Brother I hear you are agoing to be hanged, if that be so, I am come to take your place[,] I shan't suffer such a thing to happen to my Brother in my Country." The sachem then turned to the "Commanding Officer" and said "I am come for my Brother, what be you agoing to do with him." The officer replied that "he was agoing to do with them as he pleased, they were his Prisoners," which sounds more like the characteristically high-handed tone of many British army officers than a senior government official—Templer rather than Carleton[14]

The Kahnawake sachem was offended by the disrespectful remark, and tried to make an analogy about diplomatic principles, presumably lost on the commander who next demanded that the Stockbridges speak the message conveyed in their wampum belts. Abraham Nimham complied, but later confessed that "he left out a Part." The British officers were still unhappy. Then a French Canadian entered the scene and threw fuel on the fire by saying "he came from New York and reported that there had been a great fight there. Many Regulars were killed, and that there were Indians there fighting &c. He supposed that these Indians were sent by the Grand Congress to hire the Canadian Indians to fall upon the Regulars and kill them all." The redcoats promptly renewed their threat to hang the Stockbridge ambassadors.[15]

The Kahnawake party was insulted by the British officers' haughty, imperious attitude and "High threatening words passed between the General and the Indian Sachems." British officers said "they did not care the Snap of their Finger for all the Indians, they were not of much Importance[,] they would hang them all if they had a mind for it." The Kahnawake sachem offered this bold retort:

---

14. Nimham's Relation, July 5, 1775, Sullivan, *Minutes of the Albany Committee*, 1: 131-32.
15. Ibid.

you say I am little, you don't care the Snap of your finger for me, now I say the same to you, I don't care the Snap of my Finger for you, you call me little, it will take me a Year to go and call all my Friends together, if you think it is for your good hang them, but remember I shant forget it, You have tryed to hire me to fight for you but I love peace, and did not want to meddle with your Quarrel, I have not known yet who was my Enemy, who I ought to fight, but now I shall know who is my Enemy, who is a going to hurt me.[16]

Given the sachem's firm counter-threat with its strategic implications, the redcoat officers finally reconsidered and deemed it best to let the three Stockbridges go. They told the Kahnawakes "to take their Brothers and be gone, and if they ever came that way again, they would hang them [the ambassadors] without asking any Questions and gave them but four days to get out of their Territories." The Indians went to Kahnawake, where Nimham and his companions finally delivered their message and wampum to the council. In return, the Muhheconneocks accepted a formal reply from their hosts to deliver back to Stockbridge. Nimham and his partners departed Canada soon thereafter with five Kahnawake escorts.[17]

Reaching Crown Point by June 10, the Stockbridge ambassadors and Kahnawake escorts first met with Ethan Allen and officers in his circle. The Indians assured them that the Kahnawake people understood the war "to be a family dispute," and that they would "meddle in no way." Nimham also showed "the marks of abuse" he had suffered at British hands. Allen and the others recognized the Indians' sacrifice and service to the cause by contributing "a Present . . . Largely, out of their own Pockets" to the Stockbridges and Kahnawakes involved. Interpreter Winthrop Hoit and the Indians also met with Colonel Arnold on or before June 13, and the Kahnawakes provided additional information that their nation encouraged the American "Army to march into Canada, being much disgusted with the Regulars."[18]

From Crown Point, Nimham and his companions bore the formal Kahnawake response back home to Stockbridge, arriving on June 15.

16. Extract of a Letter from a Gentleman at Stockbridge . . ., June 22, 1775, *Pennsylvania Ledger,* July 1, 1775; Nimham's Relation, July 5, 1775, Sullivan, *Minutes of the Albany Committee,* 1: 132.

17. Nimham's Relation, July 5, 1775, Sullivan, *Minutes of the Albany Committee,* 1: 132; Ethan Allen, Samuel Elmore, etc. to Continental Congress, June 10, 1775, i162, r179, v1, p17, M247, NARA (also *AA4* 2: 958).

18. Allen, Elmore, etc. to Continental Congress, June 10, 1775, *AA4* 2: 958; Arnold to the Continental Congress, June 13, 1775, *AA4* 2:976; Arnold to Jonathan Trumbull, June 13, 1775, *AA4* 2: 977-78.

Delivering a proxy speech and wampum, Nimham first conveyed the Kahnawakes' apology for British abuse of the ambassadors, saying that they "wipe the Tears from your Eyes, that comes from the Trouble that has happened to your Young Men." After that formality, the Canada Indians declared their agreement with the key points of the Muhheconneocks' outreach. They promised to keep "the road," or flow of communications, open between them, and would remember "the agreement of friendship, that our fathers have made—Let us hold that fast—Let no one break that, so as to divide us." Finally, and most importantly for the Americans, the Kahnawakes proclaimed, "there is seven Brothers of us (meaning seven Tribes) we are all agreed in this—Now we say to you—I would have you sit still too, and have nothing to do with this quarrel; but be strong in your hearts, and we intend to do the same." At face value, the Muhheconneocks appeared to have secured a tremendously important promise of Seven Nations confederacy neutrality.[19]

Missionary John Sergeant and the Stockbridge town committee were encouraged by the party's results and asked the Massachusetts Provincial Congress to compensate Nimham for his losses and suffering; he soon received thirty-six shillings. Town leaders also sent transcripts of the Muhheconneock and Kahnawake speeches to the Continental Congress and Albany Committee of Correspondence. In a letter probably enclosed with the messages delivered to Philadelphia, a gentleman at Stockbridge—presumably Sergeant or Timothy Edwards—wrote: "This event turned much to our advantage, and has fully fixed the minds of the [Seven Nations] Indians there against the regulars," and that "The Canadian Indians farther told our Indians, That if they did fight at all, they would Fight Against the Regulars, for they did not like them."[20]

This information reached Congress on June 29, a particularly important time for assessing the threat from Canada. Just three days earlier, Congressional delegates had been alarmed by an apparently reliable report from the Albany Committee of Correspondence that "the French Caughnuago Indians had taken up the Hatchet" to serve with Governor Carleton and the British. That account, in turn, had prompted Congress to grant Maj. Gen. Philip Schuyler authority to invade Canada "and pursue any other measures . . . which may have a tendency

19. Answer to a Speech to the Caughnawagas . . . sent by the Stockbridge Indians, returned June 15, 1775, *Pennsylvania Ledger,* July 22, 1775 (also *AA4* 2: 1002-3).
20. Massachusetts Provincial Congress, July [3] 1775, *AA4* 2: 1480; Massachusetts Provincial Congress to the Moheakounuck Tribe of Indians, June 8, 1775, *AA4* 2: 1397; July 8, 1775, *Minutes of the Albany Committee,* 1: 129; Extract of a Letter from a Gentleman at Stockbridge . . ., June 22, 1775, *Pennsylvania Ledger,* July 1, 1775.

to promote the peace and security of these Colonies" there. The Muh-heconneocks' new information, direct from Kahnawake, served to deflate fears of imminent Indian attack on the northern frontier. Yet these two seemingly contradictory reports—from Albany and Stockbridge—are characteristic of the confusing intelligence from Canada that came throughout the summer of 1775.[21]

In reality, the Kahnawake nation would not choose sides for most of that year. Governor Carleton and his agents drew coerced promises from the village council to defend Canada if attacked, but actual Kahnawake contributions remained minimal. At the village and Seven Nations confederacy levels, they generally held to their own version of neutrality during the 1775-1776 invasion and occupation of Canada, but individual chiefs and warriors were not restrained from taking sides. The situation remained tense, confusing, and complex as different Kahnawake and Seven Nations factions cooperated with and fought alongside the Americans and the British.[22]

The actual impact of the Stockbridge diplomatic overture in May and June 1775 is impossible to assess in isolation, particularly since its message conformed with Kahnawake village and confederacy predispositions. However, the redcoats' mistreatment of the three Muhheconneock Indian ambassadors undoubtedly served to push Seven Nations fence-sitters away from the king and to encourage Kahnawake village's substantial anti-British/pro-American faction. That abusive episode in Montreal also had direct influence on at least one future Native diplomatic episode.

In the critical first weeks of the American invasion of Canada, an Oneida delegation visited Kahnawake just as many Seven Nations chiefs and warriors appeared ready to throw their support to the British. The Oneidas delivered a message, ostensibly from the Six Nations confederacy, promoting full neutrality for the Canada Indians. In an attempt to blunt the impact of the Oneidas' message, British officials

21. Albany Committee to Continental Congress, June 21, 1775, Sullivan, *Minutes of the Albany Committee,* 1: 94-95; June 26, 27 and 29, 1775, Worthington C. Ford, ed. *Journals of the Continental Congress, 1774-1789* (Washington, DC, 1904-37), 2: 108-11; Connecticut Delegates to Jonathan Trumbull, Sr., June 26, 1775, and John Hancock to George Washington, June 28, 175, Paul H. Smith, et al., eds. *Letters of Delegates to Congress, 1774-1789,* volume 1 (Washington, DC: Library of Congress, 1976), 1: 542-43, 555. The text of the Kahnawake response to Stockbridge was printed in *The Pennsylvania Ledger,* July 22, 1775.

22. For additional information on the very complex Seven Nations political scene in 1775, see Mark R. Anderson, *Down the Warpath to the Cedars: Indians' First Battles in the Revolution* (Norman: Oklahoma University Press, 2021), chapters 1 through 3.

invited them to visit Montreal for talks. The Kahnawakes, however, warned the Indian diplomats not to go, "lest they should be served like the Stockbridge Indians, and be made prisoners." As a result, the Onei-das declined the invitation, stayed at the council-fire village, and suc-cessfully persuaded the Seven Nations to maintain neutrality—thereby precluding most confederacy members' direct participation in the fight-ing that fall when the American invasion was quite precarious. So, while Abraham Nimham's mission to Kahnawake may not have had decisive effect on its own, it undoubtedly nurtured diplomatic relations between two key northern Indian nations that were inclined towards the Americans. Perhaps more significantly, the Montreal incident fueled Indian factions' anti-British sentiments, favoring a confederacy-level neutrality and indirectly limiting the scope and scale of Seven Nations involvement as the Revolutionary War continued to grow.[23]

---

23. Report of the Deputies of the Six Nations of their mission to the Caughnawagas, September 24, 1775, *AA4* 3:798; Anderson, *Down the Warpath,* 25-27, 155.

Ethan Allen's "Motley Parcel of Soldiery" at Montreal

＊＊ MARK R. ANDERSON ＊＊

When Ethan Allen described his defeat and capture outside Montreal at Longue Pointe on September 25, 1775, he observed that "it was a motley parcel of soldiery which composed both parties." The enemy included Canadian Loyalists, British regulars, Indian Department officers, and a few Native warriors. In the autobiographical *A Narrative of Colonel Ethan Allen's Captivity*, Allen only provided the broad outlines of his own force, which "consisted of about one hundred and ten men, near eighty of whom were Canadians," and he curiously described the rest as "about thirty English Americans."[1]

Heavily reliant on Allen's vague descriptions, with few other substantial sources to turn to, historians and biographers have often resorted to informed speculation as to who these Canadians and Americans were, and how they came to join Allen on his mission to take Montreal. Like many historical investigations, answering these questions has been analogous to solving a jigsaw puzzle missing many pieces, and without a reference picture. The digital age, however, has provided new pieces and shown new connections, producing a far more complete image of the men who fought alongside Allen in his last military battle.

Allen's movements in the week before Longue Pointe form the puzzle frame. In September 1775, Ethan Allen was no longer the head of the Green Mountain Boys, who had recently been formed into a Continental regiment. He lacked a military command of his own and joined the invasion of Canada as a volunteer officer, with only an honorific title of colonel. Maj. Gen. Philip Schuyler and Brig. Gen. Richard

---

1. Ethan Allen, *Narrative of Col. Ethan Allen's Captivity* (Albany: Pratt and Clark, 1804), 15-16, 19. The first printing was in 1779.

Montgomery focused their Northern Army's efforts on a siege of the well-defended British border post at Fort Saint Johns. Meanwhile, they sent Allen around the enemy fort and north through the Richelieu River valley to Chambly, to act as a liaison with Canadian Patriots and the Kahnawake Indian nation. He returned to headquarters after a successful first tour of several days' duration. Then, on September 18, Allen was sent back out. Still a volunteer, any men with him were attached for specific duties or missions. A camp journal recorded his departure: "Colonel Allen with Captain Duggan and 6 or Seven men went off to Chambly in Order to raise a Regiment of Canadians." This entry describes the first, smallest part of the "motley parcel" that would grow in the following week.[2]

The "captain" Jeremiah Duggan who left the camp with Allen is a key piece of the puzzle, as he connects many elements of the force that ultimately went to battle outside Montreal on September 25. Duggan was an emerging Richelieu Valley Patriot leader, second only to James Livingston that fall in directing Canadian irregular military recruiting and field operations. The Irish-born Duggan's fifteen years of marriage to a *Canadienne*, and his few years as a wheat merchant in the lower Richelieu community of St. Ours, undoubtedly equipped him with essential French language skills and an important local network. None of the other men leaving headquarters with Allen on September 18 were specifically identified by name, but Pvt. Jean-Jacques Bourquin of the 1st New York Regiment was almost certainly among them. Captured with Allen a week later, the Swiss-born Bourquin would have been an obvious choice to be Allen's French interpreter from the start.[3]

---

2. Ethan Allen to Philip Schuyler, September 6, 1775 [sic], Peter Force, ed. *American Archives, Fourth Series* (Washington, DC: M. St. Clair Clarke and Peter Force, 1837-1846), 3: 742-43 (*AA4*); Allen, *Narrative*, 13; Benjamin Trumbull, "A Concise Journal or Minutes of the Principal Movements Towards St. John's ... in 1775," *Collections of the Connecticut Historical Society* 7 (1899): 145 (manuscript available at Connecticut Historical Society, Diaries or journals kept by Benjamin Trumbull, 1775-1777, collections.ctdigitalarchive. org/islandora/object/40002%3A5088#page/1/mode/2up. For all applicable *American Archives* citations, the author also referred to copies in the Papers of the Continental Congress, RG360, M247, National Archives and Records Administration (NARA).

3. Hector Cramahé to Earl of Dartmouth, September 24, 1775, Historical Section of the General Staff [Canada], ed., *A History of the Organization, Development and Services of the Military and Naval Forces of Canada, From the Peace of Paris in 1763 to the Present Time*, (Quebec: 1919), 2: 81; John Livingston to Philip Schuyler, undated, *AA4*, 3: 743; Richard Montgomery to John Livingston, October 12, 1775, i41 v5 r50 p258, RG360, M247, NARA; Hugh Finlay to [Anthony Todd?], September 19, 1775, Richard A. Roberts, ed., *Calendar of Home Office Papers of the Reign of George III, 1773-1775* (London: 1899), 409; Jeremie Duggan, individual #160141, Le Programme de recherche en démographie historique, www.prdh-igd.com/en/Acces (PRDH). See Bourquin's information in Table 1.

Tasked to help recruit Canadian irregulars, Ethan Allen's initial destination was just a few miles from British-held Fort Chambly, at Pointe Olivier. There, at the north end of the Chambly basin, Canadian leader James Livingston had already assembled hundreds of locals in an armed camp. Allen did not specifically mention visiting Pointe Olivier in his own accounts, but a report from Livingston fills in this otherwise-blank section of the picture. The partisan "colonel" told Allen that there were a few weakly-manned British ships about forty miles away, sitting in the St. Lawrence off Sorel, vulnerable to capture by a surprise stroke in the character of his coup at Ticonderoga. Allen apparently took this on as a new mission, since Livingston told General Montgomery that he "sent a party each side of the [Richelieu] River, Col: Allen at their head" to take the ships. This intermediate mission connects more parts of the picture. Describing his continued trip down the Richelieu in his *Narrative*, Allen said "my guard were Canadians, my interpreter, and some few attendants excepted." Other contemporary sources confirm that this Canadian core originated from Pointe Olivier, despite frequent historical speculation that Allen had recruited most or all of them himself. The "few attendants" were probably a small bodyguard assembled from Continental soldiers who had already been operating with the Canadians at the partisan camp, under the overarching command of Maj. John Brown. In numbers, these Canadians and Continental "attendants" are the most important part of the "motley parcel" puzzle.[4]

Contemporary sources further identify three partisan "captains" among Allen's Canadians at the Battle of Longue Pointe. Based on their prominent positions in the Patriot partisan movement, Jeremiah Duggan and Augustin Loiseau almost certainly led the Canadian parties sent with Allen to capture the ships in the St. Lawrence. Like Duggan, Loiseau had been "stirring up as many of the Canadians as he possibly could" around his own home parish of St. Denis and was building a reputation as "a good soldier and staunch friend to America

4. Allen, *Narrative*, 14-15; Allen to Montgomery, September 20, 1775, *AA4*, 3: 754; James Livingston to Schuyler, undated, *AA4*, 3: 744; Simon Sanguinet, "Témoin Oculaire de l'Invasion du Canada par les Bastonnois: Journal de M. Sanguinet," in Hospice-Anthelme Verreau, *Invasion du Canada: Collection des Mémoires Recueillis et Annotes* (Montreal: Eusèbe Senécal, 1873), 44, 49; "Quebec, September 28, 1775," and "[Nauticus] To the Printer … ," *Quebec Gazette*, October 5 and 19, 1775; Hector Cramahé to Earl of Dartmouth, September 24, 1775, General Staff, ed., *History of the … Military and Naval Forces of Canada*, 2: 81. In his last letter to Montgomery, Allen boasted of his ability to raise hundreds of Canadians, and noted that they gathered fast as he ventured down the Richelieu, and his *Narrative* described that he "preached politics" on the trip and "met with good success as an itinerant"; but he never specifically claimed that he had recruited the 250 "Canadians under arms" with him at St. Ours on September 20.

& its liberties." Allen's *Narrative* battle account mentioned a third Canadian leader, Richard Young—called a "captain" in one other Longue Pointe account—who curiously left no further documentary trace.[5]

In the *Narrative*, Allen did not mention the planned capture of British ships. He only said that he was "preaching politics" as he passed "through all the parishes" down the Richelieu to Sorel. During his lower Richelieu travels, however, Allen wrote his last letter to General Montgomery on September 20, from St. Ours, and confirmed that he had abandoned the ship-capture mission. Boasting that he had 250 Canadians with him, Allen also shared his intent to return to the Fort Saint Johns siege. He offered no explanation for his subsequent decision to continue north, toward the St. Lawrence, with his attached Canadians—away from his declared destination. After the St. Ours letter, Allen's *Narrative* is the only first-person source for the rest of the mission. After reaching the mouth of the Richelieu at Sorel, he simply described following the shoreline southwest, "up the [St. Lawrence] river through the parishes to Longueil." This baffling detour from Sorel to Longueuil has been another significant gap in the puzzle.[6]

An obscure document published in nineteenth-century Canadian sources seems to fill that void, though. On the night of September 22, Capt. John Grant of the Continental Green Mountain Boys Regiment wrote to Allen for help. Grant had received intelligence that a superior enemy force was preparing to attack his sixty-three-man detachment at Longueuil. He asked Allen "to send a party or com[e] as soon as ma[y] be[,] if not needed wh[e]re you now be." Even though Allen never mentioned Grant's plea, it offers a highly plausible reason for Allen to have led his force from the Richelieu Valley to Longueuil.[7]

Grant concluded his letter with another important line, that "Col. Leviston [James Livingston] hath just sent in an express hear and their

5. Allen, *Narrative*, 14-15, 19, 20; "An Extract of a Letter from Quebec, dated Oct. 1, 1775," J. Almon, ed., *The Remembrancer; or Impartial Repository of Public Events For the Year 1776, Part 1* (London: 1776), 136; John Graham Certification for Augustin Loseau, Albany, 3 May 1779; Augustin Loizeau Petition to John Jay, n.d.; John Brown Certification for Augustin Loizeau, May 6, 1779, i147 v3 r158 pp407, 409-11, 413, RG360, M247, NARA; Sanguinet, "Témoin Oculaire," 44, 49; "Extract of a letter from an officer of rank, dated Camp before St. John's, Nov. 1, 1775," *Connecticut Courant* [Hartford], November 20, 1775. Allen's *Narrative* called Duggan "John Duggan," and never named Loiseau, who was connected to the Longue Pointe force in Sanguinet's journal.

6. Allen, *Narrative*, 14.

7. John Grant to Allen, September 22, 1775, *The New Dominion Monthly* (June 1870): 63 (cites original in possession of Montreal historian Alfred Sandham). The letter's provenance is unknown, but it may have been seized from Allen after his capture.

is a party to our assistens on their march from Shambole [Chambly] expected this night." This second party from Pointe Olivier was not initially linked to Ethan Allen, but he presumably would have met it when he arrived in Longueuil sometime on September 23. Allen's *Narrative* and the primary source record are silent about who he actually met and what he did that night upon reaching Longueuil.[8]

The *Narrative* resumed on the morning of September 24 as Allen left Longueuil for La Prairie with a "guard of about eighty men." These would have been his few American "attendants" and those Canadians under Duggan and Loiseau who elected to follow Allen even after he abandoned the original mission to capture the British ships on the St. Lawrence. Presumably, Allen intended to take them to the La Prairie-Saint Johns road, which would lead them on to the Northern Army siege camp.[9]

Just two miles out of Longueuil, Allen and his men encountered Maj. John Brown, who was directing numerous Continental detachments over a broad operations area along the southeast banks of the St. Lawrence and the lower Richelieu Valley. According to Allen's *Narrative*, Brown and other officers persuaded him in private council to join a bold bid to take lightly-defended Montreal—the mission he fatefully accepted. Apparently, Allen rushed to execute the new plan without informing James Livingston of the scheme. Three days later, when Livingston finally received word of Allen's defeat, he told General Montgomery, "Mr. Allen should never have attempted to attack the Town without my knowledge or acquainting me of his design, as I had it in my Power to furnish him with a number of men." Clearly, none of the Pointe Olivier Canadian partisans had been attached to Allen with the intent to take Montreal.[10]

After meeting Brown, Allen described his return to Longueuil to "gather canoes," and he added "about thirty English Americans" to his party there. These men have been an important, established part of the "motley parcel" picture, but their origins and connections with the others remained a significant mystery. There is still no direct documentary proof, but Captain Grant's letter seems to provide the critical link—most of the thirty Continentals who joined Allen at Longueuil had probably come with the detachment sent by Livingston two days earlier

8. Ibid.; Allen, *Narrative*, 15.

9. Allen, *Narrative*, 15; Allen to Montgomery, September 20, 1775, *AA4*, 3: 754.

10. Allen, *Narrative*, 14-15; Mark R. Anderson, "Ethan Allen's Mysterious Defeat at Montreal – Reconsidered," *Journal of the American Revolution* (October 15, 2020), https://allthingsliberty.com/2020/10/ethan-allens-mysterious-defeat-at-montreal-reconsidered/; James Livingston to Montgomery, September 27, 1775, *AA4*, 3: 953.

to reinforce Grant. Some may also have been detached from Brown's own marching party after the September 24 council.[11]

TABLE I. American Contingent[12]

REGIMENT	COMPANY	NAME	RANK	OUTCOME
1st Connecticut	Douglas	Monson, Levi	Sgt.	prisoner
4th Connecticut	Buell	Moore, Roger	Corp.	prisoner
4th Connecticut	Elmore	Goff, David	Priv.	prisoner
4th Connecticut	Elmore	Gray, William	Priv.	prisoner
4th Connecticut	Elmore	Lewis, Samuel	Corp.	prisoner
4th Connecticut	Elmore	Maxam, Adonijah	Priv.	prisoner
4th Connecticut	Elmore	Brinsmade, Zachariah	Sgt.	prisoner
4th Connecticut	Griswold	Flower, Ithuriel	Priv.	prisoner
4th Connecticut	Starr	Mayo, Jonathan	Priv.	prisoner
4th Connecticut	Starr	Drinkwater, William	Priv.	prisoner
4th Connecticut	Watson	Mack, Ebenezer	Priv.	prisoner
4th Connecticut	Watson	Barnum, Levi	Priv.	prisoner
4th Connecticut	Watson	Noble, Peter	Priv.	prisoner
4th Connecticut	Watson	Stewart, Charles	Corp.	prisoner
5th Connecticut	Benedict	Cann, Barney	Priv.	prisoner
Easton's (Mass.)	Cochran	Cross, Uriah	Sgt.	retreated
Easton's (Mass.)	Cochran	Malleroy, Nathaniel[13]	Priv.	retreated
Easton's (Mass.)	Cochran?	Burk, Jonathan	Priv.	retreated
Easton's (Mass.)	Cochran?	Luttington, John	Priv.	retreated
1st New York	Mott	Bourquin, Jean Jac	Priv.	prisoner
2nd New York	Fisher	Gray, John	Priv.	prisoner
2nd New York	Graham	Denton, Preston	Priv.	prisoner
LIKELY PARTICIPANT				
2nd New York	Van Dyck	Rose, John[14]	Priv.	prisoner/ escaped

11. Allen, *Narrative*, 15-16; Trumbull, "Concise Journal," 146-47.
12. List of the Rebel Prisoners put onboard the Ship *Adamant*, November 9, 1775, CO 42/34 fols. 255-56, (microfilm) Library and Archives Canada; "American Prisoners in Halifax," Peter Force, ed. *American Archives, Fifth Series* (Washington, DC: M. St. Clair Clarke and Peter Force, 1848), 1: 1283-1284 (*AA5*). The author consulted local histories, *Daughters of the American Revolution Lineage Books*, and other minor sources for the most appropriate spelling of names. On the Halifax list Cann is identified as Barnabas Castle.
13. Malleroy, Burk, and Luttington are identified in Uriah Cross, "Narrative of Uriah Cross in the Revolutionary War," ed. Vernon Ives, *New York History* 63 no.3 (July 1982): 288. There are no extant rolls of Cochran's 1775 company, but limited evidence suggests that Burk and Luttington came from that unit.
14. In his pension narrative, John Rose stated that he was captured with Allen, but escaped when "he jumped over board from" HM Brig *Gaspée*, "swam ashore and again joined the army under Gen. Montgomery," John Rose, S43940, p50, RG15, M804, NARA. See also

POTENTIAL PARTICIPANT
2nd New York   Graham   Scott, Edward[15]   Priv.   retreated/WIA

Assembling all these pieces of the picture, and shifting known elements around with likely connections, it appears that Allen's force had three key components when he led it across the St. Lawrence to the Island of Montreal on the night of September 24-25. First were the few men directly connected to Allen's September 18 departure from the Northern Army camp. The largest and most important contingent came from about eighty Canadian irregulars and a small Continental entourage, originally detached from Pointe Olivier to join Allen for the projected St. Lawrence ship-capture mission. The third component consisted of the thirty-some Continentals who joined him at Longueuil on the day before the battle—probably from the detachment that John Grant said Livingston was sending from Chambly (Pointe Olivier)

There are even more pieces of the puzzle that add detail and refine the image of these three main contingents. Two British lists of Longue Pointe prisoners describe specific members of the American contingent. Twenty-two are specifically identified by name—a large sample size from a group of about thirty. These men, all Continentals, were drawn from six different regiments. Thirteen came from the 4th Connecticut Regiment, up to four from James Easton's Massachusetts Regiment, at least two from the 2nd New York, and there was one each from the 1st and 5th Connecticut, and 1st New York; but no more than five came from the same company. How did these seemingly odd, unconnected elements come together to form the American contingent?

The Americans' apparently scattershot unit assignments are explained in Northern Army commanders' tendency to rely on volunteers for dangerous missions away from the main camp—as documented in orderly books and pension narratives. Except for 2nd New York Regiment units that moved to La Prairie in late September, the companies listed in Table 1 all remained with the main army around Fort Saint Johns while detached volunteers roamed the Richelieu Valley and banks

---

Philip D. Weaver, "William Dickens, John Rose, and William Turnbull: Soldiers of the 2nd New York Regiment," *Journal of the American Revolution* (August 5, 2020), allthingsliberty.com/2020/08/william-dickens-john-rose-and-william-turnbull/.

15. Circumstantially, Scott may have been at Longue Pointe. A 1789 compensation petition recorded that he was "wounded near Montreal on the 24th. of Septr. 1775 in his Right Shoulder." Since there is no record of any firefights in the area on the 24th, Longue Pointe is the most likely engagement where he suffered the wound; Report of the New York Commissioners of Invalids, 29 October 1789, in Kenneth R. Bowling, et. al., eds., *Petition Histories: Revolutionary War Related Claims* (Baltimore, MD: Johns Hopkins University Press, 1998), 7: 425.

of the St. Lawrence. The high ratio of non-commissioned officers to privates—at least one to three—further indicates that these were volunteers or handpicked men. Early twentieth-century Allen biographer John Pell was broadly correct when he surmised that the Longue Pointe party's Americans had "a diversity which indicates that the men had individually volunteered."[16]

Two of the Americans also provided pension narratives that give hazy, but valuable, insight into their individual paths to Longue Pointe. Their accounts do not specifically explain how and when they joined Allen, but still fit within the established framework. Private Adonijah Maxam recounted his departure from the main camp outside Fort Saint Johns, beginning:

> Capt. [John] Watson of Canaan, Capt. [Joseph] McCracken of the [2nd] New York troops and Major Brown went with a large party of men of whom I was one, for the purpose of penetrating thro the wood to Chambly in Canada. We lay at Chambly a few days & then I went to keep guard below Chambly [the Pointe Olivier camp]. Col Ethan Allen came to us there. We crossed the St. Lawrence River in the night with Col Allen a little below Montreal and while preparing breakfast the British force came upon us. We retreated & finally I was with Col Ethan Allen and others taken prisoner by the enemy.[17]

Maxam's vague account seems to imply that he joined Allen near Chambly. He may have been one of the "few attendants" who joined Allen from Pointe Olivier for the initial ship-capture and recruiting mission on the lower Richelieu.

Another one of Allen's Continentals, Sgt. Uriah Cross, wrote a pension account that was later published from a family-held manuscript. Cross described his departure from the main army camp as a participant in a fight on the night of September 17–18, at the crossroads immediately north of Fort Saint Johns: "I was now with Col Butler [Timothy Bedel] and Major Brown['s] Regement who met a number of teams going to St Johns with provisions which was taken. Brown marched and took Cheamblee [Chambly]." His grasp of chronology had faded by the time this narrative was recorded in 1828, most notably in that

16. September 10 and September 16 entries, 5th Connecticut Orderly Book, Early American Orderly Books, p25, 27, Reel 2, no. 17, (microfilm) New-York Historical Society; Cross, "Narrative," 287–88; Petitions from Jonathan S. Alexander, W[no number], p4; Roswell Smith, S14490, p4; and Alpheus Hall, W19717, p9, RG15, M804, NARA; John Pell, *Ethan Allen* (Lake George, NY: Adirondack Resorts Press, 1929), 117; David Bennett, *A Few Lawless Vagabonds: Ethan Allen, the Republic of Vermont, and the American Revolution* (Havertown, PA: Casemate, 2014), 83.
17. Petition of Adonijah Maxam, W5345, p5, RG15, M804, NARA.

Brown would not capture Fort Chambly until almost a month after Longue Pointe.[18]

From Chambly, Cross resumed: "I now with a number of others volunterd to go with Eathen Allen as our commander to take Montreal. We marched to longale [Longueuil] where we was met by the enemy and defeated." Longueuil and Longue Pointe had merged into a single place in his distant memories. While Cross's narrative gap between Chambly and volunteering to join Allen leaves room for interpretation, it is possible that he had been in the detachment sent from Pointe Olivier to reinforce Captain Grant at Longueuil, where he would become one of the thirty "English Americans" who joined Allen on September 24.[19]

The breadth of primary sources illuminates the American contingent's diverse origins and varied paths to the ultimate assembly point at Longueuil. It is worth noting that even with all of the information now available about Allen's Americans at the Battle of Longue Pointe, there is still no documentary evidence to support early Vermont historian Zadock Thompson's suggestion that "Allen's force was made up of Green Mountain Boys and Canadians." If any Continental Green Mountain Boys participated in the operation, they were not only a minority, but they *all* managed to escape capture or death at Longue Pointe.[20]

TABLE 2. Canadian Contingent[21]

PARISH	LAST NAME	FIRST NAME	AGE	PARISH RECORD	OUTCOME
St Denis	Loiseau	Augustin	35	#104876	retreated
St Denis	Frechette	Pierre	19?	? #176882	prisoner

18. Cross, "Narrative," 280, 288. A second, later Cross narrative in government records only described serving with Brown around Chambly in the fall campaign, without mentioning Allen or Longue Pointe; Petition of Uriah Cross, S10499, p5, RG15, M804, NARA.

19. Cross, "Narrative," 288.

20. Zadock Thompson, *History of the State of Vermont: Natural, Civil, and Statistical*, Part Second (Burlington, VT: Chauncey Goodrich, 1842), 35; Bennett, *A Few Lawless Vagabonds*, 83. Uriah Cross, and perhaps some others, had peripheral contact with the Green Mountain Boys in the summer of 1775, but none appear to have had an enduring association with the militia group.

21. List of the Rebel Prisoners put onboard the Ship *Adamant*. In the *Adamant* list, Frechette is spelled Trichet, Maillott is spelled Mayotte, and Plouf is spelled Pluse. Parish Record numbers are from PRDH: Frechette, Trudeau, and Lamarche are possible parish record matches; St. Laurent and Louis Laroche do not have region-appropriate parish records matches. Belisle died as a prisoner off Cape Fear, NC in 1776; "American Prisoners in Halifax," AA5, 1: 1283-84.

St Denis	Gauthier	Michel	18	#181137	prisoner
St Denis	Trudeau	Louis	24?	? #16549	prisoner
Beloiel	Laroche	Pierre (Amable)	36	#81160	prisoner
Beloiel	Livernois	Francois	44	#147422	prisoner
Beloiel	Maillott	Augustin	26	#207687	prisoner
St Ours	Duggan	Jeremiah	Unk	#160141	retreated
St Ours	Plouf	Alexis	22	#171510	prisoner
Chambly	Lamarche	Jean(-Baptiste?)	16?	? #186475	prisoner
Deschaillons	St. Laurent	Francois	unk	N/A	prisoner
Longueuil	Laroche	Louis	unk	N/A	prisoner
Montreal?	Young	Richard	unk	N/A	retreated
St Charles	Belisle	Antoine	21	#174853	prisoner

POSSIBLE PARTICIPANT

| Unk | Brosseau | François | 33 | #110512 | died |

In contrast to the reasonably well-developed picture of the American contingent, the depiction of the Canadians still lacks many pieces. Beyond leaders Duggan and Loiseau, the only meaningful source of information about specific Canadian contingent members comes from one British prisoner list, which identified eleven men taken with Allen. Nine of them came from lower Richelieu parishes between Chambly and Sorel, the heartland of the Fall 1775 Canadian Patriot uprising. Three dwelt in Loiseau's home parish of St. Denis; one came from Duggan's in St. Ours. Louis Laroche from Longueuil may have been a late addition to the force, perhaps joining at the canoe crossing to Longue Pointe. Burial records circumstantially suggest one more Canadian Patriot battle participant. Allen wrote that after his surrender, "the wounded were all put into the hospital at Montreal," and on the day of the battle, François Brosseau died in the city's General Hospital of the Gray Sisters.[22]

The relatively scant information gleaned from Canadian prisoner demographics still fits within the established framework of Allen's path to Longue Pointe—with the vast majority of the men apparently being first attached to Allen from the Pointe Olivier partisan camp for the ship-capture mission. In any case, a sample size of just eleven or twelve Patriot Canadian fighters is too small to draw any firm conclusions about the seventy- or eighty-man contingent; it only depicts Allen's

22. Sanguinet, "Témoin Oculaire," 44, 49; "[Nauticus] To the Printer ...," *Quebec Gazette*, October 19, 1775; James Livingston to Montgomery, September 27, 1775, *AA4*, 3: 953; James Livingston to Schuyler, undated, AA4, 3: 743-744; Bennett, *A Few Lawless Vagabonds*, 77; "Marie Joseph François Brousseau Brosseau," individual #110512, PRDH; Allen, *Narrative*, 27.

Canadian die-hards—those who stuck with him to the point of surrender or death.

There are still many missing pieces and substantial gaps, but the partially-complete jigsaw puzzle picture that can be rendered from expanded, digitally-supported documentary analysis helps dispel some historians' well-intentioned speculations and offers two key conclusions about Allen's "motley parcel of soldiery" at Longue Pointe. First, the Americans were a composite contingent of volunteers drawn from several Continental units, attached to Allen at multiple points in his path to Longue Pointe. Second, most of the Canadians were sent from James Livingston's Pointe Olivier partisan camp—undoubtedly under the immediate leadership of Jeremiah Duggan and Augustin Loiseau—following Allen as his mission evolved into their catastrophic attempt on Montreal.

The Devil at the Helm:
A Quote That Went Astray

✺ DON N. HAGIST ✺

John Marshall Deane was a soldier in the 1st Regiment of Foot Guards, among the oldest established regiments of the British army, in March 1708 when his regiment, serving in Belgium, was ordered to Scotland. They marched from Ghent to the port of Ostend where they boarded transports on March 15. They spent five weeks on board, waiting for favorable winds, sailing part of the way to their destination, learning that their mission was cancelled, and returning to Ostend where they disembarked on April 21.

Deane wrote a memoir of his service in Belgium, or Flanders as it was called at the time, which was not published until 1840. Of his time shipboard, he wrote,

> While we lay on board we had continual Distruction in ye foretop; ye Pox above board; ye Pleague between Decks: hell in ye forecastle, and ye Devil at ye Helm.[1]

The printed edition of his journal, presumably emulating his handwriting, used the "y" character to emulate a handwritten character that gave the "th" sound, a style of writing that had largely fallen out of use by the end of the eighteenth century and which causes modern readers to read "ye" instead of "the."

Deane's language is colorful, and may be familiar to students of the American Revolution, because at some point in the late nineteenth century an author incorrectly stated that it was written about a voyage from England to New York in 1776. Since that first error, it has been widely repeated—the passage appears in Richard M. Ketchum's *Decisive Day*

1. John Marshall Deane, *A Journal of the Campaign in Flanders 1708* (no publisher, 1846), 6.

(1974)[2] and John Ferling's *Almost a Miracle* (2007),[3] among other books. The spelling is usually modernized.

The passage caught my attention while working on my book *Noble Volunteers: the British Soldiers Who Fought the American Revolution*. I'd seen it before, but took notice of it in Edward R. Curtis's *The Organization of the British Army in the American Revolution*, where it is attributed to "an officer of the Guards, who was going with a detachment to join Howe at New York."[4] I've made it a point to seek out and read every known account by British officers and soldiers who served in America, so I immediately wanted to know which officer wrote this, and what else he had to say. Curtis's footnote, though, cited another book rather than the original writer—Henry Belcher's *The First American Civil War*, published in 1911. Checking that book aroused my suspicions, because Belcher attributed the quote to "a non-commissioned officer of the Guards" rather than an officer.[5] A small difference, but an indication that something was amiss. And it whetted my appetite, because writings by non-commissioned officers are exceedingly rare. But Belcher gave no source for the quotation.

Today we have an advantage that these previous writers did not: the Internet. A few minutes of searching took me to a book from the nineteenth century that cited the passage correctly to Deane's journal of the 1708 campaign, and with the correct title it was easy to find the original published source. Belcher was the earliest work I found that incorrectly dated the passage to 1776; he may have taken it from an earlier secondary source, or gotten his notes mixed up.

Deane's writing about his time on a transport is amusing and vivid, but has nothing to do with the American Revolution. Its frequent misuse illustrates why *Journal of the American Revolution* insists that contributing authors rely mainly on primary sources—just because a quotation appears in the work of a credible author doesn't mean that it is accurate.

---

2. Richard M. Ketchum, *Decisive Day: the Battle for Bunker Hill* (New York: Doubleday, 1974), 13.

3. John Ferling, *Almost a Miracle* (London: Oxford University Press, 2007), 126.

4. Edward R. Curtis, *The Organization of the British Army in the American Revolution* (New Haven: Yale University Press, 1926).

5. Henry Belcher, *The first American civil war* (London: MacMillan and Co., 1911), 255.

Thomas Knowlton's Revolution

❦❧ DAVID PRICE ❦❧

The story of Thomas Knowlton in the American Revolution is brief but meaningful. He was only thirty-five at his death, arguably a full-fledged hero in what George Washington termed "the "glorious Cause"[1] of American independence. The Connecticut colonel remains largely obscure in our collective historical consciousness but has been long recognized by serious students of the Revolution for his stellar personal qualities and the dynamic role he played in the early stages of the conflict.

Knowlton was born in West Boxford, Massachusetts, just north of Boston, on November 22, 1740[2] to William and Martha Knowlton, his family of English origin being among the earliest settlers in the colony. William moved the household to Ashford in eastern Connecticut when Thomas was eight. The boy's formal learning was limited to the narrow course of study generally characterizing instruction in the common schools at that time. As a strapping fifteen-year-old, he took up arms with the Anglo-American forces in the French and Indian War, rising to the rank of lieutenant in a provincial unit by age twenty and surviving the Battle of Wood Creek in 1758, the campaign to capture Fort Carillon (Fort Ticonderoga) in 1759 and the siege of Havana in 1762.

Knowlton married Anna Keyes of Ashford at age eighteen, and between them they raised nine children. He became a prosperous farmer and at age thirty-three was chosen as a member of the local board of selectmen, the functional equivalent of a municipal council member.

1. George Washington's Address to Congress, June 16, 1775, in *This Glorious Struggle: George Washington's Revolutionary War Letters*, ed. Edward G. Lengel (Charlottesville, VA: University of Virginia Press, 2007), 4.
2. Ashbel Woodward, *Memoir of Col. Thomas Knowlton, of Ashford, Connecticut* (Boston: Henry W. Dutton & Son, 1861. Reprinted by Andesite Press, 2015), 3. The author inferred Knowlton's birthdate from church baptismal records.

Being six feet tall, the lean and youthful New Englander was an imposing figure. Dr. Ashbel Woodward, his nineteenth-century biographer who lived in Ashford as a boy, described his subject as having a naturally bright intellect and recalled the enthusiasm and affection with which the colonel's surviving contemporaries always spoke of him.[3]

Knowlton became actively involved in the rebellion against Britain when news came to Ashford of the shooting that had erupted at Lexington and Concord on April 19, 1775. He was unanimously chosen as captain of his militia unit, the Ashford Company, which became the first to enter Massachusetts from another colony when he led these armed farmers across its boundary to support the Massachusetts militia who had engaged the redcoats. The Ashford volunteers were reorganized into the 5th Company of the 3rd Connecticut Regiment under Gen. Israel Putnam—with whom Knowlton had served in the last war—as the various contingents of citizen-soldiers gathering in Cambridge, just west of British-occupied Boston, attempted to form some semblance of an army.

On June 17, Captain Knowlton played a significant leadership role at the Battle of Bunker Hill on the Charlestown peninsula outside Boston. About two hundred men were under his command that day as part of a larger force led by Col. William Prescott.[4] Ordered by Colonel Prescott to oppose the advance of the British grenadiers, Knowlton's force took up a position on the eastern slope of Breed's hill facing the Mystic River along a livestock fence that stretched for several hundred yards from the center of the peninsula nearly to the river. The captain's men reinforced this barrier with rails and posts taken from other fields while filling any openings with newly cut grass and hay to create a suitable breastwork. "Here they received the enemy to very tolerable advantage," according to Capt. John Chester.[5] Knowlton's unit held its place until a general retreat was ordered, losing only three soldiers in the struggle. Functioning as a rearguard, it was among those providing protective cover as the entire rebel force was forced to withdraw once they had depleted their ammunition. For his role in the defense of Breed's Hill, an image of Knowlton—wearing a white shirt and pointing his musket at the oncoming British regulars—is prominently in-

3. Woodward, *Memoir of Col. Thomas Knowlton*, 15.
4. William Prescott to John Adams, August 25, 1775, in *The Spirit of 'Seventy-Six: The Story of the American Revolution As Told by Participants*, eds. Henry Steele Commager and Richard B. Morris (New York: Harper & Row, Publishers, 1967), 125.
5. John Chester to Joseph Fish, July 22, 1775, in Richard Frothingham, *History of the Siege of Boston, and of the Battles of Lexington, Concord, and Bunker Hill* (Boston: Little, Brown and Company, 1873), 390.

cluded among the various figures portrayed in John Trumbull's cele-
brated painting *The Death of General Warren at the Battle of Bunker's
Hill, June 17, 1775*, currently displayed at the Museum of Fine Arts in
Boston.[6]

The defenders exacted a heavy price in exchange for the ground they
stubbornly yielded to His Majesty's forces, causing one British officer
to lament that "from an absurd and destructive confidence, carelessness
or ignorance, we have lost a thousand of our best men and officers and
have given the rebels great matter of triumph by showing them what
mischief they can do us."[7] In a letter to her husband John—then attending Congress in Philadelphia—from their home in Braintree, Massachusetts, Abigail Adams took satisfaction from the attackers' tally of
dead and wounded, which exceeded American casualties by more than
two to one, even as she bemoaned the devastation of Charlestown by
British cannons:

> My Father has been more affected with the destruction of charlstown
> than with any thing which has heretofore taken place. Why should not
> his countenance be sad, when the city, the place of his Fathers Sepul-
> chers lieth waste, and the gates thereof are consumed with fire, scarcly
> one stone remaineth upon an other. But in the midst of sorrow we have
> abundant cause of thankfulness that so few of our Breathren are num-
> bered with the slain, whilst our enemies were cut down like the Grass
> before the Sythe. But one officer of the welch fuzelers remains to tell
> his story. Many poor wretches dye for want of proper assistance and
> care of their wounds.[8]

The scenes of desperate fighting at Breed's Hill were recorded by
one of the rebel combatants, upon whom the bloodshed left an indelible
impression long afterwards:

> The firing on the part of the British commenced at an early hour in
> the morning from their ships and batteries. But the engagement did
> not become general until a little after noon, when their forces crossed
> Charles River and attempted to dislodge the Americans from the re-

6. Joseph J. Ellis, *Revolutionary Summer: The Birth of American Independence* (New York:
Alfred A. Knopf, 2013), 153; Arthur S. Lefkowitz, *Eyewitness Images from the American
Revolution* (Gretna, LA: Pelican Publishing Company, 2017), 78; Paul Staiti, *Of Arms and
Artists: The American Revolution through Painters' Eyes* (New York: Bloomsbury Press, 2016),
180; Woodward, *Memoir of Col. Thomas Knowlton*, 17.
7. Letter of a British officer, July 5, 1775, in *The Spirit of 'Seventy-Six*, 135.
8. Abigail Adams to John Adams, June 25, 1775, in *My Dearest Friend: Letters of Abigail
and John Adams*, eds. Margaret A. Hogan and C. James Taylor (Cambridge, MA: The Belk-
nap Press of Harvard University Press, 2007), 65.

doubt which they had erected the previous night. The battle was severe and the British repulsed at every charge until, for want of ammunition, the Americans were compelled to retire. The awful solemnities of that day are still deeply impressed upon declarant's mind, and the scenes of carnage and death . . . appear as vivid as if the events of yesterday.[9]

Knowlton was named major in Benedict Arnold's 20th Continental Regiment on January 1, 1776 and led a successful raid on January 8 that set fire to eight of the fourteen houses still standing in Charlestown—those that had escaped the fires sparked by cannon fire during the Breed's Hill battle—in order to prevent their being occupied by British patrols or used as firewood by the redcoats. The intruders captured five British soldiers while barely firing a shot and without losing a single man[10] The other side's response was much more clamorous. Writing to his friend Mercy Otis Warren from Braintree that night, John Adams reported what he saw and heard of this action: "A very hot Fire both of Artillery and small Arms has continued for half an Hour, and has been succeded by a luminous Phoenomenon, over Braintree North Common occasioned by Burning Buildings I suppose."[11] In his general orders the following day, Washington thanked Knowlton

> and the Officers and Soldiers, who were under his command last night; for the Spirit, Conduct and Secrecy, with which they burnt the Houses, near the Enemy's works, upon Bunkers-hill—The General was in a more particular manner pleased, with the resolution the party discover'd in not firing a Shot; as nothing betrays greater signs of fear, and less of the soldier, than to begin a loose, undirected and unmeaning Fire, from whence no good can result, nor any valuable purposes answer'd.[12]

Aaron Burr, a fellow officer who became acquainted with Knowlton during their military service, is said to have remarked years later, "It was impossible to promote such a man too rapidly."[13] The rising Continental advanced to the rank of lieutenant colonel of the 20th Regiment on August 12, 1776, and at Washington's direction formed a

9. Jonathan Brigham, Military Pension Application Narrative, in *The Revolution Remembered: Eyewitness Accounts of the War for Independence*, ed. John C. Dann (Chicago: University of Chicago Press, 1980), 4.

10. George Washington to John Hancock, January 11, 1776, *Founders Online*, National Archives. founders.archives.gov/?q=Thomas%20Knowlton&s=1511311111&r=7.

11. John Adams to Mercy Otis Warren, January 8, 1776, *Founders Online*, National Archives. founders.archives.gov/?q=Thomas%20Knowlton&s=1511311111&r=1.

12. General Orders, January 9, 1776, *Founders Online*, National Archives. founders.archives.gov/?q=Thomas%20Knowlton&s=1511311111&r=6.

13. Woodward, *Memoir of Col. Thomas Knowlton*, 11.

contingent known as "Knowlton's Rangers" or the "Connecticut Rangers," which included about one hundred and thirty soldiers from Connecticut, Massachusetts and Rhode Island. Regarded as an elite unit, its purpose was to meet the general's desperate need for information about the British forces opposing him, he being "extremely anxious to learn the strength and contemplated movements of the enemy."[14] The army's commander-in-chief betrayed this anxiety when he wrote on August 26 from his headquarters in New York city to the manager of his Mount Vernon estate, cousin Lund Washington, and confessed to uncertainty about his adversary's intentions in the wake of their landing "a pretty considerable part of their force" on Long Island: "What their real design is I know not; whether they think our works round this City are too strong, and have a Mind to bend their whole force that way—or whether it is intended as a feint—or is to form part of their Attack, we cannot as yet tell."[15] Washington's lack of information about enemy troop totals and dispositions prior to and during the Battle of Long Island on August 27, which eventuated in a near-catastrophe for his army, convinced him that he needed a singular force dedicated to this purpose, which would report directly to him.

In the wake of the Long Island debacle, Washington turned to Knowlton to provide a special scouting service in order to obtain accurate information about the enemy's strength and positions on British-occupied Long Island. Accordingly, the colonel called on his captains to find a volunteer from among the Rangers who was willing to go behind enemy lines, but only one man agreed to do so—twenty-one-year-old Capt. Nathan Hale. Hale consented after Lt. James Sprague refused the "application" to serve as a spy on the grounds that "he was ready to fight at any time or place however dangerous but never could consent to expose himself to be hung like a dog."[16] Knowlton inadvertently created a legendary hero by accepting Hale's offer to undertake the information-gathering mission ordered by Washington, even though the youthful captain, who was described as "peculiarly free from the shadow of guile . . . however imperious circumstances of personal safety might

14. Woodward, *Memoir of Col. Thomas Knowlton*, 13.

15. George Washington to Lund Washington, August 26, 1776, in *This Glorious Struggle*, 59.

16. Jasper Gilbert to Cyrus P. Bradley, January 9, 1836, in *Documentary Life of Nathan Hale, Comprising All Available Official and Private Documents Bearing on the Life of The Patriot, Together with an Appendix, showing the background of his life; including his family circle; his college friends; his friends made as a school-master and in the army; with many illustrations, portraits and buildings that knew his footsteps*, ed. George Dudley Seymour (New Haven, CT: Privately printed, 1941), 339.

demand a resort to duplicity & ambiguity," was temperamentally ill-suited to such an endeavor, as his fate would attest.[17]

Departing the American encampment at Harlem Heights during the second week of September, Hale dressed as a schoolmaster and crossed to Long Island, where he was captured by the British on September 21. Gen. William Howe, the British army's commander, ordered the prisoner to be executed as a spy the following day. The next morning, prior to his hanging on Manhattan Island, Hale dashed off a report to Knowlton that was included among the young captain's last letters, unaware that his commanding officer was no longer alive.[18] One British officer observed that Hale "behaved with great composure and resolution, saying he thought it the duty of every good Officer, to obey any orders given him by his Commander-in-Chief; and desired the Spectators to be at all times prepared to meet death in whatever shape it might appear."[19]

Nathan Hale's demise followed by six days that of his colonel. Thomas Knowlton had suffered a mortal wound at the Battle of Harlem Heights on upper Manhattan Island on September 16 while leading his men during what proved to be a rare triumph in an otherwise dismal New York campaign for the Patriot cause. Washington's battered and weary soldiery had retreated in haste up the island the day before to elude the pursuing Anglo-German invaders who came ashore at Kip's Bay (the site of 34th Street today), but now they turned to face their attackers. The latter "met with a very different kind of Reception from what they did the day before," according to Washington's youngest general, Nathanael Greene, who was experiencing his first taste of battle.[20] The King's soldiers, he wrote, "flushed with the successes of the day before, approached and attacked our Lines, which I had the Honor to Command. The Action or rather Skirmish lasted about two hours; our people beat the enemy off the ground."[21] The redcoats ultimately withdrew through a field of buckwheat on the grounds now occupied by Barnard College and Columbia University, and Col. George Wee-

17. William W. Saltonstall to Cyrus P. Bradley, March 1, 1837, in *Documentary Life of Nathan Hale*, 349.
18. M. William Phelps, *Nathan Hale: The Life and Death of America's First Spy* (New York: Thomas Dunne Books, 2008), 189.
19. Lt. Frederick MacKenzie, diary entry of September 22, 1776, in *Documentary Life of Nathan Hale*, 292.
20. Nathanael Greene to Nicholas Cooke, September 17, 1776, in *The Papers of General Nathanael Greene*, ed. Richard K. Showman (Chapel Hill, NC: The University of North Carolina Press, 1976), 1:300.
21. Greene to [William Ellery?], October 4, 1776, ibid., 1:307.

don of the 3rd Virginia Regiment encapsulated the outcome of this encounter for their foe: "Upon the whole they got cursedly thrashed."[22]

Notwithstanding the fact that the repulse of the British advance at Harlem Heights would do nothing to alter the larger dynamic of the New York campaign, Washington could take heart from his troops' determined resistance and the positive, if fleeting, impact it had on their morale: "This Affair I am in hopes will be attended with many salutary consequences, as It seems to have greatly inspirited the whole of our Troops."[23] This occasion, the first battlefield success of his army, was marked by a significant development. The participation of units from Connecticut, Maryland, Massachusetts, Rhode Island and Virginia in a concerted effort that transcended regional factionalism gave evidence that Washington was slowly, if painfully, building a national army that could, under the right circumstances, offer effective resistance to the Crown's forces. In addition, this action provided valuable combat experience for some of his men that hardened them for the lengthy struggle ahead, as these novice soldiers were being forced to acclimate themselves to the reality of an austere military existence. Pvt. Joseph Plumb Martin of the Connecticut militia illustrated this phenomenon when he related the following incident: "While standing on the field, after the action had ceased," one of the men in his unit complained of being hungry and the officer nearby, "putting his hand into his coat pocket, took out a piece of an ear of Indian corn, burnt as black as a coal, 'Here,' said he to the man complaining, 'eat this and learn to be a soldier.'"[24]

Martin, who claimed to have met Colonel Knowlton years before, recounted the stand made by his Rangers and the Virginians accompanying them in the Harlem Heights clash:

> We lay that night [September 15-16] upon the ground, which the regiment occupied when I came up with it. The next day, in the forenoon, the enemy, as we expected, followed us 'hard up,' and were advancing through a level field; our rangers and some few other light troops, under the command of Colonel Knowlton, and Major Leitch of (I believe) Virginia [Maj. Andrew Leitch commanding riflemen from Weedon's 3rd Virginia Regiment], were in waiting for them. Seeing them advancing, the rangers, &c. concealed themselves in a deep gully overgrown with bushes; upon the western edge of this defile was a post and rail fence . . .

22. George Weedon to John Page, September 20, 1776, in *The Spirit of 'Seventy-Six*, 471.
23. George Washington to Hancock, September 18, 1776, *Founders Online*, National Archives. founders.archives.gov/documents/Washington/03-06-02-0264.
24. Joseph Plumb Martin, *Memoir of a Revolutionary Soldier: The Narrative of Joseph Plumb Martin* (Mineola, NY: Dover Publications, Inc., 2006), 25.

Our people let the enemy advance until they arrived at the fence, when they arose and poured in a volley upon them. How many of the enemy were killed and wounded could not be known, as the British were always as careful as Indians to conceal their losses. There were, doubtless, some killed, as I myself counted nineteen ball-holes through a single rail of the fence at which the enemy were standing when the action began. The British gave back and our people advanced into the field.

Martin recalled that,

The action soon became warm. Colonel Knowlton, a brave man, and commander of the detachment, fell in the early part of the engagement. It was said, by those who saw it, that he lost his valuable life by unadvisedly exposing himself singly to the enemy. In my boyhood I had been acquainted with him; he was a brave man and an excellent citizen. Major Leitch fell soon after, and the troops, who were then engaged, were left with no higher commanders than their captains, but they still kept the enemy retreating.[25]

Another officer in Knowlton's Rangers, probably Capt. Stephen Brown, wrote to a friend,

My poor Colonel . . . was shot just by my Side, the Ball entered the small of his Back—I took hold of him, asked him if he was badly wounded? He told me he was; but, says he, I do not value my Life if we do but get the Day: I then ordered two men to carry him off. He desired me by all Means to keep up this Flank. He seemed as unconcern'd and calm as tho' nothing had happened to him.[26]

Sgt. David Thorp of Woodbury, Connecticut, remembered that "we had a very severe battle with the enemy . . . and brave commander Colonel who fell in the battle—He did not say 'go boys,' but 'come boys,' and we always were ready and willing to follow him, until he fell within six feet where I was—He begged to be moved so that the enemy should not get possession of his body—I was one who helped put him on soldiers shoulders who carried him off—He expired in about one hour."[27]

25. Ibid., 24-25.
26. Excerpt from a letter from an officer to his friend in New London, Connecticut, September 21, 1776, in Henry P. Johnston, *The Battle of Harlem Heights, September 16, 1776; With a Review of the Events of the Campaign* (New York: The MacMillan Company, 1897. Reprinted by Franklin Classics, 2018), 155.
27. David Thorp, Military Pension Application Narrative, in Johnston, *The Battle of Harlem Heights*, 195.

With his dying words, the stricken colonel reportedly urged his eldest son Frederick, then serving under him and not yet sixteen years of
age, to fight for his country.[28] In death, he was lauded by Washington
in his general orders as "the gallant and brave Colonel Knowlton who
would have been an honor to any Country"[29] and in a letter to congressional president John Hancock as one whose "fall is much to be regret-
ted, as that of a brave & good Officer."[30]

The sentiments expressed by the commander-in-chief were widely
echoed by other soldiers and friends of the Revolution. The army's adjutant general, Col. Joseph Reed, writing to his wife about the Harlem
Heights engagement, observed that "our greatest Loss was a brave Officer from Connecticut whose Name & Spirit ought to be immortal-
ized, one Col Knowlton—I assisted him off & when gasping in the
Agonies of Death all his Inquiry was if we had drove the enemy."[31] Lt.
Col. Tench Tilghman, an aide-de-camp to Washington, praised the
fallen Knowlton as "one of the bravest and best officers in the army"
and noted that despite his fate, the Rangers had "persisted with the
greatest bravery" during the balance of the engagement.[32] Gen. George
Clinton, in recounting the events of September 16, referred to Col.
Knowlton as "a brave Officer who was killed in the Action."[33] Governor
Jonathan Trumbull of Connecticut, a staunch supporter of the Revolution, added to this mournful litany when corresponding with his son
Joseph, the Continental Army's commissary general: "I lament the loss
of the brave Lt. Col. Knowlton—would others behave with the spirit
and bravery he did, our affairs would soon put on a different aspect."[34]

Knowlton was buried in an unmarked grave along what is now Saint
Nicholas Avenue between 135th and 145th streets in New York City.[35]

28. Frederick Knowlton returned home upon his father's death. See Johnston, *The Battle
of Harlem Heights*, 192. Thomas Knowlton's older brother Daniel, who was serving as an
ensign with the Rangers, was captured by the British at Fort Washington in November
1776. See Johnston, *The Battle of Harlem Heights*, 190.

29. Washington's General Orders, September 17, 1776, in Johnston, *The Battle of Harlem
Heights*, 162.

30. George Washington to Hancock, September 18, 1776 *Founders Online*, National
Archives. founders.archives.gov/documents/Washington/03-06-02-0264.

31. Joseph Reed to his wife, September 17, 1776, in Johnston, *The Battle of Harlem Heights*,
135.

32. Tench Tilghman to his father, September 19, 1776, in *The Spirit of 'Seventy-Six*, 470.

33. George Clinton to Peter Tappan, in Johnston, *The Battle of Harlem Heights*, 143.

34. Jonathan Trumbull to Joseph Trumbull, September 21, 1776, in I.W. Stuart, *Life of
Jonathan Trumbull, Sen., Governor of Connecticut*. (Boston: Crocker and Brewster, 1859.
Reprinted by Kessinger Publishing, LLC, 2010), 275.

35. Johnston, *The Battle of Harlem Heights*, 79.

According to Gen. William Heath, a fellow New Englander, the colonel's remains "were interred with military honours" the day after the Harlem Heights battle.[36] A monument of Knowlton, standing defiant with sword in hand, has stood on the state capitol grounds in Hartford, Connecticut, near the corner of Trinity Street and Capitol Avenue, since 1895, the creation of sculptor Enoch Smith Woods. The following dedication is inscribed on the east side of its base:

> In memory of Colonel Thomas Knowlton of Ashford Conn. who as a boy served in several campaigns in the French and Indian Wars, shared in the siege and capture of Havana in 1762, was in immediate command of Connecticut troops at the Battle of Bunker Hill, was with his commands closely attached to the person of Washington, and was killed at the Battle of Harlem Heights, September 16, 1776, at the age of thirty-six.[37]

Today, the date 1776 on the U.S. Army Intelligence Seal denotes the formation of Knowlton's Rangers as the forerunner of the present-day army's intelligence branch. In June 1995, the Military Intelligence Corps Association (MICA) established the "Knowlton Award" in the colonel's honor to recognize MICA members who have made significant contributions to the corps, which encompasses the army's various military intelligence components and their personnel. Those who are so recognized must exhibit the highest standards of integrity and moral character as well as outstanding professional competence.[38] The award is a fitting tribute to a man who by all accounts demonstrated the competence, courage and resolve that endeared him to Washington, his fellow officers and the common soldiers with whom he served.

36. William Heath, *Memoirs of Major-General William Heath*, ed. William Abbatt (New York: William Abbatt, 1901. Reprinted by Sagwan Press, 2015), 53.

37. Dave Pelland, "Colonel Thomas Knowlton Monument, Hartford." CT Monuments.net: Connecticut History in Granite and Bronze. October 21, 2013, ctmonuments.net/2013/10/colonel-thomas-knowlton-monument-hartford/. Knowlton was actually two months shy of turning thirty-six when he was killed, so the inscription errs on his age at death.

38. "Knowlton Award," Military Intelligence Corps Association, www.mica-national.org/awards/knowlton-award/.

Major Robert Rogers and the American Revolution

SCOTT M. SMITH

After his exploits during the French and Indian War, Robert Rogers (1732-1795) was indisputably the most famous military leader born in the thirteen colonies; however, he played only a cameo role in the Revolution because both the British and American commanders-in-chief, Thomas Gage and George Washington, not only scorned him but actually arrested him for treason. Rogers' self-promotion, his financial debts, his indifference to the politics of the times, and his penchant for alcohol all contributed to his demise, but he was far from the only leading man of his day to suffer these faults.

Rogers' humble roots in the New Hampshire wilderness, combined with his daring escapades, inspiring leadership, and courage under fire fueled a steady stream of publicity in the burgeoning broadsheets of the day. After the First Battle on Snowshoes in 1757, the *Boston Gazette* blazed: "The brave Rogers is acquiring glory to himself in the field and in some degree recovering the sunken reputation of his country."[1] When Rogers straggled back to Crown Point in 1759, barely alive but victorious from his raid on the Abenaki village of St. Francis deep inside the Canadian wilderness, the *Boston Weekly Newsletter* headlined: "What do we owe to such a beneficial Man? And a Man of such an enterprising genius?"[2] After he accepted the French surrender at Detroit in 1760 and returned east, the *New Hampshire Gazette* boomed: "As soon as the arrival of the Gentleman was known, the people here [Philadelphia] . . . immediately ordered the bells to be rung."[3] Of

1. John F. Ross, *War On The Run* (Bantam Books, New York, 2009) (imputed page#)121/(Kindle location)1994; *Boston Gazette* February 14, 1757, 2.
2. Ross 284/4678; *Boston Weekly Newsletter*, February 7,1760; 1.
3. Ross 323/5310; *New Hampshire Gazette*, February 27, 1761.

course, the headlines glossed over the rumors of scalpings, prisoner executions, cannibalism and massacres that earned Rogers the respect of the Native warriors as well as the Abenaki nickname *Wobomagonda*, White Devil.[4]

Unfortunately, Rogers borrowed heavily (roughly $200,000 in today's currency) to recruit, train, and outfit his regiment, aptly nicknamed Rogers' Rangers. These debts would force him away from the American scene for much of the next fifteen years, essentially crippling him for the rest of his life. When Parliament passed the Stamp Tax in March 1765, Rogers was in London evading his creditors while also hoping to raise the funds to repay them. Accordingly, he missed the virulent debates in the colonies that led the Crown to rescind the hated tax a year later.

While in London, he self-published his *Journals* in 1765, followed by an encyclopedic *Concise Account of North America* shortly thereafter; both became "best-sellers." The longest chapter by far in *Concise Account* is entitled "Customs and Habits of the Indians." Throughout, the author conveyed both detailed knowledge and great respect: "Avarice is unknown to them . . . they are not actuated by the love of gold . . . [their] great and fundamental principles are . . . that every man is naturally free and independent; that no one . . . on earth has any right to deprive him of his freedom and independency and nothing can compensate him for the loss of it."[5] The Natives believed that land, if it was "owned" at all, belonged to the tribe, not the individual, a far cry from the rapacious approach of the British. Most notably, Sir William Johnson, Secretary of Indian Affairs and Gage's mentor, personally owned hundreds of thousands of acres making him the second largest landowner (lagging only William Penn) in the colonies by 1770.

Also in *Concise Accounts*, Rogers boasted: "Certain I am that no one man has traveled over and seen so much as I have done."[6] In fact, he dreamed of traveling further—all the way across the continent to the Pacific Ocean, if he could get funding. Given the sorry state of the Crown's balance sheet after the Seven Years War, the likelihood of receiving cash upfront was low, but the government was offering a 20,000 pound reward upon discovery of the fabled Northwest Passage.[7]

4. Stephen Brumwell, *White Devil: A True Story of War, Savagery and Vengeance in Colonial America* (De Capo Press. Cambridge, MA, 2004).
5. Ibid., 167.
6. Robert Rogers, *A Concise Account of North America* (original edition London 1765; Heritage Books, Westminster, MD 2007), VI.
7. mynorth.com/2010/05/before-lewis-clark-carver-tute-set-out-to-find-the-northwest-passage/.

On October 16, 1765, Rogers had the honor of an audience with King George III at St. James Palace. In a tone-deaf move befitting royalty, King George not only appointed Rogers commandant of Fort Michilimackinac, the Crown's westernmost outpost in North America, but also requested Thomas Gage, who held a longstanding grudge, to reimburse Rogers for past expenses. Gage would be apoplectic when the King's directive reached New York, immediately convening a commission to review Rogers expenses, delaying compensation yet again. As galling, the famous Rogers would now be in position to challenge Johnson as the Crown's primary liaison with the powerful Native tribes out west who were critical to the supply of fur pelts that fueled Johnson's trading and real estate empire.

While revolutionary sentiment boiled in the eastern seaboard cities of the colonies, Rogers was at Michilimackinac, planning his expedition to seek the Northwest Passage and again borrowing heavily to do so. Gage and Johnson plotted as well, arresting Rogers for treason on trumped up charges in December 1767 and keeping him in chains for most of 1768. A court martial acquitted Rogers on all counts in October 1768 but Rogers' name was forever stained.[8] Furthermore, Gage did not reinstate Rogers to his command or even give him permission to travel until March 1769.

More heavily in debt than ever, Rogers returned to London, seeking to restore his reputation and fortune at King George's court. Accordingly, he was absent from the colonies when British regulars fired into a crowd of Bostonians outside the customs house in March 1770, the shots that stoked the flames of Revolution. After waiting three years while Rogers unsuccessfully pleaded his case, Rogers' creditors finally had him committed to debtor's prison on October 16, 1772.[9] It would be his home for the next two years, isolating him from the incendiary Boston Tea Party in December 1773 and Parliament's response, the four Coercive (Intolerable) Acts, in the spring of 1774.

While Rogers rotted in prison, Gage, son of a First Viscount, and George Washington, well-ensconced in Virginia society after his marriage to Martha Custis in 1759, renewed their acquaintance in New York, having served together under Gen. Edward Braddock during the French and Indian War. Needless to say, neither Gage nor Washington could come close to matching Rogers' accomplishments during this global conflict, yet both "gentlemen" emerged in far superior po-

8. David A. Armour, *Treason? At Michilimackinac: The Proceedings of a General Court Martial held at Montreal in October 1768 for the Trial of Major Robert Rogers* (Mackinac Island State Park Commission 1967), 9.
9. Ross, *War On The Run*, 423/6956.

sitions for advancement than the backwoodsman with an affinity for the Natives.

After the ambush on the Monongahela River in July 1755, Gage, a lieutenant colonel at the time and commander of the British vanguard, was publicly criticized by Robert Orme, Braddock's aide, for "falling back in great confusion" when he should have pushed forward. Gage denied the accusation, flipping the blame back on Braddock. Other accounts noted that Gage fought well, albeit in covering the pell mell British retreat.[10]

Gage's hesitancy was again visible in in 1758 during the first, disastrous assault on Fort Ticonderoga under Gen. James Abercrombie as well as in 1759 when he waited for reinforcements rather than attack Fort Galette in Canada, earning the ire of his superior Lord Jeffrey Amherst. Amherst essentially demoted Gage to the back of the formation in favor of Rogers' Rangers during the second, and successful, siege of Fort Ticonderoga later that year. Gage, however, enjoyed the last laugh as he was promoted to commander-in-chief of North America in 1763 after Amherst was recalled following Pontiac's Rebellion.

The start of the French and Indian War was no more flattering for Washington. He blundered into battle at Fort Necessity in 1754, and, accordingly, was relegated to a volunteer role in the 1755 campaign. Nevertheless, he rallied the fleeing redcoats after Braddock fell mortally wounded. He later noted: "The Virginians behaved like men and died like soldiers . . .[unlike] the dastardly behavior of the English."[11]

Despite this scathing critique, Gage complimented Washington: "I shall be extremely happy to have frequent News of your Welfare, & hope soon to hear, that your laudable Endeavours, & the Noble Spirits you have exerted in the Service of your Country; have at last been crowned with the Success they merit."[12] The *Boston Gazette* could only pay Washington a backhanded laurel when he visited Massachusetts Gov. William Shirley seeking an officer's commission in 1756, calling Washington "a gentleman who has a deservedly high reputation of military skill, integrity, and valor, though success has not always attended his undertakings."[13] After Washington's petition was again rejected, he

10. John R. Alden, *General Gage in America* (Louisiana State University Press, Baton Rouge, Louisiana; 1948), 26.
11. Ron Chernow, *Washington: A Life* (Penguin Books, New York 2010), 59; George Washington to Robert Dinwiddie July 18,1755, founders.archives.gov/documents/Washington/02-01-02-0168.
12. Thomas Gage to Washington, November 23,1755, founders.archives.gov/documents/Washington/02-02-02-0183.
13. *Boston Gazette*, March 1, 1756.

retired to life in Virginia in 1758, captaining its militia most commend-ably for three years before settling into the life of a prosperous planter, devoted husband, and local politician.

Through 1773, Washington conducted his business as appropriate for a well-heeled colonist in the British Empire. Upon visiting New York to install his stepson, Jackie, at King's College, he stopped at the Kemble estate in New Jersey, family home of Gage's wife Margaret, for tea, attended a dinner in the city honoring Gage on May 27, and dined personally with the commander-in-chief on the 30th.[14] Over the course of the year, Washington worked through British government channels to expand his personal landholdings out west, noting to his surveyor: "no time should be lost in having them surveyed, lest some new revo-lution should again happen in our political System"[15] and petitioning Lord Dunmore, Virginia's royal governor, for more acreage.

By 1774 Washington's sympathies had become more radical. He noted in a July letter to his friend William Fairfax: "Are not all these things self-evident proofs of a fixed & uniform Plan to Tax us? If we want further proofs, does not all the Debates in the House of Com-mons serve to confirm this? and hath not Genl Gage's Conduct since his arrival . . . exhibited unexampled Testimony of the most despotic System of Tyranny that ever was practiced in a free Government."[16] In September, Washington embarked for Philadelphia as one of Virginia's delegates to the Continental Congress; his interest in land, particularly his own land, never subsided as his letters home throughout his military service would attest.

In July 1774, the tide also began to turn in Robert Rogers' affairs when Sir William Johnson passed away from natural causes. Shortly thereafter, Rogers was released from prison, albeit penniless. While he still collected his military pension, King George prohibited him from obtaining any actual command as retribution for a lawsuit Rogers had filed against Gage, who was still in favor at court.[17] Rogers focused in-stead on resurrecting his dream of exploring the Northwest Passage but, unsurprisingly, could only secure lukewarm support among his contacts in Parliament.

14. Alden, *General Gage in America*, 30.
15. Washington to William Crawford September 25, 1773, founders.archives.gov/docu-ments/Washington/02-09-02-0255.
16. Washington to Bryan Fairfax July 20,1774, founders.archives.gov/documents/Wash-ington/02-10-02-0081.
17. John R. Cuneo, "The Early Days of the Queen's Rangers August 1776-February 1777," *Military Affairs*, Vol. 22, No. 2 (Summer, 1958), 65-74; Memorandum of King George, April 1, 1775, Sir John Fortescue, ed., *The Correspondence of King George the Third*. Vol. III, July 1773-December 1777 (London, 1928), 195-196.

Fortunately, as the rebellion in Massachusetts surged, Gage's star dimmed. Unlike Monongahela, Ticonderoga and Galette, Gage was in charge now and could not pass the blame upward. His inability to curb the Sons of Liberty was public for all to see, earning him the nickname "the old woman."[18] In April 1775, Gen. William Howe sailed from London ostensibly to assist Gage, but, in reality, to replace him.

Rogers scraped together enough funds to embark for North America in June 1775, shortly after news of the battles at Lexington and Concord had reached England.[19] Was he simply going home, or looking for some way to plunge into the fight, or returning to Michilimackinac and the western frontier? Rogers left no written record of his intentions.

After docking in Baltimore in August, Rogers trudged up to Philadelphia to renew old contacts and assess the political situation. Upon arriving, he was greeted with an interrogation by the Committee of Safety, not the ringing of bells. He was able to secure a meeting with John Adams, who wrote: "The famous Partisan Major Rogers ... thinks we will have hot Work, next Spring. He told me an old half Pay Officer, such as himself, would sell well ... when he went away, he said to Sam Adams and me, if you want me next Spring for any Service, you know where I am, send for me. I am to be sold."[20] In the meantime, Rogers assumed the role of private citizen with landholdings and family up north; however, his commission in the British Army, his only source of income, proved an anchor around his neck.

After a month of pleading with Congress, Rogers finally received a pass to travel, providing he agreed not to scout or bear arms for the British. He journeyed next to New York, meeting with Gov. William Tryon to confirm his land grants, then to Albany to visit his brother, and finally to New Hampshire to see his wife and son after a five-year hiatus.

En route, Rogers likely heard the good news that Gage had sailed for England on October 11. While he did not have a close personal relationship with William Howe, a noted light infantry commander in his own right, Rogers had to have known that his prospects in the British Army had just significantly improved. Coincidentally or not, Rogers ended his conjugal visit after only a two-week stay and jour-

18. George Athan Billias, *George Washington's Opponents;* (New York: William Morrow, 1969), 26.
19. www.history.com/topics/american-revolution/battles-of-lexington-and-concord.
20. John Adams Diary, September 21, 1775, Massachusetts Historical Society, www.masshist.org/digitaladams/archive/doc?id=D24&hi=1&query=Rogers&tag=text&a rchive=diary&rec=1&start=0&numRecs=7.

neyed towards Boston which was surrounded by a cordon of Continental army fortifications.

Upon his arrival on the outskirts he notified George Washington, somewhat obsequiously and possibly duplicitously: "I do sincerely entreat your Excellency for a continuance of that permission for me to go unmolested where my private Business may call me as it will take some Months from this time to settle with all my Creditors—I have leave to retire on my Half-pay, & never expect to be call'd into the service again. I love North America, it is my native Country & that of my Family's, and I intend to spend the Evening of my days in it."[21]

Rogers did not know that Washington had already received a letter from Rev. Eleazar Wheelock, president of Dartmouth College, passing on rumors that Rogers had been sighted with the British forces in Canada as well as having "been in Indian habit through our encampments at St. Johns."[22] The tabloids, once Rogers' friend, also reported on his travels, going so far as to label him the commander-in-chief of the Indians.

Washington assigned Brig. Gen. John Sullivan, a New Hampshire lawyer who had yet to see combat, to interview Rogers before granting his continuance. Sullivan reported: "I am far from thinking that he has been in Canada but as he was once Governor of Michilimackinac it is possible he may have a Commission to Take that Command & Stir up the Indians against us & only waits for an opportunity to get there."[23] In true lawyerly fashion, Sullivan suggested that Washington allow Rogers to travel on his existing pass, rather than grant him a new one, so that "Should he prove a Traitor Let the Blame Centre upon those who Enlarged him."

Rogers continued on to New York to review again his land grants with Governor Tryon, but he also met with General Clinton, who was en route from Boston to South Carolina. Likely unbeknown to Rogers, a January 5 letter from Lord Germain to Howe had returned Rogers to good graces. In a memorandum, Clinton noted that he had probed Rogers about assuming a command, but Rogers demurred citing his promise to the Continental Congress.[24] Clinton's account is somewhat suspect since it is unlikely that he saw Germain's letter before he sailed from Boston.

21. Robert Rogers to Washington, December14, 1775, founders.archives.gov/documents/Washington/03-02-02-0505.

22. Eleazar Wheelock to Washington, December 2, 1775, founders.archives.gov/documents/Washington/03-02-02-0429.

23. John Sullivan to Washington, December 17, 1775, founders.archives.gov/documents/Washington/03-02-02-0522.

24. Cuneo, "The Early Days of the Queen's Rangers," 66.

Regardless of Rogers' intentions, his wanderings clearly gave the appearance of espionage. With tensions running high, New York's Committee of Safety banished him and other known Tories from the city over the course of the spring.

Rogers' whereabouts are unknown until late June when he was arrested in New Jersey on General Washington's orders. Washington was likely reeling from the discovery that week of the Hickey plot to assassinate him, fomented by Governor Tryon. It did not matter that Rogers was never incriminated in any way in this affair.

Washington interviewed Rogers personally, the only known meeting between the two tall warriors, both standing over six feet. Washington's report to John Hancock, president of the Continental Congress, highlighted his distaste for Rogers, bordering on personal jealousy, despite Rogers' professed desire to serve the Glorious Cause: "Upon information that Major Rogers was travelling thro' the Country under suspicious circumstances I thought it necessary to have him secured . . . the Major's reputation, and his being an half pay Officer has increased my Jealousies about him . . . The Business which he informs Me he has with Congress is a secret Offer of his Service . . . I submit it to their Consideration, whether it would not be dangerous to accept."[25]

While Washington was incarcerating Rogers, he was also corresponding with John Hancock to gain approval to employ Indians in the army.[26] Rogers might have assisted in this regard, yet Washington obviously had no interest in his help. Perhaps Washington felt his war council already had enough former British officers. Major Generals Charles Lee and Horatio Gates (who resigned their British commissions in 1772 and 1769, respectively), were already scheming against him.

Nevertheless, respectful of the travel pass granted by Congress, Washington allowed Rogers to go on to Philadelphia, albeit under guard. The city was agog with rumors of the Hickey plot, as Thomas Jefferson wrote to a friend: "the famous Major Rogers is in custody on violent suspicion of being concerned in the conspiracy."[27] Fortunately for Rogers, Congress had much more important matters that month than an investigation of his activities, so his case was remanded to New Hampshire for adjudication.

25. Washington to John Hancock, June 27, 1776,
founders.archives.gov/documents/Washington/03-05-02-0079.
26. Washington to Hancock, June 8, 1776, founders.archives.gov/documents/Washington/03-04-02-0367; Hancock to Washington June 18,1776, founders.archives.gov/documents/Washington/03-05-02-0018.
27. Thomas Jefferson to William Fleming, July 1, 1776, founders.archives.gov/documents/Jefferson/01-01-02-0175.

Rogers had already been shipped across the continent to stand trial once in his life, he was not going to let it happen again. In an ironic twist, he escaped from Philadelphia while Congress finalized the Declaration of Independence. Eluding bounty hunters, he turned up on General Howe's flagship off the coast of Staten Island ten days later.

With the King's approval in hand, Howe commissioned Rogers to raise a regiment, the Queen's American Rangers, which he did with gusto primarily in Long Island and Westchester. While his regiment once again bore the sobriquet Roger's Rangers, little else resembled the famed unit of the French and Indian War. His recruits now were primarily "city" boys and farmers, many motivated by the opportunity to plunder their rebel neighbors, rather than hardened backwoodsmen defending their homes. Also, the terrain of battle had changed from impenetrable wilderness to coastal towns and plains, similar to the battlefields of Europe. Finally, the British army now had its own grenadiers and light infantry, drilled in ranger tactics right out of Rogers' own handbook.

Although Rogers and his new unit met with skepticism, if not outright disdain, on their own side, they were monitored with more respect by their enemy. On August 30 William Duer, a prominent businessman and member of New York's Committee of Safety, warned Washington: "one [William] Lounsbery in Westchester County who had headed a Body of about 14 Tories was kill'd by an Officer nam'd Flood, on his Refusal to Surrender himself Prisoner—That in his Pocket Book was found a Commission sign'd by Genl Howe to Major Rogers empowering him to raise a Battalion of Rangers."[28]

Washington had much more to worry about than Rogers at the time. After saving his troops with a fortuitous naval evacuation from Brooklyn on August 30, he needed to regroup on Manhattan before the British launched another attack. He also faced the gut-curdling realization that the Continental Army could simply denigrate and disintegrate. On September 22, he wrote despairingly to Hancock: "Every Hour brings the most distressing Complaints of the Ravages of our own Troops who are become infinitely more formidable to the poor Farmers & Inhabitants than the common Enemy."[29]

While Rogers and his Rangers were quite busy terrorizing rebel homes in September, Rogers also recorded his lone accomplishment of the Revolution, the capture of the Continental Army spy, Nathan Hale,

28. William Duer to Washington, August 30, 1776,
founders.archives.gov/documents/Washington/03-06-02-0137.
29. Washington to Hancock, September 22, 1776,
founders.archives.gov/documents/Washington/03-06-02-0287.

on Long Island on the 21st, whom he transported to Manhattan. Hale was executed the next day at the artillery park near Howe's country residence, the Beekman Mansion. His body hung for three days as a warning before being buried in an unmarked grave. Since Hale was likely sent out under direct orders from Washington, his apprehension might well have provided Rogers with a measure of revenge for his arrest earlier that summer.

Washington finally reacted to Duer's warning on September 30 when he forwarded the news to Connecticut's Governor Jonathan Trumbull: "Having received authentic advice . . . that the Enemy are recruiting a great number of men with much success . . . several have been detected of late who had enlisted to serve under their Banner and the particular command of Majr Rogers."[30] Although Washington knew of Hale's demise by then from a prisoner exchange conference conducted the day after his hanging, he might not have known Rogers' role. Regardless, the commander-in-chief never formally recognized Hale's sacrifice during or after the Revolution.

On October 4, Washington did petition Hancock, again invoking Rogers by name: "Nothing less in my opinion, than a suit of Cloaths annually given to each Non-commissioned Officer & Soldier, in addition to the pay and bounty, will avail, and I question whether that will do, as the Enemy . . . are giving Ten pounds bounty for Recruits; and have got a Battalion under Majr Rogers nearly compleated upon Long Island."[31]

On October 12, a four thousand man British force marshaled by Howe himself sailed east from New York, final destination uncertain. As the British hopscotched along the Westchester coast, threatening Connecticut, Trumbull tracked Rogers: "a plan is forming by the Noted Majr Rogers a famous Partisan or Ranger in the last War now in the Service of Genl Howe on Long Island where he is Collecting a Battallion of Tories . . . who are perfectly acquainted with every inlet and avenue into the Towns of Greenwich, Stamford & Norwalk where are Considerable quantities of Continental Stores."[32]

Rather than attack the supplies in Connecticut, Howe's goal was to cut across Westchester from the Sound to the Hudson, trapping the Continental Army between British land and sea forces. When Howe

30. Washington to Jonathan Trumbull, September 30, 1776, founders.archives.gov/documents/Washington/03-06-02-0340.
31. Washington to Hancock, October 4, 1776, founders.archives.gov/documents/Washington/03-06-02-0358-0001.
32. Trumbull to Washington, October 13,1776, founders.archives.gov/documents/Washington/03-06-02-0422.

finally marched inland on October 18, heading towards White Plains, he relied on the Queens American Rangers to secure the village of Mamaroneck and protect his eastern flank, a testament to his confidence in Rogers.[33]

In the same vein, the Americans realized that a defeat of Rogers would be both a tactical and publicity coup. As Washington marched north to counter Howe's thrust, one of his most trusted generals, William Alexander, Lord Stirling (who had led the valiant but doomed charge against the Old Stone House in Brooklyn, been captured, and then exchanged) received intelligence on October 22, confirmed by the glow of campfires, pinpointing Rogers' position. He dispatched Col. John Haslet and 750 of his Delaware Blues, battle hardened in Brooklyn, to surprise the Rangers that night.

Local guides directed Haslet to approach the Rangers' encampment from the west, the direction of the main body of British troops, assuming correctly that sentries would be weakest here. Rogers headquartered in a school house in the village while his men, roughly 400 strong, bivouacked on nearby Heathcote Hill. Late that evening, the major, his battlefield senses as sharp as ever, repositioned a company of sixty men directly in Haslett's path. The Continentals attacked, easily overrunning the newly established forward post, but the crack of muskets and shouts of melee awoke Rogers and his men. When Haslet pressed forward, falsely believing he had routed the enemy, his troops met with fierce resistance from the Rangers occupying the hillside. As Rogers personally rallied his men to withstand the rebel charge, Haslet withdrew, not only claiming victory but also the embarrassment of the vaunted Rogers.

On October 23 an unidentified officer wrote: "A party was detached against him [Rogers]; they killed many, took thirty-six prisoners, sixty-five muskets, and as many blankets, and completely routed the rest of the party. This blow will ruin the Major's Rangers."[34] A few days later, Haslet himself wrote of "Colonel Rogers's, the late worthless Major. On the first fire, he skulked off in the dark."[35] On a more realistic note, Lt. Col. Robert Hanson, Washington's aide, reported to John Hancock: "by some accident or Another, the expedition did not succeed so well as could have been wished."[36] On the British side, Howe explained to

33. Cuneo, "The Early Days of the Queen's Rangers," 70.

34. Peter Force, ed., *American Archives*, Fifth Series. Vol. II (Washington, DC: Peter Force, 1851), 669.

35. Ibid., 701.

36. Robert Hanson Harrison to Hancock, October 25, 1776, founders.archives.gov/documents/Washington/03-07-02-0021.

Lord Germain: "the carelessness of his sentries exposed him [Rogers] to a surprise from a large body of ye enemy by, w'h he lost a few men killed or taken; nevertheless by a spirited exertion he obliged them to retreat."[37]

While Rogers did not play a notable role in the Battle of White Plains on October 28, the Rangers regrouped and continued to harass patriots, soldiers and civilians alike. Charles Lee delayed responding to Washington's request in November to march to New Jersey in order to chase down a Rogers sighting in Westchester; after the Rangers "contracted themselves into a compact body very suddenly," Lee chose to retreat rather than challenge the vaunted Rogers in combat.[38] In December, Westchester citizens petitioned the New York Provincial Congress for military assistance to defend their homes from both Rogers Rangers and Continental troops.

The Rangers were garrisoned at Fort Knyphausen in northern Manhattan in January 1777 when one of their captains, Daniel Strong, was captured while recruiting, and summarily executed. Rogers launched his last documented raid on January 13 against the home of Henry Williams in Bedford, absconding with a beaver hat, scarlet waistcoat, and sword among other items.[39]

By this time, Alexander Innis, newly appointed Inspector General of Provincial Forces, had launched an investigation of the regiment. Innis, a Scotsman, began his American service in 1775 as secretary to the Royal Governor of South Carolina, Lord William Campbell, implying at least a middling level of education, breeding and wealth.[40] When explaining his review process in a letter to General Clinton three years later, Innis noted: "I found the Provincial Corps in very great confusion and disorder; Several persons to whom Warrants had been granted to raise Corps had greatly abused the confidence . . . Negroes, Mulattos, Indians, Sailors & Rebel Prisoners were enlisted, to the disgrace and ruin of the Provincial Service . . . their conduct in a thousand instances was so flagrant, that I could not hesitate to tell the General [Howe], that until a thorough reformation took place he could expect no service from that Battalion."[41]

General Howe acted on Innis's recommendations, replacing Rogers and twenty-two other officers by March, although Rogers continued

37. Cuneo, "The Early Days of the Queen's Rangers," 71.
38. Charles Lee to Washington, November 30, 1776, founders.archives.gov/documents/Washington/03-07-02-0169.
39. Cuneo, "The Early Days of the Queen's Rangers," 73.
40. www.battlefields.org/learn/biographies/alexander-innes.
41. Ibid.

to recruit through the spring. While the Rangers clearly were not gentlemen, they were likely no worse than many other troops on both sides of the conflict. Notably, Howe did not court martial any of the officers, instead retiring them with three months' pay. There is no record that Rogers protested either Innis's report or Howe's action, perhaps a bargain he made with Howe in exchange for leniency towards his men.

Were Innis's motives prejudiced against the "rabble" of the Rangers or purely for the good of the Army? Col. Rudolph Ritzema, who deserted from patriot forces in November 1776 after a falling out with General Stirling and served the British Army through 1778, described Innis as "a man, whose haughty and supercilious conduct has estranged more minds from His Majesty and the British Govt. than perhaps all the other blunders in the conduct of the American war put together."[42] Nevertheless, Innis continued to serve with distinction. After completing his stint as a staff officer, he returned to the front lines, leading troops into battle at Musgrove's Mill in South Carolina in 1780 where he was wounded and subsequently dropped from view.

In April, George Washington again voiced his personal concern, noting, "Rogers is an active instrument in the Enemy's hands, and his conduct has a peculiar claim to our notice . . . If it is possible, I wish to have him apprehended and secured."[43] He need not have worried.

Rogers headed steadily downhill after his dismissal by Howe. Now an "old man" of forty-five, weakened by years of captivity and alcohol, he tried one more time to raise a company of Rangers, but ended up once again in jail. His wife divorced him in 1778, while his older brother sadly apologized in 1780: "the conduct of my brother of late almost un-mans me . . . I am sorry his good talents should so unguarded fall a prey to intemperance."[44]

Rogers ultimately returned to England with the evacuating British troops in 1783 and died destitute in London in 1795. Perhaps his greatest "crime" was his rise from low birth to great fame. Robert Rogers was always a backwoodsman, never an aristocrat, plantation squire, lawyer, bookseller, or prosperous merchant as were the other leading military figures of his times. On the other hand, Rogers' legacy of ranger tactics, wilderness exploration, and continental expansion has endured. "Rangers lead the way" remains the motto of the US Army Ranger Corps to this day.

42. E. Alfred Jones, "A Letter Regarding the Queen's Rangers," *The Virginia Magazine of History and Biography*, vol. 30, no. 4 (1922), 368–76.
43. Washington to Trumbull April 12, 1777, founders.archives.gov/documents/Washington/03-09-02-0137.
44. Ross, *War On The Run*, 456/7504.

La Petite Guerre and Indian Irregular Manner of War: Siblings, But Not Twins

BRIAN GERRING

When the major European powers began to use light troops in the mid-eighteenth century, they typically employed them in a manner of war that the French labeled as *la petite guerre*. Troops participating in *la petite guerre* operated separately from the main army, often using speed and maneuver for quick attacks and ambushes in support of an army's goals. Concurrent with this European development was warfare between North American Indian tribes and American colonists, an on-going clash beginning in the sixteenth century. In their conduct of war, Indians typically operated using similar tactics to European light troops—maneuver and speed for sudden attacks and ambushes—while also utilizing the wooded North American terrain to their advantage. In a sermon concerning Maj. Gen. Edward Braddock's defeat, William Vinal declared that "as to the *General*, he was an experienced warrior, in the *Regular Way* . . . But he had not opportunity to acquaint himself with the *Irregular Manner* of fighting in this country [italics in the original]."[1] Because of the similarities between European *petite guerre* and the North American Indian irregular manner of war, there is an assumption that the two forms of warfare were the same. From the primary sources, however, it is clear that, while similar in conduct, Europe's *petite guerre* and the Indian's irregular manner of war were two distinct forms of warfare for most of the eighteenth century.

There is no exact phrase for regular European warfare in the primary sources. After all, it was the regular way that armies conducted warfare,

1. William Vinal, *A Sermon on the Accursed Thing that Hinders Success and Victory in War* (Newport, RI: James Franklin, 1755), 14.

which consisted primarily of infantry-based armies, supported by cavalry and artillery, battling in open terrain or conducting well-ordered sieges. During regular warfare, European armies conducted battles using linear tactics, which involved lines of troops maneuvering in orderly fashion and firing in massed volleys. The purpose of this type of warfare was to bring an overwhelming amount of musket fire against an enemy, which only massed formations of soldiers could accomplish. Once these massed volleys sufficiently broke the enemy's forces, the army would initiate a bayonet charge that would drive the enemy from the battlefield—the shock assault. The intent of both *la petite guerre* and the Indian irregular manner of war was not to engage and defeat massed armies on the traditional, or regular, battlefield. Instead, operations of *la petite guerre* were ancillary to regular operations in eighteenth century warfare, and the irregular manner of war was a way of war that was opposite of regular eighteenth century warfare.

The first treatises promoting the usefulness of *la petite guerre* were Armand François de La Croix's *Trait'e de la Petite Guerre pour les Compagnies Franches* (1752), Turpin de Crissé's *Essai sur L'Art de la Guerre* (1754), and Thomas Auguste le Roy de Grandmaison's *La Petite Guerre* (1756). These treatises originated from the French military experiences during the War of the Austrian Succession (1740-1748), a conflict that shaped the European concept of the usefulness of *la petite guerre* during war. Although *la petite guerre* is a French term, it remained untranslated when used by English speakers; however, English speakers did translate the definite article *la* so that the standard use of the term was *the petite guerre*. This is apparent in Maj. Lewis Nicola's 1777 translation of Grandmaison's work where he translates the entire text, except for the phrase *petite guerre*.[2] The French treatises are known to have been in possession of Continental Army officers, including Gen. George Washington who recommended the reading of these treatises.[3] The Continental Congress also advocated the study of these treatises; they authorized the establishment of a "military school for young gentlemen," which would contain "a regimental library of the most approved authors on tactics and the *petite guerre*."[4] From theory and practice,

2. Thomas Auguste le Roy de Grandmaison, *La Petite Guerre*, trans. Lewis Nicola (Philadelphia: Robert Bell, 1777), 5.
3. Johann Ewald, *Diary of the American War: A Hessian Journal Captain Johann Ewald Field Jäger Corps*, trans. Joseph P. Tustin (New Haven: Yale University Press, 1979), 108; George Washington to William Woodford, November 10, 1775, *Founders Online*, National Archives, founders.archives.gov/documents/Washington/03-02-02-0320.
4. *Journals of the Continental Congress, 1774-1789*, vol. 8, *1777* (Washington, DC: Government Printing Office, 1907), 485.

troops conducting operations in the *petite guerre* were separate or detached from the main army—the grand army—and they typically used quick strikes and harassment attacks against the enemy's less protected areas. Due to the separated nature of units conducting the *petite guerre*, contemporary sources also referred to this type of warfare as a war of detachments. The intent of these limited and continual harassment-type attacks was to syphon military resources away from the enemy's grand army. This understanding was made clear in Roger Stevenson's *Military Instructions for Officers Detached in the Field . . . Necessary in Carrying on the Petite Guerre* (1775), where he wrote:

> This corps is a light party . . . separated from the army, to secure the camp or a march; to reconnoitre the enemy or the country; to seize their posts, convoys, or escorts; to plant ambuscades, and put in practice every stratagem for surprising or disturbing the enemy: which is called carrying on the *Petite Guerre*.[5]

As stated, there is no exact phrase for regular European warfare in the primary sources. By the time of the Revolutionary War, the *petite guerre* was a component of regular warfare; thus, it was merely a subset within established eighteenth century European warfare. Stevenson detailed in *Military Instructions* that troops engaged in the *petite guerre* were operating against traditional military forces in support of the main army's efforts.[6] Likewise, British Maj. Robert Donkin delivered an entire section on the *petite guerre* that focused on activities designed to support the grand army.[7] Like other contemporary Europeans, Americans understood that troops operating in the *petite guerre* were supporting the main war effort.

Even though the *petite guerre* revolved around regular warfare, armies sometimes employed irregular troops so that military commanders could focus their regular troops on traditional military operations, such as battles and sieges. By the eighteenth century definition, irregulars were any soldiers that were not part of a structured, state-recognized and funded, full-time army.[8] In his *Universal Military Dictionary* (1779), George Smith noted that militia—who were part-time troops—were not "regular or stated troops."[9] Simply put, in the eighteenth century mindset, if troops were not in the regular army, they

---

5. Roger Stevenson, *Military Instructions for Officers Detached in the Field . . . Necessary in Carrying on the Petite Guerre* (Philadelphia: R. Aitken, 1775), 35.

6. Ibid., i–ii, 35–36.

7. Robert Donkin, *Military Collections and Remarks* (New York: H. Gaine, 1777), 240.

8. "Essay on Regular and Irregular Forces," *Gentleman's Magazine* 16 (1746): 30–32.

9. George Smith, *Universal Military Dictionary* (London: J. Millan, 1779), s. v. "militia."

were irregular. While the eighteenth century contains many examples of irregular troops engaged in the *petite guerre*, notable examples occurred during the War of the Austrian Succession with such units as the *hussars* and *pandours*. These organizations were irregular light troops that operated using their mobility to conduct attacks against vulnerable military targets, ambushes, reconnaissance, and scouting for the main army. Some irregular light troops, particularly the *pandours*, could be brutal in their operations because of their penchant for killing captives, mutilating the dead, and targeting non-combatants, traits indicative of savage or uncivilized warfare. The barbarity of these actions proved objectionable to the civilized notion of warfare held by most Europeans. Therefore, after the War of the Austrian Succession, European militaries began a process of normalizing irregular light troops into authorized regular light troops who were more controllable to military leaders to curtail these atrocities. Simultaneously, the French military treatises appeared promoting the usefulness of *la petite guerre* as a way to bring the conduct of that form of warfare under the umbrella of "civilized" warfare.

Warfare on the frontiers of North America between colonists and Indians during the eighteenth century often involved similarly brutal, if not identical, tactics of the *pandours*. This type of warfare typically involved attacking and burning villages and homes, destroying crops, and killing or capturing non-combatants. This type of warfare usually impacted the whole of society, not just dedicated military forces. Modern parlance calls this *unlimited* or *total war* because anyone, combatants or non-combatants, could be a target. A Jesuit priest recorded this type of warfare in 1649 as attacking Iroquois completely destroyed structures and killed or captured everyone in Huron villages.[10] This type of warfare was in direct contrast to European warfare, which, in theory, stressed "humanity . . . even in war."[11] Political theorist Emmerich de Vattel wrote in 1758 that when a nation conducts war

> let us not divest ourselves of that charity which connects us with all mankind. Thus shall we courageously defend our country's rights without violating those of human nature. Let our valour preserve itself from every stain of cruelty, and the lustre of victory will not be tarnished by inhuman and brutal actions.[12]

10. Reuben Gold Thwaites, *The Jesuit and Allied Documents*, vol. 34, *Lower Canada: The Hurons, 1649* (Cleveland: Burrow Brothers, 1898), 123-134.
11. Henry Home Kames, *Sketches of the History of Man*, 2nd ed., vol. 1 (Edinburgh: W. Strahan and T. Cadell, 1778), 386.
12. Emmerich de Vattel, *The Law of Nations*, ed. Béla Kapossy and Richard Whitmore (Indianapolis: Liberty Fund, 2008), 369.

Commenting on humane conduct of war, political philosopher Jean-Jacques Burlamaqui wrote in 1747:

> In general, even the laws of war require that we should abstain from slaughter as much as possible, and not shed human blood without necessity. We ought not, therefore, directly and deliberately to kill prisoners of war, nor those who ask quarter, or surrender themselves, much less old men, women and children.[13]

Contrasting these European ideas, Thomas Jefferson described the common understanding of North American warfare as:

> The known rule of warfare with the Indian savages is an indiscriminate butchery of men women and children. These savages . . . [fight] not against our forts, or armies in the field, but the farming settlements on our frontiers.[14]

Jefferson's quote reflects the stereotypical colonial American understanding of the Indian's conduct of war, while seemingly ignoring the fact that the Americans freely practiced the same type of warfare against Indians, such as the Conestoga massacre in 1763.[15] Americans took to this manner of warfare, particularly on the frontier, as they clashed with Indian tribes during their settlement expansions to the west. James Smith, who spent the entirety of the French and Indian War in Indian captivity and intimately understood the Indian manner of war, wrote in the early nineteenth century that "Kentucky would not have been settled at the time is was, had the Virginians been altogether ignorant of this method of war."[16] This manner of war was the opposite of the regular European way of war; thus, eighteenth century sources called it an irregular manner of war. Because of this opposition, Americans and Europeans habitually characterized the Indian irregular manner of war as "uncivilized."

Despite the prevalence of attacks on non-combatants, Indians did perform operations against military targets. Typically, when Indians conducted operations against military forces, these attacks occurred in the enclosed wooded terrain of North America, which was very different from the regular, open European battlefields. Writing shortly after

13. Jean-Jacques Burlamaqui, *The Principles of Politic Law: Being a Sequel to the Principles of Natural Law*, trans. Mr. Nugent (London: J. Nourse, 1752), 282.
14. Thomas Jefferson to William Phillips, July 22, 1779, *Founders Online*, National Archives, founders.archives.gov/documents/Jefferson/01-03-02-0052.
15. *A Narrative of the Late Massacres* (Philadelphia: 1764), 5-6.
16. James Smith, *A Treatise on the Mode and Manner of Indian War* (Paris, KY: Joel R. Lyle, 1812), 10.

the Revolutionary War, British Lt. Thomas Anburey noted that "the Indian's idea of war consists in never fighting in an open field."[17] Donkin's perception of the early years of the Revolutionary War was that the Americans fought contrary to the customary rules of war— the *ruses de guerre*. He wrote that because of "the nature of the country, and cowardliness of the rebels . . . [they] delight more in murdering from the woods, walls and houses, than in shewing any genius or science in the art military."[18] Donkin echoed the prevailing thought of the time that denoted two different forms of courage in war. Scottish philosopher Henry Home Kames summed up this concept in 1774 as *passive courage* compared to *active courage*. Kames theorized that *passive courage* was attributable to "North-American savages" because they practiced a form of warfare that relied on "stratagem and surprise" to avoid fighting in open areas; conversely, Europeans had *active courage* because they willingly conducted warfare in open areas.[19] In a letter written in 1775, shortly after the British retreat from Concord, a British soldier noted this difference. He wrote that the American militia "did not fight us like a regular army, only like savages, behind trees and stone walls."[20] While these quotes do not reflect the American reliance on traditional European tactics throughout the war—and the victories brought by such tactics—they do demonstrate a difference in the perception between civilized and uncivilized conduct in warfare.

The enclosed and shrouded forest environment of North America necessitated a closer type of warfare between combatants. The tactics for operating in this constricting terrain involved a loose order or extended way of fighting, instead of the traditional linear European tactics. During the Revolutionary War, both the American and British armies adopted extended formations while also maintaining, practicing, and performing traditional European linear tactics. Warfare in the woods typically involved sudden ambush attacks from concealed positions, a type of warfare described as "skulking."[21] Anburey concluded that the Indian way of war derived from their hunting practices. He wrote:

17. Thomas Anburey, *Travels Through the Interior Parts of North America in a Series of Letters by an Officer* (London: William Lane, 1789), 294.

18. Donkin, *Military Collections*, 223.

19. Kames, *History of Man*, 45, 47.

20. "Extracts From Several Intercepted Letters of the Soldiery in Boston," Boston, April 28, 1775, in Peter Force, *American Archive: Fourth Series*, vol. 2 (Washington D.C.: M. St. Clair Clark and Peter Force, 1839), 440.

21. Benjamin Franklin to James Parker, March 20, 1751, *Founders Online*, National Archives, founders.archives.gov/documents/Franklin/01-04-02-0037; Washington to Lord Loudon, January 1757, in John C. Fitzpatrick, ed., *The Writings of George Washington from the Original Manuscript Sources 1745-1799*, vol. 2, *1757-1769* (Washington, DC: Government Printing Office, 1931), 10.

> Every Indian is a hunter, and their manner of making war is of the same nature, only changing the object, by skulking, surprising and killing those of their own species.[22]

Virginia Lt. Gov. Robert Dinwiddie summed up Indian warfare to Maj. Gen. James Abercrombie in 1756 this way:

> Dear Sir, You are come into a Country cover'd with woods and sometimes unaccessible Mountains, &c. The European Method of Waring not practic'd here. The Indian Method is bush fighting and watching every Opp'ty to destroy their Enemys.[23]

The tactics used by Indians were contrary to the traditional and regular European warfare tactics; thus, contemporaries labeled those tactics as irregular. A British officer recorded that during Braddock's Defeat, the Indians fought in an "irregular method" by firing and moving quickly, using the trees for cover, while another British participant noted that the Indians used the terrain to their advantage by fighting "either on their bellies or behind trees or running from one tree to another."[24] However, contemporaries labeled any tactic contrary to regular tactics as irregular. The Americans defeated Col. Patrick Ferguson's forces at King's Mountain using irregular tactics; a British officer present during the battle noted that the attacking Americans used trees for cover and "poured in an irregular destructive fire."[25] Likewise, an American soldier noted that some British troops operated with "irregularity" during the New York Campaign.[26] Despite the distinction between the civilized—*la petite guerre*—and uncivilized—irregular—manners of war, the conduct for both forms of warfare frequently involved similar tactics. Because of this tactical similarity, there is a present-day perception that both forms of warfare are interchangeable. Eighteenth century sources do not reflect that interchangeability.

Did Revolutionary War-era Americans include the Indian irregular manner of war a part of the European sanctioned *petite guerre*? Primary sources suggest that they did not; both forms of warfare were distinct.

22. Anburey, *Travels*, 297.

23. Robert Dinwiddie to James Abercrombie, May 28, 1756, Williamsburg, in R. A. Brock, ed., *The Official Records of Robert Dinwiddie, Lieutenant-Governor of the Colony of Virginia, 1751-1758*, vol. 2 (Richmond: Virginia Historical Society, 1884), 425-426.

24. Charles Hamilton, ed., *Braddock's Defeat: The Journal of Captain Robert Cholmley's Batman; The Journal of a British Officer; Halkett's Orderly Book* (Norman: University of Oklahoma Press, 1959), 29, 50.

25. Quoted in W. H. Wilkin, *Some British Soldiers in America* (London: Hugh Rees, 1914), 167.

26. Quoted in Frank Moore, *Diary of the American Revolution*, vol. 1 (New York: Charles Scribner, 1860), 326.

The difference was in the perception of what constituted civilized and uncivilized warfare. Washington's writings give a clear representation of the eighteenth-century American mindset that differentiated between the irregular manner of war and the *petite guerre*. Knowing both the European and Indian styles of warfare, Washington considered the Indian tactical mode of fighting as irregular. He remarked that because of the army's "apprehension of the Indian Mode of fighting," he dispatched Col. Daniel Morgan and his rifle-armed regiment to the Northern Department in 1777 because those soldiers were capable of engaging and restraining the Indian allies of Burgoyne.[27] In 1779, he requested the states of Pennsylvania and New York to enlist rangers who were "accustomed to the irregular kind of wood-fighting practiced by the Indians."[28] In 1779, Washington ordered Maj. Gen. John Sullivan to conduct an expedition against the Six Nation Indians in western New York. Washington considered this entire expedition as an irregular operation, an operation that was separate from the Continental Army's regular operations against the British army. In gauging military allocations for Sullivan's requests, Washington wrote:

> If the operations he is to be concerned in were the regular ones of the field, his calculation would be better founded; but in the loose irregular war he is to carry on, it will naturally lead to error and misconception.[29]

Although Sullivan's Expedition was separate from the main army, it was not warfare in the realm of the *petite guerre* because it was a large military operation against irregular enemies in western New York, mostly Indians and Tories, not British regulars. The intent of Sullivan's Expedition was to devastate whole British-allied Indian tribes in western New York. Washington issued the following orders to Sullivan, which demonstrate a manner of war contrary to the regular European conduct of war:

> The expedition you are appointed to command is to be directed against the hostile tribes of the six nations of Indians, with their associates and adherents. The immediate objects are the total destruction

27. Washington to Horatio Gates, August 20, 1777, *Founders Online*, National Archives, founders.archives.gov/documents/Washington/03-11-02-0012.
28. Washington to Joseph Reed, March 3, 1779, *Founders Online*, National Archives, founders.archives.gov/documents/Washington/03-19-02-0360; Washington to George Clinton, March 4, 1779, *Founders Online*, National Archives, founders.archives.gov/documents/Washington/03-19-02-0368.
29. Washington to John Jay, August 15, 1779, *Founders Online*, National Archives, founders.archives.gov/documents/Washington/03-22-02-0115.

and devastation of their settlements and the capture of as many prisoners of every age and sex as possible. It will be essential to ruin their
crops now in the ground and prevent their planting more.[30]

This order reflects the irregular manner of war that Sullivan was to
carry out. Conversely, from his experience and education, Washington
understood to whom the *petite guerre* applied; namely, troops involved
in the main war effort. When Washington departed New York for Virginia in 1781, he used the term to describe the permissible activities
for the remaining troops under the command of Maj. Gen. William
Heath. Washington instructed:

> Altho your general Rule of Conduct will be to act on the defensive
> only, yet it is not meant to prohibit you from striking a Blow at the En-
> emys Posts or Detatchments, should a fair Opportunity present itself.
> . . [including] annoying the Enemy, & covering the Country, as for the
> Security & repose of your own Troops . . . to hold the Enemy in Check,
> & carry on the Petit Guerre with them.[31]

This quote reflects a nearly textbook description for the *petite guerre*.
The 1783 Encyclopedia Britannica defines the *petite guerre* as involving
the tactics of "secret marches, occupying, defending, or attacking posts,
reconnoitering countries or the enemy, placing of ambuscades, &c.,"
which is similar to Stevenson's *Military Instructions* quoted above.[32]

After the Revolutionary War, Americans, at times, began to use the
term *petite guerre* to describe the Indian way of war, as Jefferson did in
1787 when he remarked that "the *petite guerre* always waged by the Indians" did not dissuade Americans from settling Kentucky.[33] John Connolly, a Loyalist during the war, writing about his time as a provincial
soldier during Pontiac's Rebellion several decades later, noted that he
"had an opportunity of observing the great difference between the *petite
guerre* of the Indians, and the military system of the Europeans."[34] This
change reflects the changing perception of war in the post-Revolution-

30. Washington to John Sullivan, May 31, 1779, *Founders Online*, National Archives,
founders.archives.gov/documents/Washington/03-20-02-0661.
31. Washington to William Heath, August 19, 1781, *Founders Online*, National Archives,
founders.archives.gov/documents/Washington/99-01-02-06729.
32. *Encyclopedia Britannica*, vol. 10 (Edinburgh: J. Balfour, 1783), 8840.
33. Jefferson to William Carmichael, December 11, 1787, Paris, in Albert Ellery Bergh,
ed., *The Writings of Thomas Jefferson*, vol. 5 (Washington, DC: The Thomas Jefferson Memorial Association, 1905), 382.
34. John Connolly, "A Narrative of the Transactions, Imprisonment, and Sufferings of John
Connolly, an American Loyalist and Lieut. Col. in His Majesty's Service," in *The Pennsylvania Magazine of History and Biography*, vol. 12 (Philadelphia: The Historical Society of
Pennsylvania, 1888), 311.

ary War era, where civilized and uncivilized warfare began to inter-
twine. Events in Europe further blurred any distinction between civilized and uncivilized warfare, notably from France. Concerning the
ongoing French Revolution, Edmund Burke wrote:

> The hell-hounds of war, on all sides, will be uncoupled and unmuz-
> zled. The new school of murder and barbarism, set up in Paris, having
> destroyed (so far as in it lies) all the other manners and principles which
> have hitherto civilized Europe, will destroy also the mode of civilized
> war.[35]

Subsequent events throughout the nineteenth century would continue to transform the meaning of the *petite guerre* as the traditional
perception of civilized warfare changed. As the meaning of the phrase
morphed, it began to encompass any small or limited conflict, whether
that conflict was part of a larger war strategy. While the *petite guerre* is
no longer a modern-day expression, such terms as police action, insurgency and counter-insurgency, minor operations, dirty wars, little wars,
and guerrilla and irregular warfare all have roots in the eighteenth-century phrase.

In Washington's writings, it is evident that military forces involved
in carrying out the *petite guerre* were conducting limited yet continual
operations—typically skirmishing, harassment attacks, and reconnaissance—only against British Army forces.[36] Troops conducting the *petite
guerre* could use the same tactics that Indians utilized in their manner
of war—such as maneuverability for surprise attacks, firing from concealed positions, and attacks on isolated posts. Despite the later views,
there was a differentiation between an irregular manner of war and the
petite guerre throughout most of the eighteenth century, even though
both types of warfare involved similar and, at times, identical tactics.
This distinction between the two forms of warfare originated from how
troops engaged a targeted enemy. This was a result of the perception
of the "civilized" European conduct of warfare, which involved *la petite
guerre*, and the "uncivilized" conduct of warfare of the North American
Indians, a type of warfare that colonial Americans also practiced, which
involved irregular methods.

---

35. Edmund Burke, "A Letter to a Member of the National Assembly, May 1791," in Edmund Burke, *Further Reflections on the Revolution in France*, ed. D.E. Ritchie (Indianapolis:
Liberty Fund, 1992), 55-56.
36. Washington to Philip Schuyler, February 23, 1777, *Founders Online*, National Archives,
founders.archives.gov/documents/Washington/03-08-02-0460; Washington to Heath,
January 22, 1782, *Founders Online*, National Archives, founders.archives.gov/documents/
Washington/99-01-02-07719.

George Washington and the First Mandatory Immunization

RICHARD J. WERTHER

The debate over mandatory vaccination for Covid-19 has led to many articles referring to how George Washington handled a similar issue, this one involving smallpox, with the Continental Army early in the American Revolution. With the advantage of hindsight, the decision Washington made to fully inoculate (not vaccinate) his army may today seem obvious, but it wasn't so simple for Washington and the others who lived it in real time. It's worth revisiting exactly how this decision came to pass.

"The small Pox! The small Pox! What shall We do with it?" wrote an exasperated John Adams.[1] Good question. The story of how Washington answered it provides insight into his vaunted leadership and ability to learn and change, as well as the trust his soldiers had in him. How smallpox was handled is an underrated factor in how the army lived to fight and eventually win the war.

Caused by the variola virus and extremely contagious, smallpox was the most deforming and lethal of the plague-like epidemics of the seventeenth and eighteenth centuries. Symptoms included severe pitting of the skin, eyebrows and lashes falling out, scarring so severe as to sometimes close up the nostrils, and even blindness.[2] Persons infected with smallpox are contagious for a period of about seventeen to twenty days and afflicted for twenty-one to twenty-four days after an initial asymptomatic period. There is a period of time (generally one day) in which individuals are contagious but are either asymptomatic or have

1. John Adams to Abigail Adams, June 26, 1776, founders.archives.gov/documents/Adams/04-02-02-0013.
2. Ann M. Becker, "Smallpox in Washington's Army: Strategic Implications of the Disease during the American Revolutionary War," *The Journal of Military History* Vol. 68, No. 2 (April 2004), 384.

only begun to experience minor symptoms such as fever, headaches, body aches, nausea, and malaise, which could be attributed to other ailments.[3] The smallpox virus is capable of surviving for a considerable time (days or even weeks) outside of the human body, making it much more easily transmitted and enabling its weaponization.

Washington himself, at age nineteen, had contracted smallpox in 1751 on a trip to Barbados with his half-brother Lawrence. No records were kept as to the struggle that ensued, but a twenty-four-day gap in Washington's diary attests to the severity of the disease. Thankfully for a nation yet to be born this was another of many close brushes with death he survived, leaving him with only some of the characteristic skin pockmarking from the disease (and possibly, some theorize, rendering the future "father of his country" sterile).

Given the limited technology of the day, Washington did not have many options from which to choose in protecting his troops from contagion. There were two approaches: quarantine and inoculation. Initially, he opted for the former and opposed inoculation. His eventual conversion to inoculation illustrated his ability to learn and change based on new information and necessity, but this conversion didn't come easily.

The close quarters in which an army unit works and their movement around the country made them excellent vectors for spreading such a highly communicable disease both to one another and to the general population. As Jonathan Trumbull, Sr. was to later observe, "our returning Soldiers have spread the Infection into almost every Town in the State, a Mischief that cannot happen when the Distemper is out of the Army."[4] The best available treatment, in Washington's early view, seemed to be to quarantine infected people so they would not expose others. For an army on the move, this was difficult and ineffective. Inoculation, although it also required quarantines, would seem to be a much more effective option, at least in retrospect.

It is important to understand exactly how inoculation (sometimes called "variolation") worked, as it is different than the modern and familiar solution, vaccination, and the two are sometimes confused.

To inoculate a person, you had to make an incision (usually in the arm or leg) and insert a thread containing live smallpox taken from a current sufferer. The result was that the inoculated person got a (usually) milder version of the disease and, if they survived, would have im-

3. Elizabeth Fenn, *Pox Americana: The Great Smallpox Epidemic of 1775-1782* (New York: Hill and Wang, 2001), chart on page 19.
4. Jonathan Trumbull, Sr. to George Washington, February 24, 1777, founders.archives. gov/documents/Washington/03-08-02-0466.

munity against future exposure. This differs from vaccination, where in its initial forms a milder version of the virus was injected into the patient.

The basis for the first widespread and successful method of vaccination came in 1796 from British physician Edward Jenner, based on his observation that people milking cows on the farm seemed to have an immunity to smallpox. Jenner made the connection that this immunity resulted from their exposure to the cow pox. By injecting people with this less virulent version of the smallpox virus he was able to give them immunity. Viruses were unknown, but doctors were able use what they observed worked. But this tool was not at Washington's disposal in 1775, leaving him to consider inoculation as the only alternative to quarantine.

Inoculation had some distinct disadvantages: First, inoculated people could easily spread the virus if not strictly quarantined, risking starting an epidemic of your own making. The potential for spread is why many leaders of the day opposed inoculation. The requirement for a tight quarantine made inoculation on a large scale difficult. In addition, doing this on a mass scale put a large portion of military forces under quarantine, making ill and healthy forces alike vulnerable to enemy attack. Washington was already working with an inexperienced and shorthanded force, so purposely disabling a large portion of troops, despite a longer-term gain (immunity), would be highly risky and would have to be done in the strictest of secrecy.

Last, there was a still a dash of superstition and doubt about the efficacy inoculation and the risks it entailed. Rev. Cotton Mather, a famous inoculation advocate during the severe Boston smallpox epidemic of 1721, was taken to task for committing "acts against god" for promoting inoculation. Feelings ran so strongly that someone attempted to bomb Mather's home.[5] John Adams was an early convert among the founders, successfully inoculated in 1764. While the process was not without its risks, the death rate from inoculations was roughly 2 percent. Smallpox contracted "in the wild" could have a death rate that reached over 40 percent depending on time and place.[6]

The perception of danger resulted in inoculation being made illegal in a number of colonies, a list that at one time or another included New York, New Hampshire, Connecticut, Virginia, Maryland, and Massachusetts, the latter where Washington was operating in 1775. Captur-

5. Becker, "Smallpox in Washington's Army," 387.
6. Fenn, *Pox Americana*, 21.

ing much of the thinking behind these bans, Trumbull observed in a letter to Philip Schuyler, subsequently relayed by Schuyler to Washington, that "innoculation for the small pox I find has been practised by Troops on the March to join your Army—I hope a practice so pernicious in every Respect will be discouraged . . . Indeed Sir if it is not timely restrained it appears to me it must prove fatal to all our operations and may ruin the Country"[7] If Washington had any thought of mass-inoculation of his forces, he had some minds besides his own to change.

The Boston that Washington held under siege in 1775 through early 1776 had a number of smallpox outbreaks. It is likely that the presence of smallpox in the city was to some degree responsible for Washington's reliance upon siege rather than attacking the British during the fall and winter.[8] During the siege, Washington's army had its share of outbreaks as well, which he tried to control with quarantines of infected soldiers. At this point, in conjunction with local authorities, inoculation was, at least officially, off the table, although there may have been scattered "rogue inoculations" among his troops.

Obedient to the prevailing laws, Washington was still advocating the quarantine approach, setting up a smallpox hospital for that purpose near Fresh Pond, about a mile and a half west of the Cambridge common. A sentry was deployed to ensure that anyone coming or going had proper clearance from the medical staff. Any man suspected of having the disease was to be removed at once to this quarantine location. To further mitigate against the spread of the disease, Washington issued a July 4, 1775 General Order that included a provision that "No Person is to be allowed to go to Fresh-water pond a fishing or on any other occasion as there may be danger of introducing the small pox into the army."[9]

The British, in Washington's opinion, may have been using smallpox to prolong the siege. "the small pox rages all over the Town, Such of the Military as had it not before are now under innoculation—this I apprehend is a weapon of Defence they Are useing against us"[10] The

7. Peter Force, *American Archives—A Documentary History, Series Five* (Washington: M. St. Clair Clarke and Peter Force, 1833), 1116.

8. Mary C. Gillet, "The Army Medical Department 1775-1818," *US Army Medical Department Office of Medical History, Army Historical Series*, 56, history.army.mil/html/books/030/30-7-1/index.html.

9. General Orders, July 4, 1775, founders.archives.gov/documents/Washington/03-01-02-0027.

10. Washington to John Hancock, December 14, 1775, founders.archives.gov/documents/Washington/03-02-02-0503.

danger that smallpox held for the army not only influenced Washington's decision to lay siege upon Boston for many months, but also explained his extreme caution when he moved to occupy Boston after the siege.[11] After the British abandoned Boston on March 17, 1776, Washington singled out one thousand troops who already had immunity to be the first to re-occupy the city. Smallpox continued to swirl around Boston as people sought to return to their homes or reunite with friends and family.

Boston would take until mid-September 1776 to get the upper hand on this round of the epidemic.[12] Meanwhile, Washington's force moved on to New York. Smallpox was still a factor, and Washington was still in quarantine mode. On May 26, 1776, he issued a general order directing that "Any Officer in the Continental Army, who shall suffer himself to be inoculated, will be cashiered and turned out of the army, and have his name published in the News papers throughout the Continent, as an Enemy and Traitor to his country."[13]

A few soldiers were surreptitiously inoculated, but despite the tough talk "none of the officers found to have gotten inoculated appear to have been punished. Nor are there more penalties noted in the general orders. No names were 'published in the News papers throughout the Continent.'"[14] As in Boston, Washington established a smallpox isolation hospital, this time on an island in the East River, and ordered a halt to all inoculations. The general warned that "any disobedience to this order will be most severely punished." The Continental Congress supported Washington, and when a private physician in the State of New York was caught inoculating soldiers, he was jailed.[15]

While this was Washington's official posture, his thinking was starting to shift toward the possibility of pursuing a policy of mass inoculation. First, smallpox gave the British Army a strategic edge, in that many of the troops had been exposed at an early age growing up on the European continent,[16] and the British routinely practiced inoculation. It is unclear whether the British army required inoculation, but for many soldiers it was already unnecessary. At peak, it has been estimated

11. Becker, "Smallpox in Washington's Army," 402.

12. Fenn, *Pox Americana*, 34.

13. General Orders, May 26, 1776, founders.archives.gov/documents/Washington/03-04-02-0312.

14. J.L. Bell, "Thereby prevent Inoculation amongst them," boston1775.blogspot.com/2021/05/thereby-prevent-inoculation-amongst-them.html.

15. "A Deadly Scourge: Smallpox During the Revolutionary War," www.armyheritage.org/soldier-stories-information/a-deadly-scourge-smallpox-during-the-revolutionary-war.

16. Fenn, *Pox Americana*, 49.

that 30-35 percent of Washington's force was unable to fight due to illness, much of it smallpox,[17] a disadvantage he could ill afford.

Second, inoculation would reduce his exposure to what we now call "biological warfare," a tactic allegedly used by the British against the Indians in the Seven Years' War.[18] During the siege of Boston, British Gen. William Howe released people from the city, ostensibly due to food shortages, and the subsequent introduction of smallpox to the colonial forces sustained the standoff, effectively preventing a military confrontation Howe was not confident of winning.[19] Washington suspected that these refugees were infected with smallpox and intended by Howe to infect his army. "General Howe has ordered 300 inhabitants of Boston to Point Shirley in destitute condition," wrote Washington to Congress. "I . . . am under dreadful apprehensions of their communicating the Smallpox as it is rife in Boston." Later, "four British deserters arrived with frightening news. Howe, they claimed, had deliberately infected fugitives with a design to spread the Small-Pox among the Troops."[20] Washington was disinclined to believe Howe was capable of such an atrocity—"I coud not Suppose them Capable of [deliberately passing on the infection]—I now must give Some Credit to it"[21]—but at the same time he redoubled his quarantine efforts and was careful to isolate refugees from his troops where he could.

Third, inoculation improved recruiting and decreased desertion rates for the chronically undermanned Colonial forces. The prospect of being exposed to smallpox in its "wild" form was much more daunting than that of undergoing a much less risky inoculation. If recruits could be inoculated upon entry into the army, they would be safe from the pox and more likely to stay.

Fourth, and probably most compelling, was experience, not only from Boston but from the disastrous outcome in the Battle of Quebec. The disaster at Quebec had occurred in late December 1775, and the more details that came out the worse it sounded, and smallpox was the culprit. "The Situation of our Affairs in Canada is truly alarming" Washington wrote to Phillip Schuyler.[22] Just prior to the retreat, Gen.

17. Becker, "Smallpox in Washington's Army," 393.

18. Ibid., 400.

19. Ibid., 401.

20. Elizabeth Fenn, "The Great Smallpox Epidemic," *History Today* Volume 53 Issue 8 (August 2003).

21. Washington to Hancock, December 11, 1775, founders.archives.gov/documents/Washington/03-02-02-0487.

22. Washington to Phillip Schuyler, June 7, 1776, founders.archives.gov/documents/Washington/03-04-02-0363.

John Thomas, a doctor himself who eventually succumbed to the disease, reported that only 1,000 of the force of 1,900 were combat ready, primarily due to smallpox. Engaging in a little germ warfare of his own, Sir Guy Carlton, in charge of British forces in Canada "apparently sent smallpox victims into the American lines,"[23] adding momentum to the already burgeoning outbreak. Despite the dismal failure in Canada, Washington was reluctant to consider inoculation of the troops because of the way undisciplined and haphazard efforts at inoculation (sometimes self-inoculation) had spread the disease among the troops.[24]

In January 1777, Dr. William Shippen, Washington's director general of hospitals, was authorized to perform some inoculations. Shippen reported that "I found a great number of your troops here in a miserable situation, which I have the pleasure to inform you are now in a comfortable situation."[25] Still, Washington would not cross the threshold to a full inoculation order. He wrote to Shippen on January 28, 1777 again demurring on issuing a full order: "In your last you mentioned your Intention of innoculating all the Recruits who had not had the small Pox, this would be a very Salutary Measure if we could prevent them from bringing the Infection on to the Army, but as they cannot have a change of Cloathes, I fear it is impossible."[26] On the same date, he asked Horatio Gates, whose troops were due to undergo a similar regimen, to halt the process. "I am very much afraid that all the Troops on their march from the Southward will be infected with the small pox, and that instead of having an Army here, we shall have an Hospital . . . Doctor Shippen wrote to me that he intended to inoculate the Troops as they came in, but that never can safely be done, except innoculation was to go thro' the whole Army."[27]

Reconsidering, Washington decided to take the plunge. In a February 5, 1777, letter to John Hancock, the President of Congress, he wrote:

> The small pox has made such Head in every Quarter that I find it impossible to keep it from spreading thro' the whole Army in the natural way. I have therefore determined, not only to innoculate all the

23. James Kirby Martin, *Benedict Arnold—Revolutionary Hero* (New York: New York University Press, 1997), 163.

24. Becker, "Smallpox in Washington's Army," 403-404.

25. William Shippen, Jr. to Washington, January 25, 1777, founders.archives.gov/documents/Washington/03-08-02-0163.

26. Washington to Shippen, Jr., January 28, 1777, founders.archives.gov/documents/Washington/03-08-02-0182.

27. Washington to Horatio Gates, January 28, 1777, founders.archives.gov/documents/Washington/03-08-02-0180.

Troops now here, that have not had it, but shall order Docr Shippen to innoculate the Recuits as fast as they come in to Philadelphia.

A letter to Shippen went out the next day. The original draft of Washington's letter to Hancock testifies to his ongoing ambivalence. That draft read:

> The small Pox is making such Head in every quarter that I am fearful it will infect all the Troops that have not had it. I am divided in my opinion as to the expediency of innoculation, the Surgeons are for it, but if I could by any means put a Stop to it, I would rather do it. However I hope I shall stand acquitted if I submit the Matter to the Judgment and determination of the medical Gentlemen.[28]

So what finally changed the General's mind? It appears to have been an accumulation of information rather than one specific event. The dominos fell quickly from here. On February 6, he wrote Dr. Shippen, "Finding the Small pox to be spreading much and fearing that no precaution can prevent it from running through the whole of our Army, I have determined that the troops shall be inoculated . . . I trust in its consequences will have the most happy effects."[29] Congress, in receipt of the February 5 letter to Hancock, ordered "That the Medical Committee write to General Washington, and consult him on the propriety and expediency of causing such of the troops in his army, as have not had the small pox, to be inoculated, and recommend that measure to him."[30] The Medical Committee followed a day later with a response to Washington that Congress "directed [us] to request your Excellency to give Orders that all who have not had that Disease may be Inoculated, if your Excellency Shall be of Opinion that it can be done without prejudice to your Operations."[31]

With this decision to proceed, one of the concerns about using inoculation now surfaced—the process took about four weeks. This made

---

28. Washington to Hancock, February 5, 1777, founders.archives.gov/documents/Washington/03-08-02-0268.

29. Washington to Shippen, Jr., February 6, 1777, founders.archives.gov/documents/Washington/03-08-02-0281. Fenn's book, referencing this letter from an earlier compilation of Washington's writings, identifies it as having been written on January 6, 1777, changing the sequence of events as she describes it. In Founders Online, a footnote indicates that at one point the transcript was inadvertently dated "Jany 6th." by the copyist. I am assuming the more recent transcription, bearing the February 6 date, is correct.

30. Journals of the Continental Congress, February 12, 1777, memory.loc.gov/cgi-bin/query/r?ammem/hlaw:@field(DOCID+@lit(jc00739)).

31. Continental Congress Medical Committee to Washington, February 13, 1777, founders.archives.gov/documents/Washington/03-08-02-0349.

secrecy imperative. If the British caught wind of the fact that this much of the already low fighting force was out of commission, a timely attack could make quick work of the rest. Much of the critical work was done in the winter quarters in Morristown in early 1777, but some was even done during the difficult next winter in Valley Forge. Secrecy held in both instances. Washington, writing to Trumbull in a letter which must have been somewhat satisfying due to the former's earlier opposition to inoculation, Washington wrote in January 1778, "Notwithstanding the Orders I had given last year to have all the Recruits innoculated, I found upon examination, that between three and four thousand Men had not had the Small Pox. That disorder began to make its appearance in Camp, and to avoid its spreading in the natural way, the whole were immediately innoculated."[32]

The Continental Army had executed the first large-scale, state-sponsored immunization campaign in American history.[33] As British medical writer Hugh Thursfield later wrote "I think it is fair to claim that an intelligent and properly controlled application of the only method then known of defeating the ravages of smallpox, which in the years 1775-76 threatened to ruin the American cause, was a factor of considerable importance in the eventual outcome of the War of Independence."[34] More broadly, the example set by Washington's inoculation program was a positive contribution to public health, legitimizing inoculation until Jenner's vaccine made its appearance.

32. John C. Fitzpatrick, ed., *The Writings of Washington*, Volume 11 (Washington, DC: United States Government Printing Office, 1934), 182.
33. Fenn, *Pox Americana*, 102.
34. F. Fenner et al, *Smallpox and Its Eradication* (Geneva: World Health Organization, 1988), 240.

French Adventurers, Patriots, and Pretentious Imposters in the Fight for American Independence

⊱ ARTHUR S. LEFKOWITZ ⊰

France was defeated in the Seven Years War. The defeat resulted in France losing valuable colonies, and prestige and influence in Europe. Desperate to regain her past glory, France began to modernize and rearm its army and navy. Realizing that its defeat in the Seven Years War was mainly the result of a weak navy, France undertook an ambitious program of building new and modern warships to rival Britain's Royal Navy.

Tension in America suited France's aims. The French became interested in the Americans and sent spies to report back on the growing unrest. Once the rebellion began, the French wanted to keep the war going and they supplied the rebels with war materials. Everything the French did was kept secret to avoid a war with Britain until they were ready.

The French rearmament program included purging the army of mediocre officers.

Europe was at peace at the time and these jobless officers were hard pressed to find employment as mercenaries. Other French officers were frustrated by their inability to advance in rank or gain valuable experience. Thus, these often-unemployed and destitute officers turned to the war in America as their salvation.

One of the most enduring stories from the American Revolution is the capture of Maj. Gen. Charles Lee, who was taken after leaving the safety of his army at Bernardsville, New Jersey on the afternoon of December 12, 1776. Accompanied by a few guards, Lee spent the night at the isolated Widow White's Tavern. Loyalists alerted the British to Lee's position and a detachment of intrepid dragoons surrounded the tavern on the following morning. After they chased off his bodyguards, Lee surrendered and was brought to British held Pennington, New Jersey.

Two French officers were with Lee when he was taken prisoner, René Gaiault de Boisbertrand and Jean Louis de Vernejout.[1] The French did not enter the war as America's ally in 1778, raising the question of why two French Army officers were with Lee two years prior to the French alliance.

Surprisingly, there were many Frenchmen embedded with the Continental army prior to the entry of France into the war and the arrival of a French army in America; in fact, France provided the majority of the European officers who joined the Patriot cause. Virtually all of these foreigners were either French army officers, trained in France or encouraged by the French government to volunteer for the war in America. Examples include Kazimierz (Casimir) Pulaski. Although Pulaski was Polish, he was in France at the start of the American Revolution where he was recruited to join the Patriot Army. Andrew Thaddeus Kosciuszko was another Polish national who was educated in French military schools. Bavarian-born Johann Kalb (better known as Baron de Kalb) was a lieutenant-colonel in the French Army. The so called Baron von Steuben was an unemployed Prussian officer who was introduced to Benjamin Franklin in Paris by agents of the French government.

Just how many Frenchmen volunteered to join the Continental army is difficult to determine. One problem is that some of them failed in their efforts to be appointed as officers in the Continental army and returned to France or the French West Indies. Another is that Americans were unfamiliar with foreign languages. As a result, they were spelling the names and titles of the French volunteers different ways. Washington, for example spelled Kosciuszko's name eleven different ways.[2] There are clues to the numbers including a letter Washington wrote to Congress on February 20, 1777. In his missive, Washington said that the aspirants were "coming in swarms from old France and the [West Indies] Islands."[3] In another letter written during the same

1. Jean Louis de Vernejout was commissioned a captain in the Continental Army on September 19, 1776. Maj. Gen. Charles Lee, *The Lee Papers*, 4 vols. (New York: The New York Historical Society, 1871-1874), 1: 389. His surname is spelled Virnejoux in *The Lee Papers*.
2. Alex Storozynski, "The Fiasco of July 4, 1777." *Huffington Post* Blog, May 25, 2011. For example, in a letter to Henry Laurens dated August 31, 1778, Washington spelled Kosciuszko's name as Cosciusko.
3. George Washington to John Hancock, February 20, 1777, in Edward G. Lengel et al., eds., *The Papers of George Washington, Revolutionary War Series* (24 vols. to date) Charlottesville: University of Virginia Press, 1985-2016), 8: 382 (*PGW*).

period, Washington described them as "the shoals of French Men that are coming on to this Camp."[4] Writing in August 1777, Washington referred to "the numberless applications for Imployment by Foreigners."[5]

Some French volunteers were not commissioned was because they could not speak English. Washington mentioned this problem in a letter to Congress dated October 7, 1776: "I must take the liberty to observe that I am under no small difficulties on account of the French Gentlemen that are here ... Their want of our language is an objection to their being joined to any of the Regiments." To communicate with them Washington appointed men as aides-de-camp who spoke French: Tench Tilghman, Alexander Hamilton and John Laurens. As the war expanded to include contact with Spain, Washington added Dr. James McHenry, who was fluent in Spanish, to his staff.

More French officers were rejected as the Americans became aware that the majority of them were adventurers (an old term to describe mercenaries) who came to sell their services to the Patriots. This was a typical practice in European armies; for example, a quarter of the French army at the time was composed of foreign mercenaries.

French officers mustered out of the army following the end of the Seven Years War (1756-1763) were looking for a war to add to their military experience, prestige at home through higher rank in a foreign army, and to make money. To improve their chances for a commission in the fledging Continental army, the Frenchmen often disguised their true motivation with expressions of their love of liberty and commitment to the Patriot cause. General Washington soon caught on to this masquerade. Writing to Gen. William Heath on July 27, 1777, the commander in chief warned his subordinate, "however modest, they may seem at first to be, by proposing to serve as volunteers, they very soon extend their views, and become importunate for offices they have no right to look for."[6] In another letter, Washington described his experience with French officers: "Men who in the first instance tell you, that they wish for nothing more than the honor of serving in so glorious a cause, as Volunteers—the next day solicit rank without pay—the day following want money advanced them—and in the course of a week want further promotion, and are not satisfied with anything you can do for them."[7]

4. Washington to Horatio Gates, February 20, 1777, in *PGW*, 8: 378.
5. Washington to Benjamin Harrison, August 19, 1777, *PGW*, 11: 4.
6. Washington to William Heath, July 27, 1777, *PGW*, 10: 438.
7. Washington to Gouverneur Morris, July 24, 1778, *PGW*, 16: 153-154.

Another objection to commissioning French volunteers was expressed by Gen. Nathanael Greene. Writing to John Adams in 1777, Greene said that having foreign officers in the army was "an injury to America." Greene said that he looked upon them as "so many spies ready to take their measure as their interest may direct," that is, they were vulnerable to being bribed by the British. The general lectured John Adams that it was important for Americans to lead the army, "for the multiplying of foreign officers gives us no internal strength. A good nursery of officers, nursed by experience, firmly attached to the interest of the country, is a great security against foreign invaders."[8]

The first French volunteers arrived randomly during 1775 and 1776, many from the French West Indies. These early arrivals were later described by the capable Chevalier Dubuysson des Hayes, an aide-de-camp to Lafayette, as "officers who are deeply in debt and discharged from their units in Europe." He accused the governors of the Caribbean islands of getting rid of them by sending them to America with glowing letters of recommendation.[9]

These unemployed French officers arrived with inflated resumes and elegant uniforms to improve their changes for a commission. They had to make a favorable impression as they paid for their voyage and expenses with no financial aid or recognition from the French government. For example, in 1777 a French merchant ship was intercepted and boarded by a Royal Navy cruiser. The British found three French officers and two sergeants onboard bound for America. They arrested the lot. When confronted with the incident, the Comte de Vergennes, the French foreign minister, replied, "having left France without permission to serve the Americans, the representative of the [French] King cannot involve himself in their situation."[10]

Some early French arrivals were successful, commissioned by Congress as captains, majors and colonels in the army and shipped off to General Washington's headquarters. This arrangement was disruptive, as evidenced by a letter the commander in chief wrote to John Hancock, the President of the Continental Congress, written from Morristown in February 1777. The General declared, "You cannot conceive what a weight these kind of people are upon the service and upon me in particular; few of them have any knowledge of the branches which

8. Nathanael Greene to John Adams, May 7, 1777, Richard K. Showman et al., eds., *The Papers of General Nathanael Greene*, 13 vols. (Chapel Hill, The University of North Carolina Press, 1976-2005), 2: 70-71.

9. Robert K. Wright, Jr., *The Continental Army* (Washington, DC: U.S. Government Printing Office, 1983), 129.

10. Harlow Giles Unger, *Lafayette* (New York: John Wiley & Sons, Inc., 2002), 28.

they profess to understand and those that have, are entirely useless as officers from their ignorance of the English language."[11]

At Washington's urging, Congress took steps in March 1777 to curtail the appointment of Frenchmen in the Continental army. Their actions included a resolution advising American ministers in Europe to "discourage all gentlemen from coming to America with expectation of employment in the service, unless they are masters of our language and have the best recommendations."[12]

Contributing to the Patriots' cynicism was the conspicuous failure of several early French volunteers who were commissioned as generals by Congress—Philippe-Hubert, Chevalier de Preudhomme de Borre, a sixty year old former French Army lieutenant colonel; Frederick William baron de Woedtke, who claimed to be an aide to King Frederick the Great; and Matthias-Alexis, Chevalier de La Rochefermoy, an indigent officer living in the French West Indies. De Borre, who barely spoke English, was unable to prevent the disorderly retreat of the Maryland brigade he commanded at the Battle of Brandywine. He claimed that it was not his fault if "the American troops run away from the first fire of the enemy."[13] Infuriated by criticism of his leadership, de Borre tendered his resignation, which was accepted by Congress.[14]

Baron de Woedtke served as a major in the Prussian Army. He later went to Paris where he was appointed a captain and inspector of cavalry in the French Army. When he heard about the war in America he decided to go. De Woedtke arrived in Philadelphia with bogus credentials invented by friends in France describing him as "late a Major General of Cavalry in the Prussian Service and Aid du Camp to that King, and celebrated for his love of Liberty and Military Knowledge."[15] The gullible members of Congress appointed him a brigadier general in the Continental Army on March 16, 1776. De Woedtke, who was thirty-six years old at the time, was ordered to join the American troops fighting in Canada. He was described as "a very heavy drinker" and "not the best bred up by his Prussian Majesty."[16] The Baron lasted only three weeks as an American general. According to Dr. Benjamin Rush, de

11. Washington to Hancock, February 11, 1777, *PGW*, 8: 305.

12. Worthington Chauncey Ford, ed., *Journals of the Continental Congress 1774-1789*, 25 vols.(Washington, DC: Government Printing Office, 1904-22), 7: 174.

13. Thomas J. McGuire, *The Philadelphia Campaign*, 2 vols. (Mechanicsburg, PA: Stackpole Books, 2006-2007), 1: 223.

14. Louis Clinton Hatch, *The Administration of the American Revolutionary Army* (New York: Longmans, Green and Co., 1904), 64.

15. Mark R. Anderson, *The Battle for the Fourteenth Colony* (Hanover, NH: University Press of New England, 2013), 302.

16. Ibid.

Woedtke died on July 28, 1776 "from the effects of hard drinking."[17] Commenting on the news of his death, John Adams wrote, "The Baron is dead—has not left a very good Character."[18]

Matthias-Alexis, Chevalier de La Rochefermoy was another conspicuous failure. He was particularly artful in getting his appointment as a brigadier general (he was a captain in the French Army) with extravagant claims that he was a confidant of the French royal family. Rochefermoy served with the Northern Army and was stationed at Fort Ticonderoga in July 1777. When the fortress proved untenable, its commander, Gen. Arthur St. Clair, ordered a nighttime evacuation on July 5 with no lights or sounds to alert the nearby enemy. Rochefermoy failed to notify all of the troops under his command of the retreat and compounded his incompetence by setting fire to his headquarters, illuminating the night sky. His error alerted the British to the American evacuation. He later had the audacity to defend his action and demand a promotion to major general. Rejected by Congress, Rochefermoy resigned his commission and returned to the West Indies.

The trickle of French officers who arrived in 1775 and 1776 increased to a torrent in 1777 through the single-handed activities of Silas Deane. A Connecticut merchant and former Congressman, Deane arrived in Paris in July 1776, his mission to secure military aid and loans from the French government. Deane was also given blank Continental army commissions. The rationale behind this action can be traced back to a July 10, 1775 letter General Washington wrote to Congress in which he mentioned "a want of engineers to construct proper works."[19] Benjamin Franklin visited Washington's headquarters in Cambridge, Massachusetts a few months later. During his visit, Washington told Franklin that he had an urgent need for at least two engineers.[20] Franklin was a member of the Continental Congress's Secret Committee whose purpose was to seek aid from France and other European nations. It was the Secret Committee that arranged for Deane to go to the French capital. Remembering Washington's request for engineers, Franklin's committee instructed Deane to recruit French army engineers, and gave him blank Continental army commissions to expedite his recruiting efforts.

17. Benjamin Rush to Jacques Barbeu-Dubourg, September 16, 1776, Paul H. Smith et al., eds., *Letters of Delegates to Congress 1774-1789*, 26 vols. (Washington, D.C.: U.S. Government Printing Office, 1976-2000), 5: 283-184.
18. Adams to Francis Dana, August 16, 1776, ibid, 4.
19. Washington to the President of Congress, July 10, 1775, *PGW*, 1: 85.
20. Milton C. Van Vlack, *Silas Deane, Revolutionary War Diplomat and Politician* (Jefferson, North Carolina: McFarland & Company, 2013), 87.

The parochial Deane, from rustic Wethersfield, Connecticut, was dazzled by Paris and the procession of French officers who called upon him. He was impressed with their smart uniforms, claims of military prowess and connections to the French government and the Royal family. Deane believed he was aiding the Patriot cause by issuing commissions to the most impressive French officers he met in Paris. His disciples arrived in Philadelphia where they presented their commissions to Congress. The delegates were befuddled and solved the problem by sending the Frenchmen to Washington's headquarters.

One of Deane's seemingly promising recruits was Thomas Conway, an Irish-born colonel in the French army. French officers had been arriving in America individually, but Conway arrived in Portsmouth, New Hampshire on April 22, 1777 accompanied by thirty-one additional French volunteers. He joined the army as a brigadier general in the following month.

Conway proved to be a troublemaker who was barely able to conceal his contempt for Washington's generalship. His criticism fueled the so called Conway Cabal in 1778 which was quickly squashed by Washington and led to Conway's resignation.

Noteworthy among the officers who arrived with Conway was Denis-Jean Florimond de Mautherville, chevalier du Bouchet, who commanded a company of Morgan's Rifle Corps during the Saratoga campaign. Du Bouchet was cited for his "distinguished service and notable bravery" at Saratoga by General Horatio Gates.[21]

Washington patiently cooperated with Congress to handle the influx of French volunteers until an arrogant French officer named Philippe Tronson du Coudray showed-up at headquarters. Du Coudray was a talented but egotistical artillery major in the French Army. In 1775, he was ordered by the French government to visit the nation's ten arsenals and prepare a list of surplus artillery and muskets that could be sold to the rebels. After completing his mission, the major convinced Deane to appoint him a major general and commander of the Continental army's artillery and engineering corps. Deane signed a contract with the Frenchman on September 11, 1776.

In December 1776, Benjamin Franklin arrived in France to assist Deane and was promptly introduced to du Coudray. Franklin endorsed du Coudray's appointment after learning of the major's reputation and high regard by the French government.

---

21. Stanley J. Idzerda, et al., eds., *Lafayette in the Age of the American Revolution*, 5 vols. (Ithaca, New York: Cornell University Press, 1977-1783), 1: 162.

Du Courday arrived in Boston in April 1777 accompanied by twenty-seven French officers and twelve artillery sergeants. The delegates to Congress were stunned by this latest invasion and directed their anger at Deane. They insisted that Deane had no authority to grant commissions and paid for the majority of the Frenchmen to return home.[22] Du Coudray stayed and proved to be a pompous windbag who was finally mitigated by appointing him Inspector General of Ordnance and Military Manufactories. While crossing the swollen Schuylkill River in a flatboat on September 15, 1777, Du Coudray insisted on remaining on his horse during the dangerous crossing. He drowned when his skittish horse plunged into the river with the insolent Frenchman in the saddle.

Meanwhile Deane was recalled, leaving Franklin as the principle American envoy in France. Franklin became the new target for French officers eager to join the Continental army. Franklin claimed that he was hounded at every dinner or ball he attended "by some officer or officer's friend . . . who begins his attack upon me" for a commission in the Continental army. Harassed by applicants "from morning to night . . . the noise of every coach now that enters my court terrifies me."[23]

While he did not issue commissions, Franklin wrote glowing letters of recommendation and encouraged French applicants to journey to Philadelphia to offer their services to the Continental Congress. One result was that Henry Laurens, the president of Congress at the time, wrote from the rebel capital complaining that "French officers beset my door like bailiffs watching a debtor."[24]

General Washington was also hounded by "foreign gentlemen." He constrained his volatile temper in favor of calm reasoning with the venerated Franklin. Writing to the elder statesman on August 17, 1777 Washington explained, "Our corps being already formed and fully officered, and the number of foreign gentlemen . . .continually arriving with fresh applications, throw such obstacles in the way of any future appointments, that every new arrival is only a new source of embarrassment to Congress and myself." Washington continued, "as they have come over in such crowds, we either must not employ them, or we must do it at the expense of one half the officers in the army."[25]

In time Franklin realized the trouble he was creating back home by helping the friends and families of unemployed or derisory French of-

---

22. *Journals of the Continental Congress,* 9: 877-878.
23. Hatch, *The Administration of the American Revolutionary Army,* 47.
24. Ibid.
25. Washington to Benjamin Franklin, August 17, 1777, *PGW,* 10: 647.

ficers who hounded him. He wrote, "frequently if a man has no useful talents, is good for nothing and burdensome to his relations, or is indiscreet, profligate and extravagant, they are glad to get rid of him by sending him to the other end of the world."[26]

Despite the reality of the situation, the romantic notion that French Army officers volunteered because of their love of liberty remains embedded in our culture based on a handful of outstanding French volunteers, the most famous of them Marie Jean Paul Joseph Roche Yves Gilbert du Motier, Marquis de Lafayette. Lafayette was a wealthy and venerated young French aristocrat enthralled by the rebellion in America. He was introduced to Deane in November 1776, their meeting arranged by retired French army Lt. Col. Johann Kalb who was also interested in joining the rebels. Kalb, a native of Bavaria, was described as "one of the bravest and most skillful soldiers in France."[27] Deane signed a contract with Lafayette and Kalb on December 7, 1776, appointing them major generals in the Continental army.

The two Frenchmen arrived in Charleston, South Carolina in 1777 with an entourage of fellow French army volunteers. They traveled overland to Philadelphia where they arrived late in July 1777. Congress gave Lafayette and his cadre a cool reception. The best that the wealthy Lafayette could achieve was to serve as an unpaid volunteer. Many of the other French officers who arrived with him were turned away and returned to France. Kalb remained behind; he was fluent in English and had toured America in 1768 as a secret agent of the French government to evaluate the colonists' "seeds of discontent."[28] His persistence was rewarded and Congress appointed him a major general in September 1777. Lafayette was also ultimately appointed a major general.

Franklin was also responsible for recruiting the Baron von Steuben, a talented, unemployed Prussian officer living in Paris. Franklin was introduced to the Prussian by Comte de Saint-Germain, the French minister of war, who believed that von Steuben's military experience would be useful in organizing the rebel army and disciplining its troops.[29]

There were other French volunteers who proved to be valuable Continental army officers. One of the lesser known ones was Charles Noël

26. Stacy Schiff, *A Great Improvisation* (New York: Henry Holt and Company, 2005), 14.
27. Josephine Fennell Pacheco, *French Secret Agents in America, 1763-1778*, PhD Dissertation, The University of Chicago, 1950, 152.
28. Alexander Graydon, *Memoirs of His Own Time* (Philadelphia: Lindsay & Blakiston, 1846), 65.
29. Hatch, *The Administration of the American Revolutionary Army*, 61.

Romand, Sieur de l'Lisle. Appointed a major in the Continental army, Lisle married an American woman with whom he had several children. One of Major Lisle's progenies founded the Lisle Corporation, a tool manufacturer that continues to operate as a family owned business to the present day.

It was in the field of military engineering that the French arguably made their most valuable contribution to the Patriot cause. The Americans were desperate for engineers who could design resilient fortifications. Writing to Washington in July 1777, influential Congressman James Lovell mentioned that French engineers were held in high esteem: "The corps of Engineers is very honorable in France; and officers from it are sought by different European Powers."[30]

Early in the war, Washington was fooled by several French officers claiming to be engineers. They turned out to be frauds. The commander in chief warned Richard Henry Lee, a delegate to Congress, of French officers posing as engineers, telling him, "Gentleman of this profession ought to produce sufficient and authentic testimonials of their skill and knowledge, and not expect that a pompous narrative of their services, and loss of Papers (the usual excuse) can be a proper introduction into our army."[31]

The lack of trained engineers was evident in the ill-fated November 1776 American defense of Fort Washington. The fort, built on the highest point of northern Manhattan, was considered virtually impregnable by the Patriots, but its garrison of 2,700 men surrendered after a four-hour assault by British and Hessian troops.

There was one French trained engineer in America when Fort Washington surrendered in late 1776, Thaddeus Kosciusko. A Polish national, Kosciusko spoke fluent English. He attended a military school in Warsaw after which he was awarded a scholarship to attend the prestigious Ecole Royal Militaire (Royal Military School) in Paris. While in Paris, he also studied painting and architecture at the Academie Royale de Peinture et de Sculpture (Royal Academy of Painting and Sculpture). He next attended the Ecole du Corps Royal du Génie Militaire (Royal Engineering School) located in Mézières, France. Kosciuszko returned to Poland in 1774 to find the country in chaos. With no prospects to pursue his military career at home, he returned to France. It was there that he met other ambitious young officers talking about the war in America. Perhaps with a letter of introduction to the General Charles Lee, who had served in the Polish Army,

---

30. James Lovell to Washington, July 24, 1777, *PGW*, 10: 386.
31. Washington to Richard Henry Lee, May 17, 1777, *PGW*, 9: 454.

Kosciuszko arrived in Philadelphia in August 1776. He petitioned Congress for a commission on August 30. While waiting for an answer, he got a job as a civilian engineer with the Pennsylvania Committee of Defense and set to work fortifying the Delaware River. Impressed with his engineering skills, Congress commissioned Kosciusko on October 18, 1776 as a colonel in the Continental army. He was only one man, however, and the Americans desperately needed other competent engineers.

The French government came to the rescue of the rebels by secretly loaning them four outstanding French army engineers in a clandestine arrangement negotiated by Franklin and Deane with the French minister of war and signed in Paris on February 13, 1777. The senior French army engineer sent to America was Antoine-Jean-Louis LeBègue de Presle Duportail, thirty-four years old and a member of a noble French family. Duportail was commissioned a colonel in the Continental army on July 8, 1777 and soon given command of the Patriots Engineering Corps. The three other engineers who accompanied Duportail were also commissioned as officers in the Continental army, Bailleul La Radière, Obry Gouvion and Jean-Baptiste-Jospeh, Comte de Laumoy.

The French engineers first demonstrated their expertise by constructing two temporary bridges across the Schuylkill River at Swede's Ford (modern Norristown) during the night of December 12, 1777. They brought a bridging train, a convoy of wagons loaded with building materials including lumber and tools, to the site. Using this material, the Frenchmen built one bridge by laying a wooden roadbed over floating rafts. The other bridge was made by placing thirty-six wagons in the shallow ford with wooden rails across them.[32]

The French government aided the rebels with military equipment as well as talented engineers during the first years of the American Revolution. Why would France, which was ruled by a king, support a revolution whose goal was to overthrow a fellow monarch and establish a representative government? The answer is that the colonist's rebellion was looked upon by King Louis XVI and his minsters as a golden opportunity to weaken Britain. They reasoned that the war would compel Britain to send part of its army and navy to America to suppress the uprising, easing the way for a French invasion of England. The Revolution would also force Britain to borrow money to fight the rebels, making it more difficult for them to finance a war with France. Thus, it was in France's best interest to keep the Revolution going as long as

---

32. Wright, *The Continental Army*, 131.

possible by aiding the rebels. The outcome of the war was of little interest to France in 1775-1777. King Louis just wanted the fighting to continue to bleed Britain's military power while France prepared for war.

On March 1, 778, a treaty of cooperation between France and America was announced at the Valley Forge encampment. The often-repeated story that France entered the war as America's ally because of the Patriot victory at Saratoga is an oversimplification. Burgoyne's surrender at Saratoga influenced the French but they were determined long before the Saratoga campaign to declare war on Britain. The alliance was the result of several years of negotiation by the Patriots, which included the Declaration of Independence that convinced France that the Americans were fighting for independence. Without this assurance, France would be concerned that the colonists might rejoin the British Empire and unite to seize France's remaining rich Caribbean island colonies.

France's entry into the war ended the flow of volunteer French officers to America, closing a unique chapter in the story of the American Revolution.

The Cherokee-American War from the Cherokee Perspective

JORDAN BAKER

In the early years of the American Revolution, the northern theater raged in Massachusetts with famous battles like Lexington and Concord. The southern theater, however, looked far different. From Virginia to Georgia, newly elected Revolutionary governments and self-styled Patriots both looked west at the trans-Appalachian region, hoping to finally traverse the stern border the British had set. The only problem was that the land was already inhabited. The Choctaw, Chickasaw, and Cherokee, to name the most prominent, had inhabited the land for centuries, and didn't exactly welcome Anglo-American settlement.

Conflict between American settlers/revolutionaries and the Cherokee nation erupted in the early years of the Revolution. This conflict is particularly interesting when viewed from the perspective of the Cherokee, especially two of their most prominent leaders, Dragging Canoe and Nancy Ward (or Nan-ye-hi in Cherokee).

A BRIEF INTRODUCTION TO THE CONFLICT

The tensions that eventually boiled over into the Cherokee-American War went back decades, if not longer. Sometimes allies, sometimes enemies, the Cherokee and British had been involved in a series of colonial wars dating back to the early eighteenth century. The most recent, the Anglo-Cherokee war, a regional offshoot of the Seven Years' War, where the two sides faced off as opponents, left relations frosty.

On the Cherokee side, they had successfully pushed back several encroaching Anglo-American frontier settlements in the Carolinas. These victories kept Cherokee sovereignty undiminished and even strengthened their diplomatic importance in the southeast. Despite this, the war also saw British forces destroy half of all Cherokee villages. Due to the violence of the British military campaign, as well as disease and famine that wreaked havoc throughout the nation, the Cherokee population took a huge hit. What's more, by the end of the war, the new British superintendent of Indian Affairs, Jeffrey Amherst, made the Cherokees' ability to carry on lucrative trade with the British all but impossible. Now finding it difficult to procure ammunition for their winter hunts, as well as other necessities, many Cherokee felt the British were actively endangering their way of life.[1]

On the colonists' side, the Anglo-Cherokee war left lasting distrust of their neighbors. To many, Cherokee raids on frontier farmsteads proved right the misgivings most British colonists had felt toward Native Nations since their arrival in the Western Hemisphere. Adding insult to injury, the end of the Seven Years' War saw the British government issue a Royal Proclamation that set a boundary line, called the Indian Boundary, that prohibited American settlers from crossing into the Appalachian and trans-Appalachian regions. To American settlers of the old west, this came as a slap in the face. The French crown had ceded vast swaths of territory to Britain that its citizens were now barred from inhabiting. As part of the laws surrounding this proclamation, the British government recognized the right of Native Nations to drive white settlers from their territory and would even send troops of their own to rout out trespassers.[2]

Nevertheless, Americans persisted in crossing into Cherokee territory. Unsurprisingly, these actions only took a tense situation from bad to worse. People from up and down the Cherokee Nation became increasingly incensed as white colonists continued to settle on their hunting grounds, chipping away at their borders and way of life with each new farmstead.

The most famous of these settlements was Watauga. Founded in 1769 in what is now Elizabethton, Tennesee, British colonists rented a huge tract of land from a Cherokee noble who agreed to the terms without the consent of the Cherokee powers that were.[3] For the next five years, the governments of Virginia and North Carolina continued to declare Watauga illegal, but the settlers did not move.[4]

---

1. Fred Anderson, *Crucible of War: The Seven Years' Ware the Fate of Empire in British North America, 1754-1766* (New York: Knopf Doubleday Publishing Group, 2000), 469-471.
2. Nadia Dean, "A Demand of Blood: The Cherokee War of 1776," *American Indian Magazine*, vol. 14, no. 4 (Winter 2013), www.americanindianmagazine.org/story/demand-blood-cherokee-war-1776.
3. Natalie Inman, "'A Dark and Bloody Ground'": American Indian Responses to Expansion during the American Revolution," *Tennessee Historical Quarterly*, vol. 70, no. 4 (Winter 2011), 262.
4. Ibid.

Then, in 1774, a North Carolina land speculator by the name of Richard Henderson negotiated with the Cherokee. The result was the Treaty of Sycamore Shoals, in which Henderson claimed the Cherokee not only ceded the land upon which Watauga was built, but "all of their hunting grounds south of the Ohio and Kentucky Rivers and north of the Cumberland River." Basically, Henderson claimed the Cherokee had ceded all of what would become Kentucky and Middle Tennessee.[5]

In a letter dated February 22, 1774, a British emissary to the Cherokee named John Stuart wrote to the governor of North Carolina, saying "I received a message from the Cherokees . . . The Nation is extremely uneasy at the encroachments of the white people on their hunting ground."[6] Stuart also warned of the "the consequences" of this settlement and that it "may in a little time prove fatal" as the Cherokee would seek to "redress themselves" should the Watauga settlers "neglect to move off." Speaking on behalf of the Cherokee, Stuart's writings tell us that they were none too happy when it came to the issue of the Watauga settlement.

The colonial governments went along with Henderson's suggestions, the governor of North Carolina even issuing a proclamation "enjoining . . . the said settlers immediately to return from the Indian Territory." If they didn't, they could "expect no protection from his Majesty's government."[7]

Despite this hardline stance by the colonial governors, the revolutionary governments that came to power during the American Revolution were more than happy to treat Sycamore Shoals as a legitimate accord.

THE TREATY OF SYCAMORE SHOALS

At this time, the Cherokee Nation was not a unified state, but rather a complex web of villages and clans who each had their own leaders. So, as white settlers began to move into Cherokee territory as a result of the Treaty of Sycamore Shoals and the towns in Watauga became an increasingly larger issue, the most important people within the nation convened on how to deal with the threat.

Unfortunately for the Cherokee, these leaders proved divided. On the one hand, famed diplomat Little Carpenter and military leader Oconostota wished for peace, feeling their country had found itself in

5. Ibid.

6. E. Raymond Evans, "Dragging Canoe," sites.rootsweb.com/~tnpolk2/DraggingCanoe Bio.htm.

7. Evans, "Dragging Canoe," sites.rootsweb.com/~tnpolk2/DraggingCanoeBio.htm.

the middle of one European conflict too many. The other faction, led by Dragging Canoe, who was, in fact, Little Carpenter's son, wanted war. To Dragging Canoe, force was the only means by which the Cherokee could retain their sovereignty.[8] In a stirring speech, he addressed the grievances of his people and put forth an ominous, though rather prophetic, message:

> We had hoped that the white men would not be willing to travel beyond the mountains. Now that hope is gone. They have passed the mountains, and have settled upon Cherokee land. They wish to have that usurpation sanctioned by treaty. When that is gained, the same encroaching spirit will lead them upon other land of the Cherokees. New cessions will be asked. Finally the whole country, which the Cherokees and their fathers have so long occupied, will be demanded, and the remnant of Ani-Yunwiya, the Real People, once so great and formidable, will be compelled to seek refuge in some distant wilderness. There they will be permitted to stay only a short while, until they again behold the advancing banners of the same greedy host. Not being able to point out any further retreat for the miserable Cherokees, the extinction of the whole race will be proclaimed. Should we not therefore run all risks, and incur all consequences, rather than submit to further loss of our country? Such treaties may be alright for men who are too old to hunt or fight. As for me, I have my young warriors about me. We will have our lands. I have spoken.[9]

Ultimately, Dragging Canoe's argument carried the day. His notion that white settlers wished "to have their usurpations sanctioned by treaty" won over the minds of many of his countrymen.[10] While Little Carpenter and Oconostota had their reservations, war was now unavoidable.

DRAGGING CANOE AND THE PATH TO WAR

As tensions continued to grow between American settlers and the Cherokee, the Revolutionary governments attempted to win over Cherokee leaders by sending gunpowder and other supplies. Dragging Canoe, however, could not be deterred. The Watauga settlements had proven the Americans' true intent for his people and their land. "The white men have almost surrounded us," he told Stuart and another British agent to the Cherokee, Alexander Cameron, "leaving us only a

8. Inman, "'A Dark and Bloody Ground,'" 263-264.
9. "Cherokee Leaders Speak: Dragging Canoe," www.ncpedia.org/anchor/cherokee-leaders-speak.
10. Dean, "A Demand of Blood: The Cherokee War of 1776."

little spot of ground to stand upon, and it seems to be their intention to destroy us as a Nation."[11]

Despite his certainty that war was the only way, British representatives to the Cherokee convinced Dragging Canoe to send one final olive branch. Dragging Canoe consented and the British agents offered the Watauga settlers land in Florida if they vacated their steadings in the Appalachians.[12] This offer fell on deaf ears and, rather than choosing peace, the Watauga settlers, backed by their new revolutionary governments, began fortifying their towns.

Incensed that this final attempt at reconciliation had seemingly only put the Americans on their guard, taking away his army's advantage of surprise, Dragging Canoe officially went to war. Using the geography of the Cherokee Nation to his advantage, he divided his attack into three stages: the Upper Cherokee would attack Virginia and North Carolina, the Middle Towns would focus on North Carolina, and the Lower Towns would attack South Carolina and Georgia.[13]

The Cherokee did not go into battle alone, however. At the behest of the British lieutenant governor in Detroit, Henry Hamilton, Northern Nations, including the Shawnee, Lenape, Ottawa, and Iroquois, met the Cherokee and other prominent Southern Nations, including the Creek, Chickasaw, and Choctaw. At this meeting, in May 1776, Dragging Canoe and other Cherokee leaders accepted war belts from the Northern leaders, cementing a Native Nation alliance determined to halt American encroachment on their lands.[14]

At this meeting, Dragging Canoe also affirmed his continued friendship with those British subjects who did not endanger Cherokee land or sovereignty. "If any of you choose to join the war, I will be glad, but I will not insist upon any of you going."[15]

THE CHEROKEE-AMERICAN WAR BEGINS

The conflict began on the frontiers of South Carolina, in the space between American and Cherokee soil. In late June, 1776, the Lower Towns sent their troops against the western settlements of South Carolina. A few days later, on July 1, Cherokee forces from the Middle Towns (as well as from smaller districts called the Out and Valley

11. Evans, "Dragging Canoe," sites.rootsweb.com/~tnpolk2/DraggingCanoeBio.htm.
12. Ibid.
13. William L. Anderson and Ruth Y. Wetmore, "Cherokee," www.ncpedia.org/cherokee/revolutionarywar.
14. Chuck Hamilton, "Cherokee-American Wars, 1775-1795," www.academia.edu/1196 3611/Cherokee_American_Wars_1775_1795.
15. Evans, "Dragging Canoe," sites.rootsweb.com/~tnpolk2/DraggingCanoeBio.htm.

Towns) launched their attack on the frontier settlements of North Carolina. The third prong was then launched against the American settlements of the Upper South, in what is now North Carolina, Tennessee, and Virginia.[16]

In each of these offensives, Cherokee forces went after the Anglo-American forts that dotted their eastern border. Several of these pushes seem to have been all out attacks, intended to overtake the forts and kill or push out its white inhabitants. In others, Cherokee forces attempted to besiege the forts, probably hoping to starve out the American garrisons.

While this three-pronged strategy met with moderate success, the Cherokee ultimately failed to take any forts. And, what's more, their military leader, Dragging Canoe, was wounded in the attempt. While advancing on a fort known as Eaton's Station, in what is now eastern Tennessee, Dragging Canoe faced five companies of militia, comprising some 170 men. In a brilliant maneuver, Dragging Canoe feigned retreat before ambushing the now relaxed militiamen. Forming his troops into "a cone—the apex towards the centre" of the militia's line, Dragging Canoe charged, severing the defender's line and temporarily separating their captain from the main body of their forces.[17]

Despite this initial success in what has come to be known as the Battle of Island Flats, the Cherokee forces were ultimately repelled, with Dragging Canoe taking a shot to the leg and his brother, Little Owl, somehow surviving eleven gunshot wounds.[18] A member of the militia later recounted how Dragging Canoe's troops attacked with "the greatest fury imaginable" and that "there were streams of blood" that ran "every way" after the battle.[19]

CHEROKEE TROOPS LOSE GROUND

Though the large, three-pronged attack failed to destroy their enemy's forts, Dragging Canoe and his men continued to fight on. In smaller raiding parties, they sought to ambush colonial militia and regiments of the Continental Army as they marched through mountain passes. Again, this tactic met with varying success. Several times, Cherokee parties pushed back the American troops, forcing them to wait for reinforcements.

---

16. Hamilton, "Cherokee-American Wars, 1775-1795," www.academia.edu/11963611/Cherokee_American_Wars_1775_1795.

17. Wayne Lynch, "WIlliam Cocke at the Battle of Long Island Flats, 1776", May 7, 2013, *Journal of the American Revolution*, allthingsliberty.com/2013/05/william-cocke-at-the-battle-of-long-island-flats-1776/.

18. Hamilton, "Cherokee-American Wars, 1775-1795," 17.

19. Lynch, "WIlliam Cocke at the Battle of Long Island Flats, 1776."

As the war dragged on, however, Cherokee forces began to lose ground to the relentless army of would-be settlers. All along the border, American troops launched a scorched earth campaign. And with each victory the Continental regiments earned, they burned Cherokee towns and took survivors prisoner. By the end of the campaign, they had destroyed over fifty Cherokee towns, including crops and livestock, and killed hundreds of Cherokee, enslaving the survivors and sending them as far off as the Caribbean.[20]

These losses devastated the Cherokee. Their homes razed, food destroyed, and people slaughtered, the nation's ability to continue the fight waned.

With the desire to make peace growing, Cherokee leaders met in the Overhill Towns to discuss how to move forward. Little Carpenter and Oconostota wanted to end the war however they could, no matter the cost of land. And who could blame them? With their people dying and their country being put to the torch, it may well have looked like there was no other way. In fact, their desire to end the war was so great that they even offered to give Dragging Canoe and Alexander Cameron over to the American forces in exchange for their guarantee that the Overhill Towns would be spared the same fate as so many others.[21]

LITTLE CARPENTER, NANCY WARD, AND THE PEACE FACTION

Throughout the war, Little Carpenter and his niece, Nancy Ward, stood firm as staunch advocates for peace. To them, war would only beget more conflict, thus the only true path forward that would ensure the sovereignty and borders of the Cherokee nation was peace. And one can see their point.[22] White settlers across the thirteen rebelling colonies had not proven shy about enacting violence against Native Americans when they stood in the way of American expansion. Their desire for peace was so staunch, in fact, that while Dragging Canoe's forces had the formal blessing of the Cherokee Nation, Little Carpenter and Nancy Ward continued to work toward a peace with the Watauga settlements and others.

Nancy Ward's place in this narrative is a rather special one. Born in 1738 in the prominent Cherokee town of Chota, by the time the Cherokee-American war began she was a war veteran, mother, widow, and, having married a white man in her second marriage, a go-between for Cherokee and American concerns. Given the Cherokee title of Beloved Woman, or Ghigua in Cherokee, a position of power in both

---

20. Hamilton, "Cherokee-American Wars, 1775-1795," 19.
21. Ibid
22. Inman, "'A Dark and Bloody Ground'," 263-264.

times of peace and war, Ward sat at the head of the Council of Women, could vote in the Council of Chiefs, and decided the fate of Cherokee prisoners.[23]

It is not surprising, then, that Ward came to play a prominent part in the conflict. Though her role in the war was largely diplomatic, she was not afraid to risk her own safety in an attempt to avoid casualties. In July 1776, as her cousin Dragging Canoe attempted an assault on the Watauga settlements with 600 of his troops, Ward raced ahead to warn the settlers of the impending attack. While some Wataugans escaped Dragging Canoe's forces, some were taken captive. Here again, Nancy Ward showed her commitment to peace between the two peoples. A woman by the name of Lydia Russell Bean had been captured in Dragging Canoe's attack and sentenced to death. Aided by Nancy Ward, she escaped before she could be put to the torch.[24]

TREATIES AND THE CHICKAMAUGA SECESSION

By the fall of 1776, American forces had committed themselves to an all-out defeat of the Cherokee, if not a campaign of genocide. One commander of Patriot forces showed the true intent of the war when he stated that "every Indian taken shall be the slave and property of the taker; that the nation be extirpated, and the lands become the property of the [American] public."[25]

As their forces in the field faltered, many Cherokee no doubt felt that their nation, freedom, and lives were in jeopardy. By the spring, many of the Cherokee leaders had decided to make peace. Hostilities between the two sides ended by May, when the respective leaders began agreeing to a series of treaties; but while we call these treaties, it's important to keep in mind that terms were essentially dictated to the Cherokee, rather than agreed upon by two sides that respected one another. By July, the Cherokee nation had lost five million acres.

Hoping to make an example of the Cherokee, American leaders told other Native Nations that, if they too fought, that they would be driven "out of their Country, like a Gang of Cattle & their Corn all destroyed" and "that the people over the great Water [the British] cannot help them."[26]

23. Christina Berry, "Nancy Ward: Beloved Woman Of The Cherokee," www.allthings cherokee.com/nancy-ward/.

24. Inman, "'A Dark and Bloody Ground'," 265.

25. Alan Taylor, *American Revolutions: A Continental History, 1750-1804* (New York, W.W. Norton, 2016), www.google.com/books/edition/American_Revolutions_A_Continental_ Histo/E92aCwAAQBAJ?hl=en&gbpv=1.

26. Taylor, *American Revolutions*.

Unwilling to give into the force and cruelty displayed by American forces, Dragging Canoe and his supporters broke off from the Cherokee nation and formed the Chickamauga. "My thoughts and my heart are for war," Dragging Canoe told his fellow Cherokee leaders, "as long as King George has one enemy in this country. Our hearts are straight to him and all his people, and whoever is at war with us."[27]

Due to this secession, history has gone on to give the Cherokee-American War names such as Dragging Canoe's War and the Chickamauga Wars. While we have focused on the first year of this conflict, stretching roughly from the summer of 1776 to the summer of 1777, Dragging Canoe continued to fight the good fight. Settling in what is now northwest Georgia, the Chickamauga remained at war with America for another two decades, until the conflict ultimately ended in 1795.[28]

CONCLUSION

While it is difficult to tell the story of the Cherokee-American War from the eyes of the Cherokee in great detail, given the lack of written documents produced by Cherokees at the time, I have endeavored to at least provide the general framework with which the Cherokee and their leaders approached the war and the threat of white encroachment.

By examining the American Revolution from the viewpoint of the Native Nations that fought with the British and/or against the American forces, we can gain a new perspective on how the Revolution affected the world outside the thirteen rebelling colonies and contributed to the centuries long erosion of Native American sovereignty.

27. sites.rootsweb.com/~tnpolk2/DraggingCanoeBio.htm.
28. Chuck Hamilton, "Cherokee-American Wars, 1775-1795," www.academia.edu/1196 3611/Cherokee_American_Wars_1775_1795.

The Numerical Strength of George Washington's Army During the 1777 Philadelphia Campaign

GARY ECELBARGER AND MICHAEL C. HARRIS

INTRODUCTION

Perhaps the most important facet for understanding and appreciating a military campaign is a solid grasp of the composition of the armies engaged in it; the quantity of troops shares equal importance to the identity and quality of them. The multitude of books and monographs dedicated to the 1777 Philadelphia campaign, whether in part or in entirety, estimate American troop strength because no army returns between September 1 and October 4 (the primary period of battles) were known to exist. That glaring deficiency has come to an end—at least partially. Two Continental infantry numerical strength reports have recently been unearthed from the papers of Timothy Pickering, the American adjutant general during the campaign. One tallies the entire army's Continental infantry in early September; the other does likewise near the end of the month. When combined with known returns for the beginning of November and December, these new discoveries not only fill a gap with two absolutely necessary time points, they also provide a trend line to understand how the size of the army changed during the course of the four-month campaign.

SOURCES AND METHODS

Numbers obtained from six returns develop the size of the American army in Delaware and Pennsylvania between August and December 1777. Only two of those returns have been previously published. During the American Revolution Bicentennial, Charles Lesser included the November 3 weekly return and the December 2 monthly troop-strength reports in *Sinews of Independence*, an anthology of mostly monthly returns primarily obtained from the National Archives. Those two returns depict Continental infantry numerical strength at the brigade level. They are complete for field, staff, and non-commissioned officers fit for duty, as well as both present and absent rank and file (privates) subdivided into several categories.[1]

The lacunae of troop-strength reports between May and November has forced historians to merely estimate the size of Washington's army during the most active portion of the Philadelphia campaign waged halfway between that yawning gap of known returns. Col. Timothy Pickering, the adjutant general of the army from June 1777 through January 1778, kept a copy of the December 2 return, but his copy also included a partial militia report and a Continental artillery return.

Most importantly within Pickering's collection is a revealing summary of the troop-strength return of Continental infantry ordered on September 1 and completed on September 3, as well as one reported on September 24. Unlike the brigade-level reports in November and December, these two September returns summarize the numerical strength of the total Continental infantry present, and include the total of the same officer and rank and file subdivisions that appear in the brigade-level reports later in 1777. These two returns capture the numerical strength of Washington's infantry the week before the battle of Brandywine while the army encamped in Delaware (September 3), and reveal the size of the force three weeks later (September 24)—after the Battles of Brandywine and Paoli, but only ten days before the battle of Germantown.

The September 3 return includes all ten brigades organized within five infantry divisions of the Continental army and also includes Brig. Gen. Francis Nash's North Carolina brigade. Two light infantry forces, one present and one absent, both indirectly appear on this return within a catchall category of infantry called "on command." The absent force, Col. Daniel Morgan's Virginia riflemen—estimated at 400 rank and file—were detached to the Northern Department to reinforce and assist Maj. Gen. Horatio Gates. The brand new and present force of light infantry commanded by Brig. Gen. William Maxwell was carved equally out of nine brigades. A total force of 800 rank and file is estimated for this unit; 900 including officers.

1. November 3 and December 2 return in Charles H. Lesser, ed., *The Sinews of Independence: Monthly Strength Reports of the Continental Army* (Chicago: University of Chicago Press, 1976), 50-53; September 3 and 24 returns, Timothy Pickering Papers, Massachusetts Historical Society, Boston Massachusetts; undated late September 1777 field return cited in "Council of War," September 28, 1777, in Philander D. Chase, ed., *The Papers of George Washington*, Revolutionary War Series (Charlottesville: University Press of Virginia, 2001), 12:338-39 (PGW); December 22, 1777 Weekly Report, www.fold3.com/image/9151405.

The total "on command" category on the September 3 return numbers 2,382 infantry privates, 1,182 unaccounted for after separating out the light infantry. These remaining "on command" troops are rank and file soldiers, fit for duty, but temporarily not attached to their respective regiments. In 1778, the adjutant general determined that fifty-eight percent of the unaccounted in this column were encamped with the army serving as artificers or assisting other commands, but available for service in the event of an emergency (on September 3 this amounted to 685 privates in addition to the 800 light infantry present).[2] Similarly, sixty-seven percent of soldiers columned as "sick present" were deemed by the adjutant general as healthy enough to fight if surprised by an enemy assault.[3] Obviously, soldiers appearing in the "sick absent" and "on furlough" columns were not present with the army. Forty-two percent of the unaccounted "on command" soldiers on any given return were considered detached too far from the encampment area to be relied upon for emergency service.

ESTIMATING MISSING DATA

While commissioned and non-commissioned company and regimental officers are tallied on two September returns and on the November and December ones, missing from all September returns are officers categorized as "staff" (for example, chaplains, paymasters, adjutants). This is a consistent total tally based on subsequent returns, so the November 3 total of 206 for the same regiments and brigades serving Washington in September was applied to those two returns as well. Brigade, division, and army personnel are not tallied in any returns. This includes generals (and colonels commanding brigades) and their respective military families. Also missing is Washington's Life Guard. An added factor of 150 minimally adjusts for these key personnel from September through November, and 200 for December, a month with seventeen brigade commanders and five major generals. (For example, George Washington's headquarters exceeded fifteen officers for most of this period; neither he nor anyone on his staff had ever been considered in these returns.)

Another category of missing officers in every return is "sick present" officers and those "on command" that remained on location with the army. On late-1778 returns these officers were routinely tallied, and numbers exceeding 500 were commonplace for this category in those returns. No trend can be identified in the 1778 data to estimate their numbers during the 1777 Philadelphia campaign; for this reason "sick present"

2. May 2, 1778 Weekly Report (cover), www.fold3.com/image/9151560.
3. Ibid.

and "on command" officers are entirely omitted in this analysis which assures an underestimation of the true present strength of the army.

No return previous to December 1777 has yet been discovered that captured the number of Continental dragoons and artillerists serving with Washington. December tallies of 497 horse soldiers and 620 cannoneers equates to 1,120 non-infantry Continentals. This value was applied to the September and November returns as a minimal estimate of their strength, estimating that any reinforcing artillery that arrived with the transferred brigades of the Northern Department were more than offset by the losses incurred at Brandywine, Paoli, and Germantown. Although complete militia numbers are not available in these returns, partial numbers are presented in some of them and a reasonable estimate can be determined from additional sources.

No return exists for August 1, 1777, the first morning in 1777 that most of the available Continental army awoke on the Pennsylvania side of the Delaware River. This force amounted to all but one available battery of Continental artillery, all Continental dragoons, and seven and a half brigades of Continental infantry—two regiments short of four complete divisions. Sullivan's two Maryland brigades stood six days' away by hard marching, while Nash's brigade and a battery of artillery were within a two-day march of uniting with the main army. Therefore, a reasonable estimate of numbers available on August 1 can be derived by an appropriate fraction of infantry from the September 3 data. This estimate is important to appreciate what Washington readily had available to defend against Howe's 16,000-man army had the British commander chosen to ascend the Delaware River once he entered the Capes on July 30. This method necessarily assumes no net change of numerical strength throughout August which produces a clear overestimate of the true size of the August 1 force because there is no way to capture the net gain of enlisted soldiers over departed ones that month in an army that tarried in camps for three weeks and fought no battle during that span.

It is important here to distinguish between an encampment force, a force under attack, and an attacking force. By our definition an encampment force (for example, the one in Whitemarsh on December 2) includes all present troops within two miles of the main army by foot and five miles by horse. This includes all present officers, all fit for duty and present sick rank and file soldiers, as well as fifty-eight percent of the unaccounted "on command" column. The difference between the encampment and defending force (for example at the Battle of Brandywine, September 11) is a removal of one-third of the "present sick" column which is deemed too sick to participate in a battle, even close to where they are encamped. Finally, an attacking force (for example, at the Battle of Germantown, October 4) differs from a defending force in the assumption that no "present sick" soldiers, no "staff" category of officers, and only forty percent of the unaccounted "on command" column is healthy and available to participate in an extended march and assault upon an enemy position.

Table 1 incorporates the newly-discovered September returns to capture the encampment strength of George Washington's army at three time points. The left-side column estimates the size of the force on the morning of August 1 twenty miles north of Philadelphia, the day after the bulk of his army crossed the Delaware River at Coryell's and Howell's ferries. The middle column captures by both official tally and estimates the army near Wilmington on the morning of September 3, 1777. This date is the day of the first engagement at Cooch's Bridge but also is the first day in the campaign the entire army was united in the same theater. The right-side column captures the numerical strength of the army while most of it was encamped north of Swamp Creek, near Fagleysville, Pennsylvania, and depicts the same regiments three weeks after the Delaware encampment, revealing the effects of battles and heavy marches upon its numerical strength.

TABLE 1. Numerical Strength of Washington's 1777 Army: From Crossing the Delaware Through the Battle of Paoli

Present for Duty	August 1 (derived)	September 3	September 24
Infantry rank and file	5,007	7,602	6,371
Field officers	692	976	906
NCOs	1,108	1,620	1,340
Regiment Staff (November 3)	140	[206]	[206]
General officers & their staffs (est.)	100	150	150
Present "on command"	1,005	1,474	1,148
Sick present	428	628	383
Total Continental infantry present	8,480	12,656	10,504
Militia	0	5,000	3,000
Continental Dragoons and Artillery	1,120	1,120	1,120
Total Present Force	9,600	18,776	14,624

ASSESSMENT

If General Howe had unhesitatingly ascended the Delaware River beginning on July 30, he could reasonably have disembarked his entire force at Wilmington between August 1 and August 3, and could have begun a twenty-six mile march to Philadelphia with between 16,000 and 17,000 officers and men. The size of his army alone would have dominated Washington's readily available force of fewer than 10,000 soldiers in all arms. Howe's decision to abandon the Delaware and ascend the Chesapeake allowed Washington an additional month to field nearly twice as many men as he had had on August 1. When Howe began his direct assault against Maxwell's light infantry at Cooch's Bridge on September 3, 1777, George Washington outnumbered Howe in the Maryland/Delaware theater.

Although not depicted in the table, the number of American soldiers present to fight at the Battle of Brandywine on September 11 was reduced by 2,000 militia (only 3,000 Pennsylvania militia positioned themselves at fords to defend this day),[4] and 200 fewer Continental infantry compared to September 3 as these men were calculated to be too sick to participate. These adjustments still leave a considerable force of 12,455 infantry, 1,120 cavalry and artillery, and 3,000 militia. This equates to a total defending force of 16,575 officers and men present to fight at Brandywine. This new tally is surprisingly close to a recent estimate provided in a book-length treatment of this battle.[5]

Battle casualties at Cooch's Bridge, Brandywine, and Paoli, as well as 150 miles marched in a span of twelve days, including a day where all present were subject to the most intense rainstorm of their lifetime, provided several reasons for at least the temporary loss of nearly 2,200 Continental infantry officers and men between September 11 and September 23.

OCTOBER I ARMY STRENGTH

With the discovery of two army strength returns for September 1777 in Pickering's papers, not only can we calculate a more accurate force strength for Brandywine, but also for the Battle of Germantown. Additionally, Washington provided specifics about his rank and file present and fit for duty at a September 28 council of war, perhaps as a summary of a special field report which has yet come to light. Direct and derived data from the September 24 field return and the September 28 record

4. John Armstrong to Thomas Wharton, September 8, 1777 in Samuel Hazard, *Pennsylvania Archives*, Volume 5 (Philadelphia: Joseph Severns & Co., 1853), 598.
5. Michael C. Harris, *Brandywine: A Military History of the Battle that Lost Philadelphia but Saved America* (El Dorado Hills, CA: Savas Beatie, 2014), 368.

from a council of war provides 12,602 battle-ready troops with the army camped near Faulkner's Swamp ten days before the battle of Germantown. Missing from that return is Potter's Pennsylvania militia brigade, artillery and dragoons. Also not included are the New Jersey and Maryland militia that would join the army prior to Germantown. These "missing" units added another 3,720 battle-ready troops to Washington's army. By October 1, Washington had 16,372 battle-ready troops for an attack on the British camp at Germantown, some 2,000 more than the estimate in a recent study of the battle.[6]

TABLE 2: Numerical Strength of Washington's Army on October 4, 1777: Battle of Germantown

	Attack-Ready Force	Total Present
Rank and file present fit for duty in 12 Continental Infantry Brigades (based on September 28 Council of War)	8,000	8,000
Officers & ncos present fit for duty in 11 Continental Infantry Brigades (September 24 field return) + 300 estimate for McDougal's brigade	2,589	2,589 + 206 staff officers obtained from Nov. 3 return
General officers & their staffs	150	150
Sick present (September 24 field return)	—	383
"on command" (September 24 field return)	939 (40% of total from field return)	1,362 (58% of total from field return)
Irvine's PA Militia Brigade (September 24 field return)	974	974
Potter's PA Militia Brigade (estimate)	1,000	1,000
NJ Militia Brigade (estimate)	600	600
MD Militia Brigade (estimate)	1,000	1,000
Dragoons (estimate derived from December 31 monthly return)	500	500

6. Michael C. Harris, *Germantown: A Military History of the Battle for Philadelphia, October 4, 1777* (El Dorado Hills, CA: Savas Beatie, 2020), 193.

| Artillery (estimate derived from December 2 artillery return) | 620 | 620 |
| Totals | 16,372 | 17,384 |

ANALYSIS

The difference between the battle-ready force at Brandywine versus Germantown was 203 fewer soldiers in the latter battle. George Washington's army suffered 1,700 casualties at Brandywine, the Battle of the Clouds, Paoli and other minor skirmishes over those three weeks. Also, approximately 1,000 Pennsylvania militiamen either went home at the end of their terms or deserted over that same time span. Therefore, Washington had a total loss of 2,700 troops prior to Germantown. During this span, Washington added 2,800 troops from the Connecticut Line (Brigadier General Alexander McDougall's brigade) plus New Jersey and Maryland militias. Washington should have had a net gain of 100 troops but the returns tell us he had about 200 fewer troops for Germantown. Why? That net loss could plausibly be explained by the difference of more "sick present" soldiers who could shoulder a gun in defense at Brandywine but could not be expected to conduct an overnight march to launch an attack at Germantown. Regardless, this tally of Washington's Germantown force is considerably higher than any previous estimate regarding this battle.

WHAT ELSE DO THESE NUMBERS SHOW US?

Well known and understood is the direct detrimental effect of battle losses on the strength of an army during a campaign, both in crushing defeats and in pyrrhic victories. Underappreciated is the potential crippling effects of desertions. Even wildly successful forces are not immune to this. For example, in the midst of his world-famous Shenandoah Valley Campaign of the Civil War, Gen. Thomas J. Jackson's namesake Stonewall Brigade shrunk fifty-five percent after losing 2,000 soldiers in twenty days of marching—but without fighting any battle in that span.[7] Those men, mostly new recruits, permanently deserted from a successful army.

What impact did Washington's failures throughout the Philadelphia campaign have on desertion, particularly the 2,800 temporary and permanent losses of officers and men in battle (Cooch's Bridge, Brandywine, Battle of the Clouds, Paoli and Germantown)? One might suspect that this series of defeats would swell desertion rates for several

---

7. Total desertions calculated from official returns. See Gary Ecelbarger, *Three Days in the Shenandoah: Stonewall Jackson at Front Royal and Winchester* (Norman, OK: University of Oklahoma Press, 2008), 34.

weeks after the last of those battles (Germantown, October 4). Unfortunately, neither desertions nor recruits were tabulated in extant army-sized returns in 1777.

Regardless, Table 3 attempts to capture the effects of desertions by trending the numbers of men in Continental infantry regiments present (and absent) in the first days of September and following the same units for three months into early December. Since complete data for present and absent soldiers exists only for rank and file foot soldiers, and since privates represent the bulk of Washington's army, only this category of infantry is tabulated:

TABLE 3: Numerical Strength of Continental Rank and file Infantry at Four Time Points

	Present	Absent	Total Present and Absent
September 3	9,830	3,773	13,603
September 24	7,902	4,613	12,515
November 3	8,727	4,269	12,996
December 2	9,225	4,071	13,296

The lowest total (far-right column) and present numbers as well as the highest absent numbers appear in the September 24 row; this is most likely a result of battle casualties as well as straggling and dispersed troops in the wake of the heavy marching between September 14-23. A noticeable improvement in all rows transpires over the subsequent ten weeks, even after suffering severe casualties at Germantown. This could be explained by a return of previously wounded soldiers combined with an influx of new recruits. Considering that total killed and captured infantry privates between September 1 and December 1 exceeded 1,000, then Washington's army enlisted at least 700 more rank and file soldiers than it lost by desertions or discharges during those three months. It is clear from the above table that new recruits during an active, losing campaign were surprisingly many, while desertions and discharges within the Continental ranks were apparently not detrimental at all, and may have been so insignificant as to be negligible. As catastrophic as the Philadelphia campaign outwardly appeared—it certainly injured Washington's reputation and ultimately spawned the infamous Cabal—that negative outcome in the theater, combined with escalating and crippling deficiencies in the commissary and quartermaster departments, surprisingly had no measurably adverse effect on desertions in Washington's army during the autumn months of 1777.

NOVEMBER 3 TO DECEMBER 3 ARMY STRENGTH

A weekly return for Washington's army was completed on November 3, 1777 and a monthly return was reported out on December 3. Determining the strength of Washington's force for early November requires some decisions. By this point in the campaign, fighting was raging along the Delaware River, necessitating the detour of reinforcements from the north to the river forts and detachments from the main army to operate along the river. Additionally, New Jersey militia did not migrate to Whitemarsh; instead, they moved into position in support of the river operations in southern New Jersey. As Washington was forced throughout October and November to make decisions about weakening the main army for the river operations—and harbored hopes of attacking William Howe in Philadelphia again—we have chosen to analyze the total force available for Washington in the Philadelphia region.

The November 3 weekly return delineates 12,592 troops in the Whitemarsh encampment. Missing from that return are two Rhode Island regiments garrisoning Fort Mercer. Also missing are the Pennsylvania and Maryland militia serving with the main army and the New Jersey militia operating in southern New Jersey. Dragoons and artillery are also absent from the return. Therefore, 5,170 "missing" men need to be added. In total, Washington had a force of 17,812 men operating in the Philadelphia region in early November 1777.

From the December 3 return, we can determine the strength of the army for the Whitemarsh operation as the abandonment of the forts in mid-November resulted in the concentration of the army here. The return lists 23,227 troops in the Whitemarsh encampment. Missing from that return are the dragoons and artillery, but an early December artillery return exists in Timothy Pickering's papers. A dragoon total can be estimated from the December 31 monthly return. With all soldiers accounted for, George Washington's army at Whitemarsh numbered 24,647 officers and men in all arms.

TABLE 4: The Army at Whitemarsh: Present in Camp, November 3-December 3, 1777

	November 3, 1777	December 3. 1777
Present fit for duty officers and men for 12 Continental Infantry Brigades	10,332	16,362 (includes 5 Continental Infantry Brigades & 7 independent regiments arrived since November 3)
General officers and their staffs	150	200
Sick present	889	1,691
"on command"	1,229 (58% of total from weekly return)	1,722 (58% of total from weekly return)

"confined"	9	—
"without shoes"	33	—
2 Rhode Island regiments	500 (estimate from December 31 return)	—
Pennsylvania Militia	2,100 (estimate from December 3 return)	2,364 (includes sick present & 58% of "on command")
Maryland Militia	950 (estimate from December 3 return)	938 (includes sick present & 58% of "on command")
New Jersey Militia	500 (estimate of units operating along Delaware River)	—
Dragoons	500 (estimate from December 31 return)	500 (estimate from December 31 return)
Artillery	620 (estimate from December 2 return)	870 (includes sick present & 58% of "on command" from December 2 return)
Totals	17,812	24,647

ANALYSIS

Washington's army suffered about 1,100 casualties at Germantown, Fort Mercer, and other minor skirmishes over the month of October. The only new units to join the army over that same time period were the two Rhode Island regiments. The army should have shown a net loss of 600 men between October 1 and November 3, but the returns tell us they actually gained over 600 men. Why? An impressive surge of recovered sick and wounded officers and privates as well as new recruits populated the army; this trend dovetails well with the rank and file data (see Table 3). The 17,812 men operating in the Philadelphia region on November 3 were not necessarily all attack ready, but they were present in the various camps.

Between November 3 and December 2, Washington gained 6,835 more men in one month. Considering the army suffered about 120 casualties at Fort Mifflin and other operations during this period, how did this happen? Five infantry brigades and eight independent regiments reinforced Washington from the northern army. These units added 6,712 men to Washington's force. Washington actually added 123 more men than that, which can easily be explained by the artillery batteries that came with those brigades from the northern army.

The massive army Washington perched twenty miles north of Philadelphia three weeks before the start of winter outnumbered General Howe's by fifty percent. Washington augmented his force from the victorious northern army to attack his enemy with it. On November 24, he held a council of war with subordinate officers to consider an attack plan devised by Brig. Gen. John Cadwalader of Philadelphia, and on December 3 he requested from his brigadier and major generals their input regarding "the Advisieability of a Winters Campaign, & practicality of an attempt upon Philadelphia."[8] General Howe's foray from Philadelphia to challenge Washington at Whitemarsh during the close of December's first week disrupted Washington's plan to attack him, but it did not vanquish it.

DECEMBER 18 ARMY STRENGTH:

It is instructive to look at Washington's strength the day before the Valley Forge "march in." Army strength for December 18 while they were still camped at "the Gulph" can be determined from the five known returns for the army from December—monthly returns compiled on December 2 and December 30, weekly returns completed on December 4 and December 22, and a special field report conducted on December 23.[9] An analysis of these returns reveals that Washington had 20,530 attack-ready troops and a total encamped force of 24,397 one day before entering Valley Forge.

TABLE 5: December 18 Army Strength at "the Gulph" prior to Valley Forge "march-in"

	Attack-Ready Force	Total Present with Army
Present fit for duty rank and file for 13 Continental Infantry Brigades (December 22 weekly return)	8,147	8,147
Present fit for duty officers & ncos 13 Continental Infantry Brigades (December 22 weekly return)	2,879	2,879
General officers and	200	200

8. "Brigadier General John Cadwalader's Plan for Attacking Philadelphia," c. November 24, 1777, PGW 12:371-373; "Circular to General Officers of the Continental Army," December 3, 1777, PGW 12:506.

9. December 3 return in Lesser, Sinews, 52-53; December 4 Weekly Report, www.fold3.com/image/9151401; December 22, 1777 Weekly Report, www.fold3.com/image/9151405; Field Return, December 23, 1777, www.fold3.com/image/9151423; copy of December 31, 1777 return, www.fold3.com/image/9151410; also see Lesser, Sinews, 55.

their staffs

Rank and file sick present	—	1,411
(December 22 weekly return)		
"on command" (December	1,154	1,154
22 weekly return)		
"wanting shoes (December	—	829
22 weekly return)		
7 independent regiments	924	1,017 (includes sick
(estimated from December		present & 58% of
3 and December 31 returns)		"on command")
Lord Stirling's 2 brigades	1,142	1,459 (includes
(December 23 field return)		those wanting cloathes)
2 Maryland brigades under	1,251	2,391 (includes sick
Smallwood (December 31		monthly return) present,
		wanting shoes & 58%
		of on command)
Pennsylvania Militia	2,800	2,800
(estimate from December		
3 return)		
Maryland Militia (estimate	850	850
from December 3 return)		
Dragoons (December 31	464	497 (includes sick
return)		present)
Artillery (December 22	719	763 (includes sick
return)		present & 58% of
		"on command")
Totals	20,530	24,397

ANALYSIS

Over the course of two weeks, Washington's total present force decreased by 250. This can be explained by approximately 300 casualties at Whitemarsh with fifty of them remaining in camp.

Although the Gulph encampment existed a mere five miles from Valley Forge, most, but not all of the 24,400 American soldiers did not transfer to the winter encampment the following day. The two Maryland Line brigades and all the militia did not participate in the "march in" on December 19—leaving about 19,000 troops to arrive with Washington at Valley Forge.

Notwithstanding his preparation for a winter encampment at Valley Forge for most of his army and Wilmington for his two Maryland brigades, Washington continued to seek an avenue to use his dominating numbers to attack General Howe. This included a December 23 surprise offensive against a large British foraging force, and a full-scale Christmas-time assault on Philadelphia.[10] Neither planned offensive came to fruition due primarily to quartermaster and commissary deficiencies.

CONCLUSION

Newly discovered late summer and autumn 1777 returns provide crucial data regarding George Washington's army during the Philadelphia campaign. A dedicated core of eleven infantry brigades remained intact despite significant losses on several battlefields, all the while gaining defensive and offensive battlefield experience as it was buttressed by six more brigades later in the campaign. Not only did George Washington outnumber William Howe early in September, the late September through late November reinforcements and new recruits which swelled his ranks gifted Washington with an impressive-sized army that continued to field more soldiers than the British, and eventually an army awesome in size. From Whitemarsh to the Gulph throughout the first two weeks of December, George Washington operated the largest active, single-region field army on the face of the earth, a force in numbers that exceeded the British army in Philadelphia by at least 6,000 soldiers—and exceeded the civilian population of New York, then the second largest city in the United States of America. Numbers were not the only requirement for the precise, perfectly-timed offensive that Washington sought, but the stunning size of his army provides a counter to twentieth and twenty-first century critics of Washington's mindset who belittled his late December plans to assault of Philadelphia as "a holiday-induced overindulgence in hemp or Medeira at HeadQuarters."[11]

---

10. George Washington to Henry Laurens, December 23, 1777 PGW 12:683-87; "Plan to Attack Philadelphia," PGW 12:701-703.
11. Wayne K. Bodle and Jaqueline Thibault, *Valley Forge Historical Research Report* (Washington, D.C.: United States Department of the Interior, 1980), 127.

A Reconsideration of Continental Army Numerical Strength at Valley Forge

GARY ECELBARGER AND MICHAEL C. HARRIS

On December 23, 1777, a mere four days after his Continental army entered Valley Forge, George Washington wrote to the Continental Congress expressing the dire needs of his army. He specified that due to catastrophic shortages of shoes and clothes he had "no less than 2898 Men now in Camp unfit for duty." He went on to explain that this left him with "no more than 8200—in Camp fit for duty."[1] Although Washington neither combined those numbers nor ever wrote about how many troops in total entered Valley Forge, those two figures from his December 23 letter were routinely reproduced by newspaper and book writers beginning in the middle of the 1800s in describing the Valley Forge experience and the sufferings of the 8,200 fit and 2,898 unfit soldiers who entered it.[2] The first known presentation of the total as the Valley Forge strength upon entry into the camp was within a biographical sketch of George Washington published in 1850, a monograph reproduced to a wider audience in Benson Lossing's *National History of the United States*, five years later: "When the encampment was begun at Valley Forge, the whole number of men in the field was 11,098, of whom 2,898 were unfit for duty."[3] This passage appeared in similar form for the rest of the nineteenth century.[4]

1. Washington to Henry Laurens, December 23, 1777, in Philander D. Chase, ed., *The Papers of George Washington*, Revolutionary War Series (Charlottesville: University Press of Virginia, 2002), 12: 683-87 (numbers presented on page 685).
2. "Chronology," *Williamsburgh Daily Gazette* (Brooklyn, New York), December 19, 1850.
3. "Biographical Sketch of George Washington," in Edwin Williams, *The Presidents of the United States, Their Memoirs and Administrations* (New York: Edward Walker, 1850), 43; Benson J. Lossing, *The National History of the United States*, Vol. 2 (New York: Edward Walker, 1855), 45.
4. "Washington at Valley Forge," *Frank Leslie's Illustrated Newspaper*, February 20, 1886, "The Park at Valley Forge," *Philadelphia Inquirer*, February 22, 1893.

Beginning in the 1890s, publications describing the iconic Valley Forge winter rounded this troop strength down to a simplified "11,000," an easily remembered number routinely cited for the next 125 years to the present date as Washington's entry strength on December 19, 1777.[5] From an unknown source, some publications have increased that number to "approximately 12,000 troops."[6] After consulting "the most meticulous scholars and researchers," the two authors of a recent publication accepted the range of 11,000-12,000 and also acknowledged estimates up to 2,000 higher than this for the number of soldiers that left Whitemarsh (eight days before they entered Valley Forge).[7] The traditional view is that, after entry, disease and hardships from inadequate food, clothes, and supplies reduced Washington's army significantly below 11,000. According to a National Park Service teaching guide, "It may have been as low as 5,000-6,000 at some point," before turning steeply on an upswing due to a combination of factors including several thousand new recruits and levees, and the influx of previously hospitalized and furloughed soldiers.[8]

Regardless of these scant and unattributed suggestions of a possibly higher entry force, that original figure of 11,000 as well as the revised 12,000 have never been seriously challenged. The following assessment for the first time analyzes thirty official returns: twenty-seven completed during the six-month encampment of Washington's Continental army as well as three others surrounding it. The results of this analysis should force a reconsideration not only of the traditionally accepted size of Washington's force that entered Valley Forge, but also to his army's actual numerical strength throughout the first half of 1778 in his winter encampment, and the size of the army that departed Valley Forge on June 19, 1778 to embark upon the Monmouth campaign.

HOW MANY MEN ENTERED VALLEY FORGE ON DECEMBER 19, 1777?

Record Group 93 in the National Archives contains four returns of numerical strength of the Continental army compiled in December 1777.[9] The logical starting point for a published and more legible version of half of these is Charles H. Lesser's *The Sinews of Independence*, which

5. John F. Jameson, *Dictionary of United States History. 1492-1895* (Boston: Puritan Publishing Co., 1894), 674.

6. Stephen R. Taaffe, *The Philadelphia Campaign 1777-1778* (Lawrence: University Press of Kansas, 2003), 150.

7. Bob Drury and Tom Clavin, *Valley Forge* (New York: Simon & Schuster, 2018), 107.

8. National Park Service, *Valley Forge National Historic Park Curriculum Guide* (Washington, D.C.: Department of Interior, n.d.), 21, www.nps.gov/vafo/learn/education/upload/curriculumguide.pdf.

9. These records are available at www.fold3.com.

contains all the monthly strength reports of the Continental Army, re-tabulated in columns quite different but simplified from the original reports.[10] Weekly reports and other field returns for the army were never reproduced in Lesser's publication.

To come to an understanding of how many men actually arrived at Valley Forge on December 19, 1777, we need to look back to December 3, 1777, when the previous monthly strength report was competed for the army. For this analysis all fifteen present-for-duty columns for officers and men were combined with "sick present" men and "on command" men to assess the bulk of the soldiers that comprised the main army. This gives 22,824 men in seventeen infantry brigades, five independent regiments, and the Pennsylvania and Maryland militia.[11] The December 3 strength report does not include general staff officers, Washington's Life Guard, the four regiments of light dragoons, or any of the army's artillery.

The light dragoons are included on the December 31 return with 497 men at Valley Forge which suffices as their strength four weeks earlier.[12] As estimate of 200 men will be used for generals, their military families, and Washington's Life Guard. A December 22 artillery return located in the Timothy Pickering papers lists 754 men present.[13] Therefore, 760 is a reasonable representation of their strength at the beginning of the month. When these units missing from the December 3 strength report are added to the men delineated on the report, the army had approximately 24,647 in its camps at Whitemarsh, Pennsylvania on December 3, 1777. If we accept the "traditional" number of 11,000 troops marching into Valley Forge, what happened to 13,000 men of Washington's army over those sixteen days? Maybe nothing.

Certainly, casualties were inflicted on the army at Whitemarsh, Matson's Ford, and other minor skirmishes over that time span. But those casualties only totaled approximately 300 men in these relatively minor actions.[14] That brings army strength down to 24,397 prior to December 19. Do we really believe nearly 13,000 men simply deserted or vanished in sixteen days?

10. Charles H. Lesser, ed., *The Sinews of Independence: Monthly strength Reports of the Continental Army* (Chicago: University of Chicago Press, 1976). See pages 53-78 for returns between December 1777 and June 1778.

11. December 3, 1777 report compiles troops considered as November's strength and is summarized in Lesser, *Sinews*, 53

12. Copy of December 31, 1777 return, www.fold3.com/image/9151410; also see Lesser, *Sinews*, 55.

13. Timothy Pickering Papers, Microfilm Roll 56, page 156, Massachusetts Historical Society.

14. Howard H. Peckham, ed., *The Toll of Independence: Engagements & Battle Casualties of the American Revolution* (Chicago: The University of Chicago Press, 1974), 45.

Only a few 1777 weekly reports compiled for the Continental army remain in existence today; fortunately, the December 22 report—the first and closest one for determining the number of troops that entered Valley Forge—is among those few.[15] Much like the routine monthly army returns, the template of columns and rows on the December 22 weekly report consists of twenty-one columns where numerical strength was tabulated: fourteen columns within an "Officers Present" section, a Rank & File section subdivided into six columns of present and absent categories, culminating into an aggregated "Total" for only these foot soldiers. The present-for-duty numbers do not include other men present in camp: those listed as "sick present" and "unfit for duty wanting shoes." Both must be included in the army's total presence during an encampment. There is also no accounting of sick officers that were present with the army when it marched into Valley Forge. Lastly the December 22 report enumerated infantry only; there is no accounting of artillery or cavalry personnel—numbers that would significantly add to the army's strength.

Of special importance is the "On Command" column of all weekly and monthly reports which tallies soldiers detached from their respective regiments and brigades for temporary service where additional manpower was required. Examples of this include assistance to the commissary and quartermaster departments, additional servants for officers, or household duties such as butchers or bakers. The calculation of fifty-eight percent of the "on command" force as readily available in an emergency was formulated in May, highlighting that most of these special-duty assignments were conducted within camp boundaries.[16] A much higher percentage of soldiers in the "On Command" column in the December 22 report at least marched into camp with the army before being dispersed to their respective duties. Given that the two brigades under Lord Stirling were not included in this column, it can be assumed that from the remaining thirteen brigades (approximately eighty-five percent) nearly all the reported "On Command" soldiers entered Valley Forge on December 19.

The weekly strength report for December 22, 1777 enumerates 11,026 officers and men present for duty at Valley Forge just three days after their arrival.[17] While this number approaches the "traditional" 11,000 men that entered Valley Forge, a close analysis of that number quickly sends up red flags for the careful researcher. This report was

15. December 22, 1777 Weekly Report, www.fold3.com/image/9151405.
16. May 2, 1778 Weekly Report (cover), www.fold3.com/image/9151560.
17. December 22, 1777 Weekly Report, www.fold3.com/image/9151405.

never cited in any nineteenth, twentieth or twenty-first century litera-
ture; the rounded "11,000" officers and men initially tallied in this report is purely coincidental to the 11,098 privates determined from
Washington's letter to Congress.

First, the total number of soldiers in the two Maryland brigades that
left for Wilmington, Delaware prior to the "march-in" at Valley
Forge—1,768 men—did not march into Valley Forge. Next, the three
independent regiments that were sent to Lancaster, Pennsylvania
(which departed after entry into Valley Forge and before December 22)
can be confidently added back to the march-in force by an existing tally
of their strength on December 31. Also, the two brigades of Lord Stirling's division are missing on the December 22 return, but their numbers present can be generated from a separate report of their strength
compiled the following day.[18] In addition to thousands of present but
unfit soldiers, also missing from the December 22 report are general
staff officers, Washington's Life Guard, the dragoons, and the artillerymen. Factoring in these "missing" units from the nearest existing report
of their respective strengths brings the army strength up to 19,124.
Pennsylvania and Maryland militiamen were included on the December 3 return but do not appear on the December 22 return because they
did not arrive at Valley Forge with the Continental troops.

The army George Washington marched into Valley Forge on December 19, 1777 was not the 11,000-man force "tradition" and poor
source analysis has led us to believe, nor was it the 12,000 that more
recent sources suggest. While the army did suffer about 1,800 deaths,
desertions and/or absent sick troops during the month of December,
roughly 19,000 soldiers entered Valley Forge on December 19 to begin
the winter encampment.

TABLE I. Numerical Strength of Army Entering Valley Forge, December 19,
1777

	December 22 return
Seventeen infantry brigades and seven independent regiments "present fit for duty"	13,057 (includes the two brigades of Lord Stirling's division based off December 23 return)
"sick present" & wanting shoes" officers (estimated) & men	2,749
"on command" thirteen brigades	1,900
Dragoons (exact number from December 31 return)	464
General Staff officers	200

18. Field Return, December 23, 1777, www.fold3.com/image/9151423

Artillery (exact number from   754
December 22 return)
"March-In" Total   19,124

George Washington's initial Valley Forge troop estimate of 11,098, broken down to fit and unfit soldiers on December 23, originated from a field report he ordered to be completed earlier that day, surprisingly a totally different report from the one completed the previous day.[19] The December 23 return enumerates 12,484 infantry soldiers present at Valley Forge by including noncommissioned officers not mentioned in Washington's letter to the Continental Congress. This stripped-down report omitted several thousand soldiers present in camp that day (no dragoons, artillery, commissioned officers, present sick officers and men, and shoeless officers were included).

A tremendous discrepancy exists between an equal comparison of brigades in the December 22 and 23 returns that cannot be resolved. Adding in present foot soldiers in these brigades that were tallied on December 22 as "sick present" still fails to explain the three-fold increase in naked or shoeless soldiers counted one day apart, as well as the discrepancy of 557 fewer noncommissioned officers that were enumerated in consecutive days from the exact same brigades. Given that the trend lines in the subsequent report to this (December 31) dovetails well with each category of the December 22 report—including fewer than 1,000 unfit soldiers due to poor clothing—the December 23 report cannot be considered an accurate representation of what existed at Valley Forge in the last days of 1777.

HOW MANY TROOPS WERE PRESENT IN VALLEY FORGE THROUGHOUT THE 1778 WINTER/SPRING ENCAMPMENT?

This is the appropriate question to ask as the troops residing at Valley Forge were an encampment force, not a battle-ready one. Washington's December 23 letter had emphasized the latter as he was seeking to attack the British army in Philadelphia but was forced to abandon the plan due to the high percentage of soldiers who were in camp but deemed unfit to march for a planned assault. From this point onward, Washington's prime concern was to feed and supply his professional army and prepare them for the following season of campaigning.

Fortunately, the question can be answered with a high degree of confidence, particularly in contrast to the number of troops present during the active months of the previous autumn's Philadelphia Campaign. Although merely a handful of 1777 army troop-strength reports sur-

19. Field Return, December 23, 1777, www.fold3.com/image/9151423

vive, routine monthly and nearly-weekly returns exist throughout the winter and spring of 1778. In total, twenty-seven reports were produced during the six-month encampment, six end-of-month returns, the aforementioned December 23 special field return, as well as twenty weekly reports using the same template as the monthly returns (it appears the February 2 weekly return also was used as the end-of-January monthly report).

These weekly and monthly troop-strength returns routinely consisted of twenty-nine columns: the aforementioned columns for Officers and Rank & File, and also a section for "Alterations" of officers and men, subdivided into eight more columns for permanent losses ("Deaths," "Deserted," and "Discharged") and columns for newly enlisted, recruited or leveed men all sub-grouped as "Joined." Adjutants for every Continental brigade in each winter encampment site completed a return at the end of every month as well as the time the weekly ones were due. These results were compiled in an encompassing army troop-strength report by the adjutant general for the Continental army.

To answer the question that opened this section, these returns were analyzed and pinpointed to what was routinely tallied, and what could be derived from those routine tallies. This limited the analysis to Continental army field and staff, commissioned and noncommissioned officers and privates (the latter referred to as "rank & file" in all reports), attached to infantry and artillery regiments only, present at Valley Forge only. This decision necessarily filtered out militia, even though they periodically appeared on Valley Forge returns. Continental cavalry relocated from Valley Forge in 1777 to Trenton in the winter of 1778 were also omitted from this count. Additionally, no brigade, division and army staff are included even though they were Continental officers at Valley Forge. Given that four division commanders and fifteen brigade commanders were present for nearly the entire duration, this omission removed more than one hundred professional soldiers—including every general and his staff. Most notably, George Washington and his military family of secretaries and aides were never enumerated in Valley Forge official returns.

Several hundred noncombatants who typically were present at Valley Forge throughout the six months were also left off these tabulations as they were also eliminated from the original returns. This included teamsters, household staff, artificers, enslaved persons, family members, and citizens of the region. Combining these noncombatants with the aforementioned and excluded Continentals at Valley Forge omitted several hundred temporary as well as routine residents of the encampment during those six months.

The most underappreciated aspect of the traditional history associated with Valley Forge is the number of Continental soldiers who are usually disregarded as part of Washington's winter encampment because they wintered away from Valley Forge. Gen. William Smallwood's two Maryland brigades encamped in Wilmington, nearly thirty miles south of Valley Forge. They suffered similar hardships as their Valley Forge brethren, as did isolated Continental regiments that encamped well outside the boundaries of Valley Forge, including an artillery unit also stationed in Wilmington. With the exception of December's monthly return, Continental cavalry was stationed in Trenton for most of the winter encampment, an arm of Washington's army usually tallying over 400 officers and men. During the period in which these troop-strength returns were compiled, between 1,500 and 2,500 Continental officers and men who served under George Washington were present within a two days' march from Valley Forge in other winter encampment sites.

Limited to the Continental army present at Valley Forge, four distinctive avenues exist to depict numerical strength from these returns—two of them direct and two others derived. Most directly, the number of troops tallied as present and fit for duty and on duty with their regiments is directly available from the reports without any adjustments. George Washington routinely cited this value, but did so only for infantry rank and file, omitting all artillery as well as infantry commissioned, non-commissioned and staff personnel. For this investigation, all Continental officers and privates, infantry and artillery, present and fit for duty are tabulated.

On the cover of the May 2, 1778 troop strength return, elements of a numerical formula appear which calculates a rank & file force "that might act on an emergency."[20] The clear assumption for this is to derive a strength report if the encampment came under attack. Based on the numbers scrawled, for Valley Forge and similarly for Wilmington, this is the formula:

Emergency Force = Present fit for Duty + 2/3 of sick present + 4/7 of "On Command"

This formula determined how many troops were readily available, presumably healthy enough to defend a position rather than march to and charge one. The calculation of fifty-eight percent of the "on command" force as readily available in an emergency best translates to four out of every seven of those soldiers performing those extra-service du-

20. May 2, 1778 Weekly Report (cover), www.fold3.com/image/9151560.

ties within the Valley Forge encampment. Although the likelihood that even a higher percentage of "on command" soldiers were in Valley Forge in the months preceding May, the four-sevenths calculation can be safely applied to all reports preceding May to minimally but rightfully add in soldiers routinely overlooked as present in camp within these returns.

Two considerations are required for soldiers who were in Valley Forge but not tallied in the weekly and monthly reports. One of those considerations includes officers sick and present in camp. Although the winter of 1778 tabulated only rank & file soldiers in this category, a study of the first five months of 1779 indicates these numbers existed in a separate officer's report which was likely added to the returns based on significant numbers never tallied in 1778. Similarly, the total force present at Valley Forge must be at least minimally adjusted to account for officers deemed unfit due to "Wanting Shoes and Cloathes." For both considerations, it is believed that within the officer ranks only non-commissioned personnel—sergeants, fifers and drummers—became sickened and wore out shoes and clothes at close to the rate of privates and at a much higher rate than commissioned officers and staff personnel like chaplains and paymasters. For each time point of the encampment, the percentage of noncommissioned staff present in camp but unfit due to illness or poor clothing compared to their total is likely similar to the percentage of privates present and unfit for the same reason (the calculation applied equates to three to four percentage points lower than the privates). Adjusting only for noncommissioned personnel considered present but unfit because they were ill or ill-clad makes the obviously erroneous assumption that no unfit commissioned officers and staff officers remained in Valley Forge; this assumption is nonetheless applied to insure no false inflation of the numbers in the encampment during any week or month.

Troop-strength reports exist for nearly every week of the encampment. Of these, nearly half were chosen for this analysis, representing at least two time points per complete month of the encampment. Table Two includes both raw and adjusted data to depict four different ways to represent the numerical strength of the officers and men of the Continental army at Valley Forge at fourteen time points between December 31 (twelve days after entry into camp) and June 6 (thirteen days before departure). The first column depicts all who were present and deemed fit for duty from each report. The second column adds in only privates present in camp but deemed unfit due to illness or poor shoes or clothes, as they were reported in each of the fourteen returns. The third column is the total of the first two columns plus the previously explained adjustment for "on command" rank & file still in Valley Forge, as well as the minimized correction for officers present but unfit for poor clothing and illness. This third column brings us closest to the actual number of men residing in the camp by also including an across-the-board estimate of "200" to minimally account for the Life Guard plus brigade, division and army officers as well as their staffs. These tallies are exclusive of servants and families, and other citizens and workers not considered Continental army personnel. The final column tabulates the emergent force of officers and men from the third column that could be expected to defend the camp if it came under a surprise attack. For December 31 only, an additional 600 men are added to both the third and final columns to account for Continental artillery officers and men who were indeed at Valley Forge to begin 1778, but not tabulated in that specific return.

TABLE 2. Tabulation of Numerical Presence of the Officers and Privates of the Continental Army at Valley Forge, December 1777—June 1778, obtained from Six Consecutive Monthly Reports, and Eight Weekly Reports.[21]

Date of Report	Fit for Duty and on Duty (from Report)	Fit and Unfit Present (from Report)	Total Fit and Unfit Present (Adjusted)	Total Available for Emergency
December 31	12,544	15,044	17,615	15,483
January 19	9,012	13,684	15,359	13,598
January 31	8,077	13,536	16,014	13,456
February 14	6,804	11,940	15,063	12,320
February 29	6,917	12,554	15,367	12,495
March 14	6,092	11,835	14,611	11,639
March 21	6,250	11,594	14,344	11,524
March 30	5,937	10,998	14,226	11,027
April 4	7,228	11,983	14,618	12,153
April 11	8,652	12,888	15,030	12,815
May 2	11,555	15,052	17,109	14,434
May 16	11,217	14,665	17,191	12,989
May 30	13,842	17,385	19,472	17,617
June 6*	13,513	16,651	18,839	17,038

* Fourteen brigades tallied; all other time points tally fifteen infantry brigades.

The revised data reveals that even during the leanest period at Valley Forge (the final week of March 1778), the Continental army never dipped below 14,000 officers and men present in camp. The nadir for

21. All twenty-seven reports can be found in www.fold3.com/image/9151410 thru www.fold3.com/image/9151756.

present and fit for duty numerical strength (first column) appears to be the entire month of March which may be what the published National Park Service curriculum guide alludes to; however, tracing all three weeks of that month from left to right on the table indicates how misleading this particular column truly is, even for determining a force that could defend the camp during an attack. Better appreciated is the third column which most closely represents the true total numerical presence of the Continental army that winter and spring, a population in Valley Forge that most of the time equaled or exceeded the population of Boston, then the third most populous city in the United States of America.

HOW MANY MEN DEPARTED VALLEY FORGE ON JUNE 19, 1778?

Having analyzed how many men arrived at Valley Forge with George Washington and how those numbers fluctuated during the encampment, how many freshly trained and reorganized troops left with him for the Monmouth Campaign?

A June 13, 1778 weekly return exists in the National Archives, prepared just six days prior to the army's departure for the Monmouth Campaign.[22] This strength report for the army lists 15,029 "present fit for duty & on duty" (due to blurry conditions on the original scan, present officers were calculated from a June 22 field report.[23] After adjustments, approximately 16,849 Continental troops marched out of Valley Forge with George Washington (3,600 sick men were left behind). This estimate conflicts with what Washington wrote on June 17 after a council of war. He stated the army had 12,500 men fit in case of emergency, but Washington throughout the war calculated his estimates based on musket-carrying men.[24] He rarely included officers, artillery, or cavalry in his estimates. The June 13 weekly report lists 12,777 rank and file infantry present and fit for duty which did correspond closely to Washington's June 17 estimate (not including the corrections for adding in sick and "on command" soldiers available for an emergency). En route to the battle of Monmouth nine days later, the New Jersey brigade, light dragoons, and New Jersey militia joined the army adding approximately 2,999 men to the army's strength. The army's total present strength approaching Monmouth, therefore, likely exceeded 19,000.

22. 21 June 6, 1778 weekly return, http://fold3.com/image/9151600.
23. June 22, 1778 Field Return, http://fold3.com/image/9151790.
24. "Council of War," June 17, 1778, *Papers of George Washington*, 15: 415.

TABLE 3. Tabulation of "Present" Strength of Continental army, June 19, 1778.

Present Fit for Duty and on Duty	15,029
General Staff officers and Life Guard	200
Four-sevenths (58%) of "On Command"	1,536
Sick Present	3,684 (including estimate for noncom. officers)
Total	20,449
Sick left behind	-3,600 (estimate)
"March Out" Total	16,849

An early-June commissary return indicates close agreement to the total of 20,449 tabled above (including sick present soldiers). Between June 1 and June 7, 1778, an average of 20,822 rations were drawn each day by Continental troops at Valley Forge.[25]

CONCLUSION

This is the first comprehensive analysis of present-in-camp troop strength of George Washington's army at Valley Forge between December 19, 1777 and June 19, 1778—based on a study of twenty-seven completed returns during the encampment as well as a comparison to the most immediate returns before and subsequent to these. Our analysis indicates 19,000 Continental soldiers initially marched and rode into Valley Forge, a total force that diminished to nearly 14,000 late in March at Valley Forge at its absolute nadir, before swelling to a numerical strength in May which re-established the Valley Forge encampment as the third highest population center in the United States.

The implications of this very necessary revision are far-reaching ones, particularly in understanding George Washington's supply woes in supporting an army at least 50 percent more numerous in camp than ever has been appreciated before.

---

25. "Return of Provisions and Stores Issued to the Army in Camp from the 1st to 7 June, 1778 . . . ." Gilder Lehrman Institute of American History, New York, NY.

American Indians at Valley Forge

JOSEPH LEE BOYLE

At the Bethlehem Hospital near the Continental Army cantonment at Valley Forge on November 21, 1777, John Ettwein visited a "Narragansett Indian in great distress about his soul, at the near approach of death." On March 18, 1778, Ettwein noted the passage of a company of New England soldiers that included "a few Stockbridge Indians." Ettwein was one of many to make note of the Indians, Native Americans, who served and suffered in the most famous encampment of the American Revolution.

Surgeon Albigence Waldo inoculated two Indians for small pox in the Spring of 1778, and on January 4, recorded that:

> I was call'd to relieve a Solder tho't to be dying—he expir'd before I reach'd the Hutt. He was an Indian—an excellent Soldier—and an obedient good natur'd fellow. He engaged for money doubtless as others do;—but he has serv'd his country faithfully—he has fought for those very people who disinherited his forefathers-having finished his pilgrimage, he was discharged from the War of Life & Death. His memory ought to be respected.[1]

Cato Griger/Greger, a Delaware Indian, enlisted in the 1st Massachusetts Regiment on January 20, 1778, for three years "and soon after marched . . . to Valley Forge." Griger was about thirty-six years old at the time of his enlistment.[2] In the New England regiments there were some Stockbridge Indians including Benjamin Waunechnauweet and Daniel Wauwaunpeguannant, privates in the 8th Massachusetts. A few others, such as Unkus Abimeleck, served in Connecticut regiments.

---

1. John W. Joran, "Bethlehem During the Revolution," *Pennsylvania Magazine of History and Biography* (PMHB) 13, no. 1 (1889): 77, 80; "Diary Kept at Valley Forge by Albigence Waldo," *The Historical Magazine* 5, no. 6 (June 1861): 171.
2. RG 15, Revolutionary War Pension and Bounty-Land-Warrant Files, M804, r 379, Claim W 2731. National Archives.

In April 1778, a Hessian officer saw several Mohawks in a troop of Americans at the White Horse tavern on the Lancaster Road. He reported "They are blacker, or browner, than the Delaware, have long, hanging down, very black hair, and look more evil and wilder than the others. They shoot, with bow and arrows, in a most amazing manner, as I have seen with my own eyes that they can shoot an arrow through a single bottle at a distance of 100 yards."[3]

On January 29, 1778, George Washington suggested to the committee of Congress visiting the camp that the Americans use "two or three hundred indians against General Howe's army the ensuing campaign." Operating with "some of our Woodsmen" they "would probably strike no small terror into the British and foreign troops . . . The good resulting from the measure . . . would more than compensate for the trouble and expence they might cost us."[4]

On February 20 the committee urged the employment of "a Number of Indians" to Congress. This was due to the failure of the military to bottle the British up in Philadelphia, and keep civilians from going in with supplies.

> We are of Opinion no Measure can be adopted so effectual to break off the pernicious Intercourse which the disaffected Inhabitants of this Country still hold with the Enemy from which they derive the greatest Advantages . . . it is in Contemplation to form a Flying Army composed of light Infantry & rifle Men . . . it is proposed to mix about 400 Indians with them . . . The Situation of the Oneidas to the Northward is such, that . . . bringing their Warriours to the Army, for whose Fidelity & Perseverance we shall then have the best Pledges.[5]

Congress referred the recommendation to the Board of War which concurred but "doubted the expediency of the measure, from the great difficulty and expense which will attend the raising them, and still greater in employing them to advantage, and satisfying their demands . . . and the embarrassments they create in an army."[6]

3. *Defeat, Disaster and Dedication: The Diaries of the Hessian Officers Jakob Piel and Andreas Wiederhold*, trans. and ed. Bruce E. Burgoyne (Bowie, MD: Heritage Books, 1997), 106-7.

4. Washington to the Committee of Congress with the Army, 29 January 1778, *The Writings of George Washington from the Original Manuscript Sources, 1745-1799*, ed. John C. Fitzpatrick (Washington: Government Printing Office, 1931), 10: 400-1 (WGW).

5. Committee at Camp to Henry Laurens, 20 February 1778, *Letters of Delegates to Congress, 1774-1789*, ed. Paul H. Smith et al. (Washington: Library of Congress, 1979), 9: 144-45 (LDC).

6. Ibid., 9:146; *Journals of the Continental Congress*, ed. Worthington Chauncey Ford (Washington: Government Printing Office, 1904-1937), 10: 220-21 (JCC).

Meanwhile the Committee had discussed with Baron von Steuben using Indians "to act as light Troops upon out Posts, advanced Parties and the like." On March 2, they reported to the President of Congress that Steuben liked the idea and, "the Austrians always use the Croats (a kind of white Indians) for such Purposes and to so good Effect that the King of Prussia imitated them by enrolling a Body of Irregulars to Cover in like Manner his Army." The letter concluded that a force of Indians would "keep the Enemy Compact, prevent Desertion in our Troops, make us Masters of Intelligence and give us Pledges of their Fidelity."[7]

On March 4, Congress empowered Washington to employ "a body of Indians, not exceeding 400; and that it be left to him to pursue such measures as he judges best for procuring them, and to employ them . . . in such way as will annoy the enemy without suffering them to injure those who are friends to the cause of America."[8] Washington wrote on March 13, to the Commissioners of Indian Affairs at Albany, reporting that he was authorized to employ a body of 400 Indians and:

> Divesting them of the Savage customs exercised in their Wars against each other, I think they may be made of excellent use, as scouts and light troops, mixed with our own Parties . . . The Oneidas have manifested the strongest attachment to us throughout this dispute and I therefore suppose, if any can be procured, they will be most numerous . . . If the Indians can be procured, I would choose to have them here by the opening of the Campaign, and therefore they should be engaged as soon as possible as there is not more time between this and the Middle of May than will be necessary to settle the business with them and to March from their Country to the Army.[9]

A meeting at Johnstown was held on March 7-9 with some 700 Iroquois in attendance. These were mostly Oneidas, Tuscaroras and Onondagas. James Duane reported that "The faithful Oneidas & Tuscarores were excepted and distinguished. They were applauded for their Integrity and Firmness, and assured of our Friendship and Protection."[10]

Gen. Philip Schuyler reported that "The faithful Oneidas & Tuscaroras In the presence of the others declared their determination

7. Committee at Camp to Laurens, 2 March 1778, LDC, 9: 199-200.
8. JCC, 10: 220-21.
9. Washington to the Commissioners of Indian Affairs, March 13, 1778, WGW, 11: 76-77. For the Oneidas see Joseph T. Glatthaar and James Kirby Martin, *Forgotten Allies: The Oneida Indians in the American Revolution* (New York: Hill and Wang, 2006).
10. James Duane to George Clinton, March 13, 1778, LDC, 9: 288-89; Duane to Robert Morris, March 19, 1778, ibid., 9: 309.

to Sink or swim with us" and that he had asked Lafayette for help in building a fort for the Indians. On March 22 he stated Lafayette had been promised "two or three hundred of them" and that a message was sent that day "to invite them down" for Washington's army. But Schuyler felt there was "little room to hope that we shall be able to prevail on them to Join you."[11]

The Marquis de Lafayette had arrived in Albany on February 17, and decided to attend the meeting at Johnstown as Schuyler "told me that a parcel of french men would be of some use to the cause." Lafayette brought gifts including "woollen blankets, little mirrors, and above all plenty of paint . . . There was also some gunpowder, lead, and bullets, and some silver crowns of six francs." He was adopted by the Indians and given the name "Kayewla."[12]

The commissioners agreed to build a fort for the Oneidas at Kanowalohale. On March 16 Lafayette wrote the governor of New York that he would send a French engineer for that purpose. On March 20 he informed Henry Laurens of his plan to build a fort for the "Onoyedos" and "The love of the french blood mix'd with the love of some french *louis d'or* have engag'd those indians to promise they would come with me." That day he informed Washington that he had dispatched Lt. Col. Jean-Baptiste Gouvion to build a fort for the "Onoyedas" and hoped "to bring down to your excellency some scalping gentlemen for dressing the fine hair of the *Howe* actually dancing at Philadelphia."[13]

Two days later he wrote that he had dispatched "three french men with black belts and yellow guineas to bring down as many as possible." He ordered Anne-Louis de Tousard to accompany Gouvion "to help him in building the fort of the Oneydos, and in engaging theyr warriors to join me. He will come back . . . as soon as he will be able to have collected a sufficient number of indians to march them to Albany." On

11. Philip Schuyler to Laurens, March 15, 1778, Papers of the Continental Congress, Record Group 360, M247 (PCC), r173, i173, 3: 286–92; Schuyler to Washington, March 22, 1778, Washington Papers, r48, Library of Congress; JCC, 10: 291.

12. Lafayette to George Clinton, February 27, 1778, *Lafayette in the Age of the American Revolution*, ed. Stanley J. Idzerda et al. (Ithaca: Cornell University Press, 1977), 1: 325; The Chevalier de Pontgibaud, *A French Volunteer of the War of Independence*, trans. & ed. Robert B. Douglas (1898: reprint, Port Washington, NY: Kennikat Press, 1968), 48; Idzerda, "Memoir of 1779," *Lafayette in the Age of the American Revolution*, 1: 247, Louis Gottschalk, *Lafayette Joins the American Army* (Chicago: University of Chicago Press, 1937), 143, 145.

13. Lafayette to Laurens, March 20, 1778, *Lafayette in the Age of the American Revolution*, 1: 364; Lafayette to Washington, March 20, 1778, ibid., 1: 370.

April 2 Tousard wrote from "Oneidas" to Col. Marinus Willett that the Indians "promised us to follow the Marquis delafayette where he would be pleased to go."[14]

On April 24, Duane wrote to Congress that every measure possible was being taken to forward Indians to Washington. The Oneidas would not send 200 men, but if "the Troops and Fortress which they solicited are furnished . . . they will send forward a party of their Warriors; the number they do not ascertain."[15] On April 24 "the Whole nation of Oneida" met at Fort Schuyler to receive presents. Tousard reported that after a "month of deliberations," he was granted some warriors to join Washington. The Oneida Sachems addressed the departing warriors exhorting them to their best behaviour as they will be Introduced to General Washington the Chief Warrior, and to a great officer of our father french King the Marquess delafayette at Whose particular application you go—any misconduct in you, if only a little will be of Extensive Influence—The reproach not Easily whiped away.[16]

The Indians under Tousard's leadership left Fort Schuyler on April 29. Their route is not known but on May 13 Henry Muhlenberg at Trappe, Pennsylvania, reported a party of "allied Indians" encamped in the neighborhood.[17]

In the meantime, Washington had received Schuyler's letter reporting on the proceedings at Albany. He decided from this and other accounts "there is very little prospect of succeeding in . . . engaging a body of Indians from that quarter to serve with this army." He felt that "affairs are now on such a footing as to render their aid, in the field, unnecessary, and that all we require of them is their friendship and good wishes."[18]

The Indians arrived at Valley Forge on May 13, 14, or 15 amounting to between "seven and fourthy" or fifty. Tousard had brought them down and reported that it was "a long and tedious march" and "I was

---

14. Lafayette to Washington, March 22, 1778, *Lafayette in the Age of the American Revolution*, 1: 375-76; Tousard to Marinus Willett, April 2, 1778, *Letters on the American Revolution in the Library at "Karolfred,"* ed. Frederic R. Kirkland (New York: Coward-McCann, Inc: 1952), 2: 47.

15. James Duane to Laurens, April 24, 1778, LDC, 9: 474-75.

16. Samuel Kirkland to Tousard, April 24, 1778; Tousard to Laurens, May 23, 1778, *A Salute to Courage: The American Revolution as Seen Through Wartime Writings of Officers of the Continental Army and Navy*, ed. Dennis P. Ryan (New York: Columbia University Press, 1979), 138-40.

17. *The Journals of Henry Melchior Muhlenberg*, trans. Theodore G. Tappert & John W. Doberstein (Philadelphia: The Muhlenberg Press, 1958), 3: 152.

18. Washington to Laurens, May 3, 1778, WGW, 11: 343-44.

pretty much troubled in the Road by some of the Indians who remain'd behind in order to get drinking with more ease, but the totality behaved well enough, and we arrived ... without accident nor complaints against them."[19]

On May 15 Washington asked that no more Indians be sent to him:

> I should wish the party to be stopped, or if they should be on the way and not far advanced, and it can be done without occasioning disgust, I should be glad they might return home. When my application was made for a body of Indians to join this army, our prospects were very different from what they are now ... there will be very little of that kind of service in which the Indians are capable of being useful. To bring them such a distance, while there is likely to be scarcely any employment suited to their active and desultory genius, could answer no valuable purpose; but would be productive of needless expence, and might perhaps have a tendency to put them out of humour.[20]

That day one of Washington's guards reported that "The Ingen Chief Come to Head Quarters to Congratelate with his Excelency and also Dined with him."[21] Years later a French officer remembered an Indian at dinner:

> One day we were at dinner at head-quarters; an Indian entered the room, walked round the table, and then stretching forth his long tattooed arm seized a large joint of hot roast beef in his thumb and fingers, took it to the door, and began to eat it. We were all much surprised, but General Washington gave orders that he was not to be interfered with.[22]

On May 17, Col. Daniel Morgan was ordered to select fifty men to send to White Marsh, to join a party of Indians and to act together. They were to be part of a "Considerable detachment" Washington planned to send towards the enemy. In a second letter, Morgan was

---

19. On May 16 Tousard wrote he arrived on May 13 with forty-seven Indians but on May 23 wrote he arrived on May 15 with fifty. Tousard to Marinus Willett, May 15, 1778, Emmett Collection, New York Public Library (NYPL); Tousard to Laurens, May 23, 1778, *A Salute to Courage*, 139. George Fleming noted on May 14 that "About 50 Indians are just arrived." Fleming to Sebastian Bauman, May 14, 1778, Bauman Papers, New York Historical Society. Another wrote "a Bout 50 Indians a Rived this Day thea Say there is 4 hundred moor In 2 Days March of to joine us." John Sumner to Samuel Huntington, May 14, 1778, PCC, Roll 56, i42, v7, p43.
20. Washington to Schuyler, May 15, 1778, 1934, 11: 389-91.
21. "Elijah Fisher's Diary," in Carlos E. Godfrey, *The Commander-in Chief's Guard* (1904; reprint, Baltimore: Genealogical Publishing Co.), 276.
22. Pontgibaud, *A French Volunteer*, 49.

advised that about forty Indians would either be immediately under Morgan's command or on the other side of the Schuylkill River.[23]

The next day Washington ordered Lafayette to march towards Philadelphia to block enemy parties from entering the countryside, "and obtain intelligence of their motions and designs. This last is a matter of very interesting moment, and ought to claim your particular attention." This movement was prompted by accounts that the British were preparing to evacuate Philadelphia. Washington hoped Lafayette could attack the enemy rear as they withdrew.[24] Around midnight on May 18, Lafayette left Valley Forge and crossed the Schuylkill with about 2,000 men. The march ended at Barren Hill in eastern Whitemarsh Township near the present Philadelphia County line. The Indian party, with Capt. Allen McLane's cavalry, were assigned patrol duty down the Ridge Pike.

On May 19 the British commander received information on Lafayette's position. He assembled a strong force and marched out of Philadelphia that night, hoping to trap the Americans. Divided into three columns, the British nearly caught Lafayette, but the Americans were able to retreat over the Schuylkill at Matson's Ford after several skirmishes. After Lafayette crossed to safety, Morgan was ordered to join the Marquis and plan a return over the river with up to 500 "active Volunteers." As the British had marched all the previous night they "must be much fatigued" and Morgan could "plague them and pick up some stragglers." It was suggested "If any of the Indians will go over they may do some Service."[25]

The role of the Indians in the expedition is variously stated. Lafayette wrote that "fifty of our Indian allies met fifty British dragoons. The war cries on one side and the appearance of the cavalry on the other side surprised the two parties so much that they fled with equal speed." According to Henry Dearborn "the Enimy after a small scurmish with a Party of our Anydo Indians Retired into Philadelphia . . . our only Loss was 6 of my frenchmen." Anthony Wayne, who was not with the column, stated there were no American losses and reported "some Prisoners taken by our Light Troops and Indians hanging on

23. Alexander Hamilton to Daniel Morgan, May 17, 1778, Myers Collection, NYPL; James McHenry to Morgan, Myers Collection, NYPL.
24. Washington to Lafayette, May 18, 1778, WGW, 11: 418-20.
25. Tench Tilghman to Morgan, May 20, 1778, Myers Collection, NYPL.

their Rear—the latter at one fire killed five of the Enemie's Horse, and by the war Hollow put the Remainder to flight."[26]

Tousard commanded the party which he said consisted of fifty Indians and ten frenchmen.

> I have had the occasion to acquaint the british light horses with the hollow of the Indians, and their hability in firing; but I have lost three french men on the spot . . . four were made prisoners, and myself owe my liberty, perhaps much more to two Indians, and two french men who stood constantly by me, and kill'd two Light horse at whose fire my horse had throwd me. I cannot tell the exact number of the Light horse killed . . . I have seen my self five or six killed.[27]

Lafayette lauded Tousard's efforts and told Laurens "that he has taken the greatest trouble for them." Lafayette recommended Tousard be commissioned as a major, the rank promised to him for coming to America.[28]

Elijah Fisher recorded American losses as "fore or five of our party that the Enemy's Lite horse Cut to pieces." Washington wrote that the losses were "nine men in the whole." Neither mentioned the role of the Indians.[29]

Capt. John Peebles of the British Army listed two Indians killed with no British losses. Capt. John Montresor said there were "killed on the Field, one French officer and five more Rebels and 12 Prisoners." Apparently neither were with the column. Sgt Thomas Sullivan, who was with the British force, said the Americans retreated "leaving a few men killed and wounded, and five men Prisoners. Our loss was four men wounded, and two horses killed."[30] A Hessian officer reported that Lafayette sacrificed his rear guard "part of whom were killed, wounded, and captured. Among the latter were a French major and several Indians who were armed with bows and arrows . . . said to be the

26. "Memoir of 1779," *Lafayette in the Age of the American Revolution*, 2: 7; *Revolutionary War Journals of Henry Dearborn: 1775-1783*, ed. Lloyd A. Brown & Howard H. Peckham (Chicago: The Caxton Club, 1939), 121; Anthony Wayne to Sharp Delany, May 21, 1778, PMHB 11, no. 1 (1887): 115-16.
27. Tousard to Laurens, May 25, 1778, PCC, M247, r176, i156, 9-12.
28. Lafayette to Laurens, May 25, 1778, *Lafayette in the Age of the American Revolution*, 2: 56-57; same to same, June 7, 1778, ibid., 2:71.
29. Fisher, "Diary," 277, Washington to Laurens, May 24, 1778, WGW, 11: 443.
30. John Peebles Diary, Cuninghame of Thorton Papers, Scottish Record Office (microfilm, David Library of the American Revolution); "Journals of Capt. John Montresor," ed. G. D. Scull, in *Collections of the New-York Historical Society for the Year 1881* (New York: New York Historical Society, 1882), 493; Thomas Sullivan Journal, American Philosophical Society.

Stockbridge tribe ... They were handsome well-built people, who had a rather deep yellow skin." Another Hessian mentioned sixty Indians in Lafayette's vanguard and stated that one French officer was killed and another captured with six riflemen killed and nine men captured, but "The Indians, who enjoyed undisturbed rest, returned unmolested across the Schuylkill." Gen. Wilhelm von Knyphausen recounted there were 200 Indians, and in the American rear-guard "one officer and five men were killed and some, mostly French, taken prisoners." An Anspach lieutenant who remained behind in Philadelphia heard that there were 150 Indians, four of whom were among the seventy prisoners captured.[31]

News of the action passed to civilians, who heard different stories. On May 22, Christopher Marshall at Lancaster wrote, "it's said that our Indians killed and scalped the last parcel." The next day Henry Muhlenberg at Trappe wrote he had learned of the action from his son, Gen. Peter Muhlenberg, who visited that day:

> seventy Indians of the American Army were posted as an observation corps ... The Indians were the last to cross and were surrounded by the English Light Horse in a little wood. But they retired behind the trees as their way is and made the usual horrible war-cry, which threw horses and riders into disorder and put them to flight, when the Indians shot a few cavalrymen and picked up their cloaks ... The Indians were the last to get over, and they were surrounded in a small thicket by the English light cavalry, but they retired behind the trees in accord with their custom and let loose their usual hideous war whoops, which threw the riders into confusion and sent them flying; where upon the Indians shot several of the cavalrymen and gathered up their lost cloaks.[32]

Richard Henry Lee at York wrote that "Some Oneida Indians skirmished with the enemy & killed a few of their light Horse."[33] Henry Laurens, also at York, mentioned American losses of three killed and four prisoners, that "45 Indians & about ten French Men in the Indian Corp" accompanied Lafayette and "The Enemy lost 2

31. Johann Ewald, *Diary of the American War*, trans., ed. Joseph P. Tustin (New Haven: Yale University Press, 1979), 130; *Revolution in America: Confidential Letters and Journals 1776-1784 of Adjutant General Major Baurmeister of the Hessian Forces*, trans., ed. Bernhard A. Uhlendorf (New Brunswick: Rutgers University Press, 1957), 175-76; Knyphausen to The Landgrave, May 23, 1778, Lidgerwood Collection, G.250-51, Morristown National Historical Park; Heinrich Carl Philipp von Feilitzsch, "Diary (1777-1780)," *Diaries of two Ansbach Jaegers*, trans. and ed. Bruce E. Burgoyne (Bowie, MD: Heritage Books, 1997), 38.
32. Muhlenberg, *Journals*, 3: 156.
33. Lee to John Page, May 25, 1778; LDC, 9: 748.

Horsemen killed & six or eight wounded. When the Indians had discharged their fire upon the light Horse they set up the War Whoop & according to their Custom scampered off. The British light Horse Men terrified by the yelling of the Indians fled precipitantly the other way. The Indians picked up several of their Cloaks and converted them into Boots."[34]

A newspaper carried a similar account:

> The enemy had two horsemen killed, and many wounded. When the Indians had fired off their pieces at the light horse, they set up the War Whoop, and scampered according to their Custom. The light-horse, terrified at the unusual sound, scampered off then as fast as their horses would carry them! The Indians collected some of the coats, which were dropped in the flight, and soon converted them into leggins.[35]

On December 12, 1780, Lafayette returned to Barren Hill with the Marquis de Chastellux of the French Army. Chastellux was told there were no American losses and:

> The fifty Indians who had been assigned to La Fayette were placed in the woods, in ambush, after their manner, that is to say, lying as close as rabbits. Fifty English dragoons, at the head of the column, rode into the woods. They had never seen any Indians and the Indians had never seen any dragoons. So, up jumped the savages with a savage cry, threw down their arms, and escaped to safety by swimming across the Schuylkill, while the dragoons, as frightened as they were, turned tail and fled in such a panic that they could not be stopped until they reached Philadelphia.[36]

Capt. Michel Capitaine du Chesnoy, an engineer, drew maps of the field. One version of the "Retraite de Barrenhill" indicates a spot where "les sauvages" crossed the river to rejoin Lafayette's main body.[37]

Joseph Plumb Martin remembered about a hundred Indians "from some northren tribe" who "were stout-looking fellows and remarkably neat for that race of mortals, but they were Indians." He recounted

34. Extracts from the Diary of Christopher Marshall, ed. William Duane (1877; reprint, New York: Arno Press, 1969), 182; Muhlenberg, Journal, 3: 156-57; "A Journal of Sundry Matters happening during the Stay of the Enemy at Germantown," Joseph Reed Papers, NYHS; Laurens to Francis Hopkinson, May 27, 1778, LDC, 9: 756.

35. Pennsylvania Packet, June 3, 1778.

36. Francois Jean, Marquis de Chastellux, Travels in North America in the Years 1780, 1781 and 1782, trans. Howard C. Rice, Jr. (Chapel Hill: University of North Carolina Press, 1963), 1: 171-72.

37. Peter J. Guthorn, American Maps and Map Makers of the Revolution (Monmouth Beach, NJ: Philip Freneau Press, 1966), 9-10.

when an Indian shot an arrow into a cluster of bats hanging on a church roof that "The poor bats fared hard: it was sport for all hands. They killed I know not how many." Of the skirmish itself he wrote:

> The Indians, with all their alertness, had like to have 'bought the rabbit.' They kept coming in all the afternoon, in parties of four or five, whooping and hallooing like wild beasts. After they got collected they vanished; I never saw any more of them.[38]

A plaque in St. Peter's Church Cemetery at Barren Hill honors "six indian scouts who died in battle May 1778." No one, however, except British Lieutenant Peebles, stated that Indians were killed and he mentioned only two. While casualties from Lafayette's outing may be buried there, no known records corroborate this.

On June 4 Lafayette recommended that Congress "make a present to our Indians of vermillion, looking glasses, pipes, cloathes &c. it would have a fine effect." Nearly sixty years later Peter Du Ponceau related a story about a meeting a "tall Indian figure in American regimentals and two large epaulettes on his shoulders" singing a French opera song. He said the Indian held the rank of colonel and was well educated by the Jesuits. After breakfast at Steuben's quarters, Du Ponceau never saw him again. This may have been "Colonel Louis" Atayataronghta, a Caughnawaga, who was one of the leaders of the Oneidas and Tuscaroras at Saratoga and other places. A year later Congress approved officer commissions for thirteen Oneida and Tuscarora warriors and commissioned Louis a lieutenant colonel.[39]

On June 12, Lafayette wrote to Allen McLane, responding to a request to use the Indians with his detachment. Lafayette answered he would speak to Washington about it and expected, "the Indians will do well with you in the lines." He wrote again that day that "the greatest part of them is going home to oppose the *Senecas*, whose intentions they do'nt trust upon" but "that some would stay with the army." The ones that were staying Washington wished to send to Morgan at Radnor, but they "may join you from there in some days."[40]

38. Joseph Plumb Martin, *Private Yankee Doodle*, ed. George E. Scheer (Boston: Little, Brown & Co, 1962), 118-20.

39. Lafayette to Laurens, June 4, 1778, *Lafayette in the Age of the American Revolution*, 2: 67; "The Autobiography of Peter Stephen DuPonceau," PMHB 63, no. 2 (July 1939): 221-223.

40. Lafayette to Allen McLane, June 12, 1778, Allen McLane Collection, Historical Society of Delaware; Lafayette to McLane, June 12, 1778, *Lafayette in the Age of the American Revolution*, 2: 72.

On June 13, Washington ordered Ens. Jacob Klock of the 1st New York Regiment to escort "Thirty four of the Indians . . . who are in Camp being desirous of returning home" to New York. Lafayette wrote to the commander of Fort Schuyler that "the others stay with me whose wives and children I Recommend to your attentive care. As the husbands are fighting for us, and cannot provide for them, they must be furnish'd with provisions." The departure must have been immediate as on June 14, Henry Muhlenberg recorded that a "small party of Indians returned from the American camp." On June 16 "a whole company of Indians on their way home from camp" was near Emmaus in what is now Lehigh County, Pennsylvania.[41]

Why they left is unknown. On May 29 Christopher Marshall heard from Christopher Ludwick, who had left camp the day before, that "our Indians at camp had killed three officers by mistake owing to their being dressed in the English officers' uniform." But the muster rolls show no officer casualties from the time the Indians arrived, nor is the incident mentioned by anyone else.[42]

The departure of the Indians may have been due to ravages by other tribes. Spring brought renewed raids on the frontier in Western Pennsylvania and other areas. On May 16 Timothy Matlack, secretary of the Supreme Executive Council of Pennsylvania, wrote of information from the west "which makes it necessary to give immediate attention to the defence of that quarter against the Indians." On May 19 Henry Laurens wrote, "The Indians & Tories are exceeding troublesome on the Western frontier." One author attributed their departure to simple homesickness.[43]

By June 9 the commissioners wrote Washington of the alarm of the Oneidas and Tuscaroras in New York and enclosed a letter from them "requiring the return of their warriors for their own defence." The Commissioners suggested that they "ought not to be apprised of the message from their Sachems," until the British had evacuated Philadelphia. It is possible that Washington received this letter by June 13, the day he ordered Ensign Klock to escort them home. The remaining Indians with Washington probably traveled home with Maj. Myndert Wemple who came from Albany with a party of Senecas,

41. Washington to Jacob Klock, June 13, 1778, WGW, 12: 56; Lafayette to Peter Gansevoort, June 13, 1778, *LAAR*, 2: 76 Muhlenberg, *Journal*, 3: 163; Preston A. Barba, *They Came to Emmaus* (Emmaus, PA: Borough of Emmaus, 1959), 124.
42. Marshall, *Diary*, 184.
43. Laurens to John Rutledge, LDC, 9: 718; Timothy Matlack to John Lacey Jr., May 16, 1778, *The Register of Pennsylvania* 3, no 23 (June 6, 1829): 357; John F. Reed, "Indians at Valley Forge," *The Valley Forge Journal*, 3, no. 1 (June 1986): 32.

some Oneidas and Tuscaroras, in search of Atskeray, a Seneca warrior who had been wounded and captured near Fort Pitt. This contingent met Washington in Pennsylvania, ten miles from Coryell's Ferry (now New Hope) on June 21. Washington referred them to the President of Congress and stated that the Oneidas and Tuscaroras had "dispatches from their sachems for the immediate return of such of their Men and Warriors as were here." Washington consented to this and directed they be given presents.[44]

Benedict Arnold, then commanding in Philadelphia, was directed to provide "Trinkets &ca" to the Indians, but to have the presents and gifts to the Oneidas and Tuscaroras "greatly to exceed" those given to those Senecas. He was instructed to "Have them well *presented*, after which they may return to their nation." Arnold promised that "particular Attention shall be paid to the Contents." On June 24 Arnold wrote Henry Laurens that a "Committee" of Senecas arrived the day before in search of their captive chief.[45]

Congress was at York until June 27, and then adjourned to reconvene in Philadelphia. Apparently the Indian "Committee" grew tired of waiting and left. On July 7 the Board of War was ordered "to send for and confer with the Seneca Chiefs who have lately quitted the city of Philadelphia." They refused, however, to do so. On July 17 Major Wemple arrived at Albany "with the Senecas and the other Indians from Philadelphia." It is assumed this included the remainder of the Indians that had come to Valley Forge in May.[46]

Legends have survived among the Oneidas about those sent to Valley Forge. One is that food they brought with them saved the starving army. By the time they arrived in May, though, the food shortages had passed. No known primary-source documents mention the Indians bringing food with them. The tradition claims they brought 600 bushels of corn, amounting to twelve bushels or approximately 672 pounds per man. Supposedly the Oneidas had taught the soldiers how to prepare dry corn, but corn was already familiar to the soldiers. Part of the tradition states that an Oneida woman named Polly Cooper

44. Commissioners of Indian Affairs to Washington, June 9, 1778, PCC, r168, i152, 6: 131-34; Laurens to Schuyler, May 28, 1778, LDC, 9: 765-66; Washington to Laurens, June 21, 1778, WGW, 12: 98-99; James McHenry reported that "a deputation of the . . . Indians" had an audience with Washington. James McHenry, *Journal of a March, a Battle, and a Waterfall. . . ..* (privately printed, 1945), 2.
45. Washington to Benedict Arnold, June 21, 1778, WGW, 12: 101-2; Arnold to Washington, June 22, 1778, George Washington Papers, r50 LC; Arnold to Laurens, June 24, 1778, *Laurens Papers*, 13: 512.
46. JCC, 11: 675; Schuyler to Laurens, July 19, 1778, PCC, r173, 3: 348-51.

taught the men to properly cook corn, and the army wished to pay her but she refused; instead Martha Washington took her into Philadelphia and purchased a shawl and bonnet, and the shawl is now a treasured heirloom of the Oneida Nation. Facts argue against the truth of this tradition: Martha left for Virginia on June 8, 1778, and the British did not evacuate Philadelphia until June 18. There are no known contemporary references to an Indian woman at Valley Forge.[47]

While the stay of the Indians at Valley Forge was brief, it was a matter of interest to several civilian observers who marked their passage. In 1845, a Chester County resident still remembered them passing by her house near Zion Church, on what is now State Route 724.[48]

47. Washington to John Augustine Washington, June 10, 1778, WGW, 12: 43; Washington to Laurens, June 18, 1778, ibid., 12: 82.
48. Frederick Sheeder, "East Vincent Township, Chester County, Pennsylvania," PMHB 34, no. 2 (1910): 199.

The Discovery of a Letter from a Soldier of the First Rhode Island Regiment

✳ CHRISTIAN MCBURNEY ✳

Last spring, the Varnum Memorial Armory Museum in East Greenwich, Rhode Island, announced its discovery of a handwritten letter from a formerly enslaved man who had gained his freedom by enlisting in the First Rhode Island Regiment during the Revolutionary War. The letter, written in 1781, appears to be one of only two[1] existing let-

---

1. The other letter, dated September 30, 1776, was sent by Caesar Phelps to his master, Charles Phelps. Charles Phelps from Hadley, Massachusetts, owned large farms in the Connecticut Valley. In 1776, Charles Phelps sent Caesar in his place to fight in a Massachusetts Continental Regiment. It was not uncommon for white men, when drafted to serve in the army, to send an enslaved man in their place. Typically, the Black soldier was required to share his wages with his white owner. In the surviving letter from Fort Ticonderoga in New York State, likely written by a literate fellow soldier, Caesar Phelps complained to his master that he was not receiving his share of the wages. See Letter from Sezor (Caesar) Phelps to Charles Phelps, Porter-Phelps-Huntington Family Papers, Box 4 Folder 12, Amherst College Archives and Special Collection. For more on this letter see Cara Hudson-Erdman, "Caesar Phelps," The Porter-Phelps-Huntington House Museum, www.pphmuseum.org/slavery-and-servitude-at-forty-acres-blog/2018/6/27/caesar-phelps. The article states that Phelps served in a Continental Army regiment, but did not identify it. Phelp's letter mentions that Phelps served under Captain Cranston. Cranston served in Colonel Asa Whitcomb's Regiment, 6th Continental Regiment (and Massachusetts 13th Regiment) of the Continental Army. Whitcomb's Regiment served in northern New York in the summer and fall of 1776. See Francis B. Heitman, *Historical Register of Officers of the Continental Army During the War of Revolution* (Washington Press, 1893), 139 (Abner Cranston served as captain in Whitcomb's Massachusetts Regiment, from May to December 1775, and in the 6th Continental Regiment from January 1 to December 31, 1776); Massachusetts Society of Sons of the American Revolution, *Historical Memoranda with List of Members and Their Revolutionary Ancestors* (Published by the Society, 1897), 166 (Corporal John Ashby of Salem Massachusetts served in Captain Cranston's Company, Colonel Whitcomb's Regiment, as "was at Ticonderoga in 1776," citing Rev. Rolls, Mass. Archives); "Massachusetts Line," en.wikipedia.org/wiki/Massachusetts_Line.

ters sent by a Black soldier from a Continental Army regiment (or any other American regiment) during the Revolutionary War, and it was from a soldier serving in Rhode Island's famous "Black Regiment." This makes the find a remarkable one; indeed, it is a "national treasure" as the curator of the Varnum Armory Memorial Museum and discoverer of the letter, Patrick Donovan, states.[2] The contents of the letter are also noteworthy: the soldier makes a shocking request of his former "master and mistress" who had once enslaved him.

The letter is from Thomas Nichols of Warwick, Rhode Island. It was sent to Benjamin and Phoebe Nichols of Warwick, who had once enslaved Thomas Nichols. According to Rhode Island's 1774 census, Benjamin Nichols's household contained two adult white men, two adult white women, three white children, two Indian servants, and one Black person, who must have been the enslaved Thomas Nichols.[3] A state military census for 1777 listed Benjamin and Thomas as able-bodied men between the ages of sixteen and sixty. In mid-1778, Thomas Nichols became free, escaping enslavement by enlisting in the First Rhode Island Regiment of the Continental Army.

The First Rhode Island Regiment was re-established in February 1778 in order to entice enslaved men to join its ranks. The idea likely originated from white officers of the regiment, whose ranks had been decimated from difficult military campaigns around New York City and Philadelphia. The idea also had the implicit support of General George Washington, who had forwarded the request to re-establish the regiment with enslaved men to Rhode Island's governor.

On February 9, 1778, Rhode Island's General Assembly enacted a law providing freedom to enslaved men who enlisted in the regiment. But there were a few important conditions. First, the enslaved man had to enlist for the duration of the war. Second, the enlistee's former master or mistress was to be paid by the state an amount equal to the fair market value of the enslaved man, as determined by the state. In addition,

2. Patrick Donovan, "Thomas Nichols Letter at the Varnum Armory ... a Stunning 18th-Century African American Artifact," http://varnumcontinentals.org/2021/02/feature-article-thomas-nichols-letter-at-the-varnum-armory-a-stunning-18th-century-african-american-artifact/. Donovan's discovery was highlighted in a front-page article, Paul Edward Parker, "Echoes of the Past," *Providence Journal*, Feb. 15, 2021, 1.

3. See John R. Bartlett, ed., *Census of the Inhabitants of the Colony of Rhode Island and Providence Plantations 1774* (Providence, RI: Knowles, Anthony & Co., 1858), 64; Mildred M. Chamberlain, ed., *The Rhode Island 1777 Military Census* (Baltimore, MD: Genealogical Publishing Co., 1985), 119. The original source for Benjamin being the owner of Thomas is the *General Treasurer's Accounts* cited below. The name of Benjamin's wife is dervied from Patrick Donovan's article cited in the first note above.

under the statute's structure, both the enslaved man and his owners had to agree to the enlistment.[4]

As it turned out, there were not enough enslaved young men in Rhode Island willing to enlist to fill a regiment. About ninety enslaved men did enlist, thus gaining their freedom. Free Black men, Narragansett Indians, and other men of color filled out the ranks of privates. The officers were all white men, including the regiment's colonel, Christopher Greene of Warwick.

On May 10, 1778, Thomas Nichols enlisted in the First Rhode Island Regiment and was assigned to Captain Thomas Cole's company.[5] Nichols likely showed up at a muster organized by one of the regiment's officers, with a drummer by his side to inspire the men with a drumbeat. Joining the regiment created a path to freedom, and so Nichols, along with other similarly minded enslaved men, voluntarily enlisted for the war's duration. By virtue of joining the regiment, Nichols and the other enslaved men who had enlisted were now, according to the words of the statute, "immediately discharged from the service of his master or mistress" and "absolutely FREE." In addition, they would now be fighting for the independence of the new United States.

I discovered that probably more than a dozen of these formerly enslaved men had been born in Africa.[6] Now they would fight for the freedom of the country into which they had been forcibly carried.

On May 22, the State of Rhode Island issued a note in the amount of 120 pounds to Thomas's former owner, Benjamin Nichols of War-

4. See General Assembly Resolution, February 9, 1778, in John R. Bartlett, ed., *Records of the Colony of Rhode Island and Providence Plantations*, vol. 8 (Providence, RI: A. C. Greene & Bros., 1863), 358-60. For more on the First Rhode Island Regiment, see Robert Geake and Lorén Spears, *From Slaves to Soldiers: The 1st Rhode Island Regiment in the American Revolution* (Yardley, PA: Westholme Publishing, 2016); Daniel M. Popek, *They "... fought bravely, but were unfortunate:" The True Story of Rhode Island's "Black Regiment" and the Failure of Segregation in Rhode Island's Continental Line, 1777-1783* (Bloomington, IN: AuthorHouse, 2016).

5. See Thomas Nichols Service Records, Derived from Company Muster Rolls July 6, 1778-May 4, 1781, in Compiled Service Records of Soldiers Who Served in the American Army during the Revolutionary War, M881, Washington, DC: National Archives, Washington, DC (Thomas Nichols Service Records).

6. An incomplete muster roll lists thirty-three former enslaved soldiers from the First Rhode Island Regiment and describes eight of them has being born in Africa and one as being born in Jamaica. List of Soldiers, 1781, Regimental Book, Rhode Island Regiment, 1781-83, microfilm, R.I. State Archives. While this regimental list was compiled in 1781, it contains information relating to some privates who had enlisted in the First Rhode Island in 1778. The more than a dozen estimate is based on comparing the number of enlistees whose birthplaces are known (thirty-three) to the total number of enslaved enlistees (about ninety).

wick. Thomas must have been healthy and strong, as 120 pounds was the maximum the state would pay owners of enslaved enlistees at the time.[7]

As with all the other enlistees, Nichols would have been inoculated against the smallpox at a safe house, probably in East Greenwich. Then military training with muskets and bayonets began in the town.[8] On May 31, 1778, Dr. Joshua Babcock, from Westerly, Rhode Island, wrote his friend, Benjamin Franklin, then in France, "This sable battalion, well uniformed and well conducted, bid fair for service."[9]

The new soldiers in the First Rhode Island Regiment had little time to train or gain experience in the field before facing a fierce baptism of battle. This was at the Battle of Rhode Island, on August 29, 1778. The American army, then in the town of Portsmouth in the northern part of Aquidneck Island and seeking to leave the island, had to fend off advances of British army troops. As I describe in my book, *The Rhode Island Campaign: The First French and American Operation of the Revolutionary War*, the First Rhode Island Regiment held a key redoubt on the west side of the norther part of Aquidneck Island at the most advanced—thus exposed—position of the American line. Three times experienced German troops, allies of the British, charged the redoubt and the American lines, and were repulsed by the First Rhode Island Regiment and other Continental regiments to their rear. One German officer stated, "we found obstinate resistance, and bodies of troops behind the work [the redoubt] at its sides, chiefly wild looking men in their shirtsleeves, and among them many negroes."[10] Writing a few hours after the battle, the First Rhode's Island field commander in the battle, Major Samuel Ward, wrote, "I believe a couple of the blacks were killed and four or five wounded, but none badly."[11] It was an impressive performance by the First Rhode Island, especially considering how inexperienced in combat the men were and that as enslaved men they had never been allowed to use guns or participate in militia exercises.

Thomas Nichols likely fought at the Battle of Rhode Island. In a muster roll taken in late August 1778, Nichols is reported as with the

---

7. An Account of the Negro Slaves Enlisted into the Continental Battalions, to whom they belong, with the valuation of such Slave, and Notes Given, *General Treasurer's Accounts, 1761-1781*, Alphabetical Book, No. 6, R.I. State Archives. Bartlett, ed., *Records of the Colony of R.I.*, 8:360.

8. Christian M. McBurney, *The Rhode Island Campaign: The First French and American Operation in the Revolutionary War* (Yardley, PA: Westholme, 2014), 48.

9. Quoted in ibid., 48.

10. Quoted in ibid., 188.

11. Quoted in ibid., 245.

First Rhode Island Regiment. However, in the next month's muster roll, he is reported as "Sick in hospital."[12]

It is not clear if Nichols had been wounded during the battle or suffered from an illness. Shortly before the battle, the regiment had suffered from an outbreak of disease, and Nichols may have become a victim of the outbreak after the battle.[13] During the war, on both sides, more soldiers died of disease than from bullets and cannon fire. Based on other descriptions in regimental muster rolls of Nichols as being "sick," and that in his January 1781 letter Nichols states that he is suffering from illness and not from wounds, it appears more likely he became ill after the battle and was not wounded during the battle. Patrick Donovan appropriately wonders if Nichols suffered from PTSD syndrome.[14]

Nichols was still reported as "sick" in a muster roll return submitted in May 1779 in Rhode Island. But he had apparently sufficiently recovered after that time to be listed in subsequent muster rolls as "on command" or "on guard"—that is, in a normal capacity.[15] Nichols was with his regiment when the British evacuated Newport and American regiments re-entered it in late October 1779. The muster roll for his company on January 7, 1780, from Newport, indicated Nichols was "on command."[16] But a year later, by January 18, 1781, the date of the recently discovered letter, he had either suffered a relapse of his former illness or he had acquired a new debilitating disease.

Now let's turn to Thomas Nichols's letter. Here it is, with corrections made by me to misspellings and punctuation, and with a few words revised to reflect the intended meaning. The original text of the letter is posted at the end of this article. After the letter, I will address its substance.

Windham [, Connecticut,] January 18th, 1781
Honored Master & Mistress:
   I take this opportunity to inform you of my situation at this time and

---

12. Thomas Nichols Service Records, September. 1778 ("Sick in hospital"); December 1778 ("Sick Absent"); January 1779 ("On duty"); February 1779 ("Under guard"); April 1779 ("On guard"); May 1779 ("Sick" at Quidnessett); July 1779 ("On Guard"); August 1779 ("On Guard").
13. McBurney, *Rhode Island Campaign*, 199.
14. Same cite as in second note above. Daniel M. Popek, in his exhaustively researched work on the First Rhode Island Regiment, after studying the evidence he uncovered about the battle, leaned towards Thomas Nichols being among the regiment's men wounded in the battle. Popek, *The True Story of the "Black Regiment,"* 233-34.
15. Thomas Nichols Service Records, August 1778 to December 1779.
16. Ibid., November-Dec. 1779.

desire your aide. After I drove 3 wagons as far as Windham, a wagoner took away my badge of driving and ordered me to guard the wagons, which I refused. I turned back to Colonel Christopher Greene at Coventry and the wagoner sent back two men after me. The Colonel did not blame me but told the men and me to go on again and that I should take my wagon again. But being over worried with this tramp I got but 3 miles further than where I left the wagons in South Windham at the house of one Dan Murdock where I have been confined with my old fits. But good care is taken of me. But I have a desire to return to you. Not having any money, nor clothes fit to wear and all strangers to me makes it something difficult for me. I have had a Doctor and a Surgeon's Mate [examine] me who advise me to go to the Corps of Invalids at Boston, where I may be under half pay during the life remaining in this poor state of body. But I am not able to go there. Neither do I incline to do so without advice from you. But I have a desire that Master or Mistress would go to Colonel Greene and see if you can't get me discharged from the war, it being very disagreeable to my mind as well as destructive to my health. I suppose I could ride on a horse or at least in a slay if you could obtain a discharge for me so that I may return to my master and his family again, bearing the will of God and your pleasure. So no more at this time. But I Remain your humble and dutiful Thomas.

"N" His mark

December 31, 1780. These lines I received from the Surgeon's Mate: Whereas Thomas Nichols a soldier belonging to the First Regiment in Rhode Island State has been for some time attended with fits in this place and still likely to remain unfit for military life.

In the above letter, Nichols initially explained the incident that inspired his letter. The First Rhode Island Regiment was at the time stationed at Coventry, Rhode Island, and Nichols had been ordered to drive a wagon from there into Connecticut, probably to pick up grain or other foodstuffs and return it to Coventry for the troops. But during the trip, near Windham, Connecticut, Nichols must have become so incapacitated from the onset of an illness that he was unable to perform his assigned duty. A wagoner supervising him removed his badge that entitled him to drive a wagon for the Continental Army and ordered him to serve as a mere guard for the wagons. Nichols refused the demotion and instead drove his wagon back to Coventry to meet with the commander of his regiment, Colonel Greene. Fortunately for Nichols, Greene did not punish him for disobeying orders. Rather Greene ordered Nichols to drive his wagon back to Connecticut and try to complete the task assigned to him. Nichols made the attempt, but he got no farther than three miles from South Windham when his illness again overwhelmed him. Luckily for Nichols, a local man, Dan Murdock, invited Nichols to stay at his house and took "good care" of him. At the time he wrote the letter, January 18, 1781, Nichols still suffered from his "old fits" and was not well enough to leave Murdock's house.

Thomas desperately wanted to be discharged from military service. His reasons were that the war was "very disagreeable to my mind" as well as "destructive to my health." Thomas no longer relished being a soldier and it had ruined his health.

After providing Benjamin and Phoebe Nichols with this background, Thomas Nichols made the following startling request: "I have a desire to return to you." Later he states (in the third person) that, for reasons of his poor health, "I have a desire that Master or Mistress would go to Colonel Greene and see if you can't get me discharged from the war." He again reiterates his desire for his former owners to "obtain a discharge for me so that I may return to my master and family again."

Did Thomas Nichols want to be re-enslaved? It appears that is the case. The use of the terms "master" and "mistress" evoke the master-slave relationship and he expressed a desire to "return to my master and family *again*" (emphasis added). But the conclusion is not certain. Thomas did not use any other language indicating that he wanted to return to the legal status of enslavement. Perhaps Thomas was deliberately ambiguous. He may have wanted his former owners in the short term to take him back in and care for him, and at the same time defer until later negotiations with them over his free or unfree labor status.

Thomas Nichols must have been in a severe psychological state to have even intimated that he desired to return to a state of enslavement. But poor health, the pressures of war, and the uncertainty of his economic future due to his disability could explain a temporarily disturbed state of mind. Thomas apparently felt at the time that spending the rest of his days with his former master and mistress provided him with more security than struggling to live on his own in his unhealthy condition. It is also an indication that the white Nichols family may not have been cruel masters and that Thomas saw himself having a passably decent life in their service.

Benjamin and Phoebe Nichols might not have been able to re-enslave Thomas even if they had tried. There was no provision for it in the General Assembly's legislation authorizing the re-establishment of the First Rhode Island Regiment. For Thomas to have obtained his freedom by enlisting, he had to enlist for the duration of the war. That condition implied that if a soldier deserted the regiment, he could be returned to slavery. But if the soldier was discharged for bad health that he acquired while on duty in his regiment or for battle wounds, the Rhode Island statute provided that such soldiers were not to be returned to slavery, but instead would be supported by the state.

In addition, Benjamin and Phoebe Nichols may not have wanted to re-enslave Thomas Nichols. At the time, Rhode Island's economy was in a shambles, and the white Nichols family may not have wanted another mouth to feed. In addition, they had allowed Thomas to enlist, a condition to receiving compensation from the State of Rhode Island for his loss. They may have been concerned that the State of Rhode Island would renege on the promissory note issued to them for Thomas enlisting in the First Rhode Island Regiment.

The situation is reminiscent of the implied moral obligation of slave masters to care for their elderly enslaved people. In colonial times, it was considered cruel by masters to free an enslaved man or woman after a lifetime of unpaid service and at a time when he or she was too old or infirm to perform further useful work to support himself or herself. Thomas Nichols was in effect asking his former white owners to care for him at a time when he was unable to perform exacting manual labor. But as Benjamin and Phoebe may have viewed it, Thomas had not become incapacitated in their service; rather it was from his service in the Continental Army. At the time, the fledgling United States did not care for its wounded or ill veterans, and Rhode Island had not begun to fulfill this obligation either.

One reason Thomas Nichols found himself in this situation was because he had been enslaved. A typical white soldier would have had parents working on a family farm who made a decent living and could have taken their sick son in, cared for him, and nursed him back to health. Or other relatives could have done so. But Thomas Nichols's parents likely continued to be enslaved persons and thus were not able to perform this crucial task that families sometimes are forced to undertake to assist their children. This was yet another penalty the slave system imposed on its victims.

In his letter, Thomas Nichols describes the "poor state" of his health and dire financial situation. He did not have "any money, nor clothes fit to wear." This was the fault, of course, of Congress and Rhode Island in failing to provide properly for their soldiers. Both white and Black soldiers suffered from such lack of support, especially beginning in the winter of 1778-1779 and for the remainder of the war. This sad state of affairs led to some mutinies among white soldiers, including in Rhode Island.[17]

Nichols also explains that he had been examined by his regiment's doctor and a surgeon's mate, both of whom agreed that Nichols was not fit to perform further military service. The postscript to the letter appears to be a paraphrasing of the conclusions of the surgeon's mate. He concludes that Nichols "has been for some time attended with fits" and was "likely to remain unfit for military life." However, the regimental surgeon and surgeon's mate, rather than agree that Nichols should be discharged from military service, advised Nichols that he should be transferred to the "Corps of Invalids at Boston" where he could earn "half pay." The Corps of Invalids was filled with Continental Army soldiers from various regiments who had suffered debilitating wounds or illness, making them unable to endure the rigors of a campaign. But they were deemed healthy enough to perform less demanding tasks, such as guarding forts, prisons and hospitals.

It is not known if either Benjamin or Phoebe Nichols approached Colonel Greene about obtaining a discharge for Thomas Nichols. (It is noteworthy that Thomas was willing for Phoebe to make the request on her own, an indication of his confidence in her abilities.) They had little time to act. The muster rolls for the First Rhode Island Regiment indicate that Thomas Nichols was transferred to the Corps of Invalids on February 1, 1781.[18]

Thomas Nichols wrote his mark on the letter with an "N." Who penned the letter from his dictation is unknown. It was probably Dan Murdoch or someone who lived in his house or nearby. Common soldiers not infrequently were illiterate and had other soldiers, often corporals or sergeants, write their letters for them. But in this case, Thomas Nichols was then in the house of a civilian and not at a regimental camp.

What happened with Thomas Nichols after war's end is not known. The 1790 federal census of heads of households contains an intriguing clue. It does not mention a Black man named Thomas Nichols as heading a household in Rhode Island. However, the 1790 census contains an entry for Benjamin Nichols heading a household of ten persons. It

17. See Christian McBurney, "Mutiny! American Mutinies in the Rhode Island Theater of War, September 1778-July 1779," *Rhode Island History*, vol. 69, No. 2 (Summer/Fall 2011), 47-72.

18. See Thomas Nichols Service Records, Feb. 1780 to May 1781. Another source indicates that the transfer occurred on March 1, 1781. See Bruce C. MacGunnigle, *Regimental Book: Rhode Island Regiment for 1781 &c.* (East Greenwich, RI: Rhode Island Society of the Sons of the American Revolution, 2011), 71.

will be recalled that in the Rhode Island 1774 census, in addition to the seven white family members in Benjamin's household, there were also recorded two Indians, who must have been free servants, and one Black person, who must have been the enslaved Thomas Nichols. In the 1790 federal census, Indians and Blacks were not categories. Instead, persons of color were covered by these two categories: "All other free persons" and "Slaves." The entry for Benjamin Nichols in the 1790 census includes three white adult males, four white females, three free persons of color, and no slaves.[19] Accordingly, the size and makeup of the household was the same in 1790 as it was in 1774—seven whites and three persons of color. Perhaps the persons of color in the household in 1790 were the same two Indians who were in the Nichols household in 1774—and Thomas Nichols, but as a free man. If so, Thomas Nichols was granted his wish to return to the Nichols family, but he was able to negotiate his status to remain a free man.

The 1790 census for Stratford, Connecticut, located in Fairfield County, contains the following item: "Thomas (Neg.) Nichols." The term "Neg." was short for the word Negro. This could be a reference to Thomas Nichols, the letter writer. The entry indicates that four other nonwhite persons resided in this household, perhaps the man's wife and three children.[20] This record might tie into the fact that Thomas Nichols does not appear on a list of invalid soldiers residing in Rhode Island in 1785—he may have moved to Stratford.[21]

After this mention, the documentary record for Thomas Nichols is missing. It is not uncommon for the documentary record to be missing after a certain point in the late eighteenth century and early nineteenth century, either for a white or a Black person, but it was more likely to occur for Black people. Thomas Nichols apparently did not live long enough to apply for a veteran's pension in either 1818 or 1832. Perhaps

---

19. *Heads of Families at the First Census of the United States Taken in the Year 1790, Rhode Island* (Bureau of Census, ed.) (Washington, D.C.: Government Printing Office, 1908), 14 (under Warwick). Curiously, there is no mention of Benjamin Nichols's household in a Rhode Island 1782 census. See Jay Mack Holbrook, *Rhode Island 1782 Census* (Oxford, MA: Holbrook Research Institute, 1979).

20. *Heads of Families at the First Census of the United States Taken in the Year 1790, Connecticut*, 31. This reference was mentioned in Eric G. Grundset, ed., *Forgotten Patriots, African American and American Indian Patriots in the Revolutionary War* (National Society of the Daughters of the American Revolution, 2008), 223. No Black man named Thomas Nichols was reported as a soldier in the Revolutionary War hailing from Connecticut. See ibid, 270-295.

21. List of Invalids, June 7, 1785, in Bartlett, ed., *Records of the Colony of R.I.*, 10:162-67. The list includes several Black soldiers of the First Rhode Island Regiment.

his bad health arising from his military service finally caused his early death sometime after 1790. More research is needed to find out the rest of Thomas Nichols's story after his transfer to the Corps of Invalids in February 1781. (Due to the pandemic, I was not able to search by household federal censuses after 1790).

The Thomas Nichols letter has been professionally conserved by the Varnum Armory Memorial Museum, thanks to a grant from the Rhode Island Sons of the American Revolution. The letter is now on display in a frame in the museum's Eighteenth Century room. Patrick Donovan and the Varnum Armory Memorial Museum are to be congratulated on their spectacular discovery.

The Original of the Letter, Uncorrected

Windham January 18th, 1781
Onered Master & Mistress I take this opportunity to inform you of my citiation att this time & desire your ade = after I drove 3 waggons as far as Windham I hade waggoner tookaway my badge of driving & ordered me to gard ye waggons which I refused & turned back to colonel green att Covintree & ye wagoner sent back two men after me Ye Colonal did not blame me but told ye men and me to go on again & that I should take my waggon again but being over worried with this tramp I got but 3 miles further than where I left ye waggons in So. Windham att ye house of one Dan Murdock where I have been confined with my old fits But have good care taken of me But I have a desire to Return to you Not having any money Nor Clows fit to wair & all strangers to me makes it something difficult for me I have had a Doctor and a Surgans mate to me which advize me to go to xxx corps of invalids at Boston where I may be under half pay During Life Remaining in this poor State of Body But I ante able to go thether Neither do I incline to with out advice from you But I have a desire that Master or Mistress would go to Colonel Green & see if you cant git me Discharged from ye War it being very Disagreabell to my mind as well as Destructive to my helth I suppose I could ride on a horse or att least in a Slay if you could obtain a Discharge for me So that I may Return to my Master and his family again baring[?] the will of god & your pleasure So No more att this time But I Remain your humble & dutiful Thomas "N"
His mark
December 31 1780 These lines I recv'd from ye Surgeon's mate where as Thomas Nickols a soldier belonging to ye first Regiment in Rhode Island State hath been for some time attended with fits in this place & still likely to Remain unfit for military life.

"The Predicament We Are In": How Paperwork Saved the Continental Army

❄❄ MIKE MATHENY ❄❄

"Few people know the predicament we are in," wrote George Washington, while he expressed the Continental army's dire circumstances.[1] By January 1776, just six months into the Revolutionary War, the Continental army faced a crisis outside Boston. This particular crisis, not caused by a British attack, was a personnel issue. "Search the volumes of history through," Washington wrote, "and I much question whether a case similar to ours is to be found . . . to have one army disbanded, and another to raise, within the same distance of a reinforced enemy; it is too much to attempt—what may be the final issue of the last manouvre, time can only tell."[2] The Continental army, having grown to just over 22,000 soldiers, was about to disperse. Most soldiers' enlistment contracts expired on January 1, 1776, and less than half agreed to reenlist.[3] Entire regiments were leaving the battlefield, headed for home. Congress had not paid the army for two months in a row.[4] Their short enlistments now at an end, dissatisfied soldiers believed their commitments were done. The American Revolution almost ended before it began, not due to a battlefield defeat, but in large part to the overwhelming personnel challenges inherent in creating and maintaining the first national army.

1. George Washington to Joseph Reed, January 14, 1776, William B. Reed, *Reprint of the original letters from Washington to Joseph Reed, during the American Revolution. Referred to in the pamphlets of Lord Mahon and Mr. Sparks* (Philadelphia: A. Hart, Late Carey and Hart, 1852), 44.
2. Washington to Reed, January 4, 1776, *Letters from Washington to Joseph Reed*, 36-37.
3. Robert K. Wright Jr., *The Continental Army* (Center of Military History: United States Army, 1983), 55.
4. Washington to Reed, January 14, 1776, *Letters from Washington to Joseph Reed*, 43.

Historians frequently highlight the tremendous challenges the Continental army endured. The army's early rabble nature faced many leadership, training, discipline, and logistical weaknesses. One of the most frustrating issues was its specific *personnel* problems. The army's manpower shortage, recruitment and reenlistment crises, and financial woes, comprised a unified theme. They all related to the often unglamorous and tedious topic of personnel management, or in modern terms, "human resources." The army only survived by successfully coping with these challenges through strength reporting that gave it an ability to see itself, improvisation in recruiting and reenlistment to retain its force, and short-term fixes in finances to keep the army together long enough to win the war. Personnel management was a vital factor in the success or failure in the fight for independence, one which, had the Continental army not sufficiently coped with, the American Revolution might have quickly collapsed under British occupation.

BUILDING (AND RE-BUILDING) THE ARMY

The Continental Congress created a national army with initially modest proportions that reorganized multiple times to cope with personnel challenges. After the first armed conflict occurred at Lexington and Concord in April 1775, Congress created the Continental army on June 14, 1775. Starting from scratch, the very first Continental army establishment included only ten regiments, six from Pennsylvania, two from Maryland, and two from Virginia. The Continental army assumed temporary control over the New England militia forces mustering outside Boston and attempted to incorporate them into the army on a formal basis. The total force authorized by Congress in 1775 was 22,000 men, a number which the army exceeded by October 1775.[5]

The Continental army reorganized itself frequently as a coping mechanism to handle its personnel shortfalls. The foremost challenge was expiring enlistments that caused an aggressive personnel turnover. Three major structural overhauls occurred in the winters of 1776, 1777, and 1780, each corresponding with a massive personnel exodus. In January 1776, less than half the army remained in service, and strength fell to under 10,500 soldiers.[6]

The crisis over the army's possible dissolution in early 1776 repeated itself in the winter of 1777 due to expiring enlistments. Washington implored Congress for assistance: "We are now as it were, upon the eve of another dissolution of our Army—the remembrance of the difficul-

5. Wright, *The Continental Army*, 24, 40.
6. Washington to Reed, January 14, 1776, *Letters from Washington to Joseph Reed*, 42.

ties which happened upon that occasion last year . . . that unless some speedy and effectual measures are adopted by Congress; our cause will be lost."[7] Washington further confided to his relative Lund Washington, "Our only dependence now, is upon the Speedy Inlistment of a New Army; if this fails us, I think the game will be pretty well up."[8] Washington pointed to personnel issues as the root cause: "ten days more will put an end to the existence of our Army . . . It is needless to add, that short inlistments, and a mistaken dependence upon Militia, have been the Origin of all our misfortunes, and the great accumulation of our Debt."[9]

To cope with the crisis, Congress reorganized the army and changed the standard enlistment from one to three years, or the duration of the war. Congress authorized the "Eighty-eight Battalion Resolve," the largest reorganization of the war, which occurred in September 1776. This began as an "army on paper" as manning levels fell to their lowest point in the war.[10] The 88 regiments expanded by December to 119 authorized regiments, but few were able to reach their full authorizations. If fully manned in 1777, the Continental army would have been over 90,000 soldiers.[11]

The Continental army never came close to half of its 1777 authorization and struggled to retain personnel throughout its existence. The last major reorganization occurred in 1780, when the three-year enlistments of 1777 expired. Congress, now practically bankrupt, reduced the army's size to only 49 regiments. After the 1780 reorganization, the army's quota settled around 35,000 soldiers for the remainder of the war.[12] This aggressive personnel turnover posed a tremendous challenge to the Continental army's administration. All the more credit was due to the individuals who eventually found solutions to make the system manageable, if not ultimately successful.

HANDLING PAPERWORK

With such a constant organizational flux, as well as battlefield losses, casualties, sickness, and desertion, the army was an administrative nightmare. The Continental army turned to the British Army as a

7. Washington to John Hancock, September 22, 1776, Lengel, ed. *This Glorious Struggle: George Washington's Revolutionary War Letters* (New York: Harper Collins Publishers, 2007), 68.

8. Washington to Lund Washington, December 10, 1776, ibid., 80.

9. Washington to Hancock, December 20, 1776, ibid., 81.

10. Robert Middlekauff, *This Glorious Cause: The American Revolution, 1763–1789* (Oxford: Oxford University Press, 2005), 372.

11. Wright, *The Continental Army*, 119.

12. Ibid., 154.

model for handling organization and administration. Several Continental officers including Horatio Gates, Charles Lee, and Washington himself had experience serving in the British Army during the French and Indian War. Washington recommended British military manuals to his officers such as Humphrey Bland's *A Treatise of Military Discipline* and William Young's *Manoeuvres, or Practical Observations on the Art of War* which included detailed descriptions on the specific duties of officers, including administrative tasks and procedures.[13] Despite having a model to follow, administering a newly created national army proved an imposing task. Washington frequently expressed the immense stress he was under, revealing: "At present, my time is so much taken up at my desk, that I am obliged to neglect many other essential parts of my duty: it is absolutely necessary, therefore, for me to have persons that can think for me, as well as execute orders."[14]

Washington's aides, whom he referred to as his "family," were essential in administering the army. Robert Harrison, Joseph Reed, Tench Tillman, Alexander Hamilton, and John Laurens were some of the more famous aides who served Washington during the war. Washington's writings reveal he placed tremendous value on his military family. For example, he implored Joseph Reed to serve as his personal aide on five different occasions in 1775 and 1776, revealing a dire urgency for administrative help: "Real necessity compels me to ask you whether I may entertain any hopes of your returning to my family?"[15] Reed eventually accepted and served as Washington's aide, as well as the second adjutant general of the army's staff in 1776.

Beyond his aides, the Continental army's staff assisted Washington. The first staff had five positions: adjutant general, commissary of musters, paymaster general, commissary general, and quartermaster general.[16] These positions were responsible for the war's basic necessities, including tracking the revolving door of personnel and their pay. The staff structure later reorganized to include an inspector general, a position made highly efficient by Baron von Steuben at Valley Forge in 1778.

---

13. Humphrey Bland, *A Treatise of Military Discipline* (London: Daniel Midwinter, John and Paul Knapton, 1743) and William Young, *Manoeuvres, or Practical Observations on the Art of War* (London: J. Millan, 1770). Also see J. L. Bell, "Washington's Five Books," *Journal of the American Revolution*, December 18, 2013, allthingsliberty.com/2013/12/washingtons-five-books/.
14. Washington to Reed, January 23, 1776, *Letters from Washington to Joseph Reed*, 50.
15. Ibid., 49. (for the five separate letters, see pages 12, 18-19, 28, 48, 54).
16. Wright, *The Continental Army*, 26-27.

The staff position most associated with personnel was the adjutant general. The Continental army's first adjutant general, Horatio Gates, joined Washington's headquarters in July 1775. He relieved Washington of many duties, including publishing the Articles of War and issuing instructions to the recruiting service.[17] The official appointees after Gates were Joseph Reed, Timothy Pickering, Alexander Scammell, and Edward Hand.[18] Timothy Pickering assigned a deputy to each territory's department to streamline strength reporting. Alexander Scammell further standardized the use of pre-printed forms and issued "blank-books" to every soldier for keeping their personal records.[19] Scammell and Hand collected the army's strength returns into a master account, one that still exists.[20] Collectively, the adjutants general were responsible for the essential personnel administrative function, strength reporting.

STRENGTH REPORTING

Washington's army was surprisingly efficient at strength reporting that allowed the Continental army to see itself and address personnel shortfalls. Strength reporting was the systematic and routine collection of numerical data that communicated an individual unit's strength and readiness. Strength returns captured a remarkable amount of data, especially surprising considering everything was calculated by hand. Returns numerically compiled units by regiment and brigade, listed officers by grade, tabulated numbers of rank and file soldiers, listed non-available statuses (sick, furlough, confined, etc.), presented alterations (gains and losses), and even included a "wanting to complete" calculation that gave recruiters their target number to complete their unit's authorized strength.[21]

Washington relied heavily on these returns for his army's capabilities and limitations. Washington complained of the tardiness in producing a strength return in January 1776 where he emphasized their importance: "it is impossible that the business of the Army can be conducted with any degree of regularity or propriety," and threatened to place his subordinate commanders "under arrest and tried for disobedience of Orders" if they did not produce them on time.[22]

17. Paul David Nelson, *General Horatio Gates: A Biography* (Baton Rouge, Louisiana State University Press, 1976), 43.
18. Charles H. Lesser ed., *The Sinews of Independence: Monthly Strength Reports of the Continental Army* (Chicago: The University of Chicago Press, 1976), xiii.
19. Wright, *The Continental Army*, 114, 145.
20. Lesser, *Sinews of Independence*, ix.
21. Ibid., 249.
22. Washington, General Orders, January 8, 1776, John C. Fitzpatrick ed., *The Writings of George Washington from the Original Manuscript Sources*, U.S. Presidential Library, Vol 4, 223.

Strength reporting was essential in accounting for non-available soldiers and determining unit readiness. Soldiers could be absent for duty for a variety of reasons, most commonly sickness. The strength returns for the army outside Boston in 1775 reported that of 22,676 total, there were 2,500 sick, 750 furloughed, and 2,400 detached on various duties.[23] This was a staggering 24 percent non-available rate, a vital planning consideration for the commander.

Sickness was a constant challenge for the army's personnel readiness. The army suffered a smallpox outbreak as early as 1775; Washington wrote "The small-pox is in every part of Boston . . . If we escape the small-pox in this camp, and the country round about, it will be miraculous."[24] The Continental army's unavailable numbers peaked in 1777, reaching as high as 35 percent unavailable due solely to sickness.[25] This was utterly crippling to the army's operations and was essential to the commander's planning. In response to sickness and injuries, the army created the "invalid corps," a category on strength returns where repurposed wounded soldiers, unfit for future battles, still performed garrison duties.[26]

Strength reporting allowed the army to track its rates of desertion, another crippling personnel issue. Washington complained that the penalty for desertion was too lax, saying "thirty and 40 Soldiers will desert at a time" and even make a game of it.[27] One estimate accounted for 1,134 men deserting from the Continental army between 1777 and 1778 alone. The number of court martial trials for desertion increased from only 19 in 1775, to 142 in 1776, and reached its peak of 157 recorded cases in 1781.[28] Congress raised the penalty for desertion to the death penalty in 1776. At times, units offered amnesty to deserters to recoup their manpower.[29] Despite the penalties, high desertion rates continued to plague the army.

RECRUITMENT AND REENLISTMENT

Tracking the unit's personnel status was imperative to a functioning army, but not as vital as recruiting these soldiers in the first place. The Continental army faced constant struggles with recruitment and reenlistment shortfalls. Many colonists' loyalties lay with the militia and in-

23. Wright, *The Continental Army*, 40.

24. Washington to Reed, December 15, 1775, *Letters from Washington to Joseph Reed*, 31.

25. Lesser, *Sinews of Independence*, xxxi.

26. PHILADELPHIA. IN CONGRESS, July 16, 1777, *The Pennsylvania Gazette*, July 23, 1777.

27. Washington to Hancock, September 22, 1776, Lengel, *This Glorious Struggle*, 72.

28. Charles Neimeyer, *America Goes to War: A Social History of the Continental Army* (New York and London: New York University Press, 1996), 136-138.

29. PHILADELPHIA, April 20, 1777, *The Pennsylvania Gazette*, April 23, 1777.

dependent state regiments, who offered more appealing opportunities than the Continental army in terms of better pay and shorter terms of service. Soldiers' motivations were another factor evident in recruitment. While patriotic rhetoric of liberty ran high in the first year of the war, it waned as time passed. The Continental army could not rely on patriotic fervor to satisfy its recruitment needs. Commanders and state officials increasingly had to improvise and switch to more coercive methods to man the army.

Recruiting reflected colonial America's localism. There was no centralized recruitment branch. Congress gave states quotas based on a percentage of their adult male population and it was up to the states to fill them. Recruiters marketed in their home communities to fill their companies. Congress forbade recruiters from crossing state lines, their "respective jurisdiction," warning that any "officer or officers who may have marched or removed from the State to whose battalions he or they belong" was committing a reportable offense.[30]

Recruiters used enlistment "bounties," cash bonuses, to attract prospective soldiers. Bounties ranged in amount, and they were a strong motivator for young enlistees. One young soldier, Joseph Plumb Martin, recalled when he was first considering becoming a soldier: "A dollar deposited upon the drum head was taken by some one as soon as placed there, and the holder's name taken, and he enrolled . . . My spirits began to revive at the sight of the money offered; the seeds of courage began to sprout . . . O, thought I, if I were but old enough to put myself forward, I would be the possessor of one dollar, the dangers of war notwithstanding."[31] To many young prospects, the enlistment bounty may have been the most amount of money they had ever earned in their life. This was a strong incentive for enlisting.

Incentive bounties brought one difficulty: bounty jumping, where a man enlisted into a unit just to collect the bonus and then immediately desert, sometimes repeating the process with other units. This was particularly outrageous to army officers. General orders in 1777 declared: "This offence is of the most enormous and flagrant nature, and not admitting of the least palliation or excuse, whosoever are convicted thereof, and SENTENCED TO DIE, may consider their EXECUTION CERTAIN and INEVITABLE."[32] To combat the problem, recruiters enforced a color-

30. PHILADELPHIA IN CONGRESS, April 14, 1777, *The Pennsylvania Gazette*, April 23, 1777.

31. Joseph Plumb Martin, *A Narrative of a Revolutionary Soldier: Some of the Adventures, Dangers, and Sufferings of Joseph Plumb Martin* (Signet Classics, 2010), 8.

32. General Orders, Headquarters Morristown, February 6, 1777, PHILLADELPHIA, *The Pennsylvania Gazette*, February 19, 1777.

coded ribbon system for new enlistees to wear on their hats, signifying they had already enlisted. New recruits had to wear the ribbon until the regiment fully assembled and joined the army, or they risked a punishment of "thirty-nine lashes."[33]

Competition with the localized military organizations detracted from Continental recruiting efforts. Many would-be soldiers, upon hearing rumors of harsh conditions in the Continental army, preferred to join independent state regiments, similar to militia, as well as privateering outfits that paid more and provided shorter enlistment terms. Washington was keenly aware of this problem, commenting: "It is in vain to expect that any (or more than a trifling) part of this Army will again engage in the Service . . . When Men find that their Townsmen & Companions are receiving 20, 30, and more Dollars for a few Months Service" in state militias.[34] Militia and state regiments offered young men with competitive options for enlisting. As Washington observed, motivations for service changed from patriotic fervor to more realistic interests such as pay.

In conjunction with recruiting, reenlistment was among the most challenging personnel issues. The army's three major personnel crises in 1776, 1777, and 1780 each corresponded directly to expiring enlistment terms. Washington referenced this issue: "Our inlistment goes on slowly by the returns last Monday, only 5,917 men are engaged for the insuing campaign; and yet we are told that we shall get the number wanted as they are only playing off, to see what advantages are to be made, and whether a bounty cannot be extorted either from the publick at large, or Individuals."[35] Soldiers waited until the last possible moment to reenlist, gaming the system, to see if they could maximize their benefits.

Short enlistments were a root cause of personnel shortages. This was among Washington's most frequent complaints, as he wrote: "No man dislikes short and temporary enlistments more than I do — No man ever had greater cause to reprobate and even curse the fatal policy of the measure than I have."[36] At the war's start, enlistment in the Continental army was for one year, but the diverse state regiments and militias had even shorter enlistment terms. Even one year enlistments were too long for some prospective soldiers, as Joseph Plumb Martin recalled

33. Ibid.
34. Washington to Hancock, September 22, 1776, Lengel, *This Glorious Struggle*, 68-69.
35. Washington to Reed, December 15, 1775, *Letters from Washington to Joseph Reed*, 29.
36. Washington to Reed, August 22, 1779, *Letters from Washington to Joseph Reed*, 127-128.

in 1776: "Soldiers were at this time enlisting for a year's service; I did not like that, it was too long a time for me at the first trial; I wished only to take a priming before I took upon me the whole coat of paint for a soldier."[37] Martin's first enlistment was for only six months in a unit he referred to as one of the "new levies." Martin's remark likely captured the general thinking of many prospective soldiers. While Martin reenlisted and endured the entire war's duration, many other soldiers did not.

Washington advocated for both a national draft and for enlistments to last for the war's full duration on multiple occasions. He wrote, "nothing is now left for it but annual and systematical mode of drafting ...I see no other substitute."[38] Congress did not attempt to implement a national draft; they left that decision up to the states. In the winter of 1777, Congress successfully extended a standard Continental army enlistment term to three years or "the duration of the war." This effectively staved off the next manpower shortage until 1780.

Disputes over expiring enlistments had disastrous consequences. Alongside crippling logistical and supply deficiencies, enlistment contracts and soldiers' pay were two most common causes for mutinies. At least fifteen major mutinies occurred during the war.[39] The largest occurred in the Pennsylvania Line on January 1, 1781, in Morristown, New Jersey. Two entire brigades, 1,500 rank and file soldiers, threatened to march on Congress in Philadelphia.

The soldiers complained their three-year enlistments were over, and they had not been paid for an entire year. Their commanding officer, Gen. Anthony Wayne, was not entirely surprised by the mutiny as he wrote months before it occurred: "Our soldiery are not devoid of reasoning faculties ... Trifling as it is, they have not seen a paper dollar in the way of pay for near twelve months."[40] The mutiny only ended when Joseph Reed, governor of Pennsylvania, personally negotiated the mutiny's end by giving in to the soldiers' demands. Over 1,300 soldiers were discharged from the army peaceably.[41]

The challenges in recruitment and reenlistment, as well as disputes of enlistment terms and ensuing mutinies, suggested that the primary motivation for enlisted soldiers in the Continental army may not have

37. Martin, *Narrative*, 15.
38. Washington to Reed, August 22, 1779, *Letters from Washington to Joseph Reed*, 127-128.
39. Neimeyer, *America Goes to War*, 164.
40. Anthony Wayne to Reed, December 16, 1780, *Life and Correspondence of Joseph Reed. Vol II* (Philadelphia: Lindsay and Blakiston, 1847), 316-317.
41. Neimeyer, *America Goes to War*, 151.

been purely patriotism, but that more tangible concerns motivated a diverse group of enlistees.

THE ARMY'S DEMOGRAPHY AND SOLDIERS' MOTIVATIONS

After the initial patriotic fervor waned, recruitment efforts evolved by increasingly relying on coercion such as state drafts and pulling from society's lower strata. The initial recruiting instructions from Horatio Gates "excluded all Negroes, vagabonds, British deserters, and immigrants."[42] The exact opposite happened. To fill their quotas, recruiters could not be so discerning in their prospective enlistees. An estimated 90 percent of privates came from the poorest two thirds of the taxable population, especially from foreign immigrants. Irish immigrants accounted for as much as 25 percent of the total army, and as high as 45 percent of Pennsylvania's recruits. German immigrants, including Hessian deserters from the British army, accounted for 12 percent of the Continentals. There was even a "German Battalion" from Pennsylvania.[43]

The Continental army also crossed racial barriers, becoming America's first racially integrated army. Disregarding official instructions, some states recruited African Americans, both slave and free, to fill their quotas. Some slave-owners sent their slaves as substitutes for the state draft. By 1778, a special return from Adjutant General Alexander Scammel reported 586 African Americans out of a total of 14,509 men (4 percent). As many as 5,000 African Americans served in the Continental army throughout its existence.[44]

Beyond crossing boundaries on race, the army's personnel also centered on youth. In one revealing letter, Washington complained: "I shall cut in it, when Inform you, that excepting about 400 recruits from the State of Massachusetts (a portion of which, I am told, are children hired at about 1500 dollars each for 9 months service)."[45] The official age range to enlist was sixteen to sixty, but many recruiters felt free to bend the rules.[46] Enlisted soldier Joseph Plumb Martin's memoir confirmed this; he was only fifteen when he enlisted in 1776. Martin further recollected that peer pressure among youth was a significant factor. He recalled of his experience upon enlisting: "the old bantering began,

42. Quoted in Nelson, *General Horatio Gates*, 43.
43. Neimeyer, *America Goes to War*, 19, 37-38, 50, 64.
44. Noel B. Poirier, "A Legacy of Integration: The African American Citizen – Soldier and the Continental Army," *Army History* no. 56 (Fall 2002): 16-25, 21, 24.
45. Washington to Reed, July 29, 1779, *Letters from Washington to Joseph Reed*, 122.
46. John Ruddiman, *Becoming Men of Some Consequence: Youth and Military Service in the Revolutionary War* (Charlottesville and London: University of Virginia Press, 2014), 7.

come if you will enlist I will, says one," as he recalled his own peers jostling his hand to sign the official papers. Martin later called enlisting his "heart's desire," expressing a youthful sense of grand adventure as part of his decision.[47]

Patriotic notions like freedom from Britain's economic tyranny may not have been the prime motivation for many enlistees. More likely, they were motivated by steady pay, meals, clothing, and social advancement. Long term service to the army was an unyielding hardship. This made the matter of financial compensation all the more urgent.

SOLDIERS' PAY

Hamstrung by a weak national authority, the Continental Congress and army were continuously unable to appropriately pay their soldiers during the war. Washington reflected on this issue: "In modern wars, the longest purse must chiefly determine the event—I fear that of the enemy will be found to be so."[48] Pay never ceased to be an issue. The lack of pay compounded all other personnel challenges. It further hindered recruitment and reenlistment, and it added to the reasons for mutinies, desertion, and indiscipline. Had the army not successfully coped with this issue, the army could have very well dissolved before its opportunity to turn the tide of the war at Yorktown.

The army used a bureaucratic structure to pay its soldiers. Army paymasters took the total numbers from their units' strength returns to request lump sums from Congress. Upon receipt, paymasters disbursed paper money to soldiers in their commander's presence. Commanding officers verified and signed monthly payroll reports recording soldiers pay due, advances, and balances. Standard pay for a private soldier in the infantry was six and two-thirds dollars per month.[49]

Correspondence from army paymasters reveals a never-ending catch-up game. The total expenses for the army between January and May 1780 amounted to $1,690,000.[50] Paymaster James Pierce com-

47. Martin, *Narrative*, 15-17.
48. Washington to Reed, May 28, 1780, *Letters from Washington to Joseph Reed*, 139.
49. Neimeyer, *America Goes to War*, 123.
50. James Pierce to the Board of Treasury, Morristown, May 6, 1780. Saffell, W.T.R., G. Washington, C. Lee, N. Greene, and United States Continental Congress, *Records of the Revolutionary War: Containing the Military and Financial Correspondence of Distinguished Officers; Names of the Officers and Privates of Regiments, Companies, and Corps, with the Dates of Their Commissions and Enlistments; General Orders of Washington, Lee, and Greene, at Germantown and Valley Forge; with a List of Distinguished Prisoners of War; the Time of Their Capture, Exchange, Etc. To Which Is Added the Half-Pay Acts of the Continental Congress; the Revolutionary Pension Laws; and a List of the Officers of the Continental Army Who Acquired the Right to Half-Pay, Commutation, and Lands* (Pudney & Russell, 1858), 66.

plained to the Board of Treasury in 1780, "I made a return for a million and a half dollars to pay the army for January and February, and have received only 500,000 dollars, being the whole that was in the treasury!"[51] Paymasters were forced to prioritize which units must be paid, and which could wait. For example, paymasters' letters included lines such as: "I rather think they will not spare any money for your department at present, as there are other demands more pressing," and "necessities of the two latter [departments] seem not to be very pressing."[52] Even if they had the money on hand, it may not have done much good due to massive inflation.

As the war ground on, the already weak dollar became worthless. Congress introduced thirty-one million dollars into the American economy by the end of 1777.[53] Its value depreciated quickly. In 1780, one-hundred dollars was equivalent to the value of seventy-four cents in 1775.[54] Congress issued depreciation certificates as a reactionary measure to assure soldiers their pay would not be worthless. By 1781, the monetary system was in complete freefall, with Continental currency not even being accepted as legal tender.[55]

The financial system's collapse severely impacted the war. Washington himself was content to serve without pay, but common soldiers were not so self-sacrificing. Speaking on the soldiers' dependence on money, Washington wrote: "there is no Nation under the sun, (that I ever came across) pay greater adoration to money than they do."[56] As seen in the Pennsylvania Line mutiny, it was not uncommon for soldiers to go long periods without receiving any pay at all. The situation was so bad that Alexander Hamilton believed restoring financial health was more important than winning battles; he wrote to Robert Morris: "'Tis by introducing order into our finances—by restoring public credit—not by gaining battles, that we are finally to gain our object."[57] Congress needed to take action to save the war effort.

51. James Pierce to the Board of Treasury, April 10, 1780, *Records of the Revolutionary War*, 62.

52. J. Burrall to Col Udney, and Thos. Reed, *Records of the Revolutionary War*, 53, 49.

53. Wayne E. Carp, *To Starve the Army at Pleasure: Continental Army Administration and American Political Culture, 1775-1783* (Chapel Hill: University of North Carolina Press, 1984), 31.

54. Clifford Rogers, Ty Seidule, and Samuel Watson eds., *The West Point History of the American Revolution* (New York: Simon & Schuster, 2017), 186.

55. Neimeyer, *America Goes to War*, 126.

56. Washington to Reed, February 10, 1776, *Letters from Washington to Joseph Reed*, 61.

57. Alexander Hamilton to Robert Morris, April 30, 1781, Founder's Online, founders.archives.gov/documents/Hamilton/01-02-02-1167.

Robert Morris, who became Congress's superintendent of finance in 1780, played an invaluable role in addressing the pay issue. No single person had more impact on soldiers' pay. He invested his own personal fortune and credit to pay the army on multiple occasions where he saved the army with immediate short-term financial fixes.

Morris's actions were vital to the army's success at Yorktown in 1781. Washington's army, having linked up with French allies under General Rochambeau, marched over 450 miles south to seize the moment at Yorktown. Stopping in Philadelphia, Washington worried a lack of funds would prevent the army's movement south and that unpaid soldiers may threaten mutiny. Washington implored Morris: "I must entreat you if possible to procure one month's pay in specie . . . those troops have not been paid anything for a very long time past, and have upon several occasions shewn marks of great discontent . . . but I make no doubt that a douceur of a little hard money would put them in proper tempter."[58] Scrambling to save the situation, Morris secured massive French loans at the last minute, allowing him to pay the army in valuable hard coin.[59] Additionally, Morris committed his personal fortune and created "Morris notes," his own personal currency, to pay Philadelphian merchants and contractors to support the army's logistical needs on the drive south.[60] Robert Morris' decisive action in allaying the army's financial straits in 1781 directly contributed to the victory at Yorktown.

CONCLUSION

Coping with the army's personnel administration challenges was absolutely necessary to the revolution's success. Many historians explain that Americans did not win, but rather they just "did not lose."[61] By this, historians mean the Continental army by itself could never defeat the British. It was only French assistance that finally enabled the decisive blow at Yorktown. Comparatively, the British were never able to depart from their footholds in the coastal cities to eradicate the Continental army. In a sense, all the Continental army had to do was simply exist for the revolution to continue. Therefore, sustaining the army's

58. George Washington to Robert Morris, August 27, 1981, Founder's Online, founders. archives.gov/documents/Washington/99-01-02-06802.

59. Robert Morris to George Washington, September 6, 1781, Founder's Online, founders. archives.gov/documents/Washington/99-01-02-06906.

60. Charles Rappleye, *Robert Morris: Financier of the American Revolution* (New York: Simon & Schuster Paperbacks, 2010), 256-262.

61. John Shy, *A People Numerous and Armed: Reflections on the Military Struggle for American Independence* (New York: Oxford University Press, 1976), 12.

personnel was an imperative task. The army's strength reporting, recruitment and retention, and financial payment were existential functions to prosecuting the revolution.

Describing a scenario in which Britain could win the war, Washington wrote: "Administration may perhaps wish to drive matters to this issue."[62] The army successfully coped with major personnel challenges. They did so despite virtual financial disaster. Last-minute tactical maneuvers of paperwork prevented the army's total collapse. Often overshadowed by more visceral military aspects, personnel administration had a crucial place in the Continental army, as it does in every military today. Army administrators, including Congress, commanders, staff officers, aides, paymasters, recruiters, and common soldiers alike, made victory possible. As these officers understood, the heart of any army, its most important resource, is its people.

62. Washington to Reed, May 28, 1780, *Letters from Washington to Joseph Reed*, 140.

Sir Henry Clinton's Generalship

JOHN FERLING

"My fate is hard," Sir Henry Clinton remarked after learning that he had been named commander of the British army in May 1778, adding that he expected to someday bear "a considerable portion of the blame" for Britain's "inevitable" lack of success.[1]

There were good reasons for Clinton's pessimism. Not only was France entering the war as America's ally, but Lord George Germain, secretary of state for America, directed Clinton to abandon Philadelphia and detach eight thousand troops elsewhere, chiefly to St. Lucia. Despite being left with thousands of fewer troops than Britain had committed to America during the previous year, Clinton was ordered to act with the "utmost vigour," seek to retain Britain's hold on New York and Newport, endeavor to bring George Washington to battle, and initiate "an attack . . . upon the southern colonies."[2]

Four years later Clinton's premonition of disaster came true, as did his fear that he would be held responsible for Britain's debacle. In the wake of Yorktown he was assailed in England as having been irresolute

1. Sir Henry Clinton to the Duke of Gloucester, October 10, 1778, Series III: Letterbooks, Vol. 254, Sir Henry Clinton Papers, William L. Clements Library, University of Michigan (SHCP); Sir Henry Clinton, *The American Rebellion: Sir Henry Clinton's Narrative Of His Campaigns, 1775-1782, With An Appendix of Original Documents*, ed., William B. Willcox (New Haven: Yale University Press, 1954), 85-86; Andrew Jackson O'Shaughnessy, *The Men Who Lost America: British Leadership, the American Revolution, and the Fate of the Empire* (New Haven: Yale University Press, 2013), 213; William B. Willcox, "British Strategy in America, 1778," *Journal of Modern History*, no. 2 (June 1947) 19:109.

2. Lord George Germain to Clinton, February 4, March 8, 21, 1778, in K. G. Davies, ed., *Documents of the American Revolution*, 21 Vols. (Dublin: Irish University Press, 1972-1981), 13:235; 15:57, 60, 74-76; O'Shaughnessy, *The Men Who Lost America*, 213.

3. Solomon M. Lutnick, "The Defeat at Yorktown: A View from the British Press," *Virginia Magazine of History and Biography*, no. 4 (October 1964): 72:471-78; William B. Willcox, *Portrait of a General: Sir Henry Clinton in the War of Independence* (New York: Alfred A. Knopf, 1962), 448-55.

and overly cautious, and as a commander without a strategic plan.[3] In the 1960s, Clinton's biographer, William B. Willcox, in collaboration with a psychotherapist, went even further. They portrayed Clinton as craving power, though subconsciously he felt that "he ought not to have it." This profound conflict rendered Clinton "unable to use" the authority he possessed, resulting in a "paralysis of will" that doomed him to failure.[4] Most historians have since depicted Clinton as capricious, indecisive, inordinately tentative, muddled, ruinously inactive, lacking a strategic vision, or fatally inhibited by his sense of inadequacy. Summarizing the judgment of two generations of scholars, one wrote that Clinton was "his own worst enemy."[5]

Perhaps the time has come to take a fresh look at Clinton's generalship, one not tethered to psychohistory and that above all considers the perplexities he faced.

During his initial four months in command Clinton faced multiple crises. He responded audaciously to each emergency. Days after assuming command, Clinton complied with Germain's order to relinquish Philadelphia, marching his army to New York rather than taking it by sea, a choice made partially from a desire to bring on an engagement with Washington. His wish came true when the Continental army attacked at Monmouth. Clinton counterattacked, forcing the Americans to retreat and take up defensive positions. Repeated British assaults were repulsed and the day's battle ended without a victor. Given that his army, accompanied by nearly three thousand displaced Pennsylvanians, was strung out over several miles, Clinton concluded that another

4. Willcox, *Portrait of a General*, xiv-xv, 52-54, 123-24, 311, 319, 394-96, 405-6, 446-48, 501-4; Frederick Wyatt and William B. Willcox, "Sir Henry Clinton: A Psychological Exploration in History," *William and Mary Quarterly*, 3d ser., no. 1 (January 1959):16:3-26; William B. Willcox, "Sir Henry Clinton: Paralysis of Command," in George Athan Billias, ed., *George Washington's Opponents: British Generals and Admirals in the American Revolution* (New York: Morrow, 1969), 73-102.
5. Franklin Wickwire and Mary Wickwire, *Cornwallis and the War of Independence* (London: Faber and Faber, 1971), 336; Eric Robson, *The American Revolution In Its Political and Military Aspects, 1763-1783* (New York: W. W. Norton, 1966), 136; Piers Mackesy, *The War for America, 1775-1783* (Cambridge: Harvard University Press, 1965), 213, 409, 515; O'Shaughnessy, *The Men Who Lost America*, 214; Robert Middlekauff, *The Glorious Cause: The American Revolution, 1763-1789* (New York: Oxford University Press, 2007), 576; Stanley D. M. Carpenter, *Southern Gambit: Cornwallis and the British March to Yorktown* (Norman: University of Oklahoma Press, 2019), 71; Ian Saberton, *The American Revolutionary War in the South: A Re-evaluation from a British Perspective in the Light of the Cornwallis Papers* (Tolworth, England: Grosvenor House Publishing, 2018), 25; Don Higginbotham, *The War of American Independence: Military Attitude, Policies, and Practice, 1763-1789* (New York: Macmillan, 1971), 69.

day of fighting would gain nothing. He resumed his march, hopeful the enemy would attack again. Washington disappointed him.[6]

Within days, Clinton faced greater troubles. A superior French squadron under Vice Admiral Comte d'Estaing arrived, posing a threat to New York. The British escaped the peril when d'Estaing concluded that his warships were too heavy to enter New York Harbor, but also as a result of Clinton's hurried response. Before d'Estaing could imperil Britain's vessels shielding the harbor, Clinton rushed 1,800 men and artillery to Sandy Hook. According to the Royal Navy's second in command, d'Estaing was foiled because Clinton's speedy action doomed the French to "lose their ships" should they sail within range of the harbor.[7]

Clinton thereafter guessed correctly that the Allies would turn to Newport, occupied by 4,700 British troops under Sir Robert Pigot. Eleven days before the Allied commanders concurred on a Newport campaign, Clinton sent Pigot more than 1,800 troops, artillery, and sufficient provisions to sustain the garrison through a lengthy siege. The reinforcements were in place thirteen days prior to d'Estaing's arrival, eighteen days before additional troops sent by Washington joined Gen. John Sullivan—commander of the Continental army in Rhode Island—and more than three weeks before the last rebel militiaman appeared.[8]

The joint Allied campaign came to naught when a thunderous Atlantic storm crippled the French fleet and forced it to limp to Boston for repairs. However, Sullivan opted to remain on Aquidneck Island, hopeful that d'Estaing would soon return. Clinton spotted an opportunity and acted boldly. He personally led a force of 4,300 men toward Newport. Clinton's plan was to trap Sullivan's army of seven thousand on Aquidneck Island between Pigot's force, advancing from the south, and his own descending from the north.[9]

6. Clinton to Germain, June 5, July 5, 1778, Davies, *Documents*, 15:132, 159-63; Clinton, *American Rebellion*, 89-92, 98.

7. Comte d'Estaing to George Washington, July 17, 1778, Philander Chase, et al., eds., *The Papers of George Washington: Revolutionary War Series* (Charlottesville: University of Virginia Press, 1985—),16:90 (*PGWR*); Editor's Note, ibid., 16:69-70n; Clinton, *American Rebellion*, 100; Willcox, *Portait of a General*, 238-39.

8. Clinton, *American Rebellion*, 100-1; Washington to Marquis de Lafayette, July 27, 1778, *PGWR*, 16:185; Editor's Note, ibid., 16:178n; Christian M. McBurney, *The Rhode Island Campaign: The First French and American Operation in the Revolutionary War* (Yardley, PA: Westholme, 2011), 50-51, 72, 101-2.

9. Clinton to Germain, September 15, 1778, Davies, *Documents*, 15:200; Clinton, *American Rebellion*, 102-3; McBurney, *The Rhode Island Campaign*, 106-47, 152-69; Willcox, *Portait of a General*, 250.

Clinton's plans derailed when his voyage was slowed by contrary winds and Sullivan learned of the impending danger. The Americans evacuated the island less than twenty-four hours before Clinton arrived. By the narrowest of margins, said Clinton, Sullivan had escaped from "being very critically circumstanced."[10]

Throughout 1778, Clinton had acted intrepidly and ably, even spectacularly. He had responded to existential challenges in New York and Newport, and he had come within a whisker of inflicting a crumpling blow to a large American army on Aquidneck Island.

Although Germain repeatedly urged him to implement a new British strategy adopted following Saratoga, Clinton was less active in 1779. Britain's latest strategic plan—the southern strategy—aimed at retaking Georgia and South Carolina, and possibly North Carolina. If the rebellion in those colonies could be quashed, Britain might emerge from the war with a vibrant American empire that included Canada, trans-Appalachia, several southern colonies, and a bevy of sugar islands in the Caribbean. Once d'Estaing's fleet departed for the Caribbean late in 1778, Germain saw nothing to prevent Clinton from carrying out the plan.[11]

Clinton had a different, and not unreasonable, perspective. With the grave threats of 1778 behind him, he at last complied with his orders to relinquish a substantial chunk of his soldiery. The "very nerves" of his army "dissolved," said Clinton, despite likely rebel threats and d'Estaing's almost certain return in the summer. Clinton maintained that he needed fifteen thousand men to adequately defend New York against a joint Allied attack, but he possessed barely thirteen thousand. "My zeal is unimpaired," Clinton told Germain, but he insisted that until he was reinforced, he must "remain on a most strict defensive" footing.[12]

In fact, Clinton was not totally inactive. In December 1778 he dispatched three thousand men to retake Savannah, a campaign that succeeded spectacularly when the city fell and Georgia's royal government was restored.[13] In May 1779 a flotilla sent to plunder in Virginia sowed

10. McBurney, *The Rhode Island Campaign*, 170-205; Clinton, *American Rebellion*, 103.

11. Germain to Clinton, August 5,December 3, 1778, March 31, September 27, December 4, 1779, Davies, *Documents*, 15:177-78, 279; 17:89, 224, 257.

12. Clinton to Gloucester, October 10, 1778, Series III: Letterbooks, Vol. 254, SHCP; Clinton to Germain, July 27, September 15, October 8, 25, 1778, May 22, June 18, July 28, August 20, 1779 Davies, *Documents*, 15:173, 201, 210, 232; 17:129, 146, 170, 188-89; Clinton, *American Rebellion*, 119; 213; Willcox, *Portrait of a General*, 252-53.

13. Clinton to William Eden, February 5, 1779, in Benjamin F. Stevens, ed., *Facsimiles of Manuscripts in European Archives Relating to America, 1773-1783*, 25 Vols. (London: Malby and Sons, 1889-1895), 12: No. 1258; Clinton, *American Rebellion*, 116-19; Clinton to Germain, May 22, 1779, Davies, *Documents*, 17:129-30.

widespread destruction and liberated over five hundred slaves.[14] Later that month Clinton seized the enemy forts at Stony Point and Verplanck's Point that covered King's Ferry in the Hudson Highlands. As his successful strike impeded the enemy's movements and interrupted their communications, Clinton believed that Washington would have to risk "an action" to recover what had been lost. Washington called Clinton's act "one of the wisest measures" he had "yet pursued," but he shrank from a fight. All "we can do is lament what we cannot remedy," Washington remarked.[15]

Clinton considered an attack on West Point, an action that unquestionably would have forced Washington to fight. Both commanders understood that if West Point fell, Britain would control the Hudson River to Albany, detaching New England from the other states and dooming the American cause. The post, remarked Gen. Henry Knox, the Continental army's artillery chieftain, was "the object of greatest importance, on the Continent, and to the maintenance of which every thing else ought to give place."[16]

Horatio Gates, the American general, believed that Clinton could have captured the post had he acted immediately after his foray at King's Ferry. Knox, however, was confident that the fortress was "too strong . . . to admit even of an Attempt[ted siege] much less a storm."[17]

Clinton chose not to attack, but his decision was not due to a paralysis of will. Mindful that the enemy would spare nothing to safeguard West Point and unaware of the installation's defenses—other than that Washington had been given nearly four years to secure the citadel—Clinton rejected a chancy campaign that might substantially reduce the prowess of his already shrunken army on the cusp of d'Estaing's expected return.[18]

Clinton instead ordered destructive raids along the Connecticut coast, hopeful the sorties might draw Washington into the field. When

---

14. Clinton to Edward Mathew, May 20, 1779, Davies, *Documents*, 17:125; Clinton to Eden, May 20, 1779, Stevens, *Facsimilies*, 9: No. 997; John Selby, *The Revolution in Virginia, 1775-1783* (Williamsburg: Colonial Williamsburg Foundation, 1988), 204-8.

15. Clinton to Eden, June 17 and 18, 1779, Stevens, *Facsimilies*, 9:No. 999; Clinton, *American Rebellion*, 122-26; Washington to William Fitzhugh, June 25, 1779, *PGWR*, 21:242; Washington to Horatio Gates, June 11, 1779, ibid., 21:129-31.

16. Henry Knox to Washington, March 29, 1780, *PGWR*, 25:223.

17. Douglas Southall Freeman, *George Washington: A Biography*, 7 Vols. (New York: Charles Scribner's Sons, 1948-1957), 5:109; Knox to Lucy Flucker Knox, June 29, 1779, in Philip Hamilton, ed., *The Revolutionary War Lives and Letters of Lucy and Henry Knox* (Baltimore: Johns Hopkins University Press, 2017), 149.

18. Clinton to Germain, June 18, 1779, Davies, *Documents*, 17:146.

the American commander did not move, Clinton concluded that there was little "chance of forcing Washington to [a general] action."[19]

Since Savannah's fall the previous December, Germain had prodded Clinton to act to restore royal rule in South Carolina. Clinton, in turn, advised London that he would unleash the campaign in October when the miasmic southern summer ended. However, late that summer Clinton learned that d'Estaing was returning. Certain that the enemy's target was New York, Clinton consolidated his army, recalling the troops near King's Ferry and withdrawing all British forces from Rhode Island, a step that Germain had sanctioned.[20]

Clinton soon discovered that d'Estaing's objective was Savannah, though he believed that following his success there, the French admiral would sail for New York. Both Clinton and Washington prepared for that eventuality, but d'Estaing never came north. His assault on Savannah ended disastrously, after which he returned to France. An elated Clinton called d'Estaing's repulse "the greatest event that has happened [in] the whole war." Eager to take the field, Clinton, rapidly prepared for his long awaited move against Charleston. "This is the most important hour Britain ever knew," he said. "If we lose it, we shall never see such another."[21]

Britain could not have had a better-prepared leader for conducting the Charleston campaign. Clinton was contemplative, intellectually curious, a voracious reader—especially on military history and the art of war—and was widely regarded as a superior strategist. He had entered the army while in his teens, served with distinction in two conflicts before the War of Independence, and arrived in America shortly after Lexington and Concord. During the next three years Clinton compiled a commendable record, including command of a 1776 expedition that reclaimed Newport. When General John Burgoyne was trapped in New York in 1777, he appealed to Clinton for help. Clinton acted immediately, capturing three rebel forts well up the Hudson. At Fort Clinton, he spurred on his men "by scal[ing] the top of the mountain, himself carrying the British colors, which he kept holding aloft while his troops . . . carried the post." But as this occurred during Gen.

19. Clinton to Eden, September 4, 1779, Stevens, *Facsimilies*, 10: No.1066; Clinton to Gloucester, December 10, 1779, Series III: Letterbooks, Vol. 254, SHCP.
20. Germain to Clinton, September 25, 1778, March 21, September 27, 1779, Davies, *Documents*, 15:208; 17:89, 224; Clinton to Germain, August 21, September 26, 30, October 28,1779, ibid., 17:190, 222, 230, 236-37; Clinton, *American Rebellion*, 145-49, 152.
21. Clinton to Eden, November 19, December 11, 1779, Stevens, *Facsimiles*, 10: Nos. 1032, 1034.

William Howe's invasion of Pennsylvania, Clinton lacked the manpower and naval arm to save Burgoyne's ill-fated army.[22]

Just after Christmas, 1779, Clinton with 8,700 men sailed south and carried out a textbook siege of Charleston. It culminated in May with the surrender of more than five thousand American defenders. Clinton's triumph was America's Saratoga. He had accomplished more than any British commander in the six-year-old war, and his victory triggered celebrations throughout England. One onlooker thought Clinton was "the most *popular* man in England" and some believed his conquest enabled war-weary Britain to remain at war.[23]

A jubilant Clinton giddily exclaimed that he had "conquered the two Carolinas in Charleston." His confidence swelled when thousands of Loyalists signaled an eagerness to take up arms and the colony's former royal attorney-general advised that it would be "very practicable" to reestablish British control. [24] In June, Clinton put Charles, Earl Cornwallis, in charge of the pacification of South Carolina and Georgia, leaving him with nearly 8,500 regulars that he expected to be augmented by large numbers of Loyalists. Clinton felt that Cornwallis would have sufficient numbers to successfully complete his mission, unless a "superior fleet shows itself."[25]

22. Willcox, *Portrait of a General*, 3-39, 48; 115-16, 153-55; O'Shaughnessy, *The Men Who Lost America*, 215-20; Clinton, *American Rebellion*, 55-56, 61-62, 70-84; Marquis de Chastellux, *Travels in America in the Years 1780, 1781 and 1782*, Howard C. Rice, ed., 2 Vols. (Chapel Hill: University of North Carolina Press, 1963), 1:96.

23. Clinton to Germain, May 13, 1780, Davies, *Documents*, 18:86-89; Clinton, *American Rebellion*, 158-59, 164, 171, 177, 189; 171, 177, 189; Carl P. Borick, *A Gallant Defense: The Siege of Charleston, 1780* (Columbia: University of South Carolina Press, 2003), 34-36, 49-65, 71-73, 96-108, 121-26, 130-34, 145-60, 247-50; Jim Piecuch, *Three Peoples, One King: Loyalists, Indians, and Slaves in Revolutionary South Carolina, 1775-1782* (Columbia: University of South Carolina Press, 2008), 181; John S. Pancake, *This Destructive War: The British Campaign in the Carolinas, 1780-1782* (Tuscaloosa: University of Alabama Press, 1985), 148.

24. Clinton to Gloucester, May 12, 1780, Series III: Letterbooks, Vol. 254, SHCP; Clinton to Eden, May 12, 1780, Stevens, *Facsimilies*, 7: No. 726; Clinton to Germain, May 14, June 4, 1780, Davies, *Documents*, 18: 90, 102; James Simpson to Clinton, May 15, 1780, ibid., 18:94-95.

25. Clinton to Charles, Earl Cornwallis, June 1, 3, 1780, in Ian Saberton, ed., *The Cornwallis Papers: The Campaigns of 1780 and 1781 in the Southern Theater of the American Revolutionary War*, 6 Vols. (Uckfield, England: The Naval and Military Press, 2010), 1:56-64 (*CP*); Sir Henry Clinton, *Observations on Some Parts of the Answer of Earl Cornwallis to Sir Henry Clinton's Narrative* (1783), in Benjamin F. Stevens, ed., *The Campaign in Virginia, 1781: An Exact Reprint of Six rare Pamphlets on the Clinton-Cornwallis Controversy* (London: 4 Trafalgar Square, Charing Cross, 1888), 105; Willcox, *Portrait of a General*, 320. Hereafter *The Cornwallis Papers* are cited as Saberton, *CP*.

Meanwhile, convinced that Washington was likely in a "state of un-suspecting security" at Morristown, Clinton planned to assail his foe with land and naval forces when he came north. The plan went awry when the army in New York, unaware of the commander's intentions, landed troops in New Jersey, bogged down, and suffered heavy losses. Clinton had no choice but to call off his attack and extract the endan-gered force.[26] As at Aquidneck Island, ill fortune may have cheated Clinton out of a breathtaking achievement.

Nevertheless, Clinton was upbeat, even thinking the rebellion might be "near its end." The American economy had collapsed, morale ap-peared to be sagging within the enemy camp, a Franco-Spanish inva-sion of England had failed, and Cornwallis's initial reports were optimistic. Furthermore, Cornwallis destroyed General Gates's rebel army at Camden in August, the fourth crushing blow that the Amer-icans had experienced in the South in twenty months, with losses to-taling more than eight thousand.[27]

Amidst the tsunami of welcome tidings, an enemy naval squadron—which included a French army under General le Comte de Rocham-beau—arrived in Newport in July 1780. During the next two months Clinton faced crucial decisions about how to respond to the threat, and the choices he made provided fuel for the later charges that he was ir-resolute and inordinately cautious.

While the French fleet was still at sea, Clinton—hoping to assault Rochambeau before he could establish adequate fortifications—mobi-lized a force of six thousand that was to be unleashed the moment he learned of the enemy's arrival. But a crucial week passed between the French landing and Clinton's notification that his foe had come ashore. Furthermore, neither Clinton nor the navy was aware of the enemy's size. Both wanted more information before acting, which delayed the operation. Once they agreed to strike, further delays arose owing to the navy's need to take on water and its inability to sail due to adverse winds. By the time Clinton could move—three long weeks after the French landing—intelligence reported that Rochambeau commanded upwards of six thousand regulars, who would be augmented by rebel militia, and that all the while he had buttressed his defenses. Clinton knew of the excessive losses that d'Estaing's numerically superior force

26. Clinton, *American Rebellion*, 191-92.
27. Clinton to Eden, April 4, 1779, Stevens, *Facsimilies*, 12: No. 1280; Cornwallis to Clin-ton, June 30, August 23, 1780, Saberton, *CP*, 1:161-63; 2:15-16; Cornwallis to Clinton, August 21, 1780, Davies, *Documents*, 18:148-52; Clinton to Germain, August 25, 1780, ibid., 18:153-54; Germain to Clinton, September 27, 1779, ibid., 17:225.

had suffered when assaulting a smaller entrenched adversary at Savannah. He also recollected all too well the British catastrophe in attacking amateur colonials ensconced in entrenchments constructed the night before at Bunker Hill. Clinton cancelled the strike.[28]

A successful attack would have had a momentous impact on the course of the war. A massive failure would have erased the gains made at Charleston and bolstered American morale. No one can know what would have happened had Clinton attacked, although Rochambeau contended that twelve days after landing—which would have been at least five days, and probably more, before the British could have struck—his "position was rendered respectable."[29] In light of Rochambeau's assessment, Clinton appears to have made the proper choice.

Rhode Island would not go away. In mid-September, Admiral Sir George Rodney arrived with several ships of the line, causing some French leaders to give "themselves up for lost." Clinton initially saw things in the same light and pledged men for an attack, but his ardor soon cooled. The French had now been given seventy-five days to prepare their defenses. In addition, a siege was "impractical," both because Rodney could not stay for long and the British would have inadequate artillery, given that Clinton—fearing that Washington would assail Manhattan while thousands of British troops were elsewhere—was not about to remove his heavy guns from New York.[30] Victory would hinge on a bloody assault. Success was far from predicable.

However, Clinton did not turn away from fear of failure. He opted instead for an alternative that offered a bigger prize with far fewer losses. He now knew unequivocally that Benedict Arnold, who commanded West Point, was ready to defect and hand the installation to the British. The West Point option was virtually certain to be the least costly and, if Arnold's treachery succeeded, America's quest for independence would be thwarted.[31]

---

28. Clinton to Germain, August 25, 1780, Davies, *Documents*. 18: Clinton, *American Rebellion*, 198-208; Clinton to Marriot Arbuthnot, July 15, 22, 30, 1780, ibid., 443-45, 447; Arbuthnot to Clinton, July 16, 18, 23, 27, 1780, ibid., 444-46; Captain Henry Savage to Clinton, July 30, 1780, ibid., 446-47; Clinton to Eden, August 18, 1780, Stevens, *Facsimilies*, 7: No. 730; Clinton to Eden, August 14, 1780, Vol. 118, SHCP.
29. Jean-Baptiste-Donatien de Vimeur, Count de Rochambeau, *Memoirs of the Marshal Count de Rochambeau* (reprint, New York: New York Times, 1971), 9.
30. Intelligence Reports to Clinton, August 31, August [?], 1780, Vol. 120, SHCP; Clinton to Sir George Brydges (Admiral Rodney), September 18, 1780, in Godfrey B. Mundy, ed., *The Life and Correspondence of the Late Admiral Lord Rodney*, 2 Vols. (London: J. Murray, 1830), 1:397-400; Willcox, *Portrait of a General*, 337; William B. Willcox, "Rhode Island in British Strategy, 1780-1781," *Journal of Modern History*, no. 4 (December 1945): 17:313-14.
31. Clinton to Germain, October 11, 1780, Davies, *Documents*, 18:183-86; Clinton, *American Rebellion*, 214; Intelligence Report to Clinton, August 19, 1780, Vol. 118, SHCP; Clinton

Arnold's treasonous plan unraveled and Clinton's gamble failed, a misstep with possibly costly consequences for Britain's war effort. However, lacking a crystal ball, Clinton could not foresee that Arnold's act of betrayal would founder.

From this point forward Clinton focused on what he thought would someday be an inevitable Allied attack on New York and, more immediately, on the southern strategy. Cornwallis's early confidence had waned in the face of robust partisan resistance, prompting him, in September, to make an incursion into North Carolina. His object was to recruit Loyalists and close the supply routes through which essential provisions flowed to the guerrillas and rebel armies in the southern theater. His foray ended in October in disaster at King's Mountain.[32]

Despite that setback, Clinton for the first time entered a new year—1781—"sanguine in my hopes" that the war could be brought to a successful conclusion in the coming months.[33] One reason for Clinton's optimism was that he had rethought his southern strategy. The result was an imaginative plan. From the outset, Cornwallis's orders had been to concentrate on crushing the insurgency in South Carolina and Georgia. He might take steps to "recover North Carolina," but only so long as doing so was "consistent with the security" of South Carolina. Cornwallis's mission remained unchanged.[34]

Clinton, too, recognized the necessity of sealing the supply routes that ran into the low country, and in December he dispatched an army under Benedict Arnold to Virginia. In March, Clinton deployed a much larger army under General William Phillips to the Old Dominion. Phillips, with 5,500 men, was to establish a Chesapeake base, raid rebel supply depots, and interdict shipments of arms and munitions to South Carolina. Clinton also anticipated that Phillips's presence would compel Virginia to "call back" its militiamen in the Carolinas, facilitating Cornwallis's suppression of the rebellion in the low country.[35]

Memo to Arbuthnot, August [?], 1780, Vol. 120, ibid; Stephen Brumwell, *Turncoat: Benedict Arnold and the Crisis of American Liberty* (New Haven: Yale University Press, 155-232, 251-61, 302, 322-23); Nathaniel Philbrick, *Valiant Ambition: George Washington, Benedict Arnold, and the Fate of the American Revolution* (New York: Penguin Random House, 2016), 243-80.

32. Cornwallis to Clinton, July 15, August 6, 12, December 4, 1780, Saberton, *CP*, 1:170, 176-77, 180; 3:38.

33. Clinton, *American Rebellion*, 274.

34. Clinton to Germain, June 4, 1780, Davies, *Documents*, 18:102; Clinton to Cornwallis, June 1, 1780, Saberton, *CP*, 1:57, 61.

35. Clinton to Benedict Arnold, December 14, 1780, Saberton, *CP*, 3:55-56; Clinton to William Phillips, March 10, 24, April 20-30, April 30-May 3, 1781, Clinton, *American Rebellion*, 495-96, 502-3, 515-16, 518-19; ibid., 273, 276; William H. W. Sabine, ed., William Smith, *Historical Memoirs, From 26 August 1778 to 12 November 1783* (reprint, New York: New York Times, 1971), 405-6.

Clinton's plan broke down following Cornwallis's return to North Carolina early in 1781 to cope with a new rebel army under General Nathanael Greene. In engagements at Cowpens and Guilford Courthouse, and a fruitless pursuit of his adversary through North Carolina's backcountry, Cornwallis lost roughly 40 percent of his army. An even greater blow to Clinton's plan occurred in April when Cornwallis, in violation of his orders, abandoned South Carolina and marched to Virginia.

Clinton might have ordered Cornwallis to return to South Carolina, but he declined to take a step that would be contrary to the wishes of Germain. The American secretary, driven by the unrealistic notion that the "speedy suppression of the rebellion" in every state below the Potomac was within reach, now advocated "pushing our conquests" in Virginia. Clinton had never entertained the "smallest idea" of attempting to conquer that large and populous province. He lacked the resources for such an undertaking while simultaneously defending New York. Twice in April, Clinton cautioned Germain that posting a huge army in Virginia would be "attended with great risk unless we are sure of permanent superiority at sea." Indeed, since early in the year Clinton's plan had been to remove all but two thousand of the troops in Virginia during the summer, and in June he ordered Cornwallis to send artillery and nearly half of his army to New York. A month later, Clinton countermanded his order when he learned of Germain's "great mortification" that any troops were to be removed from Virginia.[36] Clinton's well-conceived plan for regaining two southern colonies had been reduced to shambles.

In the spring, he learned that a French squadron under Comte de Grasse would reach North America in late summer, posing a potential threat to Britain's forces in either Virginia or New York. Five times that summer Clinton sent warnings to Cornwallis to prepare for the menace he might face.[37]

Clinton was unaware of d'Grasse's intentions, but he thought New York was the admiral's likely target. He even believed that if d'Grasse came to the Chesapeake and discovered that Cornwallis had prepared

36. Germain to Clinton, November 9, 1780, March 7, May 2, 1781, Davies, *Documents*, 18:224; 20:76, 132; Clinton to Germain, April 5-20, April 23-May1, 1781, ibid., 20:105, 114; Sir Henry Clinton, Instructions to Major General Phillips, March 10, 1781, Clinton, *American Rebellion*, 495; Clinton to Phillips, March 24, 1781, ibid., 502-3; ibid., 235, 278; Clinton to Cornwallis, June 11, July 8, 1781, Saberton, CP, 5:96, 140.
37. Clinton to Cornwallis, June 8, 19, July 8, 15, 1781, Saberton, *CP*, 5:128, 135, 142; 6:21-22; Clinton to Cornwallis, August 2, 1781, Davies, *Documents*, 20:208-14.

"a respectable defense," the French admiral would opt instead to attack New York.[38]

From mid-summer onward, Clinton was immersed in the crisis that culminated at Yorktown, an outcome that led critics to saddle him with much of the blame for the disaster. Criticism of Clinton centered on three matters.

He was accused of committing "one of the foremost blunders of the war" by having not reinforced Cornwallis in Yorktown during the summer. But Clinton had no better idea of d'Grasse's intentions than did Rochambeau and Washington, who were preparing to fight in New York if the admiral came there and in Virginia if the Chesapeake was the fleet's destination. Clinton guessed that New York was d'Grasse's target, a conclusion based on captured enemy correspondence and uncannily good intelligence that Washington and Rochambeau had agreed in May to attack New York. The "enemy will *certainly* attack" New York, Clinton predicted. If mistaken, however, he was confident that Cornwallis would have stockpiled sufficient provisions to see his army through a longer period than de Grasse could remain in the Chesapeake.[39]

Clinton was also assailed for not having struck when the Franco-American armies rendezvoused above Manhattan in early July. But persuaded that the enemy would attack New York, Clinton was not about to emerge from the sturdy defenses the British had constructed during the past five years, formidable emplacements that were a factor leading Rochambeau to favor a Chesapeake campaign over assailing New York. Clinton also knew that when augmented by militia, the Allied armies would possess enormously superior numbers. Clinton feared, too, that should de Grasse arrive during his and the navy's absence, the door would be left open for the French squadron to seize control of New York Harbor.[40]

---

38. Clinton to Cornwallis, August 2, 1781, Davies, *Documents*, 20:213.

39. Ron Chernow, *Washington: A Life* (New York: The Penguin Press, 2010), 413; Roger Kaplan, "The Hidden War: British Intelligence during the American Revolution," *William and Mary Quarterly*, 3d ser., no. 1 (January 1990): 47:133; Conference at Dobbs Ferry, July 19, 1781, John C. Fitzpatrick, ed., *The Writings of Washington*, 39 Vols. (Washington: U. S. Government Printing Office, 1931-1944), 22:396-97; Donald Jackson, et al., eds., *The Diaries of George Washington*, 6 Vols. (Charlottesville: The University Press of Virginia, 1976-1979), 3:406, 407, 409-10; Clinton to Cornwallis, June 8, 11, 1781, Saberton, *CP*, 5:124, 96; Lee Kennett, *The French Forces in America, 1780-1783* (Westport, CT: Greenwood Press, 1977), 106-7; Clinton to Gloucester, September 20, 1781, Series III: Letterbooks, Vol. 254, SHCP.

40. Clinton to Germain, August 20, September 4, 1781, Davies, *Documents*, 20:217, 221-22; Clinton, *American Rebellion*, 320-28; Kaplan, "The Hidden War," *William and Mary Quarterly*, 47:134; Willcox, *Portrait of a General*, 399.

Clinton was additionally criticized for having failed to attack the Allied armies once they crossed the Hudson on August 19 and marched south. But for the next dozen days—until they crossed the Raritan River, the unmistakable sign that they were headed for Virginia—Clinton could only guess his enemy's intent. He studied contradictory intelligence reports and the enemy took steps to fool him, which to some degree succeeded. However, Clinton's judgment was shaped more by word from Rear Admiral Samuel Hood, who arrived in New York two days before the Allies crossed the Raritan. Hood, who sailed from the Caribbean several days after de Grasse's departure, had scouted the entrance to the Chesapeake on August 25 and concluded—quite accurately—that the French squadron was not there. Sailing in faster copper-bottomed vessels, Hood had beaten his prey to the Chesapeake, but Clinton and the naval officers thought the information meant that d'Grasse was en route to New York.[41]

On August 30, the Allied armies began crossing the Raritan. Britain's, and Clinton's, military disaster played out over the next two months. From his first day as commander, Clinton had feared that the hand he was dealt would deny him success and inescapably lead others to blame him for Britain's ultimate failure. He was prescient.

But history has judged Clinton unfairly. He was a good commander whose reputation has been scarred by groundless psychological conjectures that should be laid aside. Furthermore, scholarly characterizations of Clinton as indecisive and incorrigibly inactive ignore his swift and bold responses to the threats posed by Comte d'Estaing in 1778, his adept operation to trap Sullivan on Aquidneck Island, the countless efforts he made to bring Washington to battle, his capture of Savannah and Charleston, his initiatives aimed at impeding the flow of rebel supplies to the low country, and the numerous morale-eroding raids he ordered. He was unwilling to strike West Point and Newport, but a commander's wariness to attack enemy targets about which little is known is on the whole a commendable attribute. Although portrayed by some as having no strategic plan, Clinton devised a superb formula for subduing the insurgencies in Georgia and South Carolina, and possibly North Carolina. Had it not been for Germain, a British army of only two thousand would have been posted at Yorktown after mid-

41. Clinton, *American Rebellion*, 326-28; Samuel Hood to Clinton, August 25, 1781, ibid., 562; Clinton to Cornwallis, August 27, 1781, ibid., 562; Freeman, *George Washington*, 5:314; Kennett, *French Forces in America*, 132; Kaplan, "The Hidden War," *William and Mary Quarterly*, 47:136; Nathaniel Philbrick, *In the Hurricane's Eye: The Genius of George Washington and the Victory at Yorktown* (New York: Penguin Random House, 2018), 161, 305-6.

summer 1781, a force so small that the Allies might have disregarded it and opted instead for a siege of New York.

Had Clinton made different choices during the crucial summer of 1781, the Yorktown disaster might not have occurred. Had the Royal Navy not lost its supremacy at sea for the third time in four years—a matter over which Clinton had absolutely no control—Britain would almost certainly have escaped the catastrophe at Yorktown.

Despite the staggering manpower challenges he had faced, by the spring of 1781 Clinton thought—and Washington feared—that the war might end with Great Britain in possession of New York and two or more southern provinces. To that point, Clinton's generalship had brought Britain close to realizing the ends it initially sought after Saratoga.

Clinton's generalship, like that of Washington, was a mixture of bold action and prudent caution, and for the lion's share of the period after 1778 Clinton was the more active, more daring, and more successful of the two. Yorktown turned things upside down, making Washington an iconic figure and causing Clinton to be scorned as an unfit commander.

The Varick Transcripts and the Preservation of the War

JUSTIN MCHENRY

Five years into the war, with his papers piling up and stuffed into overflowing trunks that followed the general from headquarters to headquarters, George Washington took the extraordinary step of asking for help to organize and preserve these papers, seeing them for what they were, "valuable documents" of public importance, living histories of the fight for American independence. He reached out to Congress to approve the hiring of a team of clerks to organize, transcribe, and ultimately preserve this historical record.[1] The resulting project would come to be known as the Varick Transcripts.

The project, headed by Lt. Col. Richard Varick, ultimately created a backup copy of Washington's official papers created during the American Revolution, and brought order to a large amount of material that had been schlepped around with the general from Virginia to Boston to New York, New Jersey, Pennsylvania and elsewhere. This would make it the first act of archival work sanctioned by the new country.

Throughout the war, Washington employed a small but impressive team of aides who were in charge of handling the bureaucratic morass that comes with managing a large army spread up and down the east coast from Quebec to Florida and out to the western frontiers. These administrative officers were responsible for drafting correspondence (to Congress, individual members of Congress, foreign dignitaries, state and local leaders, officers, etc.), all orders issued from Washington to his subordinates in all of the various departments, notes and proceedings taken during councils of war, and many other types of records.[2]

1. George Washington to Samuel Huntington, April 4, 1781, founders.archives.gov/documents/Washington/99-01-02-05289.
2. John C. Fitzpatrick, "The Aides-De-Camp of General George Washington," *Daughters of the American Revolution Magazine* LVII, no. 1 (January 1923): 11.

Over the course of the war, thirty-two aides served under Washington with four to seven working for the general at any given time. Typically, they were young, most in their twenties. The tasks laid upon these administrative officers were enormous: crafting a dozen or more letters a day, one to four pages in length, issuing general orders, delivering those orders, entering daily expense accounts, disbursing public funds, planning military campaigns, and worrying about supplying troops with food, clothing, and arms, ready at a moment's notice to pack it all in, march elsewhere and start in a new place the next day.[3] There was a near-endless stream of paper coming in and out of Washington's headquarters at any time. At the start of the war, importance was placed upon correspondence as time and care ensured that copies of letters and orders were entered into books in a neat and orderly fashion, but these formalities quickly devolved into a careless jumble until they stopped being copied into the books at all.[4]

After the retreat of his Army from New York City in August 1776, Washington boxed up his papers, thinking it best to keep them further away from British forces, and had them shipped to Congress, then in Philadelphia, to look after.[5] They would remain with Congress, even moving around with them as they adjourned to York, Pennsylvania. The boxes seem to have been misplaced or forgotten as they eventually ended up in Reading, Pennsylvania.[6] Meanwhile, the war churned on producing more and more records. With each move of headquarters, Washington's personal guard, Maj. Caleb Gibbs, packed the records up to be sent to the next location.[7] In February 1779, after the rediscovery of the older papers in Reading, Washington called for those papers to rejoin him.[8]

Two more years passed before Washington sought a solution to his growing records management problem. He related the poor state of his papers to President of Congress Samuel Huntington, and let it be known that his aides could not keep up with registering new records; now everything "remain in loose sheets; and in the rough manner in

3. Fitzpatrick, "The Aides-De-Camp of General George Washington," 11.
4. Ibid., 1-2.
5. Washington to John Hancock, August 13, 1776, founders.archives.gov/documents/Washington/03-06-02-0003.
6. Timothy Pickering to Washington, January 16, 1779, founders.archives.gov/documents/Washington/03-19-02-0010.
7. Fitzpatrick, "The Aides-De-Camp of General George Washington," 16.
8. Washington to Richard Peters, February 17, 1779, founders.archives.gov/documents/Washington/03-19-02-0230. Washington to Anthony Walton White, February 17, 1779, founders.archives.gov/documents/Washington/03-19-02-0234.

which they were first drawn." Cross-referencing or even finding records became nearly impossible and the situation had "a tendency to expose them to damage and loss."[9]

To rectify this, Washington proposed employing a team of transcribers to record and organize his records in what amounted to preserving them under the supervision of a "man of character in whom entire confidence can be placed."[10] It was not out of character for Washington, a man who took an active interest in the preservation and maintenance of his records, going so far as setting aside money and land in his will for the purpose of erecting a presidential library to house all of these records.[11] That there exists so many of his records, from his childhood up to his death, shows a dedication to preserving his legacy (and maybe even to shaping that legacy). It is no coincidence that as he prepared to get his papers in order, Washington decided to begin a war time diary. The two acts showcase his desire to tell his story, his way.

Upon reception of Washington's request, Congress passed a resolution on April 10, 1781 to hire another aide to alleviate the problem and bring some semblance of order to the papers. Things moved quickly in finding just the right man of character for the position.[12] After a month Washington settled on offering the position to Richard Varick, who accepted the offer only after discussing it with New York's wartime governor, George Clinton. Varick vacillated on taking the position, fearing that he wouldn't be able to find the right people, or anyone, to help him out with the enormous task. Armed with Clinton's assurances of help, Varick acquiesced.[13]

That Varick was the choice was auspicious as just months before he had faced court martial for being caught up in Benedict Arnold's treason drama. His selection was as much a testament to his commitment to the Continental cause as a demonstration of his excellent bureaucratic acumen. Varick enjoyed a quick rise through the ranks from joining the Army in the summer of 1775 and almost immediately became Gen. Philip Schulyer's military secretary, serving alongside him during the Canada campaign. In addition to his duties as a private secretary,

9. Washington to Huntington, April 4, 1781.
10. Ibid.
11. Dorothy S. Eaton, *Index to the George Washington Papers* (Washington, DC: Library of Congress, 1964), vii.
12. Samuel Huntington to Washington, April 14, 1781, founders.archives.gov/documents/Washington/99-01-02-05399.
13. Richard Varick to Washington, May 25, 1781, founders.archives.gov/documents/Washington/99-01-02-05867.

he served as quartermaster for all northern forts and as the Northern Army's deputy muster master general.[14]

During this time working closely with the Northern Army, he became friendly with Arnold. Military politics being what they were, when Horatio Gates replaced Schulyer as commander of the Northern Army Varick was left without a position. He took the opportunity to return to studying and practicing law. Arnold approached Varick during this lull and asked him to be his aide-de-camp at West Point. Three months later Arnold was found out to be a traitor and Varick was under arrest.[15]

While Varick was Arnold's aide his commander's behavior and actions raised many red flags, which were later confirmed. Varick's court-martial enabled him to showcase his lawyering skills by supplying the court with corroborating testimonies as well as eleven letters attesting to his character, ability and honesty. At a board of inquiry held early in November 1780, he was acquitted when no evidence was presented that he had anything to do with Arnold's actions.[16] With his name cleared, Varick entered back into private practice in New York for the next six months, before being summoned back into service by Washington in May 1781.

Washington wasted little time after receiving Varick's acceptance, appointing him recording secretary in a reply the same day, providing salary information, the authority to requisition supplies, and the use of two houses to do the job. In a separate letter, Washington provided detailed instructions on how he wanted the papers organized:

Instructions to the Recording Secretary at Head Quarters.

1. All Letters to Congress, Committees of Congress, the Board of War, Individual Members of Congress in their public Characters and American Ministers Plenipotentiary at Foreign Courts, are to be classed together and to be entered in the Order of their Dates.

2. All letters, Orders and Instructions to Officers of the line, of the Staff, and all other Military Characters, to compose, a second Class, and to be entered in like manner.

3. All Letters to Governors, Presidents and other Executives of States, Civil Magistrates and Citizens of every Denomination, to be a third Class and entered as aforementioned.

14. Paul Cushman, *Richard Varick: Revolutionary War Soldier, Federalist Politician, and Mayor of New York* (Albany: State University of New York Press, 2010), 12, 20.
15. Ibid., 65-66.
16. Ibid., 79-82.

4. Letters to foreign ministers, Foreign officers, and subjects of Foreign Nations not in the immediate service of America, in Virtue of Commissions from Congress, to compose another Class.

5. Letters to Officers of every Denomination in the service of the Enemy, and to British subjects of every Character with the Enemy, or applying to go in to them.

6. Proceedings of Councils of War in the Order of their Dates.

The Secretary is to assort and prepare these papers to be registered by different Clerks. He is to number and keep a List of his Deliveries of them to those persons, takg recets for them. The Lists are to specify the Dates, and to whom the Letters are directed; by which the papers after they are registered are to be carefully returned by the Clerks to the secretary, who is to compare them with the Books of Entries, and to have them neatly filed in the Order they are registered, or in such other manner, as that references may be more easily had to them. Clerks who write a fair [Hand], and correctly, are to be employed; and that there may be a similarity and Beauty in the whole execution, [all the] writing is to be upon black lines equidistant. All the Books to have the same Margin, and to be indexed in so Clear and intelligent a manner, that there may be no difficulty in the references. The Clerks must be sworn, or be upon their Honour, to be careful of the papers. To give no Copies without permission, or suffer any thing be taken with their privity or Knowledge.

Letters to me are to be Classed, in the same order as those from me, indorsed and filed in neat Order, and of easy access.

All Files are to be upon Formers of the same size, that the Folds may be the same, and the [Storage] (in proper Boxes) close and compact.

All Returns are to be properly assorted, arranged and treated in the same way. So are papers of [every other] Class, and the whole to be organized in such a manner, as that easy references may be had to them.

If you are not already furnished with a sufficient number of Books, you will apply to the Quarter Master General for as many more as you shall find necessary to compleat your Entries. All the Books are to be of the same size.

G.W.[17]

These instructions formed the road map used by Varick throughout the two and a half years it took to complete the project, describing the final shape into which the logbooks would be organized.

Varick visited Washington's headquarters at New Windsor, New York, and collected the trunks (fifteen in total of various sizes) full of

17. Washington to Varick, May 25, 1781.

records and various other items such as the general's bed, saddle and bridle, and a large map of South Carolina and Georgia.[18] He then moved to Poughkeepsie, New York to begin the project there in the house of Dr. Peter Tappen, the brother-in-law of Governor Clinton, whom he referred to as an "honest patriot." The governor provided Varick a guard to protect the sensitive records and the work being done.[19] Writers on the project had to take an oath not to disclose any information found in the documents they were transcribing, an early form of a security clearance.[20]

According to everyone who had an opinion on the matter this was the most dreadful job in America at the time. Comment after comment noted how terrible and excruciating it was for a person to spend their time copying letters into a book. Varick referred to the job as "a perfect and unremiting Drudgery."[21] Tench Tilghman, one of Washington's aides, related it to walking through "mud and mire,"[22] while one of Varick's potential assistants, John Stagg, Jr. called it "siege" work[23] (he did not accept Varick's offer to join the project). None of these complaints or comments on the work ever made it directly to Washington.

Varick the middle-manager had to deal with unique personnel problems. The first was trying to find a schedule that worked for everyone. The writing team would settle into an eight hour work day that consisted of working four hours in the morning, taking a two hour lunch break, and finishing off the day with four more hours of work. This was met with complaints from the writers as 8 AM proved too early for some (who were not able to wake up, eat breakfast and make it into the office by eight) and as the days grew shorter 6 PM was too late as there wasn't enough natural light to read and write with.[24] To be more

18. Varick to Washington, August 21, 1781, founders.archives.gov/documents/Washington/99-01-02-06748.

19. Varick to Washington, July 19, 1781, founders.archives.gov/documents/ Washington/99-01-02-06453.

20. Zack Lukels to Varick, July 25, 1781, *Richard Varick Papers, 1743-1871, Series I: Correspondence, 1775-1830, Subseries I: Letters received*, New York Historical Society, digitalcollections.nyhistory.org/islandora/object/islandora%3A116836.

21. Varick to Jonathan Trumbull, Jr., December `8, 1781, founders.archives.gov/documents/Washington/99-01-02-07557.

22. Tench Tilghman to Varick, July 21, 1781, founders.archives.gov/documents/Washington/99-01-02-06478.

23. J. Stagg, Jr. (probably John Stagg, Jr.) to Varick, June 15, 1781, digitalcollections.nyhistory.org/islandora/object/islandora%3A115876.

24. Varick to Washington, October 1, 1781, founders.archives.gov/documents/Washington/99-01-02-07071.

flexible Varick allowed his writers comp time to make up hours when they needed to.[25]

The work consisted of an early version of scanning files, which falls in line with what modern archives do in creating a backup of records while preserving, organizing and maintaining the original. Writers, as they were called, were assigned certain sets of records to transcribe. They recreated documents in letterbooks, trying to match the text precisely, a job they did well. John C. Fitzpatrick, editor of *The Writings of George Washington*, commented upon the small amount of errors between the actual text and the transcripts. Mainly, the errors amounted to minor spelling, capitalization, and punctuation deviations.[26]

Varick meanwhile did quality checks of their work, made lists of letters and copies for the writers to follow, crafted a common naming convention, numbered the letters, organized them into the proper locations, and fulfilled any request for records that came in.[27] It was a daunting task for the lawyer and it fast became apparent that this job was bigger than anyone really expected: "much more time is necessary to the business, than either your Excellency or myself was aware of, when I accepted the Office."[28] Which sounds like he had no idea what he was in for and shows a semblance of second thoughts.

For the most part the work itself continued fairly steadily. Pay for Varick and the writers was always an issue, with Varick sending many missives to Washington asking for him to intervene with Congress for back pay. This led to some writers leaving the project and others on the project becoming troublesome for attempting to rile up the others. Along with pay there was also grumbling over rations and forage that they were promised. Varick met all of this with a firm hand (or at least that is what he reported to Washington) to show them that "I am not anxious about their services and that Trifling will [not] be put up with."[29]

Throughout the process, Varick reached out to Congress and the states and individuals to fill in gaps he identified in the record[30] and

25. Varick to Washington, December 18, 1781, founders.archives.gov/documents/Washington/99-01-0207556.

26. John C. Fitzpatrick, ed., *The Writings of George Washington*, Vol. 27 (Washington DC: Library of Congress, 1932), 289, babel.hathitrust.org/cgi/pt?id=mdp.39015011913475&view=1up&seq=21&skin=2021.

27. Varick to Washington, October 1, 1781.

28. Ibid.

29. Varick to Washington, October 6, 1781, founders.archives.gov/documents/Washington/99-01-02-07112.

30. Varick to Washington, February 21, 1782, founders.archives.gov/documents/Washington/99-01-02-07858.

worked with Washington and his staff to be sent the paperwork currently being generated and not yet at Poughkeepsie.[31]

In total, the project spanned over two and a half years of work, organizing and transcribing and cross-referencing. Only one writer would stick it out over the entire period of the project, Zachariah Sickels. There were as many as three writers working under Varick at any one time, while most of the time it was Varick and two other writers.

As the work pushed into 1783, the workload slackened and writers were allowed to leave or were released and recalled as new records came into their possession. Washington came in July 1783 to take away the first batch of boxes of his records.[32] The final shipment occurred in December of that year along with the forty-four bound letterbooks Varick and the writers had filled over those years. Washington expressed his "thanks for the care and attention which you have given to this business. I am fully convinced that neither the present age or posterity will consider the time and labour which have been employed in accomplishing it, unprofitable spent."[33]

The Varick Transcripts have served as a constant for that period in Washington's life. During his life and particularly afterwards researchers and others borrowed some documents for one purpose or another, such as John Marshall's biography of Washington or Eliza Hamilton pulling together all of Alexander Hamilton's writings. The papers themselves, along with the transcripts, were purchased by the State Department in 1833. They were eventually transferred to the Library of Congress in 1904, where they can still be found and viewed online, a vast and reliable source of knowledge of the Revolution and of Washington.[34]

LIST OF CLERKS WHO WORKED ON THE VARICK TRANSCRIPTS

Richard Varick
Zachariah Sickels
Oliver Glean
John Myer
Edward Dunscomb
Peter Hughes
George Taylor

31. Varick to Washington, January 14, 1782, founders.archives.gov/documents/Washington/99-01-02-07693.

32. Trumbull to Varick, July 12, 1783, founders.archives.gov/documents/Washington/99-01-02-11590.

33. Washington to Varick, January 1, 1784, founders.archives.gov/documents/Washington/04-01-02-0002.

34. Eaton, *Index to the George Washington Papers*, vii-xvii.

"A Mere Youth": James Monroe's Revolutionary War

JOHN A. RUDDIMAN

Late in his life, after retiring the presidency, James Monroe drafted his own history. He was still struck, five decades after the War for Independence, by the "high character of that epoch and of those in whose hands its destiny fell." He looked back and saw the war as "a school of practical instruction . . . in the knowledge of mankind, in the science of government." Of even greater importance, it planted in "the youthful mind the sound moral and political principles on which the success of our system depends."[1] This was a pretty standard assessment from the elders of that generation as they looked back over their era. We know Monroe's wartime service launched his political career and his life's work as a statesman. But the mechanics across these uncertain wartime moments deserve closer attention: what was this Virginia teenager thinking, feeling, and choosing? Rather than see his war in mind of the man who would become Thomas Jefferson's ally and who would serve as a senator, ambassador, governor, and president, what does Monroe's revolution look like when we see him as "a mere youth,"[2] which is how he later described himself? Examining Monroe's correspondence and his autobiography reveals this young Virginia gentleman building relationships with patrons, seeking distinction among his peers, and making choices to advance himself on his path towards manly independence in the middle of a war for national independence.

Considering James Monroe as a youth reveals the process of political and military mobilization in the American Revolution. Benjamin Franklin notwithstanding, the "Founding Fathers" were not old men.

1. James Monroe, *Autobiography of James Monroe*, ed. Stuart Gerry Brown (Stanford: Stanford University Press, 1959), 26.
2. Monroe, *Autobiography*, 3, 26.

In 1776, Alexander Hamilton was twenty-one, Thomas Jefferson thirty-three, George Washington forty-four. More significantly, half the American population was younger than sixteen; during the long war, military labor would have to be drawn from this youthful pool. James Monroe was born in 1758 into a propertied but unremarkable Virginia family. He only knew a British empire in turmoil. When James was seven, his father, Spence, protested the Stamp Act, along with practically everyone else in the colonies. But Spence died young in 1774, leaving James and his siblings under the direction of their politically connected maternal uncle, Joseph Jones. Sixteen-year-old James was sent down to college at William and Mary. Finding himself in the political center of Virginia while that community mobilized to resist Parliament's impositions, young James Monroe began training and drilling with a politicized militia. What did all this look like from this teenager's perspective? His actions speak loudly. Those militia drills answered the call for political action and Monroe's need for fraternity in a new place and community. These connections persisted. When the fighting began in 1775, Williamsburg patriots organized a raid on Governor Dunmore's palace to seize weapons. Monroe participated, apparently the youngest in this heist crew, which carried off 300 swords and 200 muskets. He volunteered, serving under the direction of more established leaders. Getting on six feet tall, shoulders broadening, and thoroughly expendable, Monroe was useful muscle. This escapade suggests two things: Monroe was both visible to his elders in the movement and he was eager to offer his assistance to them.[3]

Patriotic enthusiasm in 1775 demanded action, and Monroe's social station pointed him towards military service as an officer. He recalled in his autobiography that he continued to pursue his studies at college until January 1776 when he said it was "essentially shut up by the procession of the war." Along with his college roommate John Francis Mercer ("and," he wrote, "several other youths of great merit"), Monroe volunteered as a cadet in the 3rd Virginia Regiment in the expanded Continental Army. Gentlemen cadets were essentially unpaid interns—potentially too young to be granted an officer's commission, but with the social status and family connections to be worthy of audition and instruction. Monroe passed muster: he was soon after "appointed a Lieutenant."[4] An officer's commission relied on and ratified social rank—an officer was a gentleman. Stepping forward to defend his

3. Harry Ammon, *James Monroe: The Quest for National Identity* (New York: McGraw Hill, 1971), 5-7; see also Tim McGrath's new biography, *James Monroe, a Life* (New York: Dutton, 2020).
4. Monroe, *Autobiography*, 22.

country satisfied multiple demands: he displayed his patriotic resolve while grabbing a rung on the ladder of Virginia's hierarchy. To be a gentleman in Virginia was to be seen and judged. With the college closed and his family property held in trust by his uncle, what else was teenaged Monroe going to do to advance himself?

Patriotism was not incompatible with personal drive; a Massachusetts lieutenant captured at Bunker Hill explained his motives: "When this Rebellion came on, I saw some . . . Neighbors get into Commission who were no better than myself. I was very ambitious, and did not like to see those men above me . . . I offered to enlist upon having a lieutenant's commission . . . I imagined myself now in a way of Promotion: If I was killed in Battle, there would be an end of me, but if my Captain was killed, I should rise in rank, and should still have a chance to rise higher."[5] Young men across the continent knew the war could advance their prospects.

Revolutionary soldiers and junior officers were young men; on average, Virginia's continental soldiers were between twenty and twenty-one years old at enlistment.[6] Paul Fussell, a literary critic and World War II veteran, rather cynically remarked that "War must rely on the young, for only they have the two things fighting requires: physical stamina and innocence about their own mortality."[7] The *rage militiaire* of 1775 points out a third component at play in the Revolution: messianic political enthusiasm. Nobody believes likes a true-believing teenager—this appears to have been the case for James Monroe.

If Monroe was naïve about what war was, the battles of 1776 quickly disabused him. The 3rd Virginia Regiment marched to New York as the campaign exploded. A British fleet disgorged thousands of professional British and Hessian soldiers; at Brooklyn, Monroe remembered, the elite Maryland and Delaware regiments were "cut to pieces." It was blind luck that Monroe's regiment had not completed its march north sooner and met the same fate. On Manhattan, Monroe heard the news that the Connecticut militia broke and ran from the British at Kips Bay. The next day, the Virginians held at Harlem, "fighting gallantly"

5. Peter Oliver, *Origin and Progress of the American Rebellion* (San Marino: Huntington Library, 1963), 129-30; see also John Shy, *A People Numerous and Armed* (Ann Arbor: University of Michigan Press, 1990), 168-71.

6. John R. Sellers, "The Common Soldier in the American Revolution," in *Military History of the American Revolution,* edited by Stanley J. Underdal (Colorado Springs: Office of Air Force History, 1976), 156; see also John A. Ruddiman, *Becoming Men of Some Consequence: Youth and Military Service in the Revolutionary War,* (Charlottesville, VA: University of Virginia Press, 2014), 7.

7. Paul Fussell, *Wartime: Understanding and Behavior in the Second World War* (New York: Oxford University Press, 1989), 52.

to check the British advance. Monroe saw his officers killed in this engagement. He then retreated with Washington's army to White Plains and stood with the rear guard at Newark, counting only 3,000 soldiers pass. Of this desperate moment, Monroe recalled seeing George Washington: "at the head of a small band, or rather, in its rear, for he was always near the enemy, and his countenance and manner made an impression on me that time can never efface." Peering back through a hazy patina laid down by decades, Monroe insisted, "A deportment so firm, so dignified, so exalted, but yet so modest and composed, I have never seen in any other person."[8] It must have been a bright spot for the young lieutenant in this dark moment of the war.

It is striking that Lieutenant Monroe volunteered to go with the vanguard unit in the Christmas surprise attack on Trenton. Was it patriotism? Ambition? Both? It is telling that he put himself forward to serve under a fellow Virginian, Capt. William Washington. His Continental service was still entwined with his home state, the men he knew, and those local relationships. With fifty men, that company cut off communications to Trenton, then led in attacking the Hessian picket, shooting down their commander and taking the cannons that would have ended the war had they been brought to bear. When his captain was shot, command devolved onto Monroe; he did his duty, advancing "at the head of the corps" and then was shot in turn, falling with a severe shoulder wound. He had proved himself diligent and brave during a desperately hopeless campaign. Promoted to captain in recognition of his service, Monroe had seen and felt the costs of war. He was only eighteen years old.[9]

With this recognition and promotion, the meaning of the war shifted for Captain Monroe, presenting new possibilities and challenges. His first task in 1777 was recruiting soldiers for the company he would command. It did not go well. He complained to his first captain that "fortune" had not thrown "more than six men, who are willing to enter into the army" in his path. He boldly wrote that he preferred the "fatigue and danger" of active service to recruiting. Young Monroe clearly cared what people thought of him: "There seems to be too generally annexed to the character [of recruiters] the Idea of Insignificancy and indolence."[10] Without men to command, Monroe could have

8. Monroe, *Autobiography*, 23-24; Ammon, *James Monroe*, 9.
9. Monroe, *Autobiography*, 25-26.
10. Monroe to John Thornton, July 3, 1777. The Digital Edition of "The Papers of James Monroe" is a documentary editing project at the University of Mary Washington; their "Monroe Catalogue Online" provides access to approximately 38,000 entries detailing his correspondence. All letters referenced in this essay can be readily found in PDF transcription within this excellent digital compilation.

found himself idled at home at this point. Indeed, this had befallen the officer to whom he was writing. But Monroe got lucky: Gen. William Alexander, Lord Stirling, knew Monroe from the New York campaign and invited him to join his staff as an aide-de-camp. Eighteenth-century army staff were termed a general's "family"—with the implications of the young officers' dependence on their elders and the reciprocal patronage to be provided by the commander. By the end of August, Monroe could write to his first captain, "I live very agreeably with Lord Stirling." The rest of that letter is also telling—Monroe reported the units potentially in need of officers, but gently dissuaded his former captain from coming to headquarters in search of a position; there was already much competition for assignments.[11] Young Monroe the aide had become a conduit to the powerful. This partly made up for an aide's secretarial and dependent status. His responsibility, he later wrote, was "to bear the orders of his general to the troops . . . and when in camp, or on the march, to take those of the commander-in-chief . . . and report them to his own general."[12] In the field, an aide spoke with the voice and authority of his general; but as exciting as that might be for a nineteen year old officer, he wasn't issuing his own commands or holding his own authority. Monroe spent the campaigns of 1777 and 1778 serving the internal bureaucracy of the army and the household of General Stirling.

Monroe recalled that his service as Stirling's aide provided an unparalleled education. "Possessing the confidence of his general," Monroe wrote of himself in the third person, "he knew all the springs of action and the principles on which every movement turned." He "became acquainted with all the general officers of the army, with their aides, and with other officers in that circle . . . Their society gave him lessons of practical instruction."[13] This service brought a new perspective, too. Like many other Continental officers, he perceived the Revolution from within its only national institution (apart from the Congress): "the members who composed it came from all the states" and he noted its "tendency . . . to break down local prejudices and attach the mind and feeling to the union."[14] Of course, he also saw these officers wrangle over rank and seniority and duel each other over perceived slights to their honor. And he counted the continued bill of wounds and death delivered to friends old and new; action at Brandy-

11. Monroe to Thornton, August 25, 1777.
12. Monroe, *Autobiography*, 29.
13. Ibid., 31-32.
14. Ibid., 32.

wine wounded both his old college roommate John Francis Mercer and his new acquaintance, the nineteen year old Marquis de Lafayette. "Many others . . . personal friends" of his old regiment, Monroe recalled, "were wounded and some of them killed in that action."[15] In his memoir Monroe repeatedly returned to the danger and costs of the war imposed on the other young men around him.

These officers were young, ambitious men, and the course of their war was neither smooth nor predictable. By the summer of 1778, the French alliance, near-victory at Monmouth, and the stalemate between British and Continental forces in the north made it appear that winning American independence was only a matter of time. That it would take four more years would have shocked them. At this point, in 1778, many Continentals started looking toward moving up or getting out. Officer resignations accelerated again in late 1778; the private soldiers of 1777 followed them, ending their three year enlistments at the end of 1779. They had to get on with their lives; it was time for others to take their place in the line. Monroe also appeared to be seeking advancement and his independence at this point in the war. In fall 1778, Monroe exchanged a fascinating set of letters with Theodosia Prevost—a New Jersey patriot who, despite her marriage to a British officer, had offered her home to General Washington as a headquarters site.

Monroe's surviving letters to Prevost reveal two things about this moment in later 1778: first, he was planning to travel to France, both to continue his studies and to participate in the diplomatic mission; he was contemplating a career shift. Second, he had convinced an unnamed young lady that she should consent to endure their temporary separation during this mission.[16] Monroe had likely met her in Theodosia Prevost's social circle, in which she brought together young officers and eligible young ladies. James McHenry, one of Washington's aides, recalled how officers "talked and walked and laughed and frolicked and gallanted" at her home, the Hermitage.[17] It is plausible Monroe was looking at a possible marriage match with this young woman—certainly elite—which would have had significant economic implications for him and his independence in the form of her likely dowry. Her consent—and her family's—to his plan for education abroad was necessary. This could lay a path leading away from the de-

15. Ibid., 28.

16. Monroe to Theodosia Prevost, November 8, 1778; Monroe to Charles Lee, June 13, 1779. Monroe meant to travel to France in fall 1779, writing "I wish to go in the character of an officer."

17. Ammon, *James Monroe*, 25-26.

pendence that marked the role of an aide-de-camp. (Though Monroe's relationship fizzled, this sort of marriage plot was exactly the path that Alexander Hamilton took in 1780, marrying Elizabeth Schuyler, linking himself to her politically powerful father, and then resigning from Washington's staff in a huff within two months' time.) In 1778, Monroe was figuring out how to keep climbing—in the army or out of it.

In his autobiography, Monroe explained his plans at this point: "Having entered the army with an enthusiastic zeal in support of our cause in his eighteenth year, he was anxious to pursue the same career until it should be accomplished. His object was now to obtain a command in the army." Monroe, like all aides, wanted a regiment of his own. Yet, "no commission could be granted to him, for no new regiments were to be raised and many officers of merit were deranged in consequence."[18] Here Monroe got creative: he resigned from Stirling's staff in December 1778 and returned to Virginia hoping to obtain a command in that state's internal forces. This proved ineffective. So Monroe hurried back north to headquarters in spring 1779. While there, he must have spoken with fellow aide Alexander Hamilton about his circumstances and ambitions. Hamilton thus wrote to John Laurens: "Monroe . . . proposes to go in quest of adventures to the Southward. He seems to be as much of a knight errant as your worship; but as he is an honest fellow, I shall be glad he may find some employment, that will enable him to be knocked in the head in an honorable way." Hamilton recommended Monroe for Laurens's plan to raise a battalion of freed black soldiers. "He will relish your black scheme if anything handsome can be done for him in that line. You know him to be a man of honor, a sensible man, and a soldier . . . You love your country . . . and he has the zeal and capacity to serve it."[19] While nothing came of Hamilton's recommendation, Monroe also secured letters from Washington and Stirling. Those recommendations did their work; the Virginia assembly granted Monroe a lieutenant colonelcy in the state line—but his recruiting efforts failed again, despite the British incursion into Georgia, and he "was in consequence thrown out of the service."[20]

Young Monroe was certainly patriotic. He sought a Virginia commission, he explained in 1779, "from my attachment to the service and desire, as I began almost with the war, to serve to the end of it."[21] But

18. Monroe, *Autobiography*, 29.
19. Hamilton to John Laurens, May 22, 1779, *Proceedings of the Massachusetts Historical Society* 58 (1924-25), 220.
20. Monroe, *Autobiography*, 29.
21. Monroe to [William Woodford], September 1779.

his effort to take the field with a command had failed. His dilemma at this point was that he was underage and "found it difficult to make such disposition of my property." His uncle still controlled his father's estate and Monroe was reduced to living under his uncle's roof. He apologized to Charles Lee: "If it was my house, my dear general, you should make it yours."[22] His only path to independence was continued military service. He framed it bluntly in his autobiography: he was "too young for civil employment."[23] By the fall, he lamented how Virginians were "neglecting the cause in which our Country is engaged." The war "makes no further impression on them than a narrative of events which might have happened in ancient Greece or Rome." While he read in the college library, he groused that his countrymen had "read and philosophized till they have philosophized themselves out of all feelings of the heart." Monroe remained adamant: "The perpetual freedom and Independence of an extensive Continent is at stake."[24] Of course, his manly independence and his identity were also at stake—all of which had been bound up with his career and character as an officer—and in a cause, he wrote, "in defense of which he had already made such exertions, and . . . nearly fallen a victim."[25]

It appears circumstances under which Monroe left the army amplified this moment of transition and personal crisis. All his plans and maneuvers for climbing in the army had failed. There may also have been complications at home. One of Monroe's biographers believes his uncle and key patron, Joseph Jones, unexpectedly fathered a son in 1779.[26] This new heir promised to displace Monroe from property and his family patron's focus, likely at the moment when his military career appeared at an end.

Dealing with all this uncertainty, by spring 1780 Monroe was completing his studies at William and Mary and preparing to read for the law, pursuing his uncle's plan for him from before the war. (Monroe's older friend Gen. Charles Lee lamented petty legal wrangling over real estate as "a most horrid narrower of the mind."[27]) But Monroe's long experience at headquarters helped direct a crucial decision—should he study with George Wythe, the preeminent legal mind in Virginia, or with Thomas Jefferson, the governor? He chose the governor. His uncle concurred with the logic of standing close to powerful men; if there

22. Monroe to Lee, June 13, 1779.
23. Monroe, *Autobiography*, 29.
24. Monroe to [William Woodford], September 1779.
25. Monroe, *Autobiography*, 32.
26. Ammon, *James Monroe*, 29.
27. Lee to Monroe, June 25, 1780.

was a campaign against the British, Jones hoped Jefferson would lead the state militia himself. "You, no doubt," Jones instructed Monroe, "will be ready cheerfully to give him your Company and assistance" in any campaign.[28] Young Colonel Monroe could go back to being an aide.

Jones' expectations were correct. Governor Jefferson, in between assigning Monroe legal reading lists, also wrote that he had "occasion, to employ a gentleman in a confidential business, requiring great discretion, and some acquaintance with military things."[29] The British had captured Charleston in May 1780. To protect Virginia, Jefferson needed intelligence and renewed communication with the scattered patriot forces. He tasked Monroe: "observe the British army and communicate their movements" and report the "resources of our friends, their force, the disposition of the people, the prospects of provisions, ammunition, arms." Jefferson instructed Monroe to tell governors and generals "that [they] may through you be enabled to correspond with me."[30] Monroe was back in his military element. Being cut adrift from the Continental army and his patrons there, as well as potentially facing a changed relationship with Jones, Monroe said, had "perplexed my plan of life." After the mission, he thanked Jefferson; without his patronage "I should most certainly have retired from society with a resolution never to have entered on the stage again." "My plan of life is now fixed."[31]

That was an easy thing for Monroe to write in a thank you note. But the war continued. The British landed at Norfolk, Virginia in fall 1780. Monroe received command of a militia regiment—likely at his suggestion, his old friend John Francis Mercer "was appointed with him" as his second in command.[32] They were only out for a month. When the British returned in greater force in 1781, Virginia's weak mobilization meant Continental forces led by Lafayette were necessary to check the invaders in the tidewater. Monroe's attempt to secure "some command in the militia" from the new governor was unsuccessful. Virginia had plenty of officers; she lacked soldiers.[33] "I could not stay at home in the present state of the country and should be happy to bear some part in her defense," explained Monroe to Jefferson. "For that purpose, I sat out to join the Marquis's army to act in any line ei-

28. Joseph Jones to Monroe, March 1, 1780.
29. Thomas Jefferson to Monroe, 10 June 1780.
30. Jefferson to Monroe, June 16, 1780.
31. Monroe to Jefferson, September 9, 1780.
32. Monroe, *Autobiography*, 32.
33. Ammon, *James Monroe*, 33; Monroe to Jefferson, October 1, 1781.

ther himself or Council would employ me in." He hoped to "join the army and serve till the enemy leave this state."[34] It wasn't to be. At the siege of Yorktown, Monroe again applied to his friend Lafayette, asking if he would "mention me to your friend General Lincoln." "My wish is merely to make my continuance temporary during the operations here, to . . . render some little service to the General and if possible to my state and at the same time enjoy the society of some excellent citizens from whom my particular circumstances alone have . . . reluctantly separated me."[35] He wasn't asking for a permanent appointment, just a continued chance to serve—and to perform. It never came. But Monroe had another iron in the fire. He had returned to planning a trip to France for study and diplomatic connections. During the Yorktown siege itself, Monroe told Jefferson he hoped to sail in November; he was still waiting on a France-bound ship in May 1782.[36]

Monroe's war had been marked by diligence and bravery, yes, but also by a subordination and dependence that echoed his relationships with his civilian patrons, Jones and Jefferson. His curmudgeon-y friend, Charles Lee, had long lamented Monroe's bashful demeanor, his submissive false modesty.[37] Lee, however, had a disordered personality and consequently did not understand the stance his young friend took in interacting with superiors. But Monroe himself was looking forward and was ready to shake this off. Would his French scheme safely cut those cords with patrons and allow Monroe to stand independent, his own man, at last? That ship never sailed. Instead, he followed the instructions of Jones, standing for election in the House of Delegates in order to burnish his legal credentials and elite Virginia contacts. Washington's and Stirling's old letters of recommendation again helped him. Without the letters, Monroe thanked them, "I could not have expected . . . to have obtained this degree the confidence of my Countrymen."[38] His fellow legislators in short order put Monroe on the executive council—before he had been admitted to the bar—likely because he had little private business to distract from the drudge work of governance. Echoes of the duties of aide-de-camp? When term-limits removed Jones from the Congress in 1783, the legislature sent Monroe up to keep his patron's seat warm. (Again, the parallels with Alexander Hamilton are fascinating. Hamilton got sent to the Congress to fill fa-

34. Monroe to Jefferson, June 18, 1781.
35. Monroe to Lafayette, September 27, 1781.
36. Monroe to Jefferson, October 1, 1781; Ammon, *James Monroe*, 34.
37. Lee to Monroe, July 18, 1780. Lee teasingly referred to Monroe's "mauvaise honte."
38. Monroe to Lord Stirling, September 10, 1782.

ther-in-law Schuyler's seat.) Even in elected political office, Monroe was a junior partner in a complex political network and chain of command.[39]

James Monroe arrived at Annapolis in December 1783 as his new Congressional colleagues prepared to ratify the final treaty of peace. Gen. George Washington rode into town a week later and then resigned his commission to the Congress two days before Christmas.[40] "The scene was highly interesting," Monroe later wrote with some understatement. He reflected how "he had served as a lieutenant under [Washington] only a few years before." In his autobiography Monroe drew a straight line from his military service and his elevation to political office: It was "gratifying," he wrote, "to recollect that his promotion had been the result of the free suffrage of his fellow citizens, founded in part, at least, on the favorable opinion entertained of his conduct in that service."[41] At the time, however, Monroe's path as a young officer and member of the rising generation of Virginia's political elite show the *persistence* of hierarchy, patronage, and dependence. Young men like Monroe were embedded in relationship webs that tied them to their elders. David Ramsay's observation in his 1789 history of the Revolution—"It seemed as if the war not only required but created talents"[42]— certainly applied to the young James Monroe. The war nurtured and drew forth his abilities. To this, however, we should add that even for the elite young men of Revolutionary Virginia, the pursuit of American Independence not only required, but continued their *dependence*.

39. Ammon, *James Monroe*, 35-39.
40. Ibid., 41.
41. Monroe, *Autobiography*, 34
42. David Ramsay, *The History of the American Revolution*, ed. L.H. Cohen (Indianapolis: Liberty Classics, 1990), 2: 631.

Haitian Soldiers in the Siege of Savannah

☗ ROBERT S. DAVIS ☗

The story of the Black Haitian soldiers serving in the French army in the battles to wrest Savannah, Georgia from the British in September-October 1779 went largely ignored until the 1950s and remains incompletely explained.[1] They have become better known, however, than the overall role of the peoples of the Caribbean in the era of the War for Independence.

What began as the American Revolution in 1775 morphed into a British war with France in 1778 and with Spain in 1779. This worldwide conflict centered on the islands of the Caribbean, which produced by slave labor hugely valuable sugar for rum. The French possessions alone had more value than all of the thirteen rebelling colonies. Britain gave priority to defending Jamaica.[2]

Peoples of these islands and Spanish Louisiana and Mexico became contractors, sailors, and soldiers in this war. To that end, in the French colony of St. Dominique (Haiti), on the island of Santo Domingo, Laurent-François le Noir (1743-1798), Marquis de Rouvray, formed ten volunteer African Haitian chasseur (light infantry) companies, each consisting of three officers, fifteen non-commissioned officers and sixty privates, as two battalions for the French army on March 12, 1779. Recruiting exceeded expectations by 49 percent and the companies were expanded to include eighty-four men and four corporals each on April 21.

1. George P. Clark, "The Role of the Haitian Volunteers at Savannah in 1779: An Attempt at an Objective View," *Phylon* 41 (Winter 1980): 358-59.
2. See Andrew Jackson O'Shaughnessy, *An Empire Divided: The American Revolution and the British Caribbean* (Philadelphia: University of Pennsylvania Press, 2000).

Half of all people in Haiti who were not enslaved were Black. Enlistment was open to all "gens de couleur" (gentlemen of color) not in slavery and to enslaved people offered freedom from bondage for service. Recruits came from across the island and from all classes, including from prominent Black landowning families. Each company eventually consisted of eighty-eight fusiliers, eight corporals, four sergeants, and a "fourrier" (forager or quartermaster). All officers, except for Colonel Rouvray, were white. Overall leadership of the Chasseurs-Voluntaries de Saint-Dominique, or the volunteer hunters, consisted of a colonel, a lieutenant colonel (Humphrey O'Dunne), a battalion commandant, and an aide-major.

Rouvray was a Black land owner in the colony who had risen through the ranks of the French army through service in Canada during the Seven Years War. As colonel of the Chasseurs-Voluntaries, he hoped to answer with courage the many indignities he had suffered in the army because of his race.[3] Allegedly Henri Christophe (1767-1820), later king of an independent Haiti, served as one of the two drummers or as a valet. According to one account, he received a battle wound in the fighting around Savannah. Other leaders of the later Haitian revolution also supposedly served in these battalions but documentation is lacking.[4]

Vice Admiral Charles-Henri Hector (1729-1794), the Comte d'Estaing, arrived at Cap-François, the capital of the colony, with sixty-five warships, and an army. His expedition had captured the islands of Grenada and St. Vincent's from the British and caused the capture or destruction of several British ships. D'Estaing secretly had one more project in mind before carrying out his orders to return to France. To that end, he took on board his fleet the white Haitian Grenadier-volunteers battalion (200 men), Rouvray's Black volunteers (750 men),

3. Gil Troy, "The Revolutionary Drummer Boy Turned Haitian King," *Daily Beast*, February 17, 2018, www.thedailybeast.com/the-revolutionary-drummer-boy-turned-haitian-king; Asa Bird Gardiner, *The Order of the Cincinnati in France* (Providence, RI: Rhode Island Society of the Cincinnati, 1905), 32; Stewart P. King, *Blue Coat or Powder Whig: Free People of Color in Pre-Revolutionary Saint Dominique* (Athens, GA: University of Georgia Press, 2007), 67-68; "Chasseurs-Volontaires de Saint-Domingue," Wikipedia, en.wikipedia.org/wiki/Chasseurs-Volontaires_de_Saint-Domingue#cite_note-FOOTNOTELespinasse1882166%E2%80%9367-2; Rita Folse Elliott, *"The Greatest Event That Has Happened in the Whole War": Archaeological Discovery of the 1779 Spring Hill Redoubt, Savannah, Georgia* (Savannah, GA: Coastal Heritage Society, 2011), 7, www.thelamarinstitute.org/images/PDFs/publication_175.pdf; Clark, "The Role of the Haitian Volunteers," 360.
4. Alexander A. Lawrence, *Storm Over Savannah: The Story of Count d'Estaing and the Siege of the Town in 1779* (Athens: University of Georgia Press, 1951, 1968 revised edition), 15-16, 153n13; Clark, "The Role of the Haitian Volunteers," 357-58.

and two white companies from Martinique for a total of 1,550 men. D'Estaing's army also included white French regular regiments from Guadeloupe, Haiti, and Martinique. This army of 3,524 left Cap-François on August 15, 1779 in almost one hundred transports and protected by a fleet of twenty-one ships of the line, nine frigates, three corvettes, and one cutter.

The Admiral was persuaded by Lt. Col. Charles-François Sévelinges (1754-1793), the self-styled Marquis de Brétigny, that the mere appearance of the French army and fleet in Georgia would compel the British garrison there to surrender. On September 4, the French fleet began to arrive off that coast. After reaching Savannah, d'Estaing's army was joined by American forces of 650 Continental and 750 militia soldiers commanded by Maj. Gen. Benjamin Lincoln (1733-1810).

British Brig. Gen. Augustin Prévost (1723-1786) prepared to surrender. The arrival of reinforcements under Col. John Maitland (1732-1779) and the strength of earthworks erected by British engineer Maj. James Moncrief (1741-1793) with Black labor around Savannah, however, persuaded him to make a stand. In all, the British forces in Savannah numbered 3,346 men fit for duty, not including Indians and enslaved people, compared to the combined American and French forces of as many as 7,722 men before the effects of sickness and desertion.

The Haitian soldiers, Black and white, were assigned to trench digging, but also did guard duty that consisted of lying down in front of the trenches or behind anything that they could to protect themselves from being shot. The Haitians served in the cold wet trenches under Louis Baury de Bellerive (1754-1807). These earthworks supported the batteries that later failed to reduce the British fortifications.

In the first use of African Americans in battle by the French army, Rouvray led his Black Haitians in repulsing an assault on the French trenches by Maj. Colin Graham and ninety-seven British light infantry before dawn on September 24. Rouvray then made the mistake of pursuing the retreating enemy to within cannon shot of the enemy's fortifications. Reportedly his men suffered 150 casualties, including 40 men killed running from the cannon fire.[5]

5. Clark, "The Role of the Haitian Volunteers," 362; David K. Wilson, *The Southern Strategy: Britain's Conquest of South Carolina and Georgia 1775-1780* (Columbia, SC: University of South Carolina Press, 2005), 250-52, 272-73; Rachel Ernest Dupuy, Gay M. Hammerman, and Grace P. Haynes, *The American Revolution: A Global War* (New York: David McKay, 1977), 90; Rita Folse Elliott, Daniel T. Elliott, and Laura E. Seifert, *Savannah under Fire, 1779: Identifying Savannah's Revolutionary War Battlefield* (Savannah: Coastal Heritage Society, 2009), 70: www.thelamarinstitute.org/images/PDFs/publication_173.pdf. Rouvray may have commanded the left column in the main attack on the British lines. Wilson, *The Southern Strategy*, 159, 307n83.

On October 9, the American and French forces were repulsed in a disastrous attack on the British lines around Savannah. Their combined forces lost 244 killed, 600 wounded, and 120 men taken prisoner. Many of the latter proved mortally wounded. British losses came to 40 killed, 63 wounded, and 52 missing. British Colo. John Maitland ordered a bayonet charge against the fleeing disorganized allied forces.

Under Gen. La Vicomte Louis-Marie Marc Antoine d'Ayen de Noailles (1756-1804), and supported by two cannon, the Black Haitian soldiers protected the withdrawal and the French camp as part of a reserve column that also included Marines and two white companies from Martinique. Reportedly, twenty-five of the Black Haitian soldiers died protecting the panicked escaping mob of American and French soldiers. One French officer claimed that the men of French army would have thrown down their weapons and surrendered if not stopped.[6] The white Grenadier-volunteers battalion with some of Rouvray's Black Haitian soldiers served in a feint attack with the American militia that failed to draw British forces away from the main assault.

During the campaign, desertions reduced Rouvray's Black volunteers to only 545 men and the white Grenadier-volunteers battalion under a Major Des Francais to only 156 men. Guards prevented further desertions from the Black troops.[7]

D'Estaing, wounded in the battle, ordered an end to the campaign. He returned to France a hero with some of his Black Haitian soldiers accompanying him and Rouvray on their arrival at Versailles for an audience with the King. The Savannah campaign almost delayed the second British invasion of the South from New York long enough that it might have never happened and could have avoided what became two of the bloodiest years of the American Revolution.

A company of sixty-two of the Black Haitian soldiers accompanied the wounded to Charleston and were among the soldiers who surrendered when the British successfully laid siege to the city in May 1780. They were subsequently sold into slavery along with their comrades captured by the British at sea. What remained of the Chasseurs-Voluntaries de Saint-Dominique regiment served out the war as garrison

6. Lawrence, *Storm Over Savannah*, 91-103; Elliott, *"The Greatest Event That Has Happened the Whole War"*, 7, 10, 17; Wilson, *The Southern Strategy*, 150, 159; Elliott, et al, *Savannah under Fire*, 70, 139, 141; Troy, "The Revolutionary Drummer Boy Turned Haitian King." Noailles later represented France in negotiating the arrangements for the British surrender at Yorktown. See Edward Martin Stone, *Our French Allies: Rochambeau and His Army* (New York: Scholars Bookshelf, 2006), 286-88.

7. Lawrence, *Storm Over Savannah*, 120.

troops in Grenada and Haiti. French officials considered forming a permanent regiment of Black soldiers in Haiti but recruitment failed.[8]

The Black soldiers in the Savannah campaign must have raised local concerns. Georgia's loyalist *Royal Georgia Gazette* argued that the use of Black soldiers by the French justified General Prévost's controversial decision to arm enslaved people.[9] George Washington and the Continental Congress had to be persuaded to keep African American soldiers in the Continental army in order to have an army and in spite of fear of slave revolts.[10] Of the thirteen original states, only Georgia and South Carolina refused to enlist enslaved people into their Continental forces in return for emancipation, although both states used Black soldiers.[11]

Where the Haitians stood at the two colonial Jewish cemeteries in Savannah is the only ground on the battlefield that remains as it was in 1779. Today a monument in the city honors the African Haitians who served in d'Estaing's army.

8. John D. Garrigus, *Before Haiti: Race and Citizenship in French Saint-Domingue* (New York: Palgrave McMillan, 2006), 208-10; Elliott, et al, Sav*annah under Fire*, 227-28; King, *Blue Coat*, 65-66; Troy, "The Revolutionary Drummer Boy Turned Haitian King." Rouvray would hold several important posts in France and Haiti after the American Revolution, before the French Revolution compelled him to immigrate to Philadelphia. He died there on July 18, 1798. Gardiner, *The Order of the Cincinnati in France*, 94.

9. Leara Roberts, "Haitian Contributions to American History: A Journalistic Record" in Doris Y. Kadish, ed., *Slavery in the Caribbean Francophone World: Distant Voices, Forgotten Acts, Forged Identities* (Athens, GA: University of Georgia Press, 2016), 83. The British continued to use African Americans as soldiers in Revolutionary War Georgia. Timothy Lockley, "'The King of England's Soldiers': Armed Blacks in Savannah and Its Hinterlands during the Revolutionary War Era, 1778-1787," in Leslie M. Harris, Diana Ramey Berry, and Jonathan M. Bryant, eds., *Slavery and Freedom in Savannah* (Athens, GA, 2014), 26-41.

10. Patrick F. Moriarty, "The Myth of the Citizen-Soldier: Black Patriots and the American Revolution" (Master's Thesis, Wesleyan University, 2014), 18; also see Alan Gilbert, *Black Patriots and Loyalists: Fighting for Emancipation in the War for Independence* (Chicago: University of Chicago Press, 2012).

11. See Bobby G. Moss and Michael C. Scroggins, *African-American Patriots in the Southern Campaign of the American Revolution* (Blacksburg, SC: Hibernia Press, 2004). Georgia granted freedom from bondage to slave Austin Dabney for his service and crippling wounds received in battle despite the state's laws prohibiting enslaved people from bearing arms or serving in the militia. Dabney became the first Black federal or state pensioner and, for almost fifty years, the only African American receiving a pension from the United States government. Robert S. Davis, "Tribute for a Black Patriot: A Pension for Austin Dabney," *Prologue Magazine* 46 (Fall 2014): 22-29.

George Washington's Culper Spy Ring: Separating Fact from Fiction

✵ BILL BLEYER ✵

The efforts of a group of self-taught Patriot spies who would later become known as the Culper Spy Ring played an important role in winning independence from Great Britain. But their story still has many missing pieces, and unfortunately legend and even unsubstantiated speculation have filled the gaps.

From experience in the French and Indian War, the Continental Army commander, Gen. George Washington, knew that gaining intelligence of British military actions through a spy network was critical if his underdog army was to have a chance of successfully fighting the one of the strongest military powers in the world. So when the British gained control of New York City and Long Island in autumn 1776, Washington began a long and difficult process of creating an espionage operation in the region.

Historians have long been fascinated by the intelligence efforts undertaken by enthusiastic amateurs. In more than a dozen books, researchers have tried to sort out who was involved and exactly what their roles were. The biggest mystery was the identity of Culper Junior, the chief spy in Manhattan in the later years of the war. Most of the spy ring operatives identified themselves or were identified after the war, but not Culper Junior. So when Long Island historian Morton Pennypacker revealed him to have been Robert Townsend of Oyster Bay in 1930 and then proved it with document analysis nine years later, it generated considerable attention.

Interest in the Patriots' intelligence network soared when the AMC television series *Turn: Washington's Spies* aired for four seasons between 2014 and 2017. Unfortunately, it took great liberties with the facts. These included having the ring created in 1776 rather than two years later, depicting Setauket as a neighborhood of stately stone homes rather than wooden structures, having the hamlet occupied by regular army redcoats rather than Loyalist troops, portraying Abraham Wood-hull's minister father as a Tory socializing with the occupiers rather than showing the reality of him being a Patriot sympathizer badly beaten by soldiers trying to find and arrest his son and, most ludi-crously, having Woodhull and the happily married and older Anna Strong engage in a secret affair. But the series did get people reading and talking about espionage during the war.

As with *Turn*, Pennypacker and many of the authors who have writ-ten about the Culper Ring subsequently have strayed from the truth. Pennypacker's books, which lack footnotes, transformed some anec-dotal information and legends into fact. And later writers have often repeated that material without researching or even questioning it. And while they may have sought information from Long Island historians who have spent decades studying the subject, they didn't always listen to them.

The most prominent writer in that category would be Fox News co-host Brian Kilmeade, who lives on Long Island. In preparing his 2013 bestseller with coauthor Don Yaeger and other writers, he convened gatherings of local historians from Culper-connected locations such as Setauket and Oyster Bay. They provided him with much information, some of which he ignored when it didn't fit into his narrative. He also strayed into historical fiction by filling the book with invented dialogue without indicating that the words were never spoken by the participants.

Kilmeade's work is also filled with supposed statements of fact that can be disputed. These start with the title and subtitle of the book: *George Washington's Secret Six: The Spy Ring That Saved the American Revolution*. In a volume lacking footnotes and offering only a smatter-ing of sources, the authors state that the spy ring consisted of exactly six individuals. Many more than that were involved in the operation, including couriers and boat captain Caleb Brewster. He played a critical role in carrying messages across Long Island Sound to get them to Washington's headquarters. Without Brewster there is no Culper Spy Ring. The authors have Robert Townsend playing the central role. While he was certainly important and the main source of information from New York City in the later years, the chief spy who coordinated the espionage throughout the war was Abraham Woodhull of Setauket. Without him, the spy ring never would have functioned.

Furthermore, Kilmeade and Yeager include two individuals among their chosen six who are questionable: James Rivington and a mysteri-ous woman they label only as "Agent 355." Local historians have con-cluded that Rivington, publisher of a Loyalist newspaper in Manhattan, is unlikely to have served as a spy and was definitely not part of the Culper Ring. They, and other historians, believe there was no Agent 355. And while other historians generally agree the Culper network played an important role, no one else goes as far as to say that it "saved the American Revolution." Their contention that the spy ring "broke the back of the British military" is hyperbole.[1]

EARLY INTELLIGENCE GATHERING

After operating with little useful intelligence before and after the Battle of Long Island in late August 1776, Washington took action to fill his intelligence vacuum in the fall. While still based in Manhattan, he instructed Col. Thomas Knowlton to select a group of men to undertake reconnaissance missions. The unit became known as Knowlton's Rangers.[2] Its most famous member, Nathan Hale, would be glorified as a hero despite his failure.

After Nathan Hale's ill-conceived solo spy mission, in 1777 George Washington tried to establish a spy network in and around New York City. The Continental Army commander in chief began by signing a contract with Nathaniel Sackett of Fishkill, who was a merchant in New York City, to gather intelligence.[3]

Washington selected a young officer, Yale College graduate Benjamin Tallmadge, a native of Setauket, Long Island, to serve as Sackett's military contact. The first spy to gather information successfully on Long Island as part of the Sackett network was Maj. John Clark, a Pennsylvania lawyer who had volunteered as a lieutenant in 1775. Clark established a network of contacts and was active on Long Island during much of 1777. He sent his messages to Washington through Tallmadge, who was responsible for transporting Clark to the island from Connecticut.[4]

Clark's intelligence was probably conveyed to Tallmadge by whaleboat captain Caleb Brewster, a friend and early classmate of Tallmadge who would become a captain in the Continental Army. When Clark, who operated in the Philadelphia area for most of the war, left the island, Washington needed another spy there or preferably a network of spies.[5]

1. Brian Kilmeade and Don Yaeger, *George Washington's Secret Six: The Spy Ring That Saved the American Revolution* (New York: Sentinel, 2013), xvii.

2. Kenneth A. Daigler, *Spies, Patriots, and Traitors: American Intelligence in the Revolutionary War* (Washington, DC: Georgetown University Press, 2014), 95-96.

3. Alexander Rose, *Washington's Spies: The Story of America's First Spy Ring* (New York: Bantam Books, 2006), 43.

4. Ibid., 46-47; Daigler, *Spies, Patriots, and Traitors*, 103.

5. Daigler, *Spies, Patriots, and Traitors*, 183; Morton Pennypacker, *General Washington's Spies on Long Island and in New York* (Brooklyn: Long Island Historical Society, 1939), 11-16.

Deciding his spymaster was better at developing successful espionage techniques than actually acquiring useful information, Washington terminated the arrangement with Sackett after two months.[6]

To his great relief, Washington received an unsolicited letter written on August 7, 1778—a day that could be considered the start of the Culper Spy Ring—from Lt. Brewster in Norwalk offering to gather intelligence on Long Island.[7] Washington instructed Brewster to "not spare any reasonable expense to come at early and true information." Brewster wrote his first intelligence report on August 27, 1778.[8]

Washington realized he needed someone in the Continental Army to manage ongoing correspondence with Brewster. The general asked Brig. Gen. Charles Scott, commander of a Virginia brigade, to assemble a spy network, and detailed Tallmadge to assist. Scott put little effort or enthusiasm into the spy operation, so much of the work fell to Tallmadge.

Letters from Tallmadge and his childhood friend Abraham Woodhull, who would become the chief spy, demonstrate that by October 1778 the espionage operation was in full operation.[9]

With Scott's approval, Tallmadge developed a list of codenames for the key players. Washington is believed to have invented the name for the network: Culper. It is thought to have been derived from the army commander's surveying work in Culpeper County, Virginia, when he was seventeen. Tallmadge became John Bolton while Woodhull became Samuel Culper. Sometime in the fall of 1778, Woodhull began traveling to Manhattan and reporting verbally to Brewster what he observed.[10]

With the spies Scott had recruited personally providing little useful information compared to those brought together by Tallmadge, Scott decided to give up not only supervision of the intelligence-gathering but also the army. Washington then elevated Tallmadge, only twenty-four, to be his "director of military intelligence."[11]

OPERATION OF THE SPY RING

Afraid of traveling to New York after being stopped and questioned repeatedly by British sentries, Woodhull realized he needed to recruit

6. Rose, *Washington's Spies*, 50-51.
7. Ibid., 47-48.
8. Ibid.
9. Ibid., 48,71; Daigler, *Spies, Patriots, and Traitors*, 174; Richard F. Welch, *General Washington's Commando: Benjamin Tallmadge in the Revolutionary War* (Jefferson, NC: McFarland & Co. Inc., 2014), 35.
10. Rose, *Washington's Spies*, 78, 87.
11. Ibid., 48, 71, 75-76.

someone else to spy there. His choice was Robert Townsend of Oyster Bay, purchasing agent in Manhattan for his prosperous merchant father, Samuel. To protect himself, Townsend adopted the alias of Culper Junior, as Woodhull was already Samuel Culper. Woodhull then became Culper Sr.[12]

To avoid areas where interception and capture were more likely, the agents and couriers carried intelligence reports from New York City across the East River, eastward on Long Island to Setauket, across Long Island Sound and then west along the Connecticut shore to Tallmadge and ultimately Washington north of the city or in New Jersey.

There are 193 known letters totaling 383 pages written by the Culper spies, Tallmadge, Washington and others.[13] The most recently discovered one—and the only surviving one between Tallmadge and Townsend—was found uncataloged in the archives of the Long Island Museum in Stony Brook in the summer of 2020.[14]

IMPROVING THE SPY CRAFT

Over the course of the conflict, the reports demonstrate an increasing level of spy craft sophistication. For the earliest letters, Tallmadge and Woodhull established a fairly simple process of hiding the identity of the members of the network by giving them codenames.

As the war wore on, security was increased by substituting numbers for people, places and things. The system devised by Woodhull and employed in his letter of April 10, 1779, used the figures 10 for New York and 20 for Setauket, for example.[15]

After inserting a few numerical ciphers in ten letters bound for New York and twenty going the other way, Tallmadge in July 1779 upgraded the system by preparing a "pocket dictionary" with an expanded code. The 710 words chosen were the ones most likely to be used, such as Congress, navy and Tory. Opposite each word was a number that would replace the word, such as "murder" being replaced by 387. Fifty-three proper nouns were given numbers ranging from 711 to 763. Thus Tallmadge became 721, Woodhull 722 and Townsend 723.[16]

The best added layer of security was using a special ink or "stain" invisible until treated with another solution. The ink was invented by amateur chemist James Jay, brother of John Jay, who became the first chief

12. Daigler, *Spies, Patriots, and Traitors*, 178-179.
13. Interview with Raynham Hall Museum historian Claire Bellerjeau.
14. Bill Bleyer, *George Washington's Long Island Spy Ring: A History and Tour Guide* (Charleston, SC: The History Press, 2021), 67.
15. Pennypacker, *General Washington's Spies*, 60, 209-10; Rose, *Washington's Spies*, 114, 120.
16. Daigler, *Spies, Patriots, and Traitors*, 182; Rose, *Washington's Spies*, 114, 120-22.

justice of the Supreme Court.[17] These espionage techniques employed by the Culper network were well-established tools of military spycraft, described in period military texts, but the Patriot spies and stain inventor James Jay developed their own variations.

Washington was excited at the prospect of improving the security of the spy ring, but it took him nearly six months, until December 1778, to receive a small initial supply of the solutions from Jay. The general did not have enough to provide any to the Culper spies until the following spring. In mid-April 1779, Woodhull finally received some stain and wrote that it "gives me great satisfaction."[18]

In the initial phase of the Culper network, chief spy Abraham Woodhull traveled from Setauket to Manhattan every few weeks to collect information and then returned home to turn it over to Caleb Brewster for the trip across Long Island Sound. Even after Woodhull recruited Robert Townsend to gather intelligence in the city, he would still make trips occasionally to New York to compile information or serve as a courier connecting with Townsend. But when a courier was available, Woodhull was able to remain relatively safe in Setauket and rely on Townsend and the rider. The most frequent and dependable courier was Setauket tavern owner Austin Roe, who began making the dangerous trips about April 1779 and continued until early July 1782, when the Culper correspondence ceased.

There are several aspects of the Culper story that have generated much debate:

USE OF A "DEAD DROP"

According to Alexander Rose, former CIA case officer Kenneth Daigler and several other authors, Austin Roe would usually or at least sometimes leave the letters from Townsend in a secret location in one of Woodhull's livestock fields in Setauket, where a "dead drop" box was hidden in the underbrush or buried. Woodhull would retrieve it later while attending to his cattle.

But Claire Bellerjeau, historian at the Raynham Hall Museum in Oyster Bay, Robert Townsend's family home, who has spent decades studying the Culper ring, discounts the idea. "I haven't seen any evidence of a dropbox" being used, she said, and there was no need for the spies in Setauket to have one because they could just hand off intelligence directly to each other.[19]

17. Rose, *Washington's Spies*, 106-107.
18. Ibid., 110.
19. Bellerjeau interview.

ANNA STRONG'S CLOTHESLINE

One of the best-known aspects of the Culper Spy Ring story is the purported role of Anna Strong's clothesline. According to family tradition, Anna Smith Strong, a neighbor and close friend of Abraham Woodhull, would hang out laundry to dry in a pattern that indicated where he should rendezvous with Caleb Brewster. Morton Pennypacker and some more current historians treat the story as fact while others say there is no historical documentation for it.

Strong supposedly would hang a black petticoat on her clothesline to alert Woodhull, who lived across the bay, when Brewster had arrived from Connecticut to retrieve or drop off messages. She would add one to six white handkerchiefs to inform Woodhull in which of six coves Brewster would be waiting.

Pennypacker noted that he and other historians had spent years trying to track down information about how Woodhull knew where to find Brewster. "Finally a clue was found among the papers of the Floyd family and when this was compared with the Woodhull account book it was discovered that the signals were arranged by no less a personage than the wife of Judge Selah Strong," Pennypacker wrote.[20] Strong family historian Kate Strong repeated the clothesline story in a chapter titled "In Defense of Nancy's Clothesline" in a 1969 book. She said it was corroborated by scraps of paper, deeds, journals and letters in her possession, as well as documents she saw or was told about by Morton Pennypacker.

Many historians subsequently have repeated the clothesline story without skepticism. The most preposterous version is presented by former Central Intelligence Agency case officer Kenneth Daigler. He has Brewster looking at Strong's clothesline through a telescope "from his base in Fairfield," Connecticut. That account ignores the long distance and curvature of the Earth that would thwart even modern telescopes. And it ignores the significant amount of land between the Sound and the Strong property. Brian Kilmeade wrote "the Strong estate, situated on a high bluff, would be visible to anyone passing by boat" on Long Island Sound.[21] But the Strong estate is not on a bluff by the Sound and its servants' quarters, where the laundry would have been hung out to dry, are near the beach, not much higher than sea level. To his credit, Kilmeade does describe the clothesline story as "local legend."

20. Kate Wheeler Strong, "In Defense of Nancy's Clothesline," True Tales from the Early Days of Long Island, (Reprinted from the Long Island Forum, Amityville, N.Y.), 1969.
21. Kilmeade, George Washington's Secret Six, 93.

Most Long Island historians who have spent decades researching the Culper network view the clothesline story the same way. "I have read all of the Culper letters and there is no reference to Anna Strong's clothesline," Bellerjeau said. Beverly Tyler, historian for the Three Village Historical Society in Setauket, agreed: "The clothesline story is apocryphal; I treat it as folklore" although "she had to communicate with him in some way, whether it was the clothesline or some other regular method."[22]

THE ROLE OF JAMES RIVINGTON

Historians disagree over the role, if any, of publisher James Rivington in the spy ring. Rivington operated a print shop in Manhattan, where he published a series of newspapers that demonstrated an extreme Loyalist point of view. In 1777 he began publishing the *Royal Gazette* at northeastern corner of Wall Street and Broadway. Rivington also operated two adjacent businesses, a coffeehouse and general store that sold stationery, which were frequented by British officers.[23]

Beyond those facts, things get iffy. Some authors have Robert Townsend working for Rivington as either a paid or volunteer reporter. These include Kilmeade, who offers that Townsend, who "had always had a knack for writing," arranged to be hired by Rivington as a reporter in "a stroke of brilliance" because now he "had the perfect excuse for asking questions."[24] Others go even further, elevating Townsend to being a co-owner of the newspaper and/or coffeehouse. Pennypacker and Alexander Rose have the two men jointly owning the coffeehouse, with Townsend spending time there chatting with British officers. But Pennypacker carries the story only so far. He believed Rivington knew nothing about Townsend's spy activity. "That James Rivington ever imagined Robert Townsend to be in the service of George Washington there is no evidence to show," the historian wrote. "In fact it is very unlikely. Rivington was not the type of man that Townsend would trust with that secret."[25]

Kilmeade is the biggest outlier when it comes to Rivington's espionage role: he portrays the publisher as a full-fledged Culper spy. He backs his contention by quoting a postwar letter from William Hooper, a North Carolina lawyer and signer of the Declaration of Independence, in which he stated that "there is now no longer any reason to conceal it that Rivington has been very useful to Gen. Washington by

---

22. Interviews with Bellerjeau and Three Village Historical Society historian Beverly Tyler.
23. Rose, *Washington's Spies*, 151.
24. Kilmeade, *George Washington's Secret Six*, 84.
25. Rose, *Washington's Spies*, 151; Pennypacker, *General Washington's Spies*, 13.

furnishing him with intelligence. The unusual confidence which the British placed in him owing in a great measure to his liberal abuse of the Americans gave him ample opportunities to obtain information which he has bountifully communicated to our friends."[26]

Claire Bellerjeau, who has spent a lot of time picking apart the Townsend-Rivington connection theories, noted that Townsend operated a store on Hanover Square. "Rivington's Gazette and his coffeehouse were right there on Hanover Square," she said. "You see in Robert's ledgers that he regularly bought Rivington's Gazette. People might say that Rivington was the spy, but Robert clearly doesn't think that Rivington is on his team because early on in 1779 in one of his spy letters he writes specifically to look in Rivington's paper and you will see that somebody knows what we're doing or has guessed very nearly. In Rivington's Gazette he is writing that there are spies in New York and everybody should be on the lookout to turn them in. So Robert complains about Rivington. How is it that they are spies together? That just makes no sense."[27]

Bellerjeau also noted there is no proof that Townsend and Rivington were partners in the coffeehouse. "There is zero evidence in his ledger books of any business connection with Rivington. The only thing we see is that he is buying his paper from Rivington. That's it."[28]

The authors who believe Townsend and Rivington had a business and/or espionage link point to the fact that Rivington is one of the names listed for substitution in the spy ring codebook. Kilmeade noted that "Rivington's name was the last to appear among the Culper code monikers, 726, indicating that Townsend had recruited him soon after his own engagement, probably by the late summer of 1779, when the code was developed."[29]

Bellerjeau countered that "we know that Rivington is one of the proper names in the Culper code. That makes you think he's a spy, right? But you've got place names, people's names on both sides of the conflict. Is Rivington's name in there as a person or for the Gazette? As far as the Culpers are concerned, I think the word Rivington in the code meant the paper." Because Tallmadge may have placed a guard to protect Rivington after the British left New York in 1783, Bellerjeau said, "Maybe Rivington had an outside deal with Washington and Tallmadge. Maybe he wasn't part of the Culper Spy Ring but was doing

26. Kilmeade, *George Washington's Secret Six*, 107-108.
27. Bellerjeau interview.
28. Ibid.
29. Kilmeade, *George Washington's Secret Six*, 106-107.

other spy work for them." It would make sense for security to keep intelligence operatives separated, she added.[30]

THE LADY OR AGENT 355

Some recent books on the spy ring, including Brian Kilmeade's 2013 bestseller, include the story of an Agent 355. She supposedly was a mysterious female Culper operative, even though a generic lady is mentioned only once in the letters. A coded letter from Abraham Woodhull to Washington dated August 15, 1779—a little over a month after Robert Townsend took over as chief spy in Manhattan from Woodhull—includes this sentence: "I intend to visit 727 [New York] before long and think by the assistance of a 355 [lady] of my acquaintance, shall be able to out wit them all."[31]

That ambiguous reference has spawned a whole subgenre of the spy ring story. Morton Pennypacker suggested that not only was there a female Culper spy with the code number 355 but she also was the mistress of Townsend. And to make the story even more juicy, she was arrested, imprisoned on the infamous British prison hulk Jersey, gave birth to his illegitimate child onboard and then died.[32]

Other writers have taken up the story, with some putting her in the social circle of British spy John André. Still others, including Alexander Rose, declare that the 355 referred to was Anna Strong. But he does not turn her into a secret agent. Rose does have Strong—without documentation—accompanying Woodhull into Manhattan and masquerading as his wife to make his trip less suspicious to the British sentries.[33] That seems a stretch because she was older than Woodhull, and it would mean leaving her young children at home for at least two days.

Agent 355 is a recurring character in Kilmeade's book. "One agent remains unidentified," he wrote. "Though her name cannot be verified, and many details about her life are unclear, her presence and her courage undoubtedly made a difference." With so little verified and so much unclear, it's questionable how the Fox News cohost was able to conclude that she made such a difference. In Kilmeade's telling, "she was somehow uniquely positioned to collect important secrets in a cunning and charming manner that would leave those she had duped completely unaware that they had just been 'outwitted' by a secret agent."[34]

30. Bellerjeau interview.
31. Pennypacker, *General Washington's Spies*, 252.
32. Ibid.
33. Rose, *Washington's Spies*, 173.
34. Kilmeade, *George Washington's Secret Six*, xviii.

Kilmeade dismissed the possibility that Anna Strong is the 355 referred to in the letter, stating

> a much more likely contender would be a young woman living a fashionable life in New York . . . [who] almost certainly would have been attached to a prominent Loyalist family . . . It is therefore possible that 355 was part of the glittering, giggling cluster of coquettes who flocked around the British spy John André as he moved around the city.[35]

Kilmeade even has his Agent 355 helping to uncover Benedict Arnold's treasonous plot to turn over West Point to the British. One also has to wonder why Kilmeade attaches his Agent 355 to Townsend in the city when the only mention of a lady in the letters is in connection with Woodhull. In Kilmeade's version, as in Pennypacker's, Agent 355 is imprisoned on the prison hulk Jersey. While Pennypacker has her dying there, Kilmeade gives her a chance of surviving the ordeal.[36]

Many current historians who have researched the spy ring scoff at the Agent 355 theories as wild speculation unsupported by facts. Daigler called it "a romantic myth" that was discredited in the mid-1990s.[37]

Setauket historian Beverly Tyler emphasized that there is only the one reference to a lady, in the August 15, 1779 letter. "That is it," he said. "Everything else is made up—the whole business of Agent 355 and Robert Townsend." Tyler is one of those who believes the lady referred to is Woodhull's Setauket neighbor. "I'm fully convinced it was Anna Strong," he said. "She had relatives who were Loyalists in New York City and she portrayed herself as a Loyalist. During the war, as far as we can tell—since we don't know the details about the spies we have to make some assumptions—she accompanied Woodhull into New York city on occasion. Anna Strong was 355. She wasn't Agent 355." He said members of the spy ring "didn't refer to each other as agents." And the spies who did have code numbers were all numbered in the 700s. "Making up the word agent and tying it to the number 355 has no validity whatsoever."[38]

Claire Bellerjeau also doubts there was anyone involved with the spy ring code-named Agent 355. But she conceded that "it's quite possible that there was a woman who was an agent and a significant role player. I wouldn't say that there is no agent, but she's never mentioned again.

---

35. Ibid., 93-94.
36. Ibid., 178, 213.
37. Daigler, *Spies, Patriots, and Traitors*, 189.
38. Tyler interview.

I think people want to have good stories about women so I can understand that people want to weave a larger story out of this one reference. It's the same thing with Anna Strong and her clothesline, even though there's no real evidence behind that."[39]

Bellerjeau disagrees with Tyler's contention that the lady helping Woodhull would have been Anna Strong. She doesn't believe it would be anyone in Setauket "because it's so far out on the island and not that important a place. What special advantage could a person out in Setauket give you? The intelligence is about what's going on in Manhattan." As for Kilmeade's speculation that the lady was a socialite in Major John André's circle in the city, Bellerjeau said, "It's certainly possible because you're looking for somebody who's in a particular position to outwit. But would a lady of high society be an acquaintance with Woodhull, a vegetable farmer from Setauket? It doesn't seem likely."[40]

HERCULES MULLIGAN

Historians agree that New York City tailor Hercules Mulligan was a spy for George Washington. But they don't agree on whether Mulligan was a member of the Culper ring, gathered intelligence independently or operated both ways.

The ambitious young man opened a tailoring and haberdashery business that catered to wealthy clients, including British officers stationed in the city after the occupation. He befriended Alexander Hamilton after he arrived from the West Indies in 1772. Hamilton lodged with Mulligan's family while attending King's College, and Mulligan helped convince Hamilton to support the Patriot cause. In March 1777, after Hamilton was appointed Washington's aide-de-camp, he recommended to the general that Mulligan become a confidential correspondent in the city. Mulligan took full advantage of his access to British officers who were customers of his tailoring business and others billeted in his house.[41]

Mulligan proved valuable by informing Washington of British and Loyalist plots to capture or assassinate the general as well as planned enemy movements. Whether Mulligan was considered a member of the ring or not, he apparently began to cooperate at times with the Culper operatives in the summer of 1779. Woodhull mentioned in an August 12 letter that "an acquaintance of Hamiltons" had relayed information about British regiments embarking on transports.[42] That was

---

39. Bellerjeau interview.
40. Ibid.
41. Rose, *Washington's Spies*, 225.
42. Pennypacker, *General Washington's Spies*, 252.

about six weeks after Townsend, who had known Mulligan since child-hood through his father, Samuel, began writing reports. According to Rose, Mulligan never wrote any known reports but provided informa-tion verbally to the Culper spies and via other routes to Washington.[43]

Daigler said there is documentation proving Mulligan did work with the ring on occasion. As evidence that he also ran his own separate net-work, he cited a letter from Tallmadge to Washington. On May 8, 1780, the spy chief stated that he did not know what Mulligan was doing and asked Washington for any information on that subject that might affect his own intelligence activities.

Bellerjeau concluded that Mulligan was not part of the Culper Ring. "However, he and Robert knew each other, evidenced through two re-ceipts," she said. "Did they know that they were both gathering intel-ligence? It's possible."[44]

The details of how the Culper Spy Ring operated will continue to intrigue historians and history buffs, but absent new discoveries, many of the questions will remain unanswered.

43. Rose, *Washington's Spies*, 226.
44. Daigler, *Spies, Patriots, and Traitors*, 188; Bellerjeau interview.

Texas, Cattle, Cowboys, Ranchers, Indian Raids, and the American Revolution

GEORGE KOTLIK

In discussions on the American Revolutionary War, the contributions of Texas are seldom brought up.[1] But in the 1770s, Texas, inhabited by Spaniards and Native Americans, was a hub of activity. While the signing of the Declaration of Independence occurred on July 4, 1776 in Philadelphia, *Tejanos* (Texans) manned outposts, guarded New Spain's claims, and reconnoitered neighboring Indian tribes.[2]

In the early 1690s, Texas secured a formal place within the Spanish Empire when it became an official province of the Viceroyalty of New Spain. By 1776 Spain had claimed dominion over what was then called New Spain, vast tracts of land in the North American Southwest, Central America, South America, and the West Indies. San Antonio de Bexar was the capital of provincial Texas. Only three civil settlements existed in Texas: the Villa de San Fernando de Bexar, La Bahia, and Villa de Bucareli (later renamed Villa de Nacogdoches in 1779).[3] Altogether, Spanish Texas boasted a population of roughly 3,000 Spanish citizens.

1. For further reading on Texas and the American Revolution see: Robert S. Weddle and Robert H. Thonhoff, *Drama and Conflict: The Texas Saga, 1776* (Austin: Madrona Press, 1976); Robert H. Thonhoff, *The Texas Connection With the American Revolution* (Burnet, Tex.: Eakin Press, 1981).
2. *Company of San Antonio de Bexar, July 4, 1776*, Roster, Bexar Archives, Dolph Briscoe Center for American History, The University of Texas at Austin, translated by Pablo P. Ruiz, Box 2C25.
3. Robert H. Thonhoff, *The Vital Contribution of Texas in the Winning of the American Revolution: An Essay on a Forgotten Chapter in the Spanish Colonial History of Texas* (Karnes City, Texas), 3-4, granaderos.org/july.pdf.

On June 21, 1779, Spain officially declared war on Great Britain, entering the Revolutionary War on the side of France and the emerging United States.[4] When news of Spain's entry into the war reached New Orleans, Louisiana Governor Bernardo de Galvez cast his gaze on British West Florida.[5] In no time, Galvez assembled an army of 7,000 troops bent on West Florida's conquest.[6] Among the many obstacles he faced throughout his efforts to procure West Florida for Spain was feeding his troops. In 1779, Galvez sent an emissary, Francisco Garcia, to Texas with a request to purchase 1,500 to 2,000 cattle. When rounding up this livestock, Texas officials made sure to send enough bulls so that the stock could procreate in Louisiana to prevent depletion or scarcity while under Galvez's command. When the herds were ready to make the trek to Louisiana, armed soldiers escorted *rancheros* (ranchers), *vaqueros* (cowboys), and their livestock to Louisiana.[7]

Throughout the process of raising enough cattle to meet Galvez's demand, Spanish officials encountered numerous obstacles that barred the smooth completion of that end. For starters, by September 20, 1779 Francisco Garcia had returned to New Orleans, even though Texas officials expected him to take charge of the herd. At the same time, concerns regarding the inability of most cattle's exportation from the El Espiritu Santo mission created a delay in the delivery of sufficient numbers of cattle to Galvez—according to Texas officials, cattle from the El Espiritu Santo mission comprised a major part of the herd that was intended for Louisiana. To counter this, Spanish officials explored alternative avenues to round up livestock, including the dispatch of unbranded cattle to Louisiana to make up the difference.[8] Despite these difficulties, the 2,000 requested cattle were procured and sent to New Orleans.[9] For every head of cattle exported out of Texas, ranchers were

4. Thomas E. Chavez, *Spain and the Independence of the United States: An Intrinsic Gift* (Albuquerque: University of New Mexico Press, 2002), 133.

5. Louisiana was a Spanish colony in North America following the Seven Years' War.

6. David F. Marley, *Wars of the Americas: A Chronology of Armed Conflict in the New World, 1492 to the Present* (Denver: ABC-CLIO, 1998), 335. Galvez initially only raised 1,400 troops, but his numbers would eventually swell to over 7,000; Cecil Johnson, *British West Florida, 1763-1783* (1942. Reprint, Hamden: Archon Books, 1971) 213.

7. *Teodoro de Croix to Domingo Cabello, August 16, 1779*, Bexar Archives, Dolph Briscoe Center for American History, The University of Texas at Austin, translated by John A. Orange Jr., Box 2C35.

8. *Domingo Cabello to Teodoro de Croix, September 20, 1779*, Bexar Archives, Dolph Briscoe Center for American History, The University of Texas at Austin, translated by John A. Orange Jr., Box 2C36.

9. *Teodoro de Croix to Domingo Cabello, November 24, 1779*, Bexar Archives, Dolph Briscoe Center for American History, The University of Texas at Austin, translated by William C. Taylor, Box 2C37.

charged two reales.[10] Proceeds were paid to the Spanish government who utilized those funds to pay for a military escort for the herds' safe delivery to Louisiana.[11]

One of the more serious difficulties encountered by Texas officials, and which paused the exportation of cattle to Louisiana, occurred sometime between January and June 1780. During that time a cattle drive was attacked by Comanche raiders, leading to the loss of enough cattle to cause headaches for Spanish officials. These depredations temporarily delayed any further transportation of cattle because no *Tejanos* wanted, "for any amount of money whatever," to expose themselves to the dangers of Comanche raids—both to protect their lives and avoid the risk of losing their herds.[12] For much of 1780, Native Americans, notably Comanches and Lipan-Apaches, terrorized Texas residents who, according to Texas governor Domingo Cabello, refused to attend to their herds out of fear of Indian hostility.[13] The Indian menace thus contributed to the limited amount of cattle, delays in the arrival of stock, and possible inability of Texas to export and deliver optimal amounts of livestock to Galvez.

Despite tensions with Native Americans, which was nothing new to the *Tejanos,* Texas cattle continued to arrive in Louisiana until 1782.[14] From 1779 to 1782, Texas delivered roughly 10,000 to 15,000 head to Louisiana for Galvez's invasion force.[15] In spite of Indian raids and delays, the supply of cattle was sufficient, and Spain conquered

10. *Proceedings concerning Marcos Hernandez' petition to export stock to Louisiana, May 30, 1780,* Bexar Archives, Dolph Briscoe Center for American History, The University of Texas at Austin, translated by John A. Orange Jr., Box 2C40.

11. *Proceedings concerning Marcos Hernandez' petition to export stock to Louisiana, May 30, 1780; Domingo Cabello to Teodoro de Croix, June 11, 1780,* Bexar Archives, Dolph Briscoe Center for American History, The University of Texas at Austin, translated by John A. Orange Jr., Box 2C41; *Teodoro de Croix to Domingo Cabello, September 10, 1780,* Bexar Archives, Dolph Briscoe Center for American History, The University of Texas at Austin, translated by John A. Orange Jr., Box 2C42.

12. *Domingo Cabello to Teodoro de Croix, July 10, 1780,* Bexar Archives, Dolph Briscoe Center for American History, The University of Texas at Austin, translated by John A. Orange Jr., Box 2C41.

13. *Domingo Cabello to Teodoro de Croix, December 20, 1780,* Bexar Archives, Dolph Briscoe Center for American History, The University of Texas at Austin, translated by John A. Orange Jr., Box 2C44.

14. *Translation of proceedings concerning Antonio Blanc's petition to export cattle to Louisiana, May 4, 1782,* Bexar Archives, Dolph Briscoe Center for American History, The University of Texas at Austin, translated by William C. Taylor, Box 2C47.

15. Thonhoff, *The Vital Contribution of Texas in the Winning of the American Revolution,* 5.

British West Florida after the siege of Pensacola.[16] Texas cattle fed the men who achieved that end.

In addition to providing cattle, some *Tejanos* served in Galvez's army, but the contributions from Texas did not end there.[17] Finances were raised in Texas to help pay for the war effort and secure North America's independence from the British Crown.[18] During the entire war, roughly 1,659 pesos were donated to the United States from among the Texas population. These finances helped pay for the sailors and provisions in French Admiral de Grasse's fleet that was pivotal in effecting the British surrender at Yorktown in 1781.[19]

Largely forgotten and ignored, Texas's role in the American Revolutionary War contributed to Spain's victory over Britain in the Gulf Coast. Spain's conquest of British West Florida threatened British control over the southern colonies. Consequently, in the wake of Spain's entry into the conflict, Britain was forced to consider channeling resources, attention, and efforts, all of which were stretched thin from fueling the Revolutionary War, away from the original thirteen colonies to protect and maintain Gulf Coast possessions. There is no doubt that the *Tejanos*, who transported thousands of cattle from Texas to Louisiana between 1779 and 1782, supported Liberty's cause, helping dislodge the British from West Florida. Additionally, the *Tejanos* who donated money to the independence movement and served in Galvez's army aided the North American rebels directly. For these reasons, the *Tejanos* should be commemorated for their contributions to the establishment of the United States of America.

16. N. Orwin. Rush, *The Battle of Pensacola: March 9 to May 8, 1781: Spain's Final Triumph Over Great Britain in the Gulf of Mexico* (Tallahassee: Florida State University, 1966), 31-32.
17. Thonhoff, *The Vital Contribution of Texas in the Winning of the American Revolution*, 5.
18. Chavez, *Spain and the Independence of the United States*, 213-214.
19. Thonhoff, *The Vital Contribution of Texas in the Winning of the American Revolution*, 6-7.

The Odyssey of Loyalist Colonel Samuel Bryan

DOUGLAS R. DORNEY JR.

Colonel Samuel Bryan is thought to be the highest-ranking Loyalist officer to remain in the United States after the Revolutionary War. Despite being a high-ranking British officer in command of hundreds of men, little is known about him and the militia unit he commanded. With the arrival of British regulars in the Carolinas in 1780, Bryan came out of hiding and fled to British lines where he was put in command of a Loyalist militia regiment named the North Carolina Volunteers. While historiography of the period relegates Bryan and his regiment as minor participants in the military contest, he would acquire a degree of infamy as a captured Loyalist. In the post-Yorktown period, Bryan and two of his officers were defendants in the highest profile treason trial of the era in North Carolina. Given their relatively high ranks, the men were not confined long, instead becoming bargaining chips in prisoner exchange negotiations among North Carolina governors, Gen. Nathanael Greene, and British Gen. Alexander Leslie. Ultimately exchanged, the men found themselves with the same uncertainties facing other Loyalists at the close of the war. Would they be allowed to remain in the United States? If so, would they be persecuted or imprisoned? Would they be able to keep (or more likely regain) their confiscated property? For Bryan, his officers, and other Loyalists, there were no clear answers to these questions in 1782. These uncertainties flung Bryan and other Loyalists to the near and further reaches of the British realm.

Samuel Bryan was born in Pennsylvania between 1721 and 1726. His father, Morgan, in the 1740s purchased 2,200 acres of land on the forks of the Yadkin River that became known as the Bryan Settlement. In what would eventually become Rowan County, North Carolina, the Bryan family went on to establish a double (perhaps triple) connection, by marriage, to pioneer and folk legend Daniel Boone whose family lived on nearby tracts of land.[1] Samuel's niece, Rebecca, married Boone. Samuel's brother, William, married Boone's sister, Mary.[2] Another niece possibly married Boone's brother, Edward. These Bryan-Boone family units were among the first of European lineage to establish settlements in the Kentucky territory before the war. Samuel Bryan cast his lot with Britain early in the revolutionary conflict. In May 1775, he was one of 194 men signing a petition of loyalty to the Crown. The men noted in their address to North Carolina Royal Governor Josiah Martin "to continue [to be] his Majesty's loyal subjects and to contribute all in our power for the preservation of the public peace and that we shall endeavour to cultivate such sentiments in all those under our care."[3] By January 1776, the political environment in North Carolina for loyal Americans had changed considerably. A nearby Moravian diarist reported the "Bryants" (as they were often called) had gone into hiding.[4] That month Governor Martin, who had fled to the sloop *Scorpion* in the Cape Fear River, granted commissions to Samuel, his brother William, and twenty-four other men to raise companies of fifty men each and march toward Brunswick on the southeast North Carolina coast.[5] This assemblage of Loyalists was met on their march by Patriot militia and defeated at the Battle of Moore's Creek Bridge in February 1776. There is no indication that Samuel Bryan was at the battle, but it is possible he and the men he raised were in the area or on their way to join the larger body of Loyalists. Bryan, in his 1783 claim with the British government, noted raising men to assist the "Scottish revolt" but said they were defeated, resulting in his going back into hiding.[6]

In 1777, Samuel Bryan left North Carolina for New York to converse with now former Gov. Josiah Martin and Gen. William Howe,

1. Adelaide L. Fries, *Records of the Moravians in North Carolina* (Raleigh, NC: Edwards & Broughton, 1922), 2:792.

2. J.D. Bryan, *The Boone-Bryan History* (Frankfort, KY: Coyle Press, 1913), 13.

3. Address of inhabitants of Rowan and Surry Counties to Josiah Martin concerning loyalty to Great Britain (no date, assumed to be sometime in 1775), William Saunders, ed., *Colonial Records of North Carolina* (Raleigh, NC: P. M. Hale, Printer to the State, 1886-1907), 9:1160 (CRNC).

4. Fries, *Records of the Moravians*, 3:1045.

5. Commission to Appoint Allan MacDonald et al. as Officers of Loyalist Militias, Josiah Martin, January 10, 1776, in Saunders, *CRNC*, 10:441-443.

6. Peter W. Coldham, *American Migrations, 1765-1799: the lives, times, and families of colonial Americans who remained loyal to the British crown before, during, and after the Revolutionary War, as related in their own words and through their correspondence* (Baltimore, MD: Genealogical Publishing, 2000), 612.

returning with "a number of proclamations and great encouragement" for Carolinians to persist in their loyalty.[7] Open support for the Crown became essentially illegal and more dangerous during this timeframe. In late 1777, the state government required all males over sixteen years of age to take an oath of allegiance to the new government. Those that refused were required to leave the state or risk having their property confiscated.[8] Samuel and eleven other Bryans are listed among men in Rowan County who were called to the court in 1778 to have their property confiscated.[9] These confiscations (or the threat of them) caused several of Bryan's relatives to relocate to Kentucky. Samuel's brother, Morgan, was one of those who did so after signing the oath of allegiance in 1778.[10]

In June 1780, after successfully hiding out for several years, Samuel Bryan and what eventually became 800 Loyalists made a perilous escape from the forks of the Yadkin River to British forces in South Carolina. The impetus for this flight were the actions of a Col. John Moore who had, against Gen. Charles Cornwallis's orders, assembled 1,100 Loyalists who were defeated by North Carolina militia at the Battle of Ramsour's Mill. After the battle, Gen. Griffith Rutherford's militia and a detachment of state cavalry under Maj. William R. Davie moved northeast towards the Yadkin River in search of Bryan and his Loyalists. Fleeing eastwards across the Yadkin and then south, Bryan and most of his contingent adeptly avoided engagements with the North Carolina militia and safely arrived at a British outpost in Cheraw Hill, South Carolina in late June 1780.

General Cornwallis was not exactly pleased to hear of Bryan within his lines, noting that he "had promised to wait for my orders, lost all patience and rose with about 800 men."[11] Other British officers were not so harsh in their assessments. Col. Francis, Lord Rawdon recalled

---

7. Claim of Samuel Bryan, August 28, 1782, Great Britain, The National Archives, American Loyalist Claims, Audit Office, Class 13, Volume 117, folios 346.
8. Robert O. Demond, *The Loyalists in North Carolina during the Revolution* (Durham, NC: Duke University Press, 1940), 103, 153-157.
9. Jo Linn White, *Rowan County North Carolina Tax Lists, 1757-1800* (Salisbury, NC: Privately Published, 1995), 181.
10. Morgan Bryan oath of allegiance, August, 1778 and Morgan Bryan power of attorney statement, September, 1779, Bryan Family Papers, Shane Collection, Presbyterian Historical Society.
11. Charles Cornwallis to Henry Clinton, July 14, 1780, Ian Saberton, ed., *The Cornwallis Papers: The Campaigns of 1780 and 1781 in the Southern Theatre of the American Revolutionary War* (East Sussex: Naval and Military Press, 2010), 1:168.

Bryan as a "shrewd man . . . with great influence."[12] Charles Stedman, Philadelphia loyalist and British army commissary, noted of Bryan's men that there "never was a finer body of men collected; strong, healthy, and accustomed to the severity of the climate." Stedman went on to add that many of them, although men of property, were clothed in rags and had been living in the woods for months to avoid Patriot persecution.[13] Josiah Martin, now accompanying Cornwallis's army, argued Bryan's men were great proof of his claims of Loyalist support in North Carolina.[14]

Were Bryan and his men the kind of "militant Loyalists" that British leadership had hoped to find in the American South? For the most part they were not. Despite the pressing need for Loyalist militia during the latter half of 1780, Bryan's newly formed militia regiment was only sparingly referenced in the hundreds of letters in British correspondence during this time. The most prevalent description of them were not as soldiers but as "refugees." Josiah Martin, while initially pleased to see so many North Carolinians join the loyal militia, had to ultimately concede that they primarily fled to safety within British lines to avoid being drafted into the Patriot militia.[15] Rawdon reported the same to Cornwallis, noting that "they had been drafted to serve in the militia and refusing to march had no alternative but joining us or going to prison."[16] Andrew Hamm of the North Carolina Volunteers later claimed that he was, for a short time, in the North Carolina militia but escaped.[17] Cornwallis, Stedman, and Lt. John Money in 1780 all referred to Bryan's men as "refugees" in their correspondence. There are a few indications by British officers that the militia as whole now with the army was a burden. Cornwallis cautioned one of his officers about undertaking to "supply too many useless mouths."[18] In September 1780,

12. Francis Rawdon to Cornwallis, July 4, 1780, in Saberton, *Cornwallis Papers*, 1:192.
13. Charles Stedman, *A History of the Origin, Progress, and Termination of the American War* (London: Printed for the Author, 1794), 2:197.
14. Vernon O. Stumpf, *Josiah Martin: The Last Royal Governor of North Carolina* (Durham, NC: Carolina Academic Press for the Kellenberger Historical Foundation, 1986), 188.
15. Josiah Martin to Lord Germain, August 18, 1780, Walter Clark ed., *State Records of North Carolina* (Raleigh, NC: P. M. Hale, Printer to the State, 1886-1907), 15:55 (SRNC).
16. Rawdon to Cornwallis, July 4, 1780, in Saberton, *Cornwallis Papers*, 1:192.
17. Claim of Andrew Hamm, February 17, 1787, American Loyalist Claims, AO 12/35/155, British National Archives.
18. Cornwallis quoted in Caroline W. Troxler, "Before and After Ramsour's Mill: Cornwallis's Complaints and Historical Memory of Southern Backcountry Loyalists," in Rebecca Brannon and Joseph S. Moore eds., *The Consequences of Loyalism: Essays in Honor of Robert M. Calhoon* (Columbia, SC: University of South Carolina Press, 2019), eBook, no page or location provided.

when he was about to invade North Carolina, Cornwallis complained of severe supply problems and of too many "mouths to feed."[19] These problems were so severe that the invasion was halted while supplies were gathered from other districts. If Bryan's militia were indeed a burden their presence was both counterproductive and ironic, as one of the main objectives of the first invasion of North Carolina was to come to the aid of Loyalists there.

Bryan's North Carolina Volunteers played no significant role in the battles of 1780 in the Carolinas. They were, however, involved in three engagements during an eighteen-day period. On July 30, 1780, about 400 North Carolina Volunteers were camped away from the main body of troops at Hanging Rock, a British outpost thirty miles north of Camden, South Carolina. At dawn they were surprised and routed by a detachment of North Carolina state cavalry and militia under the command of Maj. William R. Davie. A week later at the second Battle of Hanging Rock, the unit and the rest of the camp were surprised again by a larger force of Davie's men, Col. Robert Irwin's militia from Mecklenburg County, North Carolina, and South Carolina militia under the overall command of Gen. Thomas Sumter. Just ten days later at the Battle of Camden, the North Carolina Volunteers were placed in reserve behind Lt. Col. John Hamilton's Royal North Carolina Provincial Regiment on the far left of the British line. Of the 322 North Carolina Volunteers present, only two were wounded and none were killed.[20] Col. Samuel Bryan is not listed as having been in the action, the highest ranking officer for the militia being a lieutenant colonel.[21] Afterward, Bryan's men returned to their largely logistical role in Cornwallis's army. Commissary Stedman reported that the militia performed the all-important duty of constantly gathering provisions and "threshing" wheat for the army. In the fall of 1780, many Loyalist militia deserted. Stedman wrote that during Cornwallis's retreat to Winnsboro in October 1780 the militia were "maltreated, by abusive language, and even beaten."[22] After Camden, Bryan's status as a "Colonel" became only "nominal," he and his men now fell under the overall command of Lt. Col. Hamilton.[23]

From October 1780 to June 1781 there is little and then only conflicting information in British records about the North Carolina Vol-

19. Cornwallis to Cruger, September 4, 1780, in Saberton, *Cornwallis Papers*, 2:178.
20. Jim Piecuch, *The Battle of Camden: A Documentary History* (Charleston, SC: History Press, 2006), 147.
21. Ibid., 146.
22. Stedman, *American War*, 2:225-226.
23. Cornwallis to Wemyss, August 28, 1780, in Saberton, *Cornwallis Papers*, 2:208.

unteers. In the available muster rolls, the unit is noted only on a few occasions and never with the Royal North Carolina Regiment. Where they are noted there is a drastic reduction in men from 800 in mid-1780 to 402 in May 1781. Colonel Bryan and a portion of the North Carolina Volunteers were with Cornwallis in Virginia in mid-1781. In June Cornwallis wrote in a letter to the commandant of Charleston, Gen. Alexander Leslie, that "Bryand and all those miserable people and some Negroes to the amount of 21 persons" were sent to Cape Fear (Wilmington) and Charleston.[24] Two North Carolina Volunteers, in their claims to the British government, noted they left Virginia for Charleston, then went to Wilmington until the regular troops evacuated, and then back to Charleston again.[25] At least sixty-six North Carolina Volunteers were among the prisoners taken at Yorktown. Also among the prisoners were at least seventy-eight men from the Royal North Carolina Regiment.[26]

What precisely Col. Samuel Bryan and two of his officers, Lt. Col. John Hampton and Capt. Nicholas White, were doing in the North Carolina backcountry in early December 1781 is unknown. But on December 9, Bryan was arrested on charges of "high treason" and "spying" and remanded to the Salisbury town jail. Within a few days Hampton and White were also arrested and joined Bryan there.[27] The three men were charged under a 1777 North Carolina treason statute which prohibited residents taking commissions in the British army, enlisting and encouraging others to join, and providing them with aid and intelligence.[28]

The trials of the three men at the March 1782 Salisbury District Court session were likely the highest profile trials in North Carolina during the war. Bryan and his men were not alone in being accused of treason. At the Salisbury Court session that spring, there were 22 treason trials and over 160 more in 1783.[29] The men's trials involved the most prominent legal minds in the state at the time. The prosecution was led by North Carolina Attorney General Alfred Moore who later

24. Cornwallis to Leslie, June 3, 1781, in Saberton, *Cornwallis Papers*, 5:163.
25. Claims of James Hamilton, AO/13/119/419 and Roger Turner, T/50/5/58-59.
26. Library and Archives Canada, Ward Chipman Papers, MG 23, D1, Series I, Volume 27, 335-336, 364.
27. Salisbury District Criminal Action Papers, State Archives of North Carolina, DSCR 207.326.2.
28. Acts of the North Carolina General Assembly, 1777, North Carolina General Assembly, April 7, 1777 - May 9, 1777, in SRNC, 14:10.
29. Jethro Rumple, *A History of Rowan County, North Carolina Containing Sketches of Prominent Families and Distinguished Men with an Appendix* (Salisbury, NC: J.J. Bruner, 1881), 236-237.

served as associate Justice of the US Supreme Court. The defense consisted of attorneys William R. Davie, Richard Henderson, William Kinchen, and John Penn. Penn was a member of the Second Continental Congress and signer of the Declaration of Independence. Henderson and Kinchen had previously been prominent members of the nascent North Carolina legislature. The inclusion of the last defense lawyer, Davie, must have struck those with any knowledge of his background as an extremely ironic and even odd choice. Davie was the cavalry officer who pursued Bryan from Rowan County to South Carolina and later attacked his men twice at Hanging Rock eighteen months prior. Davie's defense of Bryan was said to have been such a "brilliant exhibition of his forensic ability" that afterward he had no rival in the state as a criminal trial lawyer.[30]

Detailed minutes of the three trials are not extant but a few accounts from nineteenth century sources exist. The most salient point made by the defense was that Bryan was, in effect, a non-citizen and as such was not bound by the treason statute. The defense "admitted that Bryan had served 'his Britanick Majesty whom the prisoner considered as his liege sovereign,' and argued that Bryan 'knew no protection from nor ever acknowledged any allegiance to the State of North Carolina' so therefore he could not be guilty of treason against the State."[31] Despite the best efforts of the defense the verdict was a foregone conclusion. On March 20 and 23 the three men were found guilty and sentenced to death by hanging. Shortly thereafter, Davie, Henderson, and Kinchen wrote to Gov. Thomas Burke asking for clemency, saying that the mens' "execution would be a [poor] reflection on our Government."[32] A subsequent judicial report sent to Burke by the presiding judges bolstered the request for a reprieve, noting that while the men were guilty under the provisions of the treason law their characters were not like that of numerous other notorious Loyalists. They were considered "very honest men" and there was "no proof of their having been guilty of any murders, house-burning or plundering."[33] By April 6, 1782, Burke had granted a reprieve until May 10 which was enough time for a response from Gen. Alexander Leslie in Charleston about

30. Blackwell P. Robinson, *The Revolutionary War Sketches of William R. Davie* (Raleigh, NC: Department of Cultural Resources, 1976), 51.
31. John V. Orth, "The Strange Career of the Common Law in North Carolina," *Adelaide Law Review*, 2015, 24-25.
32. Richard Henderson, William Richardson Davie, and John Kinchen to Thomas Burke, March 28, 1782, SRNC, 16:523.
33. Judiciary Report of Samuel Spencer and Jonathan Williams, April 5, 1782, SRNC, 16:269.

exchanging Bryan and his officers for American officer prisoners.[34] The same day, Burke also instructed Maj. Joel Lewis of the state troops to protect the men in jail from local "zealots" in the intervening time. One man, in his pension application, reported that it required the "utmost vigilance" of the guards to prevent the residents taking Bryan and his men from the jail and hanging them.[35]

Governor Burke's reprieve began a three-month, at times confused and contentious, exchange of letters among himself, his successor Alexander Martin, Gen. Nathanael Greene, and General Leslie. On April 10, Leslie wrote that if Bryan and his officers were executed he would execute an equal number of American prisoners.[36] By May 1782 there was consensus among all that Bryan and his officers would be exchanged for militia officers of the state and not Continental officers. By May 12, the new governor of North Carolina, Alexander Martin, had sent the prisoners to General Greene in South Carolina for exchange. Martin, frustrated at the lack of progress in the negotiations, countered Leslie's original threat that he would carry out the death sentence for Bryan and his men if the process were not resolved more quickly.[37] Sometime in June 1782 Bryan and his fellow officers were finally exchanged. However, the event did not go as planned as Greene's commissioner of prisoners exchanged Bryan, Hampton, and White not for North Carolina officers but prisoners from Virginia.[38]

In Charleston, Bryan and his officers rejoined their regiment and received their back pay.[39] Just a few months later in August-September 1782, the impending British evacuation of Charleston became evident to all including Greene's army outside the city. There is some indication that the North Carolina Volunteers were officially disbanded during this period.[40] On October 10, 1782, an "Agreement on restoration of

34. Thomas Burke to Rowan County Sheriffs, April 6, 1782, SRNC, 16:270.

35. Pension application of Andrew Carnahan (W8577), National Archives and Records Administration.

36. Manuscripts and Archives Division, The New York Public Library. Thomas Burke from Alexander Leslie, April 10, 1782, New York Public Library Digital Collections, digitalcollections.nypl.org/items/c02c9a3b-6707-7080-e040-e00a180631aa.

37. Alexander Martin to Nathanael Greene, May 12, 1782, Richard K. Showman, ed., et. al., The Papers of Nathanael Greene (Chapel Hill, NC: Published for the Rhode Island Historical Society [by] University of North Carolina Press, 1976), 11:185-186.

38. Greene to Martin, July 1, 1782, Papers of Nathanael Greene, 11:386.

39. Julie Murtie Clark, Loyalists in the Southern Campaign of the Revolutionary War (Baltimore. MD: Genealogical Publishing, 1981), 1:361-362.

40. Todd Braisted, "An Introduction to North Carolina Loyalist Units," The Online Institute for Advanced Loyalist Studies, www.royalprovincial.com/military/rhist/ncindcoy/ncintro.htm.

property" was signed between the South Carolina government meeting in Orangeburg and British authorities stipulating that the British would return all slaves to their former owners and that Loyalists who remained would not be arrested or their property taken.[41] Despite the protection offered, at least 9,121 people quit Charleston for England or other British territories. This number included 3,794 whites and 5,327 blacks. Forty-three percent went to Jamaica, forty-two percent to East Florida, and five percent to Nova Scotia. Other locations at less than five percent each included England, New York, and St. Lucia.[42] Surprisingly, after spending some much time hiding out in North Carolina during the war, Samuel Bryan made the fateful decision to remove himself and his family to East Florida.[43]

Gov. Patrick Tonyn noted a possible draw of such a sizable portion of southern Loyalists to East Florida may have been that "their property may be without much difficulty transported . . . and where their Negroes may continue to be useful to them."[44] Samuel Bryan is listed among the returns of refugees in St. Augustine in 1783, his household consisting only of himself and a Black woman, presumably a slave.[45] His wife and nine children appear never to have made it to St. Augustine. The same appears to be true for Bryan's officers, Lt. Col. Hampton and Capt. White, who are not named in any available documents from East Florida at this time.

British records indicate that almost 7,500 British troops, Loyalists, and other emigres (2,925 white and 4,448 blacks) arrived in East Florida in 1782. By 1783, the population of the province had grown to between 16,000 and 17,375 people.[46] By April of that year, news reached St. Augustine that East Florida was to be returned to Spain as part of the peace settlement. As might be expected, the news did not sit well with many who would now, if they chose to remain British subjects, have to uproot and relocate themselves yet again. One dejected St. Augustine resident noted that "should England be engaged in an-

41. Alexander R. Stoesen, "The British Occupation of Charleston, 1780-1782," *The South Carolina Historical Magazine*, Volume 63, No. 2 (April 1962), 81.

42. Joseph W. Barnwell, "The Evacuation of Charleston by the British in 1782," *The South Carolina Historical and Genealogical Magazine*, 1910, 26.

43. Bryan Claim, AO/13/117/346.

44. Maya Jasanoff, *Liberty's Exiles: American Loyalists in the Revolutionary World* (New York, Alfred A. Knopf, 2011), Kindle Edition, location 1095.

45. Lawrence H. Feldman, *Colonization and Conquest: British Florida in the Eighteenth Century* (Baltimore, MD: Genealogical Publishing, 2007), 29.

46. Linda K. Williams, "East Florida as a Loyalist Haven." *The Florida Historical Quarterly*, 54, no. 4 (1976), 473.

other war . . . let her not expect that, out of thousands of us Refugees, there will be one who will draw a Sword in her Cause."[47] By August 1785 the evacuation of those choosing to leave was complete. Some 3,000 returned to the new United States, and another 4,000 to lands along the Mississippi River. Much smaller proportions of Loyalists went to Jamaica, Nova Scotia, the Bahamas, or England.[48]

Samuel Bryan was one of thousands of Loyalists who returned to the United States in 1783 and the years following the Treaty of Paris. He and "several other obnoxious characters" arrived in Wilmington, North Carolina in early June 1783. Bryan and the other "fugitives" were referred to local judges who sought unsuccessfully to have them sent back to St. Augustine.[49]

While Samuel Bryan's life was spared after his conviction for treason, his property was not. Two months after his trial, in May 1782, Bryan and dozens of other men were listed in a state law of those who were to have their land or property confiscated.[50] Later in 1782 some of Bryan's land and slaves were confiscated and sold. In another instance of rather extreme irony, two Patriot officers who had previous connections to Bryan personally profited from the sale of his slaves and land. Major Lewis, who protected Bryan at the Salisbury jail, bought at least three of his slaves.[51] Gen. Griffith Rutherford, who pursued Bryan's Loyalists in June 1780, received commissions on the sold land and slaves.[52] From available records, Bryan lost or was forced to sell 576 acres of land, reduced from 900 acres at the time of his conviction down to 324 acres in 1784.[53]

Samuel Bryan died in 1798 in Rowan County on the same land where he spent the better part of his life. That Bryan did not relocate to Kentucky to start a "new life" among his siblings is a testament to both his own character and that of his neighbors who appeared to have accepted him back into the community. By the time of his return in 1783, North Carolinians (or at least their legislature) were ready to legally reconcile with Loyalists. The *Act of Pardon & Oblivion* absolved most Loyalists from future persecution and punishment.[54] Interestingly,

47. Ibid, 477.

48. Ibid, 478.

49. Letter from Archibald Maclaine to George Hooper, June 12, 1783, SRNC, 16:965-967.

50. Acts of the North Carolina General Assembly, 1782, SRNC, 24:424.

51. A.B. Pruitt, *Abstracts of Sales of Confiscated Loyalist Land and Property in North Carolina* (Rocky Mount, NC: 1989), 5.

52. Ibid, 139.

53. Ibid, 200. & Linn, *Rowan County North Carolina Tax Lists*, 223.

54. Proclamation by Alexander Martin concerning Loyalists, July 28, 1783, SRNC, 16:850-851.

the *Act* exempted men like Bryan who had been British officers and those who spent more than a year outside the state with the enemy. Despite being exempted, there does not appear to be any further sanction against him from 1783 onward. Only two known documents bear his signature in the last fifteen years of his life: his will and a letter to a brother in Kentucky. Both documents bear a decidedly religious and almost penitent tone. An abundance of gratitude to the Almighty may have been in order after his wartime trials and other tribulations. Perhaps Col. Samuel Bryan, in one way, was aware of his relatively good fortune. He was able to return home, the same home he knew before the war, and to remain there relatively peacefully until the end of his life. Some or even most Loyalist refugees, who never returned or returned to America far afield from their original homes, may have preferred a similar fate.

The author would like to thank Todd Braisted for providing both insight and documentary sources on the North Carolina Volunteers and Royal North Carolina Regiment.

"She Had Gone to the Army . . . to Her Husband": Judith Lines's Unremarked Life

JOHN U. REES

When the War of the Revolution began in April 1775 Connecticuter Judith Jeffords née Philips was nineteen years old, had been married for two years, and had at least one child. She was, in the descriptive jargon of the time, a mulatto, meaning of mixed Afro-European lineage. We would know little to nothing of Mrs. Jeffords if her second husband, John Lines (Lynes), had not enlisted in the Continental Army and applied for a veteran's pension in the early nineteenth century.[1]

Judith Philips was born on January 24, 1756, likely in Windham, Connecticut, where she grew up. Her childhood friend Zeruiah Hebard recalled,

> from my birth until June 1784 I resided in Windham Con[necticut]. (at which time I was married) . . . a near neighbor of my Father was a Mr. [Samuel] Philips who had a daughter by the name of Judith & was two years older than myself . . . when girls we attended the same school, and was quite intimate / after . . . Judith was 17 or 18 years old she did not reside so constantly at Windham[2]

Zeruiah continued, "Judith married one Jefford a colored man when she was quite young and . . . he soon died . . . to the best of my recol-

---

1. National Archives (United States), Revolutionary War Pension and Bounty-Land Warrant Application Files (National Archives Microfilm Publication M804), Records of the Department of Veterans Affairs, Record Group 15, Washington, D.C., reel 1567, John Lines, "a black man" (W26775), deposition of Judith Lines.
2. Ibid., deposition of Judith Lines, November 14, 1836; deposition of Zeruiah Hebard, March 9, 1837. For quoted manuscript passages, where periods are lacking a forward slash / has been inserted between sentences. The original spelling has also been left intact.

lection within three or four years."[3] The pension papers even have a letter to Judith from her fiancé:

> Norwich April ye 16 day AD 1773
>   My Dearly beloved Intended Intended [*sic*] Wife I am poorly but Dont let that consern your Mind but seek furst the Kingdom of Heaven and all things shall be added / So no more for I am Sick / I Love you[r?] Person and long for your Soul Redemsion
> James Jeffrey[4]

Judith herself noted, "when I was seventeen years of age I married a man by the name of James Jeffords in the month of April and I lived with . . . Jeffords three years and 11 months when he died in March by whom I had three children one son after the decease of . . . Jeffords." Examining various testimonies in John Lines' pension file, it seems certain Judith married James Jeffords in 1773 and that he died in March 1777, at which time they had had two children, plus one born after Mr. Jefford's passing.[5]

Judith Jeffords, with her three children, returned to her father's home in Windham. At some point she caught the eye of another Windham resident. Judith recalled, "I lived a widow four years as much over as from March to July & was then married to John Lines in Colchester Con[necticut]. by one Esqr. Watrous." Evidently, she had found a man who would accept a ready-made family and all the responsibility that entailed.[6]

Again, from Zeruiah Hebard; she, "does distinctly recollect that . . . Judith married a man by the name of Lines who belonged to the Army . . . [she] well remembers hearing the Phillips family tell that she was

3. Ibid., deposition of Zeruiah Hebard, November 24, 1836.
4. Ibid., James Jeffrey (Jefford) letter, April 16, 1773.
5. Ibid., deposition of Judith Lines, March 14, 1837. Laurie Weinstein, Diane Hassan, and Samantha Mauro, authors of "The Unfulfilled American Revolution" suggest that Jeffords may have died while in military service. They note that a John Jeffords served in Connecticut regiments (possibly state units) stationed in the state's eastern portion. They also include two deserter notices for a John Jeffords serving in Connecticut Continental regiments. One of those was described as an Indian. That one of these men was Jeffrey Jeffords is possible but not probable. Another possibility is that Judith Jefford's husband was serving with the state militia when he died, but at this date we do not certainly know. Laurie Weinstein, Diane Hassan, and Samantha Mauro, "The Unfulfilled American Revolution," Cosimo A Sgarlata, David G. Orr, and Bethany A. Morrison, eds., *Historical Archaeology of the Revolutionary War Encampments of Washington's Army* (Gainesville: University Press of Florida, 2019), 201-202.
6. National Archives Pension Files, John Lines (W26775), deposition of Judith Lines, March 14, 1837.

married & also remembers that they said she had gone to the Army with or to her husband."[7] Regarding his military service, John Lines noted that,

> at Windham Connecticut about the middle of October AD 1780 [he] enlisted for three years . . . as a private soldier and was honourably discharged . . . on the 15th day of November AD 1783 . . . as near as he can recollect when he first joined the Army . . . he served in the company of Capt. [Nehemiah] Rice in the 5th Regt. Col. [Isaac] Sherman Connecticut Line; that he next served in Col. Butlers [4th] Regt. same Line, in Capt Harts [Jonathan Heart's] Company, being 4th. if he rightly remembers; . . . he then next served in Col. [Ebenezer] Huntingtons [1st] Regt. same Line as waiter to the Coll. & just before his discharge he was waiter to Col. Wyllys [likely Major John Plasgrave Wyllys] same Line; . . . prior to his sd. enlistment he had served his country as a private soldier in sd. War by various enlistments, about two years.[8]

Mr. Lines was fairly accurate in this recounting, even in the shuffling and reduction of regiments in the war's final years. He did misremember his enlistment date, which his service record shows to have occurred on March 30, 1781. As for his previous service, most likely he referred to stints in the militia; There was a John Lines, also from Windham and perhaps our man, who served with Latimer's Connecticut Militia Regiment from August 24 to October 22, 1777, taking part in the Saratoga campaign. In his pension testimony Lines may have misremembered the chronology of his military career; he placed his service in the 4th Connecticut after enlisting in the 5th Regiment, but service records reveal a John Lines who served as a six-months levy in the 4th Connecticut Regiment, beginning July 12, 1780 and being discharged that October, after only three months and fourteen days service. Finally, there was a John Lyon who enlisted in Col. Roger Enos's Connecticut State Regiment for three months in 1778. That man served from July to September, and was given extra pay for two months, eight days duty at West Point, where he was sent with a "with a team" of horses. We cannot know for certain whether Lines and Lyon were the same man, but, given variations in the spelling of names (later in life he gave his name as Lynes), it is a distinct possiblilty.[9]

7. National Archives Pension Files, deposition of Zeruiah Hebard, March 9, 1837.

8. Ibid., deposition of John Lines, April 18, 1818.

9. Compiled Service Records of Soldiers who Served in the American Army During the Revolutionary War (National Archives Microfilm Publication M881), Record Group 93 (Connecticut), 5th Regiment, John Lines; (Connecticut), Enos' Regiment, John Lyon; (Connecticut) Latimer's Militia Regiment, John Lines;, and (Connecticut) 4th Regiment, John Lines.

At any rate, perhaps due to lack of work, John Lines decided to enlist in March 1781. Judith seems certain they were married that July, but John's military service record notes he was at West Point in June, July, and August of 1781. Either Mrs. Lines' memory was remiss, or John was able to travel the 130 miles from West Point, New York, to Colchester, Connecticut, to get married. Perhaps, if he was the John Lyon mentioned above, he was again put in charge of a team and wagon, and sent to Colchester to pick up cargo. Windham is fourteen miles from Colchester, and John and Judith could have taken that opportunity to marry. This is, of course, informed supposition.[10]

We do know that Judith eventually joined her husband's regiment. In 1837 she recalled, "the next summer after I got married . . . [my husband] sent for me to him I think the place was called the Highlands / at that time my . . . husband was a waiter for Col. Sherman & while at the camp I had the small Pox – I think I staid about 3 or 4 months." Based on Judith's timeline, she joined her husband in summer 1782. We do not know if she took her three children, the youngest about four years old, with her, or left them in Connecticut with family or friends. That spring and early summer the 5th Connecticut Regiment, 1st Connecticut Brigade, was at or near West Point, New York. In late August the regiment, along with most of Gen. George Washington's army, traveled by bateaux downriver to Verplanck's Point, New York, site of the main army's last field encampment. If Judith stayed for four months, she may have ended her stay at Verplanck's Point, but more likely she had already gone home, or was recovering from smallpox.[11]

In reading Judith Lines' 1837 testimony, we can easily pass over her remark, "while at the camp I had the small Pox."[12] So much lies hidden behind those words; here is historian Elizabeth Fenn's description of what she experienced, or was lucky to avoid:

10. Ibid. (Connecticut) 5th Regiment, John Lines.
11. National Archives Pension Files, John Lines (W26775), deposition of Judith Lines, March 14, 1837. Charles H. Lesser, *Sinews of Independence: Monthly Strength Reports of the Continental Army* (Chicago, Il. and London: The University of Chicago Press, 1976), 228-236. For more on women at late-war West Point and the 1782 Verplanck Point camp see, John U. Rees, "'The multitude of women': An Examination of the Numbers of Female Followers with the Continental Army," the following sections: "1781, 'The women with the army who draw provisions'"; "1782, 'Rations . . . Without Whiskey': Colonel Henry Jackson's Regimental Provision Returns"; and "1783, 'The proportion of Women which ought to be allowed . . . ,'" *The Brigade Dispatch* (Journal of the Brigade of the American Revolution), three parts: vol. XXIII, no. 4 (Autumn 1992), 5-17; vol. XXIV, no. 1 (Winter 1993), 6-16; vol. XXIV, no. 2 (Spring 1993), 2-6 (Reprinted in *Minerva: Quarterly Report on Women and the Military*, vol. XIV, no. 2 (Summer 1996)).
12. National Archives Pension Files, John Lines (W26775), deposition of Judith Lines, March 14, 1837.

early symptoms would have resembled a very nasty case of the flu. Headache, backache, fever, vomiting, and general malaise all are among the initial signs of infection. The headache can be splitting; the backache excruciating ... Anxiety is another symptom. [In one particularly virulent form] Fretful, overwrought patients often die within days, never even developing the distinctive rash identified with the disease . . . The fever usually abates after the first day or two, and many patients rally briefly ... But the respite is deceptive ... By the fourth day of symptoms, the fever creeps upward again, and the first smallpox sores appear in the mouth, throat, and nasal passages. At this point, the patient is contagious ... The rash now moves quickly. Over a twenty-four hour period, it extends itself from the mucous membranes to the surface of the skin. On some, it turns inward, hemorrhaging subcutaneously. These victims die early, bleeding from the gums, eyes, nose, and other orifices. In most cases, however, the rash turns outward, covering the victim in pustules that concentrate in precisely the places where they will cause the most physical pain and psychological anguish: The soles of the feet, the palms of the hands, the face, the forearms, neck and back are focal points of the eruption. Elsewhere the distribution is lighter.

If the pustules ... do not run together, the prognosis is good. But if they converge upon one another in a single oozing mass, it is not. This is called confluent smallpox, and patients who develop it stand at least a 60 percent chance of dying. For some, as the rash progresses in the mouth and throat, drinking becomes difficult, and dehydration follows. Often, the odor peculiar to smallpox develops ... A missionary in Brazil described a 'pox so loathsome and evil-smelling that none could stand the great stench' of its victims. Patients at this stage of the disease can be hard to recognize. If damage to the eyes occurs, it begins now. Secondary bacterial infections can also set in, with consequences fully as severe as those of the smallpox.

Scabs start to form after two weeks of suffering, but this does little to end the patient's ordeal. In confluent or semi-confluent cases of the disease, scabbing can encrust most of the body, making any movement excruciating ... Death, when it occurs, usually comes after ten to sixteen days of suffering. Thereafter, the risk drops significantly as fever subsides and unsightly scars replace scabs and pustules. After four weeks of illness, only the lesions encapsulated in the palms of the hands and the soles of the feet remain intact ... in most cases, the usual course of the disease – from initial infection [eleven days before the first symptoms occur] to the loss of all the scabs – runs a little over a month. Patients remain contagious until the last scab falls off ... Most survivors bear ... numerous scars, and some are blinded ... those who live through the illness can count themselves fortunate. Immune for life, they need never fear smallpox again.[13]

It is not known how many smallpox scars Judith retained after her recovery, but army deserter descriptions for the period 1775 to 1783 show that pox marks were common. Of seven men in Parson's Connecticut Regiment, June to August 1775, two were described as "mark'd with the Small Pox." Another soldier of the 22nd Continental Regiment in April 1776 was said to be "much pox broken."[14]

Lines' pension file also contains a singular artifact. Judith noted in her testimony, "my . . . husband used to write to me when he was in the Army & I have one of his letters now & which I give to the magistrate who takes this my Deposition it is dated November 11, 1781 & is in the hand writing of . . . my husband."[15]

> November the 11 1781 i take this Opper tuna ty to send to you my deer and loving wife to let you now that i am well and hopeing these lines may find you and the Children Well / I am Pleased [several illegible words] I shold be very glad to hear from you my deer and loveing wife / I Cant but think it hard that I havnt had one letter [several illegible words] from home and this is the six letter of [mine?] and I haven't received one / I have seen my father and my mother [is] dead and one of my brothers mother died 3 [weaks?] a go brother died 2 days a go [sic]/ i have two brothers liveing and all my sisters / father is very much pleased of you and he intends to Come and se[e] you this faal or the first of the winter / it is about six Weeks since i seen father he gives his cind Com Ply ments to you and so does all my brothers and sisters / they are at the north river a bout sixteen miles from fishkill / o my deer and loveing wife [several illegible words] the love the Cind love that I have for you / I have gon a [illegible words] for your sake and I Could not help it god bless your deep love / [illegible name] and his wife is well / Game [possibly short for Gamaliel; last name Phillingly?] was in Camp last week and he says they was all well / [I] belong to Carnol [Isaac] Shermans [5th Connecticut] Rg ment Capting [illegible] Compy ny / we lay at fishkill now / i should be ver[y] glad if you would take [two illegible words] and Send me a letter how

13. Elizabeth A. Fenn, *Pox Americana: The Great Smallpox Epidemic of 1775–82* (New York: Hill and Wang, a Division of Farrar, Straus and Giroux, 2001), 16, 18.

14. Joseph Lee Boyle, *'He loves a good deal of rum . . .': Military Desertions during the American Revolution, 1775-1783*, vol. 1 (1775-June 30, 1777), vol. 2 (June 30, 1777-1783) (Baltimore, MD: Genealogical Publishing Co., 2009), 1, 4, 36.

15. National Archives Pension Files, John Lines (W26775), deposition of Judith Lines, March 14, 1837.

you have lived this sum mer and [whether?] the house is dun and
[whether?] you kill that cow or [whether?] you have got a nother / i
want to [k]now all these things very much / i in tend to Come home
this winter if I Can but dont [k]now if i can / god bless your deer soul
if I Could se you my self then I Could talk with you my deer wife as I
like i have seen hard times [several illegible words] I have lived a-11-
day With Bread [only] / i have the [illegible word] a good deal bad so
I re mane your loveing husband un tel death John lines.[16]

This letter, the only known surviving example written by an African
American Continental soldier to his family, provides a few more insights into Mr. and Mrs. Lines' lives and wartime experiences. First,
John Lines could read and write and, as may be inferred by the fact his
wife went to school when young, Judith could read as well. The ap-
proximate literacy rate in New England at the time of the Revolution
was 80 percent for men, and 50 percent for women. One source notes
that the middle states had similar literacy levels, the southern states
less so, and people living in cities enjoyed higher levels of reading and
writing than rural populations. Where free black citizens fit into these
generalizations is not well known, but in most states, and, again, particularly in the south, they likely fared worse than white citizens.[17]

John Lines also revealed that his wife was taking care of their family,
home, and livestock, largely on her own, though she likely had some
assistance from family or neighbors. Still, a large responsibility for one
person, especially given the hard labor involved in supporting an eighteenth century household.[18]

Private Lines's note about eating only bread for eleven days rings
true with what we know of Continental Army food supply. While food
was at times varied and relatively plentiful, shortages were all too familiar, even for officers. Pennsylvania lieutenant colonel Josiah Harmar

16. National Archives Pension Files, John Lines to Judith Lines (letter), November 11,
1781. John Lines' letter is faint and hard to transcribe. I reached out for help and Philip
Mead, Chief Historian and Director of Interpretation at the Museum of the American Revolution in Philadelphia, took up the challenge and produced a comprehensive transcription.
With that in hand, I was able to fill in some of the missing parts, contribute some amendments, and add some judicious editing. My heartfelt thanks to Phil for his help.
17. "How Literacy Rates Have Improved Since 1776," The Read Center, readcenter.org/lit-
eracy-rates-improved-since-1776/#:~:text=Moreover%2C%20literacy%20rates%
20in%20America,in%20four%20Americans%20were%20illiterate. "Did Public Schools
Really Improve American Literacy?," Foundation for Economic Education, fee.org/arti-
cles/did-public-schools-really-improve-american-literacy/.
18. For insights imto the difficulties of running a house and property during that era see,
Laurel Thatcher Ulrich, The Life of Martha Ballard, Based on Her Diary, 1785-1812 (New
York: Alfred A. Knopf, 1990).

wrote on August 22, 1780, "Provisions extreme scarce; only half a Lb. Meat in three days," and three days later, "This movement of our . . . [troops] is occasioned through dire necessity, the Army being on the point of starving." While building huts in December 1779 Massachusetts surgeon James Thacher related, "notwithstanding large fires, we can scarcely keep from freezing. In addition to other sufferings, the whole army has been for seven or eight days entirely destitute of the staff of life; our only food is miserable fresh beef, without bread, salt, or vegetables." Even when life became settled, living conditions were spartan during winter months. From "Camp [at the] Jersey Hutts," Maj. John Noble Cummings noted in February 1781, "We live excellently in Camp upon a Variety of Dishes Viz: Salt Beef and Ash Cake for Breakfast D[itt]o for Dinner and the same for Supper provided there is any left."[19]

Regarding women with Connecticut Continental regiments, we have little information until the war's last year. A "Return of the number of Women and Children in the several regiments and Corps stationed at, and in the vicinity of West Point and New Windsor" is dated January 24, 1783 and includes the three remaining units from the state. At that time, while Judith was already home, John Lines had been transferred to the 1st Connecticut Regiment, which contained ten women and eight children. The 2nd and 3rd Regiments had, respectively, twelve women and eight children, and eleven women and six children.[20]

John Lines remained in the army until November 15, 1783, his discharge signed by Maj. Gen. Henry Knox, commander of the Continental Army's artillery and destined to be the United States' first Secretary of War. Lines was soon after reunited with Judith and the children back home in Windham. At the time of their marriage, Judith and John had three children, all from Judith's first marriage, As she noted in her March

19. Josiah Harmar, "Lieut. Colonel Josiah Harmar's Journal. No: 1." November 11, 1778 to September 2, 1780, p. 79, Josiah Harmar Papers, William L. Clements Library, Ann Arbor, Michigan. Microfilm, Harmar Papers, vol. 27, reel 10. James Thacher, *Military Journal of the American Revolution* (Hartford, Ct. 1862), 181. John N. Cummings to John Ladd Howell, February 24, 1781, Howell Papers, Stewart Collection, Savitz Library, Rowan State College, Glassboro, New Jersey. For more on enlisted soldiers' food see, John U. Rees, "'To the hungry soul every bitter thing is sweet.' Soldiers' Food and Cooking in the War for Independence," www.scribd.com/doc/129368664/To-the-hungry-soul-every-bitter-thing-is-sweet-Soldiers-Food-and-Cooking-in-the-War-for-Independence.

20. "Return of the number of Women and Children in the several regiments and Corps stationed at, and in the vicinity of West Point and New Windsor, that drew Rations under the late Regulation, shewing also the Number of Rations allowed for Women and Children by the present system," January 24, 1783, Revolutionary War Rolls (National Archives Microfilm Publication M246), Record Group 93 (Washington, D.C., 1980), pp. 259-260. Rees, "The multitude of women," vol. XXIV, no. 2 (Spring 1993), 2-3.

1837 depostion,"The first Child I had by my last husband was not born until we had been married about four years"; that would make the baby's birthyear about 1785. In searching the United States census records, I only found one entry that matched their family. In 1790 a Lynes family, with John listed as head of household, resided in Windham, and consisted of six "all other free persons," the euphemism for people of color. If that is the correct family, which is more than likely, by that date the Lines still had only four children. In July 1820 John mentioned his twenty-eight-year-old son Samuel (named after Judith's father), who would have been born in around 1792.[21]

That same year sixty-six-year-old Lines, then living in Vermont, submitted a schedule of his finances and belongings, a pension requirement implemented after the intitial 1818 legislation.

[Dated July 3, 1820]
Real Estate $630.00 2 Oxen 2 Cows 8 Sheep 2 Calves
1 Horse 2 Hogs 3 Pigs Household Furniture $18. in all $784.50
I justly owe sundry persons $560.05
  My occupation has been that of a Farmer am unable to do much Labour My wife Judith Lines is 64 Years of Age is sick with a disord[er] upon the liver as the doctor says My son Samuel Lines aged 28 Years has Convulsion fitts not able to do much Labour and dependent on me for his support John Lines[22]

In his 1836 supporting testimony for John Lines' pension application Peres Tracy, son of another 5th Connecticut veteran, recounted,

I was acquainted with John Lines a black man formerly of Windham Con. afterwards of Brookfield Vt. nearly fifty years ago & until his death in 1828 . . . my Father Peres Tracy was in the Army of the Revolution . . . while living in Windham Con. [as] a neighbor to . . . Lines I have heard my Father say he used to be acquainted with Lines in the Army & that he was waiter to Col. . . . Sherman & that for a considerable time during one Campaign Lines wife was with him in Camp & used to work for . . . Sherman & others[23]

21. National Archives Pension Files, John Lines (W26775), Continental Army discharge paper, November 15, 1783, and John Lines' schedule of finances and belongings, July 3, 1820. U.S Federal Census Collection, 1790-1940; 1790 census, John Lynes family, Windham, Connecticut, www.ancestrylibrary.com/search/categories/usfedcen/.
22. National Archives Pension Files, John Lines (W26775), John Lines' schedule of finances and belongings, July 3, 1820.
23. National Archives Pension Files, John Lines (W26775), deposition of Peres Tracy, November 15, 1836. Compiled Service Records of Revolutinary Soldiers (Connecticut), 5th Regiment, Peraz Tracy, enlisted July 3, 1781, discharged June 27, 1782.

Peres went on, "I moved from Windham Co. to this town [Randolph, Vermont] forty three years since & that . . . Lines and his family moved from the same place the same year to Brookfield town adjoining." That move would have been in 1793, the year following Samuel Lines' birth. The Lines family change of residence came just two years after Vermont gained statehood. When Vermont was established as a republic in July 1777 its Constitution banned slavery; another codicil decreed that currently enslaved males would gain their freedom at age twenty-one, females at eighteen, thus making it the promised land for some African Americans at the time.[24]

We do not know much of the Lines family after they emigrated to Vermont. John Lines continued farming on their new property, but did other work as well. Mr. Tracy noted, "I often labored with him & heard him relate his exploits while in the war." Reuben Peck, another resident of Brookfield, stated, "I was for many years acquainted with one John Lines a black man . . . Lines used to work for my father being a wall layer & . . . [I] deponent often heard him relate about his services & exploits in the War of the Revolution & of his wife being in the Army with him."[25]

It is notable the people who contributed testimony supporting John's and Judith's pension applications were, despite my first assumptions, all white, a fact corroborated by searching the 1790 through 1830 censuses. Sometimes the deponent's race is clear, such as when Zeruiah Hebard commented she, "was acquainted with Lines & his wife after the war both in Connecticut & Vermont and knows they were considered very reputable people & <u>for colored people</u> had a great many friends."[26]

On November 14, 1836, attempting to claim a widow's pension, Judith Lines was interviewed at home in Brookfield. Her testimony reads in part,

> Judith Lynde or Lines a resident of . . . Brookfield (who being by reason of bodily infirmity unable to attend Court) aged Eighty years the 14th. day of January last . . . She is the widow of John Lynde or Lines a black

24. National Archives Pension Files, John Lines (W26775), deposition of Peres Tracy, November 15, 1836. Samuel Lines birthdate is from ibid., John Lines' schedule of finances and belongings, July 3, 1820. Winthrop D. Jordan, *White Over Black: American Attitudes Toward the Negro, 1550–1812* (Baltimore, Md.: Penguin Books, Inc., 1971), 345.

25. National Archives Pension Files, John Lines (W26775), deposition of Peres Tracy, November 15, 1836, and deposition of Reuben Peck, March 14, 1836.

26. U.S Federal Census Collection, 1790-1940; 1790 census, John Lynes family, Windham, Connecticut, www.ancestrylibrary.com/search/categories/usfedcen/. National Archives Pension Files, John Lines (W26775), deposition of Zeruiah Hebard, March 9, 1837.

man who [was] a soldier in the War of the Revolution . . . her . . . husband died at Brookfield . . . in July 1828.[27]

After John's death his wife was entitled to a pension, but Judith had no proof of their marriage. On the 29th of the same month Assistant Judge and Clerk of the Probate Court J.K. Parish wrote J.L Edwards, Federal Commissioner of Pensions, describing the problem.

> Sir Herewith I forward to the Department the declaration of Judith Lines . . . I have been unable to ascertain by positive proof from records or from witnesses who were present at the marriage the absolute time of the marriage
>
> The testimony of Mr. & Mrs. [Diah and Zeruiah] Hebard, [Peres] Tracy and Parish [sic, possibly meant to be Reuben Peck] all go to show that she must have been married before the close of the war – There is no family record and by a letter herewith forwarded I am convinced there is no record in the Town Clerks office in Colchester Con[necticut]. & that there can be no record found made by the Justice who married her
>
> Should the Department require positive or record proof in this case I fear the claimant will fail, although I think there can be no doubt of the fact of her marriage some time previous to the close of the war, such as being in the Army &c. Her own story in short is this She married Jeffords when 17 yrs. Old & lived with him 3 years 11 months when he died, that she was a widow a month or two more than four years when she was married to Lines, that there was no wedding that she & Lines went to the Justice who married them, Lines then belonged to the Army but she thinks his time was about out & he afterwards enlisted for she thinks during the war
>
> I apprehend from enquiry of aged person they were not in those days very particular in the records of marriages of persons of colour Lines was black & his wife a mulatto
>
> I have no doubt but the decision of the Department in this case as in others will be as favourable as the rules will admit for the applicant.[28]

In the end, all these efforts succeeded, and Judith received a pension of 80 dollars per year, backdated to March 4, 1831. Her pension certificate was issued on May 15, 1837, but at age eighty-one she may not have long benefitted from her just due.[29]

27. U.S Federal Census Collection, 1790-1940, deposition of Judith Lines/Lynde, November 14, 1836.

28. National Archives Pension Files, John Lines (W26775), J.K. Parish to J.L Edwards (letter), November 29, 1836.

29. Ibid., Judith Lines Pension Certificate, awarded May 15, 1837, Windsor, Vermont.

It is only fair we give Judith Lines the last word, a recap of her life, perhaps a self-made eulogy. This is from her March 14, 1837 deposition:

> I Judith Lines of Brookfield in Orange County & state of Vermont . . . . say that I was born in Con. in the town of Windham, and that when I was seventeen years of age I married a man by the name of James Jeffords in the month of April [1773] . . . he died in March [1777] by whom I had three children one son after the decease of . . . Jeffords . . . I lived a widow four years [and four months] . . . & was then married to John Lines in Colchester Con. By one Esqr. Watrous—The first Child I had by my last husband was not born until we had been married about four years – I further . . . say that the next summer after I got married . . . [my husband] sent for me to him I think the place was called the Highlands / at that time my . . . husband was a waiter for Col. Sherman & while at the camp I had the small Pox—I think I staid about 3 or 4 months—I further . . . say that my husband had a certificate of his marriage from Esqr. Watrous but it is probably lost I have not seen it for several years . . . I further testify that my youngest son died of a wound recd. in the last war, his name was Benjamin, the wound was recd. at the Battle of Chippewa[30]

And so the rising generations mirrored their elders, and continued to serve, sacrifice, and contribute to the welfare of their country.

30. Ibid., deposition of Judith Lines, March 14, 1837. No evidence has been found of a Benjamin Lines being wounded in the War of 1812. It may be that Judith misspoke when she testified and gave the wrong name. Two soldiers seem to fit her description. John Lynes, was a private in the 25th U.S. Regiment, a unit that fought at the Battle of Chippewa, July 5, 1814. John Lynes was placed on the pension roll on January 26, 1816, to commence from September 20, 1815. He died on June 24, 1824. A more likely match is William Lynes; he enlisted in the 30th U.S. Regiment in Burlington, Vermont, and was noted to have black eyes, curly hair, and a black complexion. William fought at La Colle Mills in March 1814, and at Plattsburgh in September 1814. In the latter battle he was wounded while serving as a marine aboard the American fleet. *The Pension Roll of 1835* (Indexed Edition, in Four Volumes) vol. 1, The New England States (reprint, Baltimore, MD: Clearfield Publishing Co., Inc, 2002), Connecticut Pension Roll, 9. Thanks to my cousin Matthew C. White for finding this information.

The Yorktown Tragedy:
Washington's Slave Roundup

GREGORY J. W. URWIN

On October 19, 1781, Gen. George Washington attained his apex as a soldier. Straddling a spirited charger at the head of a formidable Franco-American army, Washington watched impassively as 6,000 humiliated British, German, and Loyalist soldiers under the command of Lt. Gen. Charles, Second Earl Cornwallis, emerged from their fortifications to lay down their arms in surrender outside Yorktown, Virginia. The following day, Washington voiced the elation filling his heart in a general order congratulating his subordinates "upon the Glorious events of yesterday." Ordinarily a stickler for discipline, Washington authorized the release of every American soldier under arrest "In order to Diffuse the general Joy through every breast."[1]

Five days later, October 25, the Continental Army's commander-in-chief issued quite a different order. Thousands of Virginia slaves—"Negroes or Molattoes" as Washington called them—had fled to the British in hopes of escaping a lifetime of bondage. Washington directed that these runaways be rounded up and entrusted to guards at two fortified positions on either side of the York River. There they would be held until arrangements could be made to return them to their enslavers. Thus, with the stroke of a pen, Washington converted his faithful Continentals—the men credited with winning American independence—into an army of slave catchers.[2]

This is not the way that Americans choose to remember Yorktown. When President Ronald Reagan attended the festivities marking the

---

1. "G.O. after orders," October 20, 1781, in George Fleming, "Orderly Book, Second Regiment of Continental Artillery, 1 October 1781-26 April 1782," MS 2003.12, Special Collections, John D. Rockefeller, Jr., Research Library, Colonial Williamsburg Foundation, Williamsburg, VA.
2. "After Orders," October 25, 1781, in Fleming, "Orderly Book."

battle's bicentennial in October 1981, a crowd of 60,000 nodded in approval as he described Washington's crowning triumph as "a victory for the right of self-determination. It was and is the affirmation that freedom will eventually triumph over tyranny."[3] For the African Americans who constituted one fifth of the young United States' population in 1781, however, Yorktown did not mark the culmination of a long and grueling struggle for freedom. Rather, it guaranteed the perpetuation of slavery for eight additional decades.

Perhaps the most striking thing about Washington's fugitive-slave roundup is that the document authorizing it has lain hidden in plain sight for more than two centuries. A copy exists among Washington's papers at the Library of Congress, and more can be found at other archives in the surviving compilations of daily orders maintained by every Continental brigade and regiment under the dauntless Virginian's immediate command. Most historians who cover Yorktown are content to celebrate Washington's military genius. The blinders imposed by the lingering effects of American exceptionalism deter them from grappling with issues that would complicate the traditional triumphalist narrative. A clear-eyed look at the sources—including those recorded by British and German participants—reveals that for the 200,000 African Americans who composed 40 percent of the Old Dominion's population, freedom wore a red coat, not blue, in 1781.[4]

In the leadup to the War of Independence, prominent white colonists feared that British authorities would liberate their slaves in retaliation for rebellion. The African-American population certainly hoped that would be the case. After conversing with two Blacks in service to a Pennsylvania family fleeing the Redcoats' advance on Philadelphia, Rev. Henry Melchior Muhlenberg, a Lutheran minister, confided

3. "Excerpts From President's Remarks," *New York Times*, October 20, 1981, A6; and Kurt Andersen, "A Last Bicentennial Bash," *Time*, 2 November 1981, 31.
4. Operational histories covering 1781 Virginia in which black lives matter little or not at all include: Henry P. Johnston, *The Yorktown Campaigns and Surrender of Cornwallis 1781* (New York: Harper & Brothers, 1881); Thomas J. Fleming, *Beat the Last Drum: The Siege of Yorktown* (New York: St. Martin's Press, 1866); Burke Davis, *The Campaign That Won America: The Story of Yorktown* (New York: Dial Press, 1970); Brendan Morrissey, *Yorktown 1781: The World Turned Upside Down* (Oxford: Osprey Publishing Limited, 1997); William H. Hallahan, *The Day the Revolution Ended, 19 October 1781* (Hoboken, NJ: John Wiley & Sons, Inc., 2004); Richard M. Ketchum, *Victory at Yorktown: The Campaign That Won America* (New York: Henry Holt and Company, 2004); Jerome A. Greene, *The Guns of Independence: The Siege of Yorktown* (New York: Savas Beatie, 2005); and Ian Saberton's otherwise perceptive *The American Revolutionary War in the South: Re-evaluation from a British Perspective in the Light of the Cornwallis Papers* (Tolworth, Surrey: Grosvenor House Publishing Limited, 2018).

to his diary on September 20, 1777: "They secretly wished that the British army might win, for then all Negro slaves will gain their freedom. It is said that this sentiment is almost universal among the *Negroes* in America."[5]

These aspirations struck George III's soldiers with shocking force once the war's focus shifted from New England and the Middle Colonies to the South in 1778. Lt. Col. Banastre Tarleton, the hell-for-leather British cavalryman, bore witness to this phenomenon following the capture of Charleston, South Carolina, in May 1780. "All the negroes," he testified, "men, women, and children, upon the approach of any detachment of the King's troops, thought themselves absolved from all respect to their American masters, and entirely released from servitude: Influenced by this idea, they quitted the plantations, and followed the army."[6] Lord Cornwallis, who would soon take command of British forces in the South, expressed his irritation at this road-choking Black exodus as he penetrated the prostrate Palmetto State. "The number of Negroes that attend this Corps," he complained, "is a most serious distress to us."[7]

This pattern of behavior continued after Virginia became the conflict's decisive theater in 1781. The Old Dominion—the largest, most populous, and richest of the young republic's thirteen states—absorbed three British invasions that year. On December 20, 1780, nearly 1,800 troops under Benedict Arnold, who had betrayed the Continental cause to become a British brigadier general, set sail from Sandy Hook, New Jersey, for Chesapeake Bay. Without pausing to give the Virginia militia a chance to mobilize, the Connecticut-born Arnold swept up the James River and became the first Yankee general to capture Richmond, the state's new capital, on January 5, 1781. Arnold then retired downstream to Portsmouth on the Elizabeth River, which he converted into a fortified naval base. More than 2,000 British reinforcements landed at Portsmouth on April 1, which facilitated another amphibious lunge up the James that culminated at Petersburg twenty-four days later. Lord

5. David Waldstreicher, *Runaway America: Benjamin Franklin, Slavery, and the American Revolution* (New York: Hill and Wang, 2004), 210; Theodore G. Tappert and John W. Doberstein, trans., *The Journal of Henry Melchior Muhlenberg*, 3 vols. (Philadelphia: Muhlenberg Press, 1942-58), 3: 78.

6. Banastre Tarleton, *A History of the Campaigns of 1780 and 1781 in the Southern Provinces of North America* (1787; reprint, New York: New York Times and Arno Press, 1968), 89-90.

7. Charles, Second Earl Cornwallis, to Sir Henry Clinton, May 17, 1780, Sir Henry Clinton Papers, William L. Clements Library, University of Michigan, Ann Arbor, MI.

Cornwallis showed up at Petersburg on May 20 with the survivors of the arduous winter campaign he had conducted in North Carolina.[8]

Along with additional British reinforcements from New York that reached Cornwallis almost immediately, he now mustered more than 6,500 fit officers and men—a big enough force to march almost anywhere in Virginia that he desired while still retaining his hold on Portsmouth. With the king's soldiers able to penetrate parts of the Old Dominion that had hitherto escaped the touch of war, more and more enslaved persons rose to meet them. As Robert Honyman, a local physician, scribbled in his diary: "Many Gentlemen lost 30, 40, 50, 60, or 70 Negroes besides their stocks of Cattle, Sheep & Horses. Some plantations were entirely cleared, & not a single Negro remained." Richard Henry Lee, a prominent leader in the independence movement, confided fearfully to his brother, "Tis said that 2 or 3000 negroes march in their train, that every kind of Stock which they cannot remove they destroy."[9]

Just one year earlier, Cornwallis had regarded fugitive slaves as impediments to his operations. Once he reached Virginia, however, he gave clear indications that he now viewed these Black freedom seekers as military assets. After the earl's army reached Dr. Honyman's neighborhood, the latter observed, "Where ever they had an opportunity, the

8. "Extract of a Letter from New-York, Dec," *St. James's Chronicle or the British Evening Post* (London), January 25-27, 1781; Johann Ewald, *Diary of the American War: A Hessian Diary*, trans. and ed., Joseph Tustin (New Haven: Yale University Press, 1979), 258-78, 294-99; John Graves Simcoe, *Simcoe's Military Journal: A History of the Operations of a Partisan Corps Called the Queen's Rangers, Commanded by Lieut. Col. J. G. Simcoe, during the War of the American Revolution* (1844; reprint, New York: New York Times & Arno Press, 1968), 159-204; Cornwallis to Clinton, May 20, 1781; Cornwallis to Clinton, May 26, 1781; "Return of the Troops sent to Virginia ————- Since Oct. 80," circa June 1, 1781; Benedict Arnold to Clinton, May 12, 1781; "Return of the Troops in Virginia on Lord Cornwallis's arrival and including the Corps with his Lordship," circa June 1781, all in Clinton Papers; Tarleton, *Southern Campaigns*, 285, 294-95; Charles Stedman, *The History of the Origin, Progress, and Termination of the American War*, 2 vols. (Dublin: P. Wogan, P. Byrne, J. Moore, and W. Moore, 1794), 2: 393-94; Johann Ewald, "Diary Kept by Captain Ewald of the Honourable Field Jager Corps concerning the Expedition under Brigadier-General Arnold," December 21, 1780—January 21, 1781, Knyphausen Correspondence, Part 2, GG 360, Morristown National Historical Park, Morristown, NJ, microfilm at the David Library of the American Revolution, Washington Crossing, PA.
9. Richard Henry Lee to William Lee, July 15, 1781, in James Curtis Ballagh, ed., *The Letters of Richard Henry Lee*, 2 vols. (New York: Macmillan Company, 1911-14), 2: 230; Richard K. MacMaster, ed., "News of the Yorktown Campaign: The Journal of Dr. Robert Honyman, April 17-November 25, 1781," *Virginia Magazine of History and Biography* 79 (October 1971): 394.

soldiers & inferior officers likewise, enticed & flattered the Negroes,
& prevailed on vast numbers to go along with them."[10]

These runaways contributed immeasurably to Cornwallis' mobility
by bringing him the choicest thoroughbreds from their enslavers' sta-
bles. This steady infusion of prime horseflesh gave the earl the most
fearsome cavalry force fielded during the Revolutionary War, and he
had enough horses left over to mount hundreds of his infantry. Some
Blacks found jobs as officers' servants, and others worked as foragers
or menial laborers. Black labor raised the fortifications that protected
Portsmouth and later encircled Cornwallis's second base at Yorktown.
A few fugitive slaves served the British as guides, and one daring man
assumed the role of a double agent, helping to lead a force of Continentals and militia into a costly ambush at Green Spring on July 6,
1781.[11]

A few weeks after that engagement, Gov. Thomas Nelson wrote
Cornwallis to enquire if there were any way Virginia planters could recover what they considered to be their property. The British commander responded with a politely worded note that gave Nelson scant
comfort: "Any proprietor not in Arms against us, or holding an Office
of trust under the Authority of Congress and willing to give his parole
that he will not in future act against His Majesty's interest, will be in-
dulged with permission to search the Camp for his Negroes & to take
them if they are willing to go with him." In other words, Cornwallis
declared he would force no enslaved person to return to an enslaver—
even those claimed by Loyalists. Had the earl prevailed in Virginia, this

10. MacMaster, "Honyman Journal," 400; Ewald, *Journal*, 335.

11. *Royal Gazette* (New York), August 29, 1781; Regimental Orders, July 28, 1781, After
Orders, August 4, 1781, Morning Regimental Orders, August 25, 1781, all in "British
Order Book: H.B.M. 43rd Regiment of Foot, General Orders, May 23 to August 25,
1781," British Museum, London; William Phillips to Clinton, April 3, 1781, PRO
30/11/5/155-62, Alexander Ross to Lieutenant Paterson, June 20, 1781, PRO
30/11/87/15-16, and Cornwallis to Charles O'Hara, August 4, 1781, PRO 30/11/89/5,
all in Charles Cornwallis: Papers, National Archives, Kew; Headquarters, Cox's Plantation,
June 5, 1781, "'Cornwallis' Orderly Book,' February 8, 1781-July 13, 1781," Orderly Book
Collection, 1764-1815, William L. Clements Library; Joseph G. Rosengarten, trans. and
ed., "Popp's Journal, 1777-1783," *Pennsylvania Magazine of History and Biography* 26
(1902): 38; Edmund Pendleton to James Madison, September 10, 1781, in David John
Mays, ed., *The Letters and Papers of Edmund Pendleton, 1734-1803*, 2 vols. (Charlottesville:
University Press of Virginia, 1967), 1: 371; Robert J. Tilden, trans, "The Doehla Journal,"
William and Mary College Quarterly History Magazine 2nd Series, 22 (1942): 243; Marquis
de Lafayette to George Washington, July 20, 1781, in Louis Gottschalk, ed., *The Letters of
Lafayette to Washington, 1777-1799* (Philadelphia: American Philosophical Society, 1976),
209; Tarleton, *Southern Campaigns*, 353.

de facto emancipation proclamation might have drastically altered the course of U.S. history. Washington and the French squelched that prospect three months later, however, when they trapped the British at Yorktown.[12]

Historians still debate over the exact number of Virginia Blacks who sought British protection in 1781. Thomas Jefferson, the Old Dominion's governor during the first half of that year, claimed that the state lost 30,000 enslaved to Cornwallis—a gross exaggeration. A database compiled from affidavits filed by Rebel planters in nineteen counties and residents of Portsmouth yielded a list of 1,119 runaways, but that figure is only a partial sample of the whole.[13]

Even if Cornwallis had achieved military success, things would have still ended tragically for many Black fugitives who joined their fortunes to his. Smallpox, possibly the eighteenth century's greatest killer, marched in the earl's ranks, and African Americans sickened and died in droves after he entered Virginia. Brig. Gen. Edward Hand, one of Washington's senior staff officers, recorded this trenchant comment during the Yorktown siege: "almost every Thicket Affords you the Disagreable prospect of a Wretched Negroes Carcase brought to the earth by disease & famine. the Poor deluded Creatures are either so much Afraid of the displeasure of their owners that they voluntarily starved to death or were by disease unable to Seek Sustenance." Among the inhabitants of Revolutionary America who gave their all for liberty, these "Wretched Negroes" should join those in the forefront.[14]

Slavery's victory at Yorktown reveals the corruption that infected the American Revolution. Throughout United States history, liberty and opportunity have been purchased for some through the oppression of others. Our revered Founders—intent on rallying mass support for a revolt intended to replace one set of colonial elites with another—in-

12. Thomas Nelson to Cornwallis, October 20, 1781, PRO 30/11/90/17-18, and Cornwallis to Nelson, August 6, 1781, PRO 30/11/90/19-20, both in Cornwallis Papers.

13. Thomas Jefferson to William Gordon, July 16, 1788, in Julian P. Boyd, et al., *The Papers of Thomas Jefferson*, 43 vols. (Princeton: Princeton University Press, 1950-2018), 13: 363-64; Cassandra Pybus, "Jefferson's Faulty Math: The Question of Slave Defections in the American Revolution," *William and Mary Quarterly* 58 (April 2005): 243, 247-48, 258-59, 261. The author and his wife, Cathy Kunzinger Urwin, constructed that database from the numerous complaints pertaining to citizens' property lost and destroyed by the British, which were sent to the Virginia General Assembly in 1782. Those records reside today at the Library of Virginia in Richmond. It bears noting, however, that the complaints from a dozen counties affected by the British invasions are missing.

14. Edward Hand to Jasper Yeates, October 12, 1781, Edward Hand Papers, 1775-1801, MssCol 17927, Archives & Manuscripts, New York Public Library, New York, NY.

dulged in egalitarian rhetoric that most of them did not believe. What redeemed the Revolution is the fact that so many common Americans took that rhetoric literally. Over the centuries, various outgroups have agitated to expand the frontiers of freedom, and their efforts have made this country a fitter place to live. If we think of the Revolution as an ongoing process rather than a sanitized relic to be cloaked by myth, that movement can still serve as a positive force in American society and its professed principles remain worthy of celebration.

Such as are Absolutely Free:
Benjamin Thompson's Black Troopers

TODD W. BRAISTED

At the Museum of the American Revolution in Philadelphia, there is an exhibit in the core gallery examining the choices, opportunities and constraints of African Americans in Virginia in 1781. Titled "Sometimes, freedom wore a red coat" it seeks to educate people on the effect the British Army had on operating in areas where slavery flourished, and the role of these former slaves in Britain's war effort. It is here where things can get murky—"joining the army" may not have meant what the phrase implies at face value.

At the very start of the war in America, the British recognized the need for locally-raised forces. American troops had been raised in the colonies for all previous conflicts fought there, and despite the nature of the newest war, the British felt confident that enough Americans remained loyal to bolster their ranks, at least until more troops could be raised in Europe. Troops raised by direction of the commander-in-chief of the Army in America, such as the Royal Highland Emigrants, would be known as Provincials. Regiments in the Provincial Establishment would receive arms, accoutrements, equipage, pay, clothing and provisions the same as British soldiers, be under the same discipline, serve for the duration of the war and be liable for service anywhere, although it was understood they would not leave North America.[1]

Not all troops raised in America would fall under this establishment. The governors of the provinces, those who still held some power or control, could call out their militia or raise new corps on their own authority, paid for by whatever funds were available to them. In Halifax,

---

1. Order to Lieutenant Colonel Allan Maclean for levying the Royal Highland Emigrants, Boston, June 12, 1775, Additional Manuscripts, No. 21,833, folios 1-2, British Library.

Gov. Francis Legge raised the Nova Scotia Volunteers;[2] in Saint Augustine, Gov. Patrick Tonyn raised the East Florida Rangers;[3] and in Virginia, Gov. the Earl of Dunmore raised two corps: the Queen's Own Loyal Virginia Regiment and the Ethiopian Regiment.[4] The latter was unique among all these corps, being composed of all black enlisted men, primarily escaped slaves.

The popular misconception is that the British would arm all escaped slaves who joined them. In the case of Dunmore's regiment, and early recruits to the Provincial Corps, this was mostly true, but the Ethiopian Regiment was a short-lived experiment. After suffering severely from disease, the corps (and the Queen's Own Loyal Virginia Regiment), evacuated Virginia with Dunmore and were disbanded on Staten Island on or about September 24, 1776.[5]

In the new corps being raised on the Provincial Establishment, some blacks did enlist as soldiers carrying arms into such units as the King's American Regiment, the Queen's American Rangers and DeLancey's Brigade. After an American raid onto Long Island in the fall of 1776 captured as many as two dozen men of the 1st Battalion of DeLancey's, one of the captors described the prisoners as "a motly herd, about one half of them being Negroes and Indians."[6] The implication was no doubt intended to portray those bearing arms for the British as something less than those fighting for independence.

The compositions of the Provincials did not seem to concern the British until irregularities caused by Robert Rogers and his corps, the Queen's American Rangers, persuaded British commander-in-chief Sir William Howe to appoint an inspector general to, among other things "attend to their good order and Discipline."[7] That person was Alexander Innes. Innes, a former British Army captain and most recently secretary to South Carolina Royal Governor Lord William Campbell, set about his duties with a ruthless zeal, removing the troublesome Rogers

2. The Earl of Suffolk to Francis Legge, Whitehall, October 16, 1775, War Office, Class 1, Volume 681, folios 59060, Great Britain, The National Archives (TNA).

3. Patrick Tonyn to Henry Clinton, Saint Augustine, April 15, 1776, Sir Henry Clinton Papers, Volume 15, item 17, University of Michigan, William L. Clements Library (CL).

4. Dunmore to William Howe, on board the Ship *William* off Norfolk, Virginia, November 30, 1775, in William B. Clark, ed., *Naval Documents of the American Revolution*, Vol. 2 (Washington DC: Government Printing Office, 1976), 1210-1211.

5. Accounts and Disbursements of John Earl of Dunmore in Virginia, 1775-1776. Audit Office, Class 1, Volume 1324, Roll 627, TNA.

6. *The Connecticut Journal* (New Haven), November 6, 1776.

7. Commission of Alexander Innes as Inspector General of Provincial Forces, January 29, 1777, Misc. Acc. 1328, Rare Books and Manuscripts, Boston Public Library.

from command along with thirty of his officers.[8] Innes next broadened his gaze to the other corps under his authority and made recommendations accordingly to Howe's staff. On March 14, 1777 Innes reported to the British adjutant general that "Negroes, Mullatoes, Indians and Sailors have been inlisted" and recommended they be discharged and none enlisted in the future.[9] Howe concurred, signifying that the intention of the corps was to be composed only of "His Majesty's Loyal American Subjects" and that all those mentioned by Innes, and "other Improper Persons," be discharged.[10] It is unknown how many men of all denominations were removed from the different units, but no less than forty-five sailors discharged from Provincial regiments were given over to the Royal Navy immediately following the above order.[11]

The one more or less unwritten caveat in the prohibition was for allowing blacks to serve in an unarmed role, that of pioneer. Pioneers, in the eighteenth century military sense, were laborers whose duties included building fortifications, removing obstacles and general maintenance. While a number of the corps would have one or perhaps two black pioneers per company, particularly in the south, there were two companies of black pioneers on the Provincial Establishment, those commanded by Captains Robert Richard Crowe and George Martin. These two units were combined in 1778 and served the remainder of the war under Capt. Allan Stewart, a North Carolina Loyalist.[12]

An additional mode of service for blacks in the Provincials was as musicians, either drummers, fifers, trumpeters or bandsman. These functions, particularly the first three, were not so much for entertainment but rather for relaying commands in battle, in camp, and on the march. In the exhibit at the Museum of the American Revolution, one of the stories presented is that of a fifteen-year-old Virginia slave named London who became a cavalry trumpeter in Benedict Arnold's regiment, the American Legion. A South Carolina former slave,

---

8. Regimental Orders of the Queen's American Rangers, March 31, 1777, Treasury Solicitor, Class 11, Volume 220, TNA.

9. "Inspectors Report to the Adjutant General 14th March 1777," Headquarters Papers of the British Army in America, PRO 30/55/441, TNA.

10. "General Orders 16th March 1777 For his Majesty's Provincial Forces," Orderly Book of the King's American Regiment, CL.

11. Muster Book of HMS *Senegal*, May 3 to June 30, 1777, Admiralty, Class 36, Volume 7770, TNA.

12. Return of the Black Pioneers, New York, September 17, 1778, Sir Henry Clinton Papers, Volume 41, item 29, CL.

Bernard E. Griffiths, aka Barney, was noted for his bravery at Spencer's Ordinary as a trumpeter with the Queen's American Rangers.[13]

Cavalry played an important role for both sides in the American Revolution. With limited regular cavalry available in America, the British by necessity turned more and more to Provincial and militia mounted troops to fill the void. Corps such as the British Legion, Queen's American Rangers and American Legion provided opportunities, albeit limited ones, for blacks to serve in an important function and be armed at least with a sword and perhaps a brace of pistols. One of these new corps, the King's American Dragoons, attempted to push the boundaries imposed by Innes and the British commanders.

The King's American Dragoons was unique in that their formation was solicited in England rather than the normal chain of command in America. Proposed in June 1780 by Daniel Murray, commander of an independent cavalry troop known as Wentworth's Volunteers, the plan was reviewed by Secretary of State Lord Germain, who laid it before King George III, who gave it his approval and encouragement.[14] The commander recommended for the corps was French and Indian War Massachusetts Gen. Timothy Ruggles, who had commanded the Loyal American Association at Boston earlier in the Revolution.[15] It is unknown whether Ruggles was even aware of his nomination, but at nearly seventy years old, his days of being a soldier were well behind him and he was never appointed to the corps. But the new regiment caught the eye of one of Germain's undersecretaries in England, Benjamin Thompson.

Benjamin Thompson was born in Woburn, Massachusetts on March 26, 1753.[16] A stout Loyalist, Thompson was settled in New Hampshire at the start of the war, already a major in the militia in his young twenties. After fleeing New Hampshire, Thompson wound up in London where he acquired the patronage of Lord George Germain, who appointed him an undersecretary of state for America. In addition to this post, he served in England under Alexander Innes as a deputy inspector, allowing him access to information on both the war and the

13. Todd W. Braisted. "Bernard E. Griffiths: Trumpeter Barney of the Queen's Rangers, Chelsea Pensioner—and Freed Slave," *Journal of the American Revolution* (February 21, 2019), allthingsliberty.com/2019/02/bernard-e-griffiths-trumpeter-barney-of-the-queens-rangers/.

14. Proposals for raising the King's American Dragoons, c-1780. Headquarters Papers of the British Army in America, PRO 30/55/2812, TNA.

15. Instructions from Ruggles to Captain Francis Green, Boston, November 15, 1775. Audit Office, Class 13, Volume 45, folio 476, TNA.

16. W.J. Sparrow, *Count Rumford of Woburn, Mass.* (New York: Thomas Y. Crowell Co, 1964), 17.

American forces fighting for Britain.[17] When Ruggles proved unwilling or unable to take charge of the then-raising King's American Dragoons, Thompson was in a position to request command of the corps with the rank of lieutenant colonel. Serving in a civil capacity in England left the actual raising of the corps to Daniel Murray, as major.[18]

After arranging for complete uniforms, accoutrements, colors and even light artillery for his new corps, Thompson joined the first available transport for America.[19] With Thompson came a handful of enlistees that he recruited, such as McQueen Bisset, the regimental armorer.[20] Also on board were four trumpeters, all recruited by Thompson that September: Daniel Green, Richard Stanley, John Frederick and William Higginson.[21] Each was a former black slave, and each was headed for South Carolina.

The fleet on which Thompson and his charges were on, some forty vessels convoyed by HMS *Rotterdam, Duc de Chartres* and *Astrea*, set out for New York, not Charleston, at the end of September 1781.[22] When this fleet of provision ships and a few recruits sailed, the war in America was still not decided. One of the passengers on board was Lord Dunmore, far removed from his days leading the Ethiopian Regiment but now ordered back to Virginia to resume his government. Cornwallis's surrender at Yorktown that October ended any dream of returning to Virginia and governing. The situation in South Carolina was little better. Despite winning most of the major battles, the British were forced to abandon the backcountry and occupied only the neighborhood of Charleston—Dumore was reduced to sitting around a house in Charleston, provided by some refugees there whom he thanked "for their attention, in the politest manner."[23] Militarily, the

17. Thompson held this last position at least as early as December 1779 and continued into 1781. Benjamin Thompson to George Germain, London, December 22, 1779, Colonial Office, Class 5, Volume 156, folios 272-273, TNA.

18. Warrant from Sir Henry Clinton to Daniel Murray to raise the King's American Dragoons, New York, February 22, 1781, Headquarters Papers of the British Army in America, PRO 30/55/3353, TNA.

19. Thompson was ordered on board HMS *Rotterdam* heading for New York with a fleet carrying recruits. John Fisher to Philip Stephens, Whitehall, September 28, 1781. Colonial Office, Class 5, Volume 255, folio 53, TNA.

20. Thompson ordered a quarterly allowance to Bisset's wife of five guineas at the insistence of her husband as a condition of his going to America and leaving her behind. Thompson to Germain, New York, September 12, 1782, Sackville-Germain Papers, Volume 16, CL.

21. Muster Rolls of the King's American Dragoons, February 24 to April 24, 1782, RG 8, "C" Series, Volume 1901, folios 4, 5, 7 and 8, Library and Archives Canada (LAC).

22. *Royal Gazette* (New York), January 5, 1782.

23. *Royal Gazette* (New York), January 19, 1782.

most pressing problem was the want of good cavalry. There were hundreds of Provincial and militia cavalry available, but no competent cavalry officer to put them in order. Lt. Gen. Alexander Leslie, commanding in South Carolina, complained that the cavalry force in the province was little better than mounted infantry.[24]

The unexpected arrival of the fleet at Charleston presented a fortuitous, if temporary, solution to the cavalry dilemma. When Thompson learned that he would not be headed to New York anytime soon, he offered his services to Leslie to put the cavalry into some sort of order, which offer was accepted. The different cavalry units were scattered but ordered to join together from John's Island and Haddrell's Point under Thompson, whose camp was an outpost four miles from the city. It included the Provincial South Carolina Royalists, along with a troop of New York Volunteers, British Legion, Queen's Rangers and North Carolinians. In addition to these he had attached to his corps "Two strong Troops of mounted militia, and a Seapoy Troop (*Gens de Couleers*)."[25] This last troop was an armed black cavalry unit of thirty officers and men commanded by a Captain March.[26] Known as the Black Dragoons or Black Pioneer Troop, it served until the evacuation of Charleston in December 1782, and thereafter in the West Indies as a part of the Black Carolina Corps. A militia unit, it was the only the only one of its kind and was unique in being officially commanded by blacks; while other blacks in the north served in refugee corps (not Provincials) with the rank of "colonel," these titles were not formal or official in any way, but were merely honorary recognition of leadership bestowed on them by their followers.

Thompson formed an instant bond with all the officers and men under his new command. "They have all been used to fire, and Sword," he wrote of his troopers "and are brave to the last degree." Thompson led the troops, both the Provincials and militia, in maneuvering twice a day, quickly bringing them into a state of proficiency.[27] That training was put to the test in grand style that February, as Thompson led his cavalry and some supporting infantry into the countryside. On February 24, 1782 Thompson's cavalry, outpacing the infantry, caught up

24. Alexander Leslie to Clinton, Charleston, December 27, 1782, Colonial Office, Class 5, Volume 104, folios 217-218, TNA.
25. Thompson to Germain, Cavalry Camp Advanced Post, January 11, 1782, Sackville-Germain Papers, Volume 15, CL.
26. Abstract of pay for the "Black Pioneer Troop" from July 1 to September 30, 1782, Treasury, Class 50, Volume 2, folio 372, TNA.
27. Thompson to Germain, Cavalry Camp near Charleston, January 15, 1782, Sackville-Germain Papers, Volume 15, CL.

with an enemy force of 500 South Carolina State Troops and militia under Col. Archibald McDonald at Wambaw Bridge. With the loss of just one man wounded, the cavalry charged the whole: "the enemy fired their pistols, broke in confusion, and were pursued with great slaughter."[28] The following day Thompson repeated his success when he marched the cavalry to Tidyman's Plantation, two miles from the previous day's battle, where he attacked none other than Francis Marion and a mixed force under his command. Employing the same tactics as the day before, the Loyalist cavalry charge broke the enemy force, with the loss of just one militiaman wounded. Marion's losses included his tent and rum.

Returning to camp, Thompson and his men, black and white, were the toast of Charleston, where people could for a moment forget that the war they were fighting had already been decided. The British commander ordered this commendation published: "Lieut. General LESLIE desires Lieut. Colonel THOMPSON, and the officers and soldiers of the Cavalry and Infantry who served under his command, will accept his best thanks for the service performed by them on the late expedition." Leslie likewise informed his superior, Sir Henry Clinton, that Thompson "has put [the cavalry] in exceeding good order, and gained their confidence and affection." The time for the fleet that brought Thompson to finally resume its voyage to New York was rapidly approaching, however, and with it, an end to Thompson's South Carolina adventure. "I have much regret to part with this enterprising young officer," Leslie continued, "who appears to have an uncommon share of merit, and zeal for the service."[29] The service of the Black Dragoons must have made a very favorable impression on Leslie, as he proposed forming an even larger corps of armed blacks, requesting Clinton "determine in what manner their Officers should be appointed and on what terms their freedom should be given them."[30] The plan went nowhere, as Clinton was on the point of sailing for home. The war in America was winding down.

When Thompson and his recruits boarded the fleet for New York that March, they were joined by twenty others recruited while in South

28. *Royal Gazette* (Charleston), February 27 to March 2, 1782.

29. Leslie to Clinton, Charleston, March 12, 1782, *Royal Gazette* (New York), September 11, 1782.

30. Leslie to Clinton, March 30, 1782, Headquarters Papers of the British Army in America, PRO 30/55/9957, TNA.

Carolina, including a soldier aptly named Horsman.[31] Thirteen of these recruits traveled on the Armed Storeship *Sally*, perhaps as a guard, while Thompson and the remainder were dispersed on other vessels.[32] On April 11, 1782 "arrived at Sandy-Hook, in 10 Days from Charlestown, South-Carolina, a Fleet of 45 Sail of Navy and Army Victuallers (most of which arrived at that Place last Fall from Europe) under Convoy of his Majesty's Ships *Carysfort*, *Duke de Chartres*, *Astrea*, *Charlestown*, and *Grana* … In the Fleet came Passengers, his Excellency the Earl of Dunmore, Governor of Virginia, Colonels [John] Small and [Benjamin] Thompson, and several other Gentlemen of high Rank."[33]

While Thompson may have been known previously to some of the officers of his regiment, many of whom were fellow New Englanders, he no doubt took some time acquainting himself with the remainder, and the enlisted men under his command. His first order of business was to enlarge the corps. "I mean to Recruit in good Earnest" he wrote Deputy Muster Master Ward Chipman on June 20, and he was as good as his word, with enlisting dozens.[34]

Upon joining the regiment at New York, Thompson made sure each of his five (and later six) troops had at least one black pioneer. These men came from quite diverse backgrounds. Peter Moses had been a slave in Virginia who had joined Lord Dunmore in 1775. Joseph Kelly was a twenty-four-year-old mulatto from Setauket, Long Island, while Andrew Hilton and Charles Allen were from Maryland, each described as "part Indian." Edward Hill and Joseph Williams were former slaves from New Jersey and North Carolina respectively but Gabriel Dickenson was a freeborn black from North Castle, New York. Thompson not only added the black trumpeters he brought from England, but replaced any white trumpeters already serving with newly recruited former slaves Charles Ferrell, Hector Munro, Edward Lloyd and Dick Jackson.[35]

Thompson's corps would recruit 388 men by the end of July 1782, and this at a time when the other Provincial units at New York were

---

31. Muster Roll of Captain James Fulton's Troop, King's American Dragoons, February 24 to April 24, 1782, RG 8, "C" Series, Volume 1901, folio 8, LAC.

32. Ship Muster Book, Armed Storeship *Sally*, April 1, 1782 to May 31, 1782, Admiralty, Class 36, Volume 9942, TNA.

33. *The New-York Gazette and the Weekly Mercury*, April 16, 1782.

34. Thompson to Chipman, Camp, Cow Neck, June 20, 1782, RG 8, "C" Series, Volume 1901, folios 44-45, LAC.

35. Examination of the Book of Negroes. Headquarters Papers of the British Army in America, PRO 30/55/10427, TNA.

struggling to replace losses from death and desertion. Not among those counted as soldiers but who nonetheless had a military role were the black servants hired by each officer. As Thompson informed Germain:

> I Permit no man to be taken from the Ranks to be made a servant of. All our Officers have Black Servants, they are all Dressed in the same Uniform, except the feathers in their Turbans, which are of different Colours according to the Troops their Masters belong to. At Reviews and on all Field Days they Parade with the Regiment and assist in managing the Guns. They get no pay from the King, but they draw Rations, their Masters paying for them at the usual rate (2½d).[36]

The guns in question were four amusettes ordered from England in September, "with Carriages & Harness complete."[37] A 1782 British Verbruggen brass amusette barrel weighed about 225 pounds, was between five and five and a half feet in length and fired a one pound shot.[38] Thompson was extremely proud of these guns, and included having them fire a "royal salute" after maneuvering on the field with the troops before His Royal Highness Prince William Henry at Fresh Meadows, Long Island on August 1, 1782 to mark the occasion of presenting the regiment with their colors.[39] Using the black servants to assist with operationing these light artillery pieces would have involved them in a fast-paced, complex procedure, as Thompson laid out to Germain shortly after the color ceremony:

> I have tried our Guns & find them to answer admirably And have lately astonished all the world by taking them up on Horse back. Three Horses carry the Gun with it[s] Carriage, Ammunition Boxes &c, with the Greatest ease, and at any Pace. I have promised to show the Commander in Chief one of them taking a flying leap at a five Barr'd Gate; and I have little doubt, but I shall be able soon to show him one swim-

36. Presumably this included Thompson's own two servants, named David and William. Thompson to Germain, New York, August 8, 1782, Sackville-Germain Papers, Volume 16, CL.
37. Germain to Lord Townshend, Whitehall, September 7, 1781, Colonial Office, Class 5, Volume 262, folios 3-4, TNA.
38. David McConnell, *British Smooth-Bore Artillery: A Technological Study to Support Identification, Acquisition, Restoration, Reproduction, and Interpretation of Artillery at National Historic Parks in Canada* (Minister of Supply and Services Canada: 1988), 51.
39. *Royal Gazette* (New York), August 7, 1782. It was noted during the account of the ceremony that a band of music played, in addition to the trumpeters of the regiment. There was indeed a band of music in the regiment, and while it was probably composed of blacks, that cannot be said with certainty. "Instruction for Collonell Tomsons Band of Music from the 24th Octobr. ending the 24 of Decemr. [1782],Ward Chipman Papers, MG 23, D 1, Series I, Volume 29, Part 1, Page 135, LAC.

ming over a River. I have contrived a Breast-Plate for the Horse, (anal-
ogom to the Cork waistcoats) which will effectually prevent his sinking
with the weight of the Gun on his back. Our men are already so expert
that they take the Gun with all its apparatus from the Horses backs, put
it together and fire it in the space of one minute and a Quarter, and in
one minute more it is on Horse back again. It carries its round shott further and truer, and shoots its grape [shot] better than any Gun in the
Service. I hit a tree the other Evening, (less than a large mans body) at
the distance of 300 Yards three time[s] in five shots, with single Bullets.[40]

Despite all New York and the Loyalists within realizing the war was
lost, with commissioners in Paris then at work hammering out the
treaty, Thompson envisioned carrying his corps to fight against the
French in India or the West Indies. In his plans, he contemplated not
just the King's American Dragoons as they then stood, but an expanded
number of artillerymen and four companies of light infantry to be
raised from among the existing Provincial units at New York. On
March 14, 1783, Thompson solicited Sir Guy Carleton, who had replaced Clinton as commander in chief the previous year, for permission
to raise just such a corps, which would include his beloved "Four Field
Pieces with their Harness &c. complete, for a Troop of Flying Artillery."[41] Exactly one week later Carleton issued Thompson a warrant
to raise and augment his new corps. Another augmentation to the corps
was in the number of black pioneers, specifying fifty-two privates, four
corporals and four serjeants, each of whom would receive one guinea
bounty along with the pay and clothing of infantry. Carleton did stip-
ulate that "care is to be taken not to permit any Negroes but such as
are absolutely free, to inlist in this Corps."[42]

In the proposed establishment of this expanded corps, it would total
700 officers and men of all ranks and types. Each new company of light
infantry was to have a black drummer and fifer each, while the cavalry
would retain their black trumpeters. The artillery would consist of no
officers, but four sergeants, four corporals, two drummers and fifty privates. Upon being formed, the artillery would follow these orders and
guidelines:

---

40. Thompson to Germain, New York, August 17, 1782, Sackville-Germain Papers, Volume 16, CL.

41. Thompson to Guy Carleton, New York, March 14, 1783, Headquarters Papers of the
British Army in America, PRO 30/55/7128, TNA.

42. Warrant from Carleton to Thompson, New York, March 21, 1783, Headquarters Papers
of the British Army in America, PRO 30/55/7178, TNA.

The Four Pieces of Cannon to be on the flanks of the Batallion, two on the Right, and two on the Left, and the Company of Artillery to be formed in two Divisions, Each Division to be under the Command of a Quarter Master. The Privates of the Company of Artillery to be Blacks. To have no other Arms but Swords, and to be Accoutered for drawing the Guns. The Non-Commissioned Officers to be Whites and to be Armed with Muskets and Bayonnettes. The whole to have Infantry Pay.[43]

Despite all his exertions, not Benjamin Thompson or any other human could change the outcome of the war. Within just a few days of his new warrant, the preliminary articles of peace arrived at New York, putting an effective stop to all plans for the West Indies and the new corps. The prospect of the British leaving America threw all the Loyalists into fear and despair, including Thompson. "It is a thousand pities so fine a Regiment should be anihilated" he lamented to Germain.[44] On April 4, 1783 Thompson formally requested leave to go to England to solicit "in behalf of himself and the Corps, that they may be employed in the East Indies" or elsewhere. In the meantime, he requested the corps be dismounted and turn in their cavalry appointments, then to do duty in Nova Scotia "till further Orders."[45]

Thompson sailed for England immediately. Upon his arrival in London, he set about writing a slew of letters, not requesting further service but that the King's American Dragoons be put on the American Establishment, and that the officers' ranks be made permanent in America and that they be entitled to half-pay upon the regiment being disbanded.[46] Thompson simultaneously lobbied for all Provincial officers to receive half-pay, he being appointed to solicit just that, which was granted.[47] This made his request for his corps more or less moot and

43. "Proposed Establishment of a Corps of Light Troops to be raised for His Majesty's Service to be Commanded by Lieutenant Colonel Thompson Commandant of the King's American Dragoons" c-March 1783, Headquarters Papers of the British Army in America, PRO 30/55/10368, TNA.

44. Thompson to Germain, New York, September 14, 1782, Sackville-Germain Papers, Volume 16, CL.

45. Thompson to Carleton, New York, April 4, 1783, Headquarters Papers of the British Army in America, PRO 30/55/7320, TNA.

46. The American Establishment, instituted in 1779, was intended for those corps that had recruited their authorized strength in men. It provided the officers with permanent rank in America and half-pay upon being disbanded, as well as having the regiment order its own clothing directly from England. Germain to Clinton, Whitehall, January 23, 1779, Colonial Office, Class 5, Volume 97, folios 2-5, TNA.

47. Thompson to Lord North, Pall Mall Court, June 8, 1783, Headquarters Papers of the British Army in America, PRO 30/55/7936, TNA.

the matter seems to have simply faded away. One last request, that which he was most adamant about, was not granted, his promotion to full colonel.[48]

Back in New York that summer, Sir Guy Carleton was fully immersed in evacuating New York City, a logistical challenge of immense proportions given the communications of the times. The one request Thompson had made to him was carried out, that of sending the regiment to Nova Scotia. While all Provincial units at New York would eventually be sent there, the King's American Dragoons were the first, and unlike any other corps continued doing duty rather than simply disbanding. "The King's American Dragoons who are dismounted, having desired to be sent to St. Johns River, Bay of Fundy, I have agreed to their request, and they will proceed directly to that place, where they are to encamp, and do duty for present," Carleton informed the British commander at Halifax on April 26, 1783.[49]

On April 23, 1783 a fleet left New York carrying nearly 2,800 Loyalists to the River Saint John, Nova Scotia (now New Brunswick). Of those, 404 men, women and children belonged to the King's American Dragoons, including no less than forty-five black trumpeters, pioneers and officers' servants, embarked on board the transport ship *Lady's Adventure*.[50] Before any of those forty-five could get on board to transport them away from America, they were questioned by commissioners from the British, determining whether or not those of color were legally allowed to leave under an agreement worked out between both sides. While the Americans were anxious to reclaim what they considered property lost to the British (and not legally allowed to be removed under the treaty of peace), the British were equally insistent in fulfilling Sir Henry Clinton's 1779 proclamation promising freedom to all blacks joining them.[51] In addition to the trumpeters and pioneers, each officer typically had one or more servants embarking with them. Lt. Alexander

48. Thompson to Lord North, Pall Mall Court, June 25, 1783, Home Office, Class 42, Volume 2, folios 286-289, TNA.

49. Carlton to James Paterson, New York, April 26, 1783, Headquarters Papers of the British Army in America, PRO 30/55/7558, TNA.

50. "Return of Loyalists and Troops sailed for the undermentioned Places. N. York 10th October 1783," War Office, Class 60, Volume 27, TNA.

51. Clinton's proclamation, issued at Philipsburg, New York on June 30, 1779, read in part "I do most strictly forbid any person to sell, or claim right over, any Negro the property of a Rebel, who may take refuge with any part of this army." Sir Henry Clinton Papers, Volume 62, item 28, CL. Commissioners appointed by the United States would arrive in New York after this initial fleet had sailed. For a fuller account of the process, read Bob Rupert "How Article 7 freed 3000 Slaves," *Journal of the American Revolution* (August 4, 2016), allthingsliberty.com/2016/08/how-article-7-freed-3000-slaves/.

Stewart's servant, for instance, was named John Stewart, a nineteen year old free-born black from Charleston, South Carolina; Cornet Arthur Nicholson's was a twenty year-old female former slave named Hester Walton, also a South Carolinian.[52] All would now be off to new lives in what remained of British North America.

Whatever duty Thompson or the British envisioned for the corps at the mouth of the Saint John River (soon to be the City of Saint John), all they appear to have done for several months was take up space, being gobbled up by more and more Loyalists from New York. They were eventually shunted further up the river, where they were joined by the remainder of the Provincials arriving from New York City at the end of September 1783. Soon thereafter, Maj. Daniel Murray, commanding the corps in Thompson's absence, received the inevitable order stating, "You are hereby directed to disband the Kings American Dragoons on the tenth Day of October Instant."[53] The officers and men of Thompson's regiment, many of whom had never fought in a battle or fired a shot in anger, would now settle into civilian lives with their families. For those of color in the corps who had left bondage and slavery, it was a chance of a free life, one shared with some 3,000 others in Nova Scotia. While old struggles were behind them, new ones lay ahead, with never-ending challenges to life and liberty.

* * *

Benjamin Thompson went on to take the title Count Rumford, wrote many scientific papers, and made significant contributions to the study of thermodynamics. He proved that heat was not a substance but a product of motion, determined that fur causes warmth by inhibiting convective cooling, invented sous-vide cooking, and established basic principles of radiant heating. He invented the double boiler, as well as an improved kitchen range and drip coffee pot, and efficient industrial furnaces; he designed an efficient fireplace design still in use today. Forty-five years after his death, Rumford Baking Powder was named after him.

---

52. Examination of the Book of Negroes, Headquarters Papers of the British Army in America, PRO 30/55/10427, TNA.
53. Henry Edward Fox to Daniel Murray, Township of Prince William, September 28, 1783, Edward Winslow Papers, Volume 18, 1783, No. 106, University of New Brunswick, Harriet Irving Library.

The King of Sweden: Friendly Foe of the United States

⛭ RICHARD WERTHER ⛭

New York City, November 16, 1783. It was finally here, Evacuation Day. The British, who had occupied Manhattan for seven long years, were finally leaving town. General George Washington and his troops paraded down Broadway, terminating their triumphant return at Fraunces Tavern at the southern tip of Manhattan. A raucous 120-person celebration, hosted by New York Governor George Clinton, ensued.[1] The toasts came fast and furious. "The United States of America." Huzzah! "His most Christian Majesty (Louis XVI of France)." Huzzah! "The United Netherlands". Huzzah! "The King of Sweden." Huzzah! "The Continental Army". Huzzah! They kept rolling until thirteen toasts in all rang out, one representing each colony.

Hold on! Back that up for a second. The King of Sweden? Coming in at number four yet? What role did the King of Sweden, Gustav III, have in supporting the Revolution? Given his position in the pecking order of Evaluation Day honorees, the answer might be surprising. Sweden, ostensibly a neutral nation (but then again, so supposedly was France for a long time), had a minor and largely unmemorable role in the waging of the war itself. So why drink to the King of Sweden? The answer is that Sweden was the first country, neutral in the just-concluded conflict, to recognize, by its own initiative, the United States by negotiating a treaty of amity and commerce.[2]

But all was not as it appeared. And now, as Paul Harvey used to say, "the rest of the story." How did the treaty happen and how did the King

---

1. Nicole Saraniero, "Evacuation Day, New York City's Forgotten November Holiday," Untapped New York (untappedcities.com).
2. Adolph B. Benson, *Sweden and the American Revolution* (New Haven: The Tuttle, Morehouse & Taylor Company, 1927), 12.

really feel about America and its Revolution? What role did Sweden play in the Revolution itself?

Although his inclusion in this toast seems to cement Gustav III's place in the pantheon of America's most ardent foreign supporters, the reality was quite the reverse. The King did express early curiosity, if not support, for the Revolution. And while he grudgingly marveled at the daring of the American project, expressing a large measure of admiration as to the building of a new republic against such long odds and presciently wondering if upcoming centuries would belong to America, he very quickly overcame any romantic admiration he might have had for the colonists in the early stages of their revolt. Gustav III's early fascination quickly turned to a marked aversion.[3]

As George III did, and as Louis XVI, in retrospect, should have considered for his own longevity as King, Gustav III reflexively opposed the American colonists because of his inherent regal prejudices about the right of kings. Some sources even identify him as the European ruler most hostile to the Revolution.[4] He indeed regarded the colonists as rebels, who could become free and independent only through the release of their oath of allegiance to the King of England.[5] He wrote to his minister at Paris in late 1778, reluctantly offering military support while at the same time expressing his ambivalence about the whole enterprise:

> The action of the French ministry (in recognizing American independence) it seems to me, has deviated both from the principles of justice and practical interests, and from state principles of nations that have been in force for centuries. I cannot admit that it is right to support rebels against their king. The example will find only too many imitators in an age when it is the fashion to overthrow every bulwark of authority. But I presume I shall have to give in in this matter [that is, agree to join the conflict].[6]

As it was with the French, much of Sweden's motivation for entering the fray stemmed from resentments of British high-handedness in trade and maritime rights left simmering from the Seven Years' War. This, combined with prospects for lucrative trade with the belligerents and slim hopes of obtaining an island possession in the West Indies, made

3. H. Arnold Barton, *Scandinavia in the Revolutionary Era, 1760–1815* (Minneapolis: University of Minnesota Press, 1982), 107.
4. Jonathan R. Dull, *A Diplomatic History of the American Revolution* (New Haven: Yale University Press, 1985), 71.
5. Benson, *Sweden and the American Revolution*, 19.
6. Ibid.

a self-interested case for Swedish involvement, hence Gustav III's grudging agreement to let his countrymen join the conflict.

There was also one specific person whose involvement may have influenced Gustav III's decision to extend limited support to the American cause. France's foreign minister driving the war effort from that country's point of view happened to be Charles Gravier, comte de Vergennes, the former French envoy to the Swedish Court. Vergennes had provided last minute help, including money and advice, to Gustav III in completing the 1772 coup d'etat which brought him to power.[7]

Gustav III's reluctant support opened the door to Swedish nationals participating in the Revolution, though they did so mostly under the flags of other countries. This gave the King what in modern terms would be called "plausible deniability" and came in handy later, enabling the United States to celebrate Sweden as the first "neutral" country to honor it with a commercial treaty. Sketchy records make it difficult to determine exactly how many participated, but it was thought to be around 200 to 300 serving with France, the Dutch or with American privateers.[8] The French Navy, for one, was on a ship-building binge and desperately needed experienced sailors. Of these, two in particular stood out: Axel de Fersen and Curt von Stedingk. Their service to the American cause earned each election to the Society of the Cincinnati, the military society formed by Continental and French officers. They were the only two from Sweden to achieve this honor. Upon their return to Sweden, however, the King did not allow them to wear the medals signifying their induction into the Society. He wrote that he could not countenance them wearing "a public mark of the success of a revolt of subjects against their rightful ruler, and above all a revolt whose cause and narratives were so unfair and so unfounded."[9]

De Ferson had the more colorful career of the two. He had a close (rumored in some quarters intimate) relationship with Marie Antoinette, was appointed the first aide-de-camp for General Rochambeau, and served with the American rebel army at the Siege of Yorktown. The coup de gras, upon his return to France, was his role in planning and personally participating in (driving the coach) the flight of the royal family from Paris during the French Revolution. We all

7. Dull, *A Diplomatic History*, 36, 38-39.

8. Barton, *Scandinavia in the Revolutionary Era*, 114. Unfortunately, at least this many and perhaps more served or, more commonly, were impressed into the British Navy. Ibid., 121.

9. C. Stedingk, et al, *Posthumous memoirs of the Feldmarechal Count of Stedingk: written on letters, dispatches and other authentic pieces left to his family* (translated title) (Paris: A. Bertrand, 1844-47), 72. This is from a letter Stedingk received directly from the King, written March 26, 1784.

know how that turned out. De Ferson was informed of the failure of the royals' escape plot after his successful escape to Belgium, writing to Gustav III on June 23, 1791 that "Everything has failed. Sixteen leagues from the frontier the King was arrested and taken back to Paris."[10]

Von Stedingk served in the French navy under Count D'Estaing in 1779, first in the successful takeover of Grenada from the British and later in a losing effort at the Siege of Savannah, which he led, where he planted the American flag before the attack was repulsed.[11] Returning to his native Sweden, Stedingk ended up having a long, distinguished career in service to his country, highlighted by a long ambassadorial posting in Russia, and a leadership role in the Swedish Army as they participated in the Napoleonic Wars. He died at the age of ninety in 1837.

After the Revolution concluded, and shortly after the Treaty of Paris formally made that official, the commercial treaty with Gustav III and Sweden was signed, though it had been in the works since 1782. Though Gustav III's motivations were strictly commercial, the claim of "first neutral nation to treat with the United States" was enough to vault him into the high status he had in the order of celebratory toasts at Fraunces. As one foreign observer commented, "if Washington's and Franklin's actions had impaired commerce, there would have been nothing but scorn for American independence" from Gustav III.[12] Even the limited military support earlier provided by Sweden also had a distinctly self-serving character, as opposed to the wide-eyed ideological commitment communicated by other foreign participants such as Lafayette or Steuben.

So, how did the treaty come about? It started on the initiative of the Swedish King, who contacted Benjamin Franklin through his envoy to France, Comte Gustaf Philip Creutz, on April 23, 1782, inquiring whether Franklin had the power to treat with the Swedes. Franklin naturally jumped at the opportunity, writing to Robert R. Livingston in Congress more to ask for forgiveness than permission, having already informed Creutz the next day that he had the power.[13] "Recollecting a

10. Mildred Carnegy, *A Queen's Knight - The Life of Count Axel de Ferson* (London, Mills and Boon, Ltd., 1912), 190.

11. Stedingk to King Gustav, January 18, 1780, as quoted in Benson, *Sweden and the American Revolution*, 166.

12. Barton, *Scandinavia in the Revolutionary Era*, 108.

13. Benjamin Franklin to Comte De Creutz, with Franklin's account of their conversation, April 24, 1782, Founders Online, founders.archives.gov/documents/Franklin/01-37-02-0143.

general Power that was formerly given to me with the other Commissioners, I answer'd [Creutz's question] in the Affirmative."[14] Franklin had been provided the draft agreement by Creutz that same month and Gustav III had insisted that Creutz negotiate with Franklin, whom he held in high esteem. Congress eventually confirmed that Franklin had the authority to reach an agreement.[15]

One motivation for the King to hasten the process was the impending recognition of John Adams as minister plenipotentiary by their commercial rivals the Netherlands. In fact, the proposed treaty Congress subsequently gave Franklin as his template for Sweden, was little more than the proposed Netherlands treaty, with Netherlands crossed out and Sweden inserted! Congress had discussed Franklin's request on September 9, 1782, and appointed a committee consisting of Arthur Lee, Ralph Izard, and James Duane to prepare the proposed treaty.[16] Franklin received this proffering, along with a letter from Congress dated September 28, 1782, which he received in November. The instructions were signed by John Hanson, then "President of the United States in Congress Assembled," the first President of the Confederation Congress. Coincidentally, Hanson was for a long time treated by historians as being of Swedish descent, though more recent scholarship has shed serious doubt upon this claim.[17]

Formal negotiations with Creutz commenced December 18, 1782.[18] Both parties to the negotiation had the same objective. Franklin's instructions from Congress stated that "the direct & essential object of the treaty is to obtain the Recognition of our Independency by another European power."[19] The King, according to notes Franklin made at the time, "desir'd it might be taken notice of in favour of Sweden that it was the first Power not at War with England that had sought our Alliance."[20]

14. Franklin to Robert R. Livingston, June 25, 1782, Founders Online, founders.archives.gov/documents/Franklin/01-37-02-0337.

15. Ibid.

16. Journals of the Continental Congress, 1774-1789, Thursday, September 19, 1782, American Memory, ammem/amlaw/lwjc.html.

17. Alan H. Winquist, Jessica Rousselow-Winquist, *Touring Swedish America* (St. Paul: Minnesota Historical Society Press, 2009).

18. The Swedish-American Treaty of Amity and Commerce, with Translation, 3 April [i.e., 5 March] 1783, Founders Online, founders.archives.gov/documents/Franklin/01-39-02-0154.

19. Continental Congress to Franklin: Commission and Instructions [September 28, 1782], Founders Online, founders.archives.gov/documents/Franklin/01-38-02-0116.

20. Franklin to the Comte de Creutz, Franklin Papers, franklinpapers.org/yale?vol=37&page=204b.

The fruit of the King's pragmatic support was the Treaty of Amity and Commerce, agreed to by Franklin and Creutz on April 3, 1783, some five months after the Preliminary Articles of Peace that effectively ended the Revolution were agreed upon. Gustav III ratified the treaty in Stockholm on May 23, and Congress, having some trouble assembling the necessary quorum of nine states, formally signed on July 29.

The fifteen-year pact was fairly routine, as agreements of this type were structured, and negotiations between Franklin and Creutz had ran smoothly, despite the fact the Sweden initially proposed twenty-seven articles and Congress's template was eighteen. The final product included twenty-seven articles plus five more added by Congress. As John Adams wrote in late 1782, expressing the enthusiasm for the pact that landed the King the cleanup spot in the batting order of Evacuation Day toasts that evening at Fraunces,

> The King of Sweden has done the United-States great honor ... by inserting, that he had a great desire to form a Connexion with States, which had so fully established their Independence, and, by the wise & gallant Conduct, so well deserved it; and his Minister desired it might be remembered, that his Sovreign was the first who had voluntarily proposed a Treaty with us.[21]

The treaty got "The Thirteen United States of North America" (as they were referred to in the document) on the board, so to speak, as far as support from neutral countries. Thus the celebratory toasts to the King of Sweden. As for Gustav III, he would be "toasted" in a different way nine years later, meeting a fate similar to that of Louis XVI. He was assassinated in March 1792, surviving the initial attack but dying two weeks later of an infection from the wound he sustained. This event does not appear to have been a reaction against monarchical power inspired by the American example, as Gustav III might have feared (and if so, it would have been a quite delayed reaction!). Internal politics within Sweden seem to have been the precipitating factor, but more idealistic factors cannot totally be ruled out. One member of the cabal which plotted the assassination, Adolph Ludvig Ribbing, fought as a naval officer in the Revolution and is considered by some historians as one of the few Swedish participants who was "genuinely inspired by the revolution in America."[22]

---

21. John Adams to Livingston, December 14, 1782, Founders Online, founders.archives. gov/documents/Adams/06-14-02-0075.
22. Barton, *Scandinavia in the Revolutionary Era*, 122.

Shifting Indian Policy of the Articles of Confederation

JOHN DELEE

While the Articles of Confederation are often viewed as a failed attempt at governing the newly independent United States, this period did provide for growth and development in the realm of how to properly interact with Native American tribes on the lands east of the Mississippi River ceded by Great Britain. The interactions of the United States with Indian Nations, especially regarding American land claims, shifted from Arthur Lee's belief in the "right of conquest" to Henry Knox's policy based upon "justice and public faith" towards the Indian Tribes.

ARTHUR LEE AND THE SPOILS OF WAR

Arthur Lee during the War for Independence served as a diplomat for the United States and was elected as a Virginian delegate to the Continental Congress where he served on the committee for Indian Affairs and as one of the five commissioners to treaty with the Native Americans at Fort Stanwix and Fort McIntosh.[1]

The Committee of Indian Affairs, of which Arthur Lee was a member, sent a report to the Continental Congress on October 15, 1783 noting that the Indians who allied with the British during the war were under obligation "to make atonement for the enormities which they have perpetrated, and a reasonable compensation for the expense which the United States have incurred by their wanton barbarity; and they possess no other means to do this act of justice than by compliance with the proposed boundaries."[2] While this report

1. Biographical Directory of the United States Congress. bioguide.congress.gov/search/bio/L000188.
2. *Journals of the Continental Congress, 1774-1789*, ed. Worthington C. Ford et al. (Washington, D.C., 1904-37), 25: 683.

focused on the tribes in the Ohio valley and western New York frontier, similar sentiments were expressed in regards to the tribes all along the frontier of the new nation.[3] This view, that the United States now owned the land after the 1783 Treaty of Paris and the Indian tribes were merely tenets upon American soil, drove many Congressional delegates to insist that "the Savages should without Compensation abandon Part of their Country to the United States who claim it by Conquest & as a Retribution" for Indian violence during the war.[4]

In March 1784, after serving on the Committee for Indian Affairs for one year, Arthur Lee was appointed to serve as a commissioner for the treaties with the tribes of the Six Nations on the frontier of New York, which resulted in the Treaties of Fort Stanwix (1784) and Ft. McIntosh (1785). Lee and the four other commissioners were directed to treat with the tribes to establish boundaries and limit interactions between settlers and Indian tribes.[5] Lee's service on the committee that created the initial report outlining America's claims to Indian lands under the "right of conquest" ensured those ideas and beliefs transferred into his diplomatic dealings with the Six Nations during the negotiations.

Although Arthur Lee and his fellow commissioners may have strongly believed in America's "right of conquest" claims, they were capable diplomats who understood they could not simply demand the tribes surrender lands without a degree of compensation to help make the negotiations less contentious. The commissioners requested $60,000 to cover the cost of gifts for the treaty negotiations.[6] This perception is borne out in Article 4 of the Treaty of Fort Stanwix, and Article 10 of the Treaty at Fort McIntosh, where the United States agreed to "provide goods to be delivered ... for their use and comfort."[7] While this may appear to be a shift away from war reparations to be paid for with Indian lands, it is more likely an effective application of diplomatic tools to strongly encourage the tribes to cede the lands peacefully.[8]

---

3. *Journals of the Continental Congress*, 27: 454-6.
4. *Journals of the Continental Congress*, 25: 684-5; Pennsylvania Delegates to the Pennsylvania Assembly, September 25, 1783, in *Letters of Delegates to Congress, 1774-1789*, ed. Paul H. Smith, et al. (Washington, D.C.: Library of Congress, 1976-2000), 20: 710-11.
5. *Journals of the Continental Congress*, 28: 134.
6. *Journals of the Continental Congress*, 26: 297.
7. *Journals of the Continental Congress*, 28: 424, 426.
8. This assumption can be later confirmed in the response and claims of invalidity given by Native Americans over the Treaty of Ft. Stanwix that arises. Weston A. Dyer, "The Influence of Henry Knox on the Formation of American Indian Policy in the Northern Department, 1786-1795" (PhD dis., Ball State University, 1970), 100.

The best method to truly understand how the United States government and Arthur Lee understood America's "right of conquest" to Indian lands is to view the Continental Congress's interactions with tribes that allied with new nation during the War for Independence. Due to "their fidelity and attachment to the United States, through all the vicissitudes of the late war," the Continental Congress directed that Indian officers who fought for the Continentals be paid "in like manner as other officers," and the Oneida and Tuscarora lands were specified and purposefully not divided as part of the Treaty of Ft. Stanwix.[9] This difference highlights how Arthur Lee based his Indian policy upon which side a tribe allied with during the War of Independence and sought retribution from those tribes that had aligned themselves with the British forces.

HENRY KNOX AND THE POLICY SHIFT

After Benjamin Lincoln departed as Secretary at War in 1783, the War Department was staffed by two clerks until January 1785, when the Continental Congress began looking for someone to head the department.[10] The roles of the Secretary at War were to oversee and maintain stores and supplies for the military, raise and train an Army whenever Congress deemed an increase in military size appropriate, and direct the mission of the military as a senior leader within the military chain of command. By the middle of 1786, Congress began to fully recognize the potential advantages of having an organized Indian Department under the Secretary of War and with the "Ordinance for regulating the Indian Department" created three geographic regions, each possessing their own superintendents who would live on the frontier to discourage "annoyance of the inhabitants of the frontiers."[11] This merger of military command and Indian policy did not exist during the Arthur Lee period, but with the merger of the War Department and the newly created Indian Department, the military's role to create and maintain rigid borders and peaceful interactions between Indian tribes and frontier settlers grew and remained a critical part of that relationship well into the nation's future.

By 1787, Secretary Knox and other national level leaders began to see illegal settlement on Indian lands as a key cause of violence between

9. *Journals of the Continental Congress*, 28: 55, 423-4.

10. Mark Puls, *Henry Knox: Visionary General of the American Revolution* (New York: St. Martin's Griffin, 2008), 190.

11. *Journals of the Continental Congress*, 30: 369.

12. Congressional delegates and Knox also saw illegal settlement on federal lands as some akin to theft, primarily because it prevented the selling of those lands to pay off national

frontier Americans and Indian tribes.[12] Treaty stipulations and directions issued by Congress to the newly appointed Indian Superintendents "prohibit the settlement of all persons, not properly authorised for that purpose, upon unappropriated lands of the United States, under the penalty of their displeasure," and allowed for the forceful removal of squatters from Indian lands.[13] While the Army attempted to ensure peace along the frontier, it often removed white squatters from Indian lands due to the individual states' lack of concern respecting the treaties signed by agents of the United States government.

The Articles of Confederation stated that Congress possessed the right to "regulating the trade and managing all affairs with the Indians, not members of any of the states," and this stipulation caused many states to be unwilling to adhere to the treaties between the Indian Nations and the United States.[14] In September of 1786, then-Congressman Arthur St. Clair introduced a motion to prevent Virginia from sending state militia into territory west of the Appalachian Mountains into lands that Virginia had not yet ceded to the United States, because he was afraid of the militia starting an Indian war.[15] Georgia and North Carolina both maintained grievances relating to the borders defined in the 1785 Treaty of Hopewell between the United States and Cherokee Indians.[16] Recommendations for solving these jurisdictional disputes ranged from the states ceding their lands claims, allowing the United States government to serve as the judge or mediator, or allowing open warfare to arise.[17] While the Congressional committee formed to handle this jurisdictional issue agreed that the states were failing in their responsibility to prevent settlement on Indian lands, they ultimately recommended (as that was the limit of Congress's power) that the states cede the disputed claims to the United States so that the federal government could deal with the Indians unilaterally.[18]

With the states pushing for the National Army along the frontier to protect them against Indians, Secretary Henry Knox saw the role of the Army on the frontier as one that "must keep both sides in awe by a strong hand, and compel them to be moderate and just."[19] By the

debt. George W. Van Cleave We *Have Not a Government: The Articles of Confederation and the Road to the Constitution* (Chicago: The University of Chicago Press, 2017), 52.

13. *Journals of the Continental Congress*, 28: 333.

14. *Journals of the Continental Congress*, 9: i-vi.

15. *Journals of the Continental Congress*, 31: 657.

16. *Journals of the Continental Congress*, 30: 187-90.

17. *Journals of the Continental Congress*, 32: 366.

18. *Journals of the Continental Congress*, 32: 454-63.

19. *Journals of the Continental Congress*, 32: 328.

middle of 1787, Congressional committees that dealt with the Virginia militia's unauthorized actions along the frontier noted that Congress had a "duty to preserve peace with Indian nations and to permit no settlements on their lands or Intrusions on lands of the United States in that part of the Country."[20] Illegal settling on Indian lands threatened to erupt into warfare along the frontier, and Congressional committees noted that war "cannot be consistent with the Interest and policy of the Union," especially due to the poor state of finances of the country under the Articles of Confederation.[21] Knox, as well as other delegates to Congress, had noted that it was cheaper to maintain peace through treaties than it was to go to war against the Indians.[22]

THE GROWTH OF A COHERENT POLICY

By 1787, Congress published instructions for the Indian super-intendents which dictated, "Justice forbids the United States from being guilty of oppression; but at the same time it dictates that their peaceable citizens shall be protected in their lawful pursuits."[23] This shift away from demanding that "the Savages should without Compensation abandon Part of their Country to the United States who claim it by Conquest and as a Retribution" brings to full light the movement away from a belief in the "right of conquest" to a policy more based upon "justice and public faith."[24] In an attempt to engage fairly with Native Americans, Congress appointed commissioners to meet with Indian tribes to renegotiate previous treaties, not to demand additional land concessions but to "remove all causes of controversy, so that peace and harmony may continue between the United States and the Indian Tribes, the regulating trade and settling boundaries."[25] This shift in mentality occurred throughout the development of the Indian Department under Secretary Knox, but was codified by late 1787.

In 1787, Knox recommended to Congress that to keep peace along the frontier and to prevent excursions by each side, a military force of 1,500 was needed to maintain order and "by force expel them (those

20. *Journals of the Continental Congress*, 32: 268.

21. *Journals of the Continental Congress*, 33: 478.

22. Massachusetts Delegates to John Hancock, May 27, 1788, in *Letters of Delegates*, 25: 116.; *Journals of the Continental Congress*, 32: 331. Knox notes that it is cheaper and more economical to request militias and attempt treaties than it was to attempt to raise and field an Army, due primarily to the failure of the United States finances and governmental system.

23. *Journals of the Continental Congress*, 32: 67.

24. Pennsylvania Delegates to the Pennsylvania Assembly, September 25, 1783, in *Letters of Delegates*, 20: 710.; *Journals of the Continental Congress*, 32: 67.

25. *Journals of the Continental Congress*, 33: 710-1.

Henry Knox, left, Secretary of War of the United States, and Arthur Lee, right, painted by John Trumbull. (*New York Public Library/Yale University Art Gallery*)

settled in a territory illegally) from their towns or extricate them."[26] While he acknowledged the financial impossibility of raising and supporting such a force, he provided a glimpse into the ideal policy that he would implement, which was not based upon seizing of lands through "right of conquest," but was instead based upon an attempt at peaceful coexistence along a defined border. Congress ultimately agreed to most of the proposed policy to "afford the most effectual protection to the frontier ... from incursions and depredations of the Indians, for preventing intrusions on the federal lands [by illegal settlers] ... prevent wanton Attacks upon the Indians by lawless men which so essentially tend to destroy all peace and friendship with the indian Nations."[27]

Knox's rebuttal of Arthur Lee's "rights of conquest," his use of the Army on the frontier, and his view of a proper policy were displayed in his report to Congress about a request from Colonel Martin of the North Carolina militia requesting troops to help maintain peace on that state's frontier. Knox claimed, "By an upright and honorable construction of the treaty of Hopewell the United States have pledged themselves for the protection of the said indians within the boundaries described by the said treaty and that the principles of good Faith sound

26. *Journals of the Continental Congress,* 32: 327-32.
27. *Journals of the Continental Congress,* 32: 372-3. Clarity to quote added by author.

policy and every respect which a nation, owes it own reputation and dignity require of the union possess sufficient power that it be exerted to enforce a due observation of the said treaty."[28] Knox's insistence that the United States consider agreements and treaties made with Indian tribes as valid and legally binding for the new nation enabled him to convince the Continental Congress to approve a measure to send US troops to North Carolina to remove illegal settlers who were residing on Indian lands.[29]

Toward the end of the life of the Articles of Confederation, a clear Indian policy emerged. Providing continuity of leadership in these matters through four iterations of congressional delegates and committee members, Secretary Knox devised a framework for interacting with Native American tribes. Tribes, and their land claims, were to be treated in the same fashion as independent nations with defined borders that were established through treaties and protected by a military force that prevented unauthorized travel and commerce. The United States had moved away from insistence of Indian lands based upon "right of conquest" and war reparations, and instead shifted to a policy which utilized the United States Army and a newly developed Indian Department to maintain a peaceful separation between Indian tribes and white settlers.

---

28. *Journals of the Continental Congress*, 34: 343.
29. *Journals of the Continental Congress*, 34: 343-44, 476-479.

Justice, Mercy, and Treason: John Marshall's and Mercy Otis Warren's Treatments of Benedict Arnold

▘▘ RAND MIRANTE ▘▘

In the early years of the nineteenth century, the founders of the new American Republic were lurching forward from the shockingly successful outcome of their increasingly remote Revolution, and finding themselves immersed in the uncharted waters of nation-building. The political landscape was inflamed by passionate partisanship and varying, often vituperatively expressed visions of what course to follow, what form the Republic ought to assume, and what guidance the past could offer for the discordant present and an uncertain future.

Squaring off contemporaneously at opposite poles of the political spectrum were two of the country's most prominent historians who were participants in the years of the Revolution: the Chief Justice of the United States Supreme Court, former staunch Federalist John Marshall, a Virginia veteran of Washington's army and subsequent survivor of Thomas Jefferson's assault on the federal judiciary; and Mercy Otis Warren, a fervent Jeffersonian Republican, iconoclastic dramatist and chronicler who found and placed herself at the Massachusetts epicenter of pivotal Revolutionary history. Marshall's platform was his multi-volume, periodically released, and unevenly focused biography of his consummate hero, under whom he served at Brandywine, Germantown, Valley Forge, and Monmouth: *The Life of George Washington*. Warren's pulpit was her comparably monumental *History of the Rise, Progress and Termination of the American Revolution Interspersed with Biographical, Political and Moral Observations*. Both works can be seen as polemical exercises that were intended to shape the future by transfiguring the past via the authors' respective ideological prisms.

To illustrate this great debate, I've chosen to focus largely the glass upon the tenor and tone of the two dueling historians' respective treatments of that iconic traitor, Gen. Benedict Arnold, and the interpretations that could be derived therefrom. It's entirely possible that Marshall briefly encountered American General Arnold at the end of the Valley Forge encampment when oaths of allegiance were administered, and Marshall's militia unit (he had been demobilized from the Continental Army in 1779) was witness to British General Arnold's 1781 onslaught in the James River area.[1] It's unlikely but not inconceivable that Warren observed the patriotic version of Arnold in Boston in 1775 just prior to his epic march on Quebec. Regardless of the at-best highly tangential nature of any first-hand meetings the authors might have had with him, Arnold's betrayal played an important role in each of their narratives.

Warren commenced *Rise, Progress and Termination*—a three-volume work with the final installment coming out in 1807—with a striking commentary on the nature of mankind, right after an attention-getting initial sentence which rather caustically described "History [as] the deposite of crimes, and the record of every thing disgraceful or honorary to mankind."[2] On the opening page, she outlined the "secret springs" which, in addition to the benign hand of providence, precipitate human events:

> The study of the human character opens at once a beautiful and a deformed picture of the soul. We there find a noble principle implanted in the nature of man, that pants for distinction. This principle operates in every bosom, and when kept under the control of reason, and the influence of humanity, it produces the most benevolent effects. But when the checks of conscience are thrown aside, or the moral sense weakened by the sudden acquisition of wealth or power, humanity is obscured, and if a favorable coincidence of circumstances permits, this love of distinction often exhibits the most mortifying instances of profligacy, tyranny, and the wanton exercise of arbitrary sway.[3]

---

1. John Marshall to Joseph Story, July 25, 1827, *The Papers of John Marshall Digital Edition*, Charles Hobson, ed. (Charlottesville: University of Virginia Press, Rotunda, 2014), rotunda.upress.virginia.edu/founders/default.xqy?keys=JNML-print-01-11-02-0017.
2. Mercy Otis Warren, *History of the Rise, Progress and Termination of the American Revolution Interspersed with Biographical, Political and Moral Observations*, 2nd ed., ed. Lester H. Cohen (Indianapolis: Liberty Fund; 1994), 3. The work was completed by the end of 1804, with all three volumes published by 1807.
3. Ibid., 3.

Here then we have Warren's central thesis, to be hammered home with myriad examples, put boldly and up front: as seen by her, the infatuation of many founders and their Federalist followers with rank and privilege, and with financial aggrandizement and predatory, speculative commercialism, was endangering the very survival of the hard-won liberties and freedoms bequeathed by the Revolution. Corruption was knocking at the door—or rather, it was already inside the edifice—and it was threatening to spread depredation and ruin, as it had "from Cesar to an arbitrary prince of the House of Brunswick." Warren plainly laid out what she believed to be at stake:

> The progress of the American Revolution has been so rapid, such the alteration of manners, the blending of characters, and the new train of ideas that almost universally prevail, that the principles which animated to the noblest exertions have been nearly annihilated. Many who first stepped forth in vindication of the rights of human nature are forgotten, and the causes which involved the thirteen colonies in confusion and blood are scarcely known, amidst the rage of accumulation and the taste for expensive pleasures that have since prevailed.[4]

Unusually for her day, Warren, whose father, brother, and husband were all prominent Massachusetts patriot leaders, had been home-schooled to a high standard; echoes of *Decline and Fall* and classical and Biblical references abound in her *History*.[5] Her polemical writing initially had taken the form of poems and plays; in the latter category, her acerbic satirical dramas, including *The Adulateur* and *The Defeat*, deriding Gov. Thomas Hutchinson (represented by her character the corrupt and treacherous "Rapatio"), achieved popularity and notoriety, although the author's identity was understandably kept secret.[6] Thus, as her Revolutionary chronicle reached the momentous year of 1780 and the spirit of patriotism was showing signs of waning, she propelled Benedict Arnold onto her stage, as though he were a stock villain in one of her dramas. General Arnold, Warren wrote, "was a man without principle from the beginning, and before his defection was discovered,

---

4. Ibid., 4.

5. On the second page of *Rise, Progress and Termination*, the author spoke of "turbulent passions" that have turned the "lower creation" into an "aceldama." Plaudits go to the reader who, unlike this writer, is not thereby compelled to reach for the dictionary!

6. For a discussion of Warren's plays, including whether or not she was the author of *The Blockheads*, lampooning the British stranglehold on Boston, see Nancy Rubin Stuart, *The Muse of the Revolution* (Boston: Beacon Press, 2008), 48-49, 51-52, 103-04. Stuart points out that the plays were meant to be read but not performed, as there was no live theater in Boston at the time, thanks to its "Puritan tradition."

he had sunk a character raised by impetuous valor, and some occasional strokes of bravery, attended with success, without being the possessor of any intrinsic merit."[7] The worship of military prowess was not for Warren, which to her was completely meaningless if not exercised for virtuous reasons, no matter how worthy the cause—for without virtuous actors, the cause itself would inevitably be corrupted, and divine providence would therefore not lend it assistance. Referring to Arnold's alleged plundering of Montreal and his "rapacity" in Philadelphia, echoing the Governor Hutchinson character, she continued:

> He had accumulated a fortune by great crimes, and squandered it without reputation, long before he formed the plan to betray his country, and sacrifice a cause disgraced by the appointment of a man like himself, to such important trusts.[8]

Here Warren castigated not just Arnold but the very act of his appointment. Leaving no room for any ameliorating traits or mitigating circumstances, she stated that Arnold was "proud of the trappings, and ambitious of an ostentatious display of wealth and greatness (the certain mark of a narrow mind)."[9] Here we have at center stage the exemplar for speculative, status-seeking, fortune-hunting post-war American leaders and their followers who were jeopardizing the moral achievements of the Revolution. Arnold verged onto the path of treason after making "exorbitant demands on congress" for reimbursements and determining upon "revenge for public ignomiy, at the expense of his country . . . after the perpetration of so many crimes" (another reference to his avaricious conduct and maladministration as military governor of Philadelphia).[10]

Warren thereupon turned her attention to British go-between Maj. John André, whom she described as "elegant in person," "amiable," "polite," "sensible," and "brave" before decrying that, due to "mistake in himself" and Arnold's "baseness" he "descended to an assumed and disgraceful character"—that is, the character of a spy.[11]

To Mercy Otis Warren, the practice of espionage was to be roundly condemned, and her condemnation wasn't limited in this instance to

---

7. Warren first introduced Arnold in connection with the Quebec expedition, where he was described as "a young soldier of fortune, who held in equal contempt both danger and principle." Warren, *Rise, Progress and Termination*, 143.
8. Ibid., 400.
9. Ibid., 400.
10. Ibid., 401.
11. Ibid., 404.

André's superior officer. In a passage striking for the breadth of the net of opprobrium thrown, she observed:

> Doubtless, the generals Clinton and Washington were equally culpable, in selecting an Andre and a Hale to hazard all the hopes of youth and talents, on the precarious die of executing with success, a business to which so much baseness and deception is attached.[12]

In addition, while Warren contrasted the brutally abrupt execution of Nathan Hale by the British with the "politeness and generosity" shown André by his captors (including their commander in chief), she nevertheless noted:

> Many persons, from the impulse of humanity, thought that general Washington might consistently with his character as a soldier and a patriot, have meliorated the sentence of death so far, as to have saved, at his own earnest request, this amiable young man from the ignominy of a gallows.[13]

Thus, early on, Warren did not exempt the paragon George Washington from criticism, and while he never came close to being a primary target, we will again see her upbraid the Father of his Country for falling short, in the postwar aftermath, of the requisite standards of republican virtue and morality.

Warren provided dramatic foils to the villainous Arnold and the corrupted André by introducing from the wings the trio of militiamen-captors, "John Paulding, David Williams, and Isaac Vanvert" (actually Van Wart). These three homespun Americans refused the British major's offered bribe, and Warren stated that their names "ought never to be forgotten" (not allowing for having herself gotten one of them wrong).[14] Their importance to her nevertheless was that they epitomized her patriotic ideal: citizen soldiers, interested only in the good of their country, impervious to subornation and showing "contempt for private interest." She favorably observed that Congress awarded the heroic trio silver medals and pensions.[15] She also noted that Arnold's "insolent and overbearing" subsequent proclamation for others to join

---

12. Ibid., 404.

13. Ibid., 406-07.

14. Ibid., 403.

15. Ibid., 408. Interestingly, after the war the trio became enmeshed in pension claims and was also the focus of some controversy as to whether or not they had pocketed the major's proffered bribe, with American admirers of André besmirching their characters and populist champions rising to their defense. See Robert E. Cray, "Major John Andre and the Three Captors: Class Dynamics and Revolutionary Memory Wars in the Early Republic, 1780-1831," *Journal of the Early Republic*, vol. 17, no. 3 (Autumn 1997).

him in switching sides "cast many indecent reflections on congress," an important point to be kept in mind when we consider Marshall's treatment of the same episode.[16]

After the American patriots' cause, aided by the intervention of the three militiamen and abetted by divine providence thanks to their righteousness, dodged Arnold's treasonous bullet and triumphed a year later at Yorktown, Warren's worries about the future really began to set in. She compared the new nation to a "young heir ... incapable of weighing the intrinsic value of his estate." She bemoaned that hard-won liberty was being "bartered away for the gratification of vanity, or the aggrandizement of a few individuals."[17] She saw—ubiquitously cropping up like the yield from maliciously sown dragon's teeth—Federalists enamored with centralized control, with the accumulation of wealth, and with fostering the corruption of speculative finance ("though the spirit for freedom was not worn down, a party arose, actuated by different principles, new designs were discovered").[18] Glimmerings of the worst traits of Arnold could be detected everywhere, and Warren warned "it is necessary to guard at every point, against the intrigues of ambitious men, who may subvert the system which the inhabitants of the United States judged to be most conducive to the general happiness."[19]

Here, then, is a sampling of the gallery of prominent patriots whose conduct and ambitions were subjected to scrutiny and criticism in *Rise, Progress and Termination*:

Benjamin Franklin—Referring to his succumbing to flattery and "unbounded applauses" that placed him under the sway of the duplicitous Charles Gravier, comte de Vergennes: "it is painful even for the impartial historian, who contemplates the superiority of his genius, to record the foibles of the man ... yet this distinguished sage became susceptible of a court influence."[20]

John Jay—As delegate to negotiate a treaty with Great Britain, he "fell from the dignified, manly, independent spirit which should have marked an American negociator."[21]

Gouverneur Morris—"A character eccentric from youth to declining age; a man of pleasure, pride, and extravagance, fond of the trappings

16. Warren, *Rise, Progress and Termination*, 407.
17. Ibid., 645-46.
18. Ibid., 698.
19. Ibid., 692.
20. Ibid., 290.
21. Ibid., 668.

of monarchy, implicated by a considerable portion of the citizens of America, as deficient in principle, was not a suitable person for a resident minister in France."[22]

Alexander Hamilton—Unsurprisingly, excoriated by Warren for his creation of the national debt, "which was probably never intended to be paid," she described him as a "young officer of foreign extraction, an adventurer of bold genius, active talents, and fortunate combinations, from his birth to the exalted station to which he was listed by the spirit of favoritism." Warren saw Hamilton as having ignited a powder train of "restless passions" and "a rage for project, speculation, and artifices . . . which finally ruined multitudes of unsuspecting citizens."[23] (It should again be noted that to Warren, bravery, genius, military prowess, fortitude, and success unaccompanied by virtue and morality were in and of themselves meaningless, as she had already made clear in her indictment of Arnold.) As a staunch opponent of standing armies, she also pointed her accusatory finger at Hamilton as "the prime mover and conductor of [the] extraordinary business" of assembling what she deemed the "dangerous engine" of the excessive force mobilized to suppress the Whiskey Rebellion in 1794.[24]

George Washington—Warren's approach here was to praise—which she did frequently—with fairly faint damnations. In becoming the president of the aristocratic and hereditary order of the Society of the Cincinnati, which she believed he should have forcefully declined, Washington should have acted upon a sense of "the impropriety of an assumption so incompatible with the principles of a young republic," instead of heading "a self-created peerage of military origin."[25]

And after reviewing Washington's farewell address admonitions, she noted that by the time he delivered them at the end of his second term,

> it was at a juncture when the citizenry were split into factions; after an exotic taste had been introduced into America, which had a tendency to enhance their public and to accumulate their private debts; and after the poison of foreign influence had crept into their councils, and created a passion to assimilate the politics and the government of the United States nearer to the model of European monarchies.[26]

22. Ibid., 671. Like her hero Jefferson (and unlike Gouverneur Morris), Warren expressed sympathy towards the French Revolution, while decrying its undeniable excesses.
23. Ibid., 668.
24. Ibid., 665, 672.
25. Ibid., 618-19.
26. Ibid., 673.

Certainly not a ringing approbation of the initial presidential administration.

John Adams—Here, toward the end of her chronicle, Warren's criticism reached an absolute crescendo directed at her former close friend, the one-term Federalist chief executive whose peremptory actions had propelled in large part Thomas Jefferson's ascension to the highest office. In her own defense, she morosely noted that "the heart of the annalist may sometimes be hurt by political deviations which the pen of the historian is obliged to record." Those deviations included "prejudices and passions . . . sometimes too strong for his sagacity and judgment," and "a partiality for monarchy"; Adams had turned into a betrayer who had "relinquished the republican system, and forgotten the principles of the American revolution, which he had advocated for near twenty years."[27] (The reaction by the prickly Adams to this harsh verdict was predictably one of wounded outrage and an outpouring of protesting correspondence.)[28]

None of these (to Warren) clay-footed icons were compared overtly to Benedict Arnold, but the lesson of Warren's morality play is clear: the American republic, established on a foundation of revolutionary virtue and dedicated to popular representation and the protection of individual freedoms (Warren was a staunch proponent of the Bill of Rights), was being betrayed and subverted again, consciously by some, inadvertently by others through their acquired weaknesses.

We now turn to Chief Justice John Marshall, Warren's contemporary counterpoint and end-of-term Adams appointee to head the Supreme Court. While on the Court, Marshall undertook the rather unorthodox and extremely demanding project of writing his hagiographic *Life of George Washington* at the urging of Washington's nephew—and Marshall's fellow justice on the Court—Bushrod Washington; his well-placed friend and colleague provided Marshall with extraordinary access to his uncle's trove of papers. The first two volumes came out in 1803 and, to Marshall's deep disappointment and chagrin, they were neither a commercial nor a critical success. (George Washington was barely mentioned in the first tome, which went badly off the rails by

27. Ibid., 675.

28. See Martha J. King, "'The Pen of the Historian'," *Princeton University Library Chronicle*, vol. LXXII, no. 2 (Winter 2011): 524-29, which includes Adams' acid assertion to Warren that "after the termination of the Revolutionary War, your subject was completed"—hardly the way she saw it.

confining itself to an exhaustive history of the colonial period.) But they and the volumes which followed (especially the final one which covered the postwar years, just as Warren's last volume had done) did spark an immensely heated political controversy, with President Thomas Jefferson referring to the completed work as a "five-volumed libel."[29]

Marshall was a distant cousin of Jefferson, and likely going as far back as the Revolution the relationship was not a cordial one; perhaps this was traceable to Marshall's perceptions of Jefferson's failure to provide frontline leadership when Arnold raided Virginia in 1781. This lack of cordiality was exacerbated by litigations involving the two "cousins" as attorneys (on opposite or even when on the same sides). It festered further when Marshall, as one of President Adams' three envoys to France, was the exasperated and offended target of Directory Minister Charles-Maurice de Talleyrand-Périgord's attempted shakedown of the United States during the "X Y Z Affair" in 1797-98, which turned into a partisan flashpoint between anti-French Federalists and pro-French Democratic-Republicans.[30] The rocky relationship completely deteriorated when Marshall was appointed to the Supreme Court in the eleventh hour of the Adams administration, and incoming President Jefferson launched his vehement but ultimately unsuccessful vendetta against a judiciary stocked with Federalists. So the two men were outright, publicly bitter enemies by the time publication of volume five of *The Life of George Washington* coincided with the momentous 1807 treason trial of Jefferson's nemesis, his former vice president Aaron Burr, a trial presided over by Marshall serving quite ironically as a circuit judge, since having to ride circuit in addition to sitting on the Supreme Court was seen as a punitive measure concocted by Democratic-Republican leaders and directed at the justices.[31] President Jefferson's unsuccessful attempts to influence the outcome of the Burr trial (actually two trials and two acquittals), including in a speech to Congress, are well-known; underscoring the level of partisan distrust was the fact that suspicions were voiced by Bushrod Washington (who was Marshall's financial partner in the proceeds of *The Life of George Washington*) that the chief executive was using the postmaster general of the

---

29. Thomas Jefferson to William Johnson, March 4, 1823, founders.archives.gov/documents/Jefferson/98-01-02-3373.

30. David Robarge, *A Chief Justice's Progress: John Marshall from Revolutionary Virginia to the Supreme Court* (Westport, CT: Greenwood Press, 2000), 160-62, for the genesis of the Marshall-Jefferson enmity, and 183-95 for an engrossing look at Marshall in Paris.

31. Jean Edward Smith, *John Marshall: Definer of a Nation* (New York: Henry Holt, 1996), 305, 308.

United States and his postal agents to interfere with the books' subscription sales.[32]

I wish to make it completely clear that in his biography's treatment (in the fourth volume) of the 1780 treason plot, Marshall in no way exculpated Benedict Arnold, nor did he diminish the severity of the turncoat's crime or the potentially disastrous impact of his betrayal (yielding up what Marshall referred to as "the Gibraltar of America"), had it been successful. There was no process of acquittal at work here, nothing comparable to that of Aaron Burr (where the prosecution was procedurally flawed and the evidence available at the time of the Burr trial was in any event quite convoluted and controversial). Arnold was strongly denounced by Marshall as "a traitor, a sordid traitor, first the slave of his rage, then purchased with gold."[33]

However—and especially when read in juxtaposition to Warren—I believe a difference in tone can be detected. Marshall did not castigate Arnold as rotten to the core from the outset (recall Warren's condemnatory "devoid of principle from the beginning"). Rather, Marshall cited Arnold's "great services and military talents," "his courage in battle," his "patient fortitude with which he bore the most excessive hardships," and "the firmness which he had displayed in the field . . . in the most adverse circumstances."[34] These character traits were not at all irrelevant to the combat-veteran Marshall. But, relieved from field command due to his wounds, in Philadelphia Arnold failed to display "that strength of principle and correctness of judgment to which his high station exposed him" (unlike in Warren, no mention was made of the much more ambiguous circumstances involving the disputation of Arnold's military accounts in Montreal).[35] Marshall almost matter-of-factly took note of Arnold's "speculations which were unfortunate," and then proceeded to recount how "his claims against the United States were great" and how Arnold became entangled in challenging reviews by the assigned commissioners and appealing to congress, where a committee was said to have reduced even what the commissioners had allowed. "Not the less soured and disgusted by these multiple causes of irritation in consequence of their being attributable to his own follies and vices, he gave full scope to his resentments . . . and gave great offence to congress."[36] Marshall opined that Benedict Arnold was now out for vengeance.

32. See ibid., 330, dismissing the veracity of the suspicion.
33. John Marshall, *The Life of George Washington* (Philadelphia: C. P. Wayne, 1805), iv: 287.
34. Ibid., iv: 271-72.
35. Ibid., iv: 272.
36. Ibid., iv: 272-73.

Marshall recounted the treason plot and its undoing, but attributed the capture of André to his "want of self-possession" that "would almost seem providential."[37] The three (unnamed) militiamen-captors were praised for "invaluable service" but not glorified to anywhere near the extent as did populist-proponent Warren. Neither was there any denunciation from the pragmatic Marshall of the practice of espionage as immoral. The Chief Justice closed his treatment of the treason episode by commenting on the turncoat's post-defection proclamation (from which he extensively quoted), in which Arnold attempted to incite others to follow his lead:

> He was profuse in his invectives against congress and their leaders generally, whom he criminated with sinister views in protracting the war at the public expense, and with general tyranny and usurpation. With these charges he artfully mingled assertions of their sovereign contempt for the people, particularly manifested in refusing to take their collective sentiments on the proposals for peace which Great Britain had made.[38]

Up to this point, the conclusion of the coverage in *Life of George Washington* of the Arnold plot, for the most part the distinctions between Marshall's treatment and that of Warren in *Rise, Progress and Termination* are nuanced and not glaringly obvious. But I believe that what immediately follows—on the very next page of the same chapter, without break or interval—is consequential in distinguishing the two works. Turning immediately and seamlessly to the state of the Continental Army in late 1780, Marshall wrote:

> Notwithstanding the embarrassments with which congress was surrounded, *and the miserable system of government to which the affairs of America were then committed*, it is not easy to find adequate reasons for the neglect ... It would seem, from private letters, as if two parties still agitated congress. The one entered fully into the views of the commander in chief; the other, jealous of the army, and apprehensive of its hostility to liberty when peace should be restored, remained unwilling to give stability."[39] (Emphasis added.)

Placed in extremely close proximity to Arnold's descent into treason, I submit that it is not too much of a leap for a reader to infer from Marshall that Arnold's "rage," while not justifying his unconscionable course

37. Ibid., iv: 280.
38. Ibid., iv: 288.
39. Ibid., iv: 292. In his advocacy for a professional, standing army, one readily discerns yet another deep divide between Marshall and Warren.

of action, could nevertheless have been to some degree provoked by "the miserable system." In other words, it's something of a wonder that Arnold was, according to Marshall, the only influential American officer who took the drastic step of re-adhering to the Crown. And whether or not the reader makes this same interpretive leap as well, the passage does provide the sharp, stark juxtaposition of contrasting fears for the nation's future held by the Federalist justice and by the Jeffersonian Republican woman of letters. For him, the threats were anarchy, the tyranny of the masses, unchecked and unbalanced populism, the spread of Jacobinism. For her, it was the restoration of the evils of monarchic privilege in republican guise, aided and abetted by the corruption of civic virtue. As Mercy Otis Warren remarked in *Rise, Progress and Termination*, the reader may draw his or her own conclusions.

A Chance Amiss: George Washington and the Fiasco of Spain's Gift Diplomacy

ELISA VARGAS

At the beginning of March 1777, Arthur Lee, a delegate to the United States Congress, urgently requested to meet with the Marquis de Grimaldi, who until just a few weeks before had been the Secretary of State of Foreign Affairs of King Carlos III of Spain, and who was now on his way to take charge of the Spanish embassy in Rome. Coming from Paris, Lee was part of the American delegation in charge of obtaining financial and logistical support for the independence cause of the thirteen colonies. Although the meeting between Grimaldi and Lee in Burgos did not result in the expected official Spanish support for the American cause, it did open the doors to important secret aid that would be channeled through the mercantile company of the man who had organized and acted as translator of this meeting: Don Diego María de Gardoqui y Arriquibar.[1]

According to Lee's information to the American Commissioners in Paris, Spain agreed to send clothes, blankets and tents from the city of Bilbao, leaving the operation in charge of Diego de Gardoqui, who would personally hire the ships and crew, and monitor the shipment of supplies to Havana and the port of New Orleans.[2] Louisiana's Governor, Bernardo de Gálvez, would add ammunition and other supplies to the rebel army's cache. Once in American waters, the rebel ships would

---

1. María Jesús Cava and Begoña Cava, *Diego María de Gardoqui: Un Bilbaíno en la diplomacia del siglo XVIII* (Bilbao: BBK, 1992), 10.
2. American Commissioners to the Committee of Secret Correspondence, Paris, March 12, 1777, founders.archives.gov/documents/Franklin/01-23-02-0305. Also see Alfonso Carlos Saiz Valdivieso, *Diego María Gardoqui. Esplendor y Penumbra* (Madrid: Muelle Uritarte Editores, 2014), 80.

be authorized to pick up the cargo in Spanish ports in America. A secret line of credit of four million *reales de vellón* (equivalent to half a million Continental dollars)[3] was established with the Spanish treasury for the purchase of medicines, muskets, tents, blankets, buttons, shoes, socks, blue woolen cloths and white fabrics to make uniforms for the continental army, as well as anchors, ropes and sails among other naval objects.

Born in 1735, Diego de Gardoqui, was heir to *Gardoqui e Hijos* (Gardoqui and Sons Co.), one of the most renowned codfish trading companies between Bilbao and North American ports. From a young age, his father entrusted him with the task of expanding the family business to other ports and commodities, and for this reason he was sent to London to study finance and learn the language, which made Diego one of the few Spaniards at the time to be fluent in English. True to the wishes of his father, Diego's brothers continued to support him after the death of the patriarch, buying him a post at the Bilbao consulate, launching a professional career that would include positions in the Bilbao City Council (from 1771 to 1776) and as advisor at the Court in Madrid (from 1777).[4] From the latter, he would launch the daring undertaking of channeling the secret Spanish aid to the United States using his family's business as cover. In fact, the *Gardoqui e Hijos* company had long been involved in supplying arms and supplies to the American revolutionaries.[5] In February 1775, a year and a half prior to the Declaration of Independence of the United States and long before the courts of France or Spain used the adventurer and writer Caron de Beaumarchais as a cover for the same purpose, the Basque company already had sent "three hundred muskets and bayonets, and almost double that number of pairs of pistols" to the American Revolutionaries.[6]

---

3. For the Spanish financial aid to the American Revolution see José Antonio Armillas Vicente, "Ayuda secreta y deuda oculta. España y la independencia de los Estados Unidos," in Eduardo Garrigues, Emma Sánchez Montañés, Sylvia L. Hilton, Almudena Hernández Ruigómez and Isabel García-Montón Garrigues, eds, *Norteamérica a finales del siglo XVIII: España y los Estados Unidos* (Madrid: Fundación Consejo España-Estados Unidos y Marcial Pons, 2008), 171-196.

4. Cava and Cava, *Diego María de Gardoqui*, 12.

5. Reyes Calderón Cuadrado, "Alianzas comerciales hispano-norteamericanas en la financiación del proceso de independencia de los Estados Unidos de América: La Casa Gardoqui e hijos," in *Norteamérica a finales del siglo XVIII: España y los Estados Unidos*, 197-218; Natividad Rueda, *La Compañía Comercial Gardoqui e hijos: 1760—1800* (Vitoria-Gasteiz: Gobierno Vasco, 1992).

6. José Gardoqui to Jeremiah Lee, Bilbao, February 15, 1775, in *Naval Documents of the American Revolution* (Washington, DC: Government Printing Office, 1964-2014), 1:401.

For two decades, Gardoqui and Sons Co. had established trade routes between Bilbao and the American ports of Salem, Newburyport, Beverly, Boston, and Gloucester in Massachusetts. Its American partners included prominent merchants closely linked to the cause of the American Revolution such as the Cabot brothers—one of the region's leading merchant families—and Elbridge and Samuel Russel Gerry, pioneers of independence commissioned by the Second Continental Congress to supply the rebel army.

The Gardoqui family knew how to take advantage of this extraordinary opportunity by identifying Spain's interests with their own. In little more than a decade, the clan increased its capital exponentially. Between 1765 and 1778, the company imported codfish, rice, tobacco and indigo from the thirteen colonies, exporting in turn wool, naval articles and iron. By 1791, the annual earnings of Gardoqui and his sons would exceed six hundred thousand *reales*, and there are even those who claim that they had an estimated capital of ten million *reales*.[7] In the first years of the American War of Independence, the role of the Gardoqui would be essential in keeping the Continental army armed and supplied, at a time when the Spanish Government's official policy regarding the conflict was, in the words of the Count of Floridablanca in 1777, to "prepare for the war, as it is inevitable, but do everything to prevent it."[8] When the British Navy closed American ports on the East Coast, Spanish aid to the American revolutionaries had to be sent through Havana and New Orleans, from where US agents would make it reach its destination by going up the Mississippi. With the entry of Spain into the war against Great Britain in June 1779, the need for secret intermediaries to send aid to the American revolutionaries would disappear; nonetheless Gardoqui continued trading with his American partners, clients and contacts.

His special relationship with John Adams, who would later become the second President of the United States and one of the most renowned ideologues within the circle of American patriots responsible

7. Andoni Artola Renedo, "El cardenal Francisco Antonio Gardoqui (1747 -1820): las claves de una carrera en la Iglesia Católica," *Bidebarriera: Revista de humanidades y Ciencias Sociales de Bilbao* 21 (2010), 47-66, 2. Álvaro Chaparro Sainz, "Diego María de Gardoqui y los Estados Unidos: Actuaciones, influencias y relaciones de un vasco en el nacimiento de una nación," *Vasconia* 39 (2013), 101-140; 120.
8. María Pilar Ruigómez de Hernández, *El gobierno español del despotismo ilustrado ante la independencia de los Estados Unidos de América: Una nueva estructura de la política internacional (1773–1783)* (Madrid: Ministerio de Asuntos Exteriores, 1978), 225. Juan Hernández Franco, *La gestión política y el pensamiento reformista del Conde de Floridablanca* (Murcia: Universidad de Murcia, 1984), 334.

for drafting the Constitution of 1787, should be noted here. Their first meeting took place by chance in 1780, in the course of Adams' travel to Paris to join the United States embassy in that capital. Adams' ship was forced to dock at El Ferrol, in the north-west coast of Spain. In the rush to reach his destination and replace Silas Deane, Adams decided to continue his journey by road in the middle of winter. According to his personal diary and his correspondence with his wife Abigail, shortly after Adams arrived in Bilbao, Diego Gardoqui knocked on his door to invite him to dinner at his house.[9] From that night on, Gardoqui became his personal guide to Spain.

Once the British army was defeated at the Battle of Yorktown in October 1781, the American Congress began to consider entering into negotiations with Spain to discuss two main points: the navigation on the Mississippi River and the definition of the borders south and west of the new nation.[10] During the peace negotiations that took place in Paris in late 1782 and early 1783, the enormous distance that separated the Spanish, French and American proposals became evident. Spain wanted its borders to start from the Gulf of Mexico, following the Apalachicola River to the Flint River and continuing through the Appalachians to Lake Erie. The United States was in a position to recognize the coasts of the Gulf of Mexico as Spanish territory as long as Spain recognized that the American borders began with the Mississippi River. France for its part proposed that the southern limit of its border with Spain should be set on the Ohio River to the east.

As Spain had not been a formal ally of the American Revolutionaries and was unwilling to recognize the Unites States as a country, the American negotiators in Paris felt no need to inform the Spanish government about their territorial agreements with the British, which established that if, at the time of the cessation of hostilities, Florida remained in the hands of the British, the southern border of the United States would be fixed at the 31st parallel. This provision directly contradicted the surrender capitulations signed by Gen. Bernardo de Gálvez and Gen. John Campbell after the British were defeated at Pensacola in May 1781. If the border was set from the 31st parallel, north of the city of New Orleans, Spain would lose a fundamental containment zone that afforded protected from constant incursions of outlaws and American militiamen.

9. John Adams to Abigail Adams, January 16, 1780, founders.archives.gov/documents/Adams/04-03-02-0201. Adams to Michel Lagoanere, January 16, 1780, founders.archives.gov/documents/Adams/06-08-02-0193.
10. Alfonso Carlos Saiz Valdivieso, *Diego María Gardoqui. Esplendor y Penumbra* (Madrid: Muelle Uritarte Editores, 2014), 108.

When, in 1784, the Spanish government decided it needed to send an official envoy to the United States it was no surprise that Gardoqui was selected for such a crucial posting, with instructions to settle the pending negotiations with the new Republic.[11] Spain's position of controlling navigation along the Mississippi was not easy to maintain as it contravened the practice of international law of the time, which established that a river's navigation rights could be transferred from one state to another—first from France to Great Britain, and after this to the United States—without the need for the consent of the third affected state, in this case Spain.[12]

At forty-nine years of age, Gardoqui presented himself as the ideal candidate to unblock negotiations with the United States, since he not only knew George Washington personally but also had an extensive network of contacts among the delegates to Congress where he was known for the role that *Gardoqui e Hijos* company had played in delivering secret Spanish aid to the American revolutionaries.[13] Richard Henry Lee, president of Congress in 1785, Arthur Lee and James Monroe demonstrated in favor of the Spanish thesis in exchange for commercial rights. These circles were keenly aware that the exports of codfish to Spain produced between four and five million dollars annually, a business that Northern States were keen to protect.

Gardoqui presented his credentials as "plenipotentiary minister" (equivalent to what is currently an ambassador, but that was at the time the highest diplomatic representative appointed to a country where there was no tradition of bilateral relations) of the Kingdom of Spain before the United States of America on June 22, 1785. From its independence in 1777 until adoption of the constitution in 1789, the young American republic was a confederation in which the central state had very little power or resources. In the absence of a president or prime minister, the most prominent figure in the executive was the Secretary of Foreign Affairs, John Jay. Between 1779 and 1782, Jay had been sent to Spain, where in the words of one historian, he spent "thirty murderous months on the periphery of the Spanish court."[14]

Although he did not succeed in attaining an alliance between the two nations nor Spanish recognition of the independence of the United

---

11. Cava and Cava, *Diego María de Gardoqui*, 28-29.
12. On the question about navigation of the Mississippi see Gonzalo M. Quintero Saravia, *Bernardo de Gálvez: Spanish Hero of the American Revolution* (Chapel Hill: University of North Carolina Press, 2018), 263-265.
13. Cava and Cava, *Diego María de Gardoqui*, 33-34.
14. Stacy Schiff, *A Great Improvisation: Franklin, France, and the Birth of America* (New York: Henry Holt, 2005), 254.

States, Gardoqui did obtain important financial aid in arms and supplies. The fact is that John Jay returned from Spain very frustrated. Without speaking a word of Spanish, he responded to his isolation with a resentment reaffirmed by the already-old Anglo-Saxon Protestant prejudices against Catholic Spain. Despite his personal views, Jay was realistic and a diplomat, aware of the weakness of his young nation that needed a long period of peace and tranquility to, in the words of the Declaration of Independence, "assume among the powers of the earth, the separate and equal station to which the Laws of Nature and of Nature's God entitle them." Even in this context, the negotiations between Jay and Gardoqui lasted for almost a year. In August 1786 Jay submitted to the American Congress a principle of agreement in which, although Spain granted certain commercial privileges to North American ships in ports of Spanish America, it denied their access to the Mississippi.

Although it obtained seven votes to five, it was not approved, as a majority of nine was required. After many negotiations with the government of Madrid, still reluctant to renounce its sovereignty over the "father of the waters," Gardoqui proposed to Jay that American merchants could navigate through the river in exchange for payment of a rate of fifteen percent of the value of the cargo in an effort to overcome the blockade. When it seemed that an agreement was feasible, a scandal broke out in Congress promoted by some delegates from the south. Jay was accused of contravening his instructions and hiding key aspects of his negotiations with Spain from that legislative body. According to a letter written to Washington by James Madison in September 1788, it was evident that John Jay was willing to relinquish navigation rights in exchange for substantial commercial concessions from Spain.[15]

Faced with this setback, Gardoqui sought the support of Washington, who despite having retired from politics and living in his Mount Vernon estate at that time, continued to enjoy enormous prestige and influence. To ingratiate himself with him, Gardoqui personally entrusted the delivery of a precious gift that King Carlos III had sent to General Washington: a donkey—politely referred to as "royal gift"—which was to become the father of a new generation of American mules. Gardoqui took advantage of the donkey's delivery to try to obtain Washington's support for the Spanish positions, but the astute Virginian gentleman limited himself to thanking him for the gift, avoiding being involved in any political or diplomatic dispute.[16]

15. James Madison to George Washington, New York, September 26, 1788, founders.archives.gov/documents/Washington/05-01-02-0005
16. Washington to Diego Gardoqui, January 20, 1786, founders.archives.gov/documents/Washington/04-03-02-0439

Just a few months later, Gardoqui insisted again asking Washington for help, this time sending him a vicuña cloth, "his majesties true manufactured cloth," that he said had been specially made for the general "of the wool of an animal of that name produced only in Buenos Aires."[17] The general, as revealed in his correspondence with the ambassador in August 1786, was especially grateful for the cloth.[18] A vicuña remnant remains in the Mount Vernon Museum awaiting identification; like the rest of Washington's clothing, it was fragmented and distributed among his extensive relatives as if it were a relic. But once again, the exquisitely educated Washington declined to intervene, referring to what Congress decided.

Despite the limited success in his previous efforts, Gardoqui would not give up in his efforts to win the support of Washington. By the end of 1787, perhaps hoping that the third time would be the charm, he again insisted with a new gift: an edition of *Don Quixote*. The idea dated back to a meeting or dinner at Benjamin Franklin's house in Philadelphia, at which Washington heard about Cervantes's character for the first time. His curiosity was awakened, and the next day he bought an English edition translated by Tobias Smollett, who had participated in the failed British attack on Cartagena de Indias in 1741 in which George Washington's half-brother Lawrence also fought. On his return to Virginia, Lawrence named his estate in honor of the English Vice Admiral under whom he served then: Edward Vernon. Gardoqui was either present or learned of Washington's interest in *Don Quixote* and did not miss the opportunity to give him what is still today considered one of the best and most luxurious editions of the work: the one commissioned by the Royal Spanish Academy in 1780.[19]

In his letter of appreciation for the four volumes of the *Don Quixote* edition, dated November 28, 1787,[20] Washington could not be more courteous but firm in reminding Gardoqui that his person had nothing to do with government affairs of the United States since he resigned his command of the Continental Army. After receiving the letter, Gar-

17. Gardoqui to Washington, June 12, 1786, founders.archives.gov/documents/Washington/04-04-02-0107
18. Washington to Gardoqui, August 30, 1786, founders.archives.gov/documents/Washington/04-04-02-0222
19. This edition of Don Quixote was commissioned by the Real Academia Española to the printer Joaquín de Ibarra and is considered to be one of the finest ever produced. Miguel de Cervantes, *El ingenioso hidalgo don Quijote de la Mancha* (Madrid: Joaquín de Ibarra, 1780).
20. Washington to Gardoqui, November 28, 1787, founders.archives.gov/documents/Washington/04-05-02-0417

doqui would not insist anymore and the correspondence between the
two would be interrupted, as if it foreshadowed the beginning of a new
era in the relations between Spain and the United States of America.
In 1788, the United States ratified its new Constitution establishing a
system of government in which the retired general would occupy its
presidency, while at the end of that same year, King Charles III died
leaving the Spanish throne to his incompetent son, Charles IV.[21]

As a diplomat, Gardoqui displayed a style unusual in a traditional
ambassador, whom some authors have described as direct and pragmatic—businesslike—that produced mixed results. While Gardoqui's
"gift diplomacy" stumbled against Washington's gentlemanly propriety
it was much more successful when applied to less morally picky politicians who had no problems in accepting Cuban cigars (like Richard
Henry Lee), or even an Arabian stallion (presented to John Jay).[22] The
little success of his intentional gifts to George Washington differed
greatly from the results obtained while negotiating the treaty with Jay.[23]
Gardoqui's business contacts served him and his company well at a time
when his main purpose should have been vested in negotiating the interests of his country. It was clear that his private and official priorities
were far from clearly separated.

In addition to his diplomatic duties, during his time as envoy of the
Spanish Crown to the United States of America, Gardoqui became involved in the task of attracting settlers to the then still very underpop-
ulated Spanish province of Louisiana. Perhaps with the best of
intentions, but in a disorderly way, he supported without too much ver-
ification several dubious initiatives that were presented to him to bring
Catholic settlers from Maryland, Virginia, Kentucky, New York or even
from Germany to that Spanish territory, in some cases advancing official funds to organizers. The very few times when Anglo-American or
German settlers did arrive in Louisiana, they completely lacked any
type of experience as peasants or farmers, generating serious problems
for the governor of Louisiana, Esteban Miró.

21. Jon Kukla, *A Wilderness so Immense. The Louisiana Purchase and the Destiny of America*
(New York: Anchor Books, 2003), 106-107.
22. Richard Henry Lee to Thomas Lee Shippen, June 4, 1785, in Paul H. Smith, et al.,
eds. *Letters of Delegates to Congress, 1774-1789*, 25 volumes (Washington, DC: Library of
Congress, 1976-2000), 22:432, memory.loc.gov/cgi-bin/query/D?hlaw:3:./temp/~ammem
_VUIX. John Jay to Gardoqui, March 1, 1786, founders.archives.gov/documents/Jay/01-
04-02-0140. Initially Gardoqui committed a faux pas with Jay's wife, Sarah, when in October
1785 left his card at their home with a "valuable present" for her. Too valuable for them to
accept it, they decided to return it. Jay to Gardoqui, October 4, 1785, founders. archives.
gov/documents/Jay/01-04-02-0088.
23. Cava and Cava, *Diego María de Gardoqui*, 34.

Diego de Gardoqui, ca. 1785. (*Wikipedia Commons/Public Domain*)

Diego de Gardoqui returned to Bilbao on July 24, 1789 aboard *San Nicolás*, possibly one of *Gardoqui e Hijos'* ships. In October 1791 he was appointed Secretary of the Treasury Office, Minister of Finance in its current name, first as ad interim and later as permanent, under the government of Prime Minister Manuel Godoy. His Anglo-Saxon education, rare for a time when most of the ruling classes looked more toward Paris than London, was essential to the introduction in Spain of Adam Smith's economic theories. In his five years as minister, he faced the expenses generated by the war against revolutionary France (1793-1795); tried to apply important reforms to increase state income (eliminating exemptions and privileges); improved the treasury administration; controlled public debt; and promoted national industry.

From his position as a member of the government of the *Prince of the Peace* (one of Godoy's peerages),[24] Gardoqui would observe with a mixture of despair and rage how the negotiations between Spain and the United States progressed, which would end in the signing, on October 27, 1795, of the Spanish-American Treaty of friendship, limits and navigation, known in Spain as the Treaty of San Lorenzo, and in the United States as Pinckney's treaty.

In this treaty, Spain acceded to each and every one of the United States' aspirations. The border was established at the 31st parallel and, under the guise of mutual freedom of navigation, which served Spanish

24. Manuel Godoy was rewarded with various titles during his political career. He was made Prince of the Peace after the Peace of Basel (July 1795) that ended the war with France.

interests little or nothing, the Mississippi was completely open to American merchants. This was exactly what Gardoqui had endeavored to avoid during his four years as "minister plenipotentiary" to the United States. Just three months after the signing of the Treaty of San Lorenzo, Diego de Gardoqui was appointed ambassador to the Kingdom of Sardinia, with its capital in Turin. In fact, it was an honorable way out for someone who had long since fallen from grace. In his diaries, The Spanish politician and writer Gaspar Melchor de Jovellanos wrote that Gardoqui received "his belated justice and goes as ambassador to Turin, where he will no longer be able to prevaricate or to . . . ."[25]

In his two years in Turin, Gardoqui had the opportunity to see first-hand how the order of the old regime was beginning to collapse at the hands of the young general Napoléon Bonaparte, who in northern Italy was leading revolutionary France from victory to victory. On the very day of his sixty-third birthday, November 12, 1798, Diego de Gardoqui died in Turin. He is today remembered in both Spain and the United States as a statesman and diplomat who helped found the relationship between the two nations.

---

25. In the first published version of Jovellanos' Diaries the editor inserted here three dots while in the original manuscript was written "steal." Gaspar Melchor de Jovellanos, *Obras de Gaspar Melchor de Jovellanos, Diarios (Memorias íntimas) 1790–1801* (Madrid: Sucesores de Hernando, 1915), entry of October 27, 1776, 322.

The Constitutional Convention Debates the Electoral College

⊱ JASON YONCE ⊰

In the last two decades, the Electoral College has come under harsh, though derivative, criticism as a result of the presidential elections in 2000 and 2016. Comparing the Electoral College at its inception to the Electoral College of 2020 is a distortion. For one, the twelfth amendment ended the practice of affording the presidency and vice-presidency to the first and second place finishers in the electoral vote. Secondly, by 1830, all but South Carolina had adopted the "winner take all" distribution of the electoral vote which, aside from the contentious 1800 election, has been the primary cause of strife than the Electoral College itself.

On the surface, the Electoral College is no more than a double majority check; one of many that are present in the Constitution. The reason for double majorities is simple: changes to government or to laws should require very strong support. This is true not only in federalist systems but in unitary governments as well. In the United States, the first and most easily identifiable majority required is the quorum.[1] Prior to the ratification of the 1787 constitution, the American government's relationship with quorums was problematic at best. The Confederation Congress struggled to produce a quorum even to ratify the Treaty of Paris in 1783. Yet, the Annapolis Convention convened, drafted its recommendations, and adjourned without a quorum in 1786.[2] Other examples of these double—and multiple—majorities in the Constitution include the passage of bills in two houses and the multilayered process to amend the Constitution.

1. United States Constitution, Article I, Section 5, Clause 1. The Constitution is notoriously fickle about what a quorum is.
2. Jason Yonce, "The Annapolis Convention Of 1786: A Call For A Stronger National Government," *Journal of the American Revolution,* May 27, 2019, allthingsliberty.com/2019/05/the-annapolis-convention-of-1786-a-call-for-a-stronger-national-government/.

Even eminent historians have fallen prey to notions that the Electoral College is a uniquely American institution. These historians, along with critics of the institution, place the formation of the Electoral College in a historical vacuum. Systems of using electors were well-known before the Constitutional Convention. Even among the states, indirect suffrage systems—to include the use of electors—were already established.

At the Constitutional Convention of 1787, the debates over the best method of electing the executive branch were subordinate to other discussions about executive power. In fact, as contentious as the Electoral College is today, the actual issue of electing the president was mostly considered a settled matter during the first month of the convention. Both the Virginia and New Jersey Plans, which differed so greatly on the legislative branch, were in unison over the election of the executive. Specifically, the executive—whatever that would be—would be chosen by the legislature. Had it not been for the insistence of three men in particular—Elbridge Gerry, James Wilson, and Alexander Hamilton— it is questionable whether we would even be having a discussion of the Electoral College today. Other framers would grow more prominent in this debate as it ensued.

During the first month of the convention, the committee of the whole pored over the broad strokes of the new government. Questions about the executive were less contentious than those about the legislative but discussions did center around a few primary concerns: how many executives, how long would they serve, could they serve again, who should they be, and can they be removed? The question of "who chooses them" did not take precedence but that is not to say that it avoided discussion altogether.

By May 29, the discussion in the committee of the whole had finally reached the questions concerning the executive and the judiciary branches. Even if the executive branch had not roused quite the same furor that the legislative had, it was the question that spoke to the nature of the new terms of confederation that the convention had hoped to achieve. Perhaps it would have been less prickly to have had an executive council drawn from the states, but the bulk of the opinion leaned toward a unified executive. For states that had maintained a large degree of independence under the confederation government, a unified executive vested in a single person represented a massive shift in the nature of the government. The frequently-underestimated Charles Pinckney of South Carolina and Delaware's George Reed were the expositors of this supreme executive.

On the question of how this executive was to be chosen, the answer seemed obvious to the committee: the congress would select them for a term of seven years. William Paterson's notes are the only set attesting to this selection process, other framers who bothered taking notes for posterity seemed entirely unconcerned with the matter by May 29 and 30. The diversity of opinions on how elections should take place reflected the immense diversity of thought among the states. Each state delegate carried to the convention its preference. Caleb Strong of Massachusetts, as well as other New England Federalists, brought a preference for annual elections and a greater degree of democracy. Other states, like South Carolina, did not popularly elect the governor. James Wilson of Pennsylvania was the most disposed toward popular elections for every branch and house to include the senate.

Elbridge Gerry's opinions were difficult to predict, a common complaint among his contemporaries. Gerry later favored a slightly more democratic approach to electing the executive in contrast to his earlier criticism that "excess democracy" was a scourge to resist. To re-emphasize Gerry's fickle nature, he would change his mind again by the close of the committee's deliberations on June 19. In the interim, Gerry and Wilson drew towards the center of a compromise to allow for electors to choose the executive on behalf of the states' residents.

This idea was not a new one to the framers. Maryland's 1776 constitution created an electoral college to elect its state senate. Maryland was not unique in its undemocratic property requirements for suffrage or to run for office, but their initial constitution, post-independence, left little reason to question aristocratic control. A slate of twenty-four electors—two from each county plus one each from Annapolis and Baltimore—were elected by county freeholders to convene and choose the fifteen members of the senate for five-year terms. They were at liberty to choose the senators from their own ranks as well. If the question of senatorial election roused much debate in the 1776-7 convention, it was not recorded. The first President of the Senate in Maryland was high federalist tobacco planter Daniel of St. Thomas Jenifer. Ten years later, Jenifer attended the Constitutional Convention as a delegate from Maryland.[3]

James Madison and Rufus King objected to this framework initially. Selection by Congress, or through electors, would reduce confidence in the new government. King's notes from the convention calculated how far removed certain positions were away from the people's votes. This speaks to the notion that King figured state governors or legisla-

3. *The Decisive Blow is Struck: A Facsimile Edition of the Proceedings of the Constitutional Convention of 1776 and the First Maryland Constitution* (Annapolis: Hall of Records Commission of the State of Maryland, 1977).

tures would choose the electors, a notion that would later be the case in some states. A president chosen by way of electors, chosen by state legislators, then certified by a national congress hardly seemed pragmatic let alone a system that would instill much confidence that the government truly represented the will of the people. In Maryland there would be yet another layer of electors as well!

Gerry and Wilson's efforts notwithstanding, the matter was settled in committee. The overwhelming number of state delegations rejected popular election of the executive and the use of electors. On June 7, Gerry—perhaps changing his mind or attempting to reinvigorate the discussion via a new proposal—proposed that state governors select the president. The discussion was brief and the committee did not divert from course. The New Jersey Plan came to the floor on June 15 and, despite its many objections to the Virginia Plan, was basically in agreement that the congress should choose the executive.

Outside of the example of Maryland, several European nations had used indirect electors since the middle ages. The best-known example was the Holy Roman Emperor who, since the Golden Bull of 1356, was chosen via powerful electors scattered throughout the continent. While hardly a democratic election of a monarch, the recognition of electors was also, in some manner, the recognition of states and territories within the Holy Roman empire that was later realized in 1648 in the Treaty of Westphalia.

If this seems like a distant and overreaching example of electors to support the idea of an electoral college, it was not so for the constitutional framers. In particular, a young Alexander Hamilton invoked the examples of European electors in his first major speech to the convention on June 19. Hamilton, for all his later esteem, had not spoken much during the first month of the convention, which Madison attributed to his age and political differences from the other New York delegates. Age was inhibiting for some—Jonathan Dayton of New Jersey barely spoke at the convention. For others, like Charles Pinckney, it made little difference. However, Madison was understating the differences between Hamilton and his fellow New York delegates, John Lansing and Robert Yates. Both were unwavering anti-Federalists who later left the convention in protest and rallied a great deal of support against ratification in what would be the closest ratification vote of any state until Rhode Island's in 1790.

Hamilton described "elective monarchies" but carefully avoided the unease associated with the idea of monarchy by stating that these elective monarchies were often in tumultuous governments. Hamilton, more than any other to this point, made the case for what would become the

Electoral College. Drawing from Maryland's example, Hamilton also endorsed a similar indirect suffrage scheme for the senate. Once the full convention met in July, however, the Electoral College was again rejected and congressional appointment again moved forward.

Despite these votes, the question of executive elections arose numerous times between July and September. A play-by-play of each instance would be rather redundant. There were patterns within the individual debates that are worth treating generally rather than specifically, but the changes in the state voting blocs prove interesting. By September, only South Carolina and North Carolina continued to oppose any direct or indirect scheme of electing the executive. Even as this majority formed, one debate became intractable: how would states choose the electors? At this point Hamilton had left the convention and would not return again until September. After July 10 none of the New York delegation remained; as noted, John Lansing and Robert Yates had exited the convention in protest. New Hampshire's pair of delegates would not arrive until July 21. Of those that remained, the most vocal members of this debate were James Wilson, Elbridge Gerry, Gouverneur Morris, James Madison, and George Mason. It would be up to Connecticut, in the persons of Roger Sherman and Oliver Ellsworth, to rescue the convention from utter fracture as they did with the warring between the Virginia and New Jersey Plans.

Debate on the executive question quieted for some time while the convention moved on to the judiciary. It would be a recurring, and tiring, theme all the way until September, such that delegates grew restless about presidential selection. Connecticut maneuvered to offer a compromise. While Sherman had not necessarily been opposed to legislative appointment, it was clear by July that the idea was going nowhere even though it has previously garnered support. Connecticut delegates refined the Electoral College idea and proposed the now-familiar formula of apportioning the electors by state. In this first model, states could have one to three electors. Though this motion passed with only a divided Massachusetts and the Carolinas opposed to it, the debate would re-emerge and continue. The Connecticut plan nonetheless became the foundational compromise that united a majority of the state delegations.

To get a sense of what problems the Electoral College solved, one has to shake off any contemporary notions - which goes without saying in historical analyses - but it requires stepping away from the convention itself. The confederation government lacked an executive. Despite many extraordinary claims to the contrary, the president of the confederation congress was not an executive figure.

If the problem of legislative elections nearly drove the convention into chaos, the question of electing an executive that had hitherto not existed would prove even more difficult. This is especially true given the fears many of the framers harbored of having an executive figure at all. This probably spurred much of the early support for congressional appointment of the president. The British had an evolving "head of government" but what those in the present would think of as a Prime Minister was foreign to many at the time and repugnant to men who were even given the title.

There was very little consistency among the states for guidance. Many states lacked direct election of their governors. South Carolina did not popularly elect a governor—or presidential electors - until after the Civil War. Pennsylvania existed under a directorial system with an executive council like contemporary Switzerland. Outside of James Wilson, and the example of some New England delegates, the thought of direct elections was simply unpalatable.

George Mason considered it a paradox that so many of the framers were agitating for a stronger, more energetic legislature but thought it would be too corrupt to choose an executive. Yet, the fears of cabal and legislative intrigue with selecting the executive were likely realistic. It would hardly be fair to call the executive branch a distinct branch at all if that were the case. Gerry pitched gubernatorial or state legislative election as an alternative but this received even less consideration than direct elections. The fears of leaving the executive too beholden to the state governments was palpable. That would come near to defeating the designs of many who had called the convention which had even considered, abortively, to give national veto power over state legislatures.

While much of the preceding focuses on the internal debate, a look at state delegation votes is instructive as well. Though the topic of electing the executive ebbed and flowed, a few dates are important for consideration in 1787: June 2, July 17, July 19, July 24, August 24, and September 5.[4]

Maryland, already comfortable with using electors, and Pennsylvania, whose club of exclusively Philadelphia delegates were friendly to the idea of popular elections, were reliably on the side of using electors while the other states were not. With little variation those two states were always predictable. Equally predicable were the southern states of

---

4. Information on votes are drawn from Max Farrand, *The Records of the Federal Convention of 1787* (New Haven: Yale University Press, 1937), 1: 77-31, 149-181 and 2: 29-120, 397-406.

North Carolina, South Carolina, and Georgia for opposing anything except for congressional appointment. Georgia would prove interesting later.

The other states dithered on the subject. New York was rarely even featured in these votes, and when they were the deep ideological divide between John Lansing and Robert Yates versus Alexander Hamilton kept the delegation divided. As noted earlier, eventually none of them would be present for the convention.

On on July 17 the same basic voting pattern held as it did on June 2. On a third vote, congressional appointment was unanimous. Two days later almost every small state, barring Georgia, had flipped sides. It was around this same time that questions about representation, via the Connecticut Compromise, were finally getting ironed out and probably alleviating much of the anxiety among small states. Jacob Broom of Delaware seconded the motion to vote on the Electoral College both times and Connecticut itself would switch sides to employing electors to vote on the president. Oliver Ellsworth of Connecticut actually initiated the motion on July 19. Questions about the Senate lingered for a few days.[5]

A week later, on July 24, William Houstoun and James Dobbs Spaight, of Georgia and North Carolina respectively, attempted another change to carve out a provision for national appointment of the electors. This succeeded briefly and every small state except for Connecticut voted in favor of the idea. New Hampshire's late arrival complicated matters again because they did not support the use of electors and formed a bloc with the southern states during the August vote. With New York missing, and Massachusetts strangely absent, the even split led to a rejected motion.

Finally, on September 5, the small states except for New Hampshire fell in line and Georgia defected to the Electoral College bloc leaving only the Carolinas. John Langdon and Nicholas Gilman were from two separate factions in New Hampshire politics. Langdon's faction was his own and not particularly inclined toward nationalization; Gilman was more independent friendly to a faction of nationalists.[6] South Carolina's

5. Broom's appearances in the record are infrequent as were his personal documents left to posterity. This and his fight against premature adjournment without a drafted constitution are the only notable mentions, although Broom was fairly successful in both business and politics. See M.E. Bradford, *Founding Fathers* (Lawrence: University Press of Kansas, 1994), 108-109. Bradford lists Broom as an attendee of the Annapolis Convention but this is not borne out in the records of that meeting.

6. Forrest McDonald, *The Economic Origins of the Constitution* (Chicago: University of Chicago Press, 1958), 21-38.

delegation was largely dominated by John Rutledge who opposed the Electoral College, although Charles Pinckney also held great sway with matters and, at least in 1800, appeared to have been friendly to the Electoral College.[7]

Georgia had proven pivotal before on the question of representation. Abraham Baldwin cast the deciding vote on the Connecticut Compromise after befriending the delegation in other votes. Georgia, like New York, had an interesting delegation. William Few was serving concurrently in the Confederation Congress and absent for much of the deliberations until the final signature in September. William Pierce left to engage in a duel after a falling out with a business partner.[8] William Houstoun had been the nay vote to Baldwin's yea on the representation question but was also absent by the end of July.

This was the quandary. Bruce Ackerman noted that popularity played little to no role in the framers' calculus for choosing an executive. He argues that this became a feature of elections after the Adams-Jefferson battle in 1800. Electors seemed like a good middle ground but not if they were simply going to vote for the most popular man in their state. Therefore, it was settled that each elector would cast two ballots and one could not be from his state. This seems to have been an innovation of North Carolina's Hugh Williamson. If this system failed then it became a matter of concern for the House but, in this sole instance, the House would vote in state blocs rather than as individuals. It is worth noting here that the Constitution forbade members of congress from also acting as electors. Even setting aside the problems that have arisen in the ensuing 233 years with the Electoral College, this system was far from ideal. One only has to envision a fifth-place finisher currying enough favor in the new House to suddenly become the president.

While imagining other systems of executive selection in 1787 could be useful as a counterfactual exercise, very few alternatives could be serious. Even analyzing the possibility of direct election would be fruitless given the still-limited suffrage in the period. Congressional appointment is the lone alternative that seemed to have been taken seriously

7. Farrand, III:382-390.

8. Gerald J. Smith, "Abraham Baldwin," *New Georgia Encyclopedia*, University of Georgia Press, November 11, 2005, www.georgiaencyclopedia.org/articles/history-archaeology/abraham-baldwin-1754-1807. Sam Fore, "William Pierce," *New Georgia Encyclopedia*, University of Georgia Press, November 14, 2008, https://www.georgiaencyclopedia.org/articles/history-archaeology/william-pierce-1753-1789. Also, Lee Ann Caldwell, "Georgia and the U.S. Constitution," Augusta University, accessed May 31, 2020, www.augusta.edu/library/resources/constitution_day/ga.php.

at the convention. This arrangement would still have been a republican method. Roger Sherman pointed out in early July that the Congress were to be the representatives of the people. Gouverneur Morris, who stood flatly opposed to both term limits and congressional appointment, tethered the question to another: impeachment. If there was to be the threat of impeachment then it followed that a powerful enough cabal could simply appoint the president at will and could dangle the threat of impeachment over his head to induce him to do their bidding.

Legislative selection of some sort did have a pragmatic appeal to many of the delegates: it was cheap. Charles Pinckney of South Carolina spoke of "designing men" gaining the presidency in a popular election scheme, but the large geographic expanse of the original colonies made the idea of convening a one-time body to elect the president unattractive given the large distances. Madison was also aware of what a popular election scheme would entail for the south in an election where the three-fifths compromise would hold no leverage. Any election that required forming a majority would benefit the north; the number of southern freemen would be far too few to have any equal footing.[9]

The final report from September 4 combined all of the elements that permitted compromise on the matter of executive elections. As Jack Rakove observed, "the political logic of the electoral college almost exactly replicated the debate over representation." This observation holds true in the latter half of the convention, although by appearances the more pragmatic concerns held more weight in the first.

There were too many questions of intrigue in congressional appointment. Popular election would be a wonderful boon to large states or would benefit a popular tyrant. Even electors, if they were apportioned, could simply be a way for the largest states to wrest all the power. But if the electors were chosen at the state level, they would have to at least consider a single candidate outside of their state and, failing that, the House could vote on the president but not as individuals. For all of the contemporary criticism of the United States' complex electoral mechanism, other countries can pose equally, and arguably more, complicated structures. One need only take a cursory glance at Belgium, The Netherlands, Bosnia-Herzegovina, Lebanon, or Myanmar to feel even more overwhelmed. Laws to get on the ballot in France are equally perplexing. A popular election scheme may be far simpler to grasp, and seem fairer and more democratic overall, but the basic problems of each

---

9. Jack Rakove, *Original Meanings: Politics and Ideas in the Making of the Constitution* (New York: Vintage Books, 1996), 89-93, 259-75.

system have not changed in 233 years. As one of many mechanisms of consent in the Constitution, it permits some parity among the various states when it comes to electing the President that helps to avoid delegitimizing the election by placing its outcome solely in the urban centers of the country. However, even a cursory glance of the historical record shows that the idea was not exactly sacrosanct in the minds of the Framers and that the Electoral College's creation was borne of political expediency rather than a generally accepted idea of its usefulness. Nevertheless, casting it aside should require dialogue about the possible consequences at least on par with the dialogue that surrounded its creation.

Respected Citizen of Washington City: The Mystery of Will Costin, Freed Mount Vernon Slave

꿔 DAVID O. STEWART 샣

Will Costin was found dead in his own bed on the morning of May 31, 1842. Washington City's leading newspaper, the *Daily National Intelligencer*, reported the passing of this "free colored man, aged 62 years," then praised Costin's years of service to the Bank of Washington, the capital's largest. Costin's job sounds modest today—he was "Porter to the bank"—but the *Intelligencer* stressed that he held "the unlimited confidence" of the bank's officers. In his work, the newspaper continued, "millions of money were allowed to pass through [Costin's] hands," yet "in no one instance . . . was there discovered the slightest defalcation." In gratitude, the bank directors approved a final payment of fifty dollars to his family.

The newspaper added that Costin's "colored skin covered a benevolent heart," having raised not only his own children but also four orphans. With Dickensian sentimentality, the *Intelligencer* concluded that "The tears of the orphan will moisten his grave, and his memory will be dear to all those (a numerous class) who have experienced his kindness."[1] Forty miles away, the *Baltimore Sun* noted that Costin's funeral

1. *Daily National Intelligencer*, June 1, 1842. It is easy to wonder how a bank "porter" handled millions of dollars. Official government publications of the era confirm that Costin handled large amounts of money. In reports of the U.S. Treasurer in 1838 and 1839, Costin is listed dozens of times as the recipient of warrants issued by different agencies of the government, including the Navy Department and the Post Office. The amounts confided to him on those occasions were often many thousands of dollars; one warrant was for $50,000. Plainly, Costin's duties included more than hauling furniture and running errands. Public Documents, Senate of the United States, 26th Cong., 2d Sess., Vol. II, Blair & Rives (1841), pp. 230, 258; U.S. Doc. 445, Index to Executive Documents, 26th Cong., 1st Sess. (Doc. No. 29), pp. 18, 20, 24, 26, 132, 134, 136, 140, 82-86, 191-95.

was attended by "nearly two hundred hacks [carriages] and other vehicles in line, besides a great many people on horseback." That report urged that Costin's "excellent example be followed, and his many virtues imitated by the whole colored population of this country."[2]

Even Congress heard about Costin's virtues. Former president John Quincy Adams, then serving in the House of Representatives, pointed to the bank porter as a reason for opposing legislation to deny the vote to Blacks in Washington City. Costin, Adams thundered,

> was as much respected as any man in the District; and the large concourse of citizens that attended his remains to the grave—white as well as black—was an evidence of the manner in which he was estimated by the citizens of Washington. Now, why should such a man as that be excluded from the elective franchise, when you admit the vilest individuals of the white race to exercise it?[3]

These tributes omitted Costin's many efforts to advance other Blacks. He helped secure the freedom of nearly twenty enslaved people, most of them his own relatives. In 1821, Costin courageously challenged a law that required free Blacks in Washington City to register annually; his lawsuit won some relief for free Blacks.[4] When his Methodist church relegated Black parishioners to the balcony, he cofounded a new congregation that spawned the still-thriving Metropolitan AME Church of Washington. Costin ran or supported charitable organizations to benefit Black citizens, including three schools.[5] Few African Americans of his generation could point to such extensive accomplishments.

The 1842 tributes to Costin also failed to mention that he claimed a blood relationship to Martha Washington, the nation's first First Lady. That claim, largely neglected since it emerged in an obscure public document in 1871, was probably true.

WHO WAS WILL COSTIN'S MOTHER?

The 1871 publication, ostensibly about public education in the District of Columbia, reported that Costin's descendants stated that his mother was Ann Dandridge, half-sister to and childhood playmate of Martha Dandridge (later Martha Washington). The family asserted that Ann

---

2. *Baltimore Sun,* June 3, 1842.
3. *Congressional Globe,* 27th Cong., 2d Sess., pp. 569-70 (June 2, 1842).
4. *Costin v. Corporation of Washington,* 2 Cranch 254 (October Term 1821).
5. Hillary Russell, "The Operation of the Underground Railroad in Washington, D.C., c. 1800-1860," (July 2001) (Historical Society of Washington, D.C. & National Park Service).

and Martha shared the same father, John Dandridge, so Will Costin was Martha's nephew. Ann's mother, the family continued, was a slave of African and Cherokee descent. Pointing to that supposed Indian heritage, the family asserted that Will was born free in 1780. At the age of twenty, according to the family, Will married a Mount Vernon slave, Philadelphia Judge (known as Delphy), who was inherited in 1802 by Martha Washington's granddaughter, Eliza Parke Custis Law. After Delphy was freed "on kind and easy terms," the family concluded, the Costins' children were born free.

Elements of this family account cannot be proved, or are wrong. For example, under Virginia law, the child of an Indian mother was not born a slave, unless the mother also had African forebears. If Ann Dandridge's mother had mixed ancestry, she might not have been deemed an Indian mother.[6] Nor were the children of Will and Delphy Costin born free. The inconsistencies are not surprising. The lives of the enslaved, and of mixed-race relatives of prominent families, were not well-documented. Nevertheless, the connections among Will Costin, Mount Vernon, and Martha Washington's grandchildren lend weight to the Costin family's account that they were related to the Dandridges.[7]

THE BURNED-RECORD COUNTY

Many Virginia slaveholders fathered mixed-race children with slaves. Those offspring were born into slavery and thus increased the owners' wealth. Thanks to studies by Annette Gordon-Reed, formal tours at Monticello now announce that Thomas Jefferson had four mixed-race children with the enslaved Sally Hemings. Martha Washington's first husband had a mixed-race half-brother. In the nineteenth century, mixed-race Virginians claimed descent from Martha Washington's grandson, George Washington Parke Custis.[8]

No records survive of Ann Dandridge, in part because the Dandridge family's home was in New Kent County, a "burned-record

6. Virginia's racial distinctions among Whites, Blacks, and Indians insisted that slave status was inherited through the maternal line. "Comment: Making Indian's 'White': The Judicial Abolition of Native Slavery in Revolutionary Virginia and Its Racial Legacy," 159 U. Pa. L. Rev 1457 (2011).

7. *Special Report of the Commissioner of Education on the Condition and Improvement of the Public Schools in the District of Columbia*, 41st Cong., 2d Sess., ex. Doc. No. 315, submitted to the Senate June 1868 and to the House of Representatives June 1870 (Government Printing Office, 1871), 203-04. This account was reproduced, largely verbatim, in George W. Williams, *History of the Negro Race in America from 1619 to 1880* (New York: G. P. Putnam's sons, 1882), 2:193-94.

8. *'The Only Unavoidable Subject of Regret,': George Washington, Slavery, and the Enslaved Community at Mount Vernon* (Charlottesville: University of Virginia Press, 2019), 144-46.

county" east of Richmond. The term, familiar to Virginia historians, reflects Union Army soldiers' tendency to burn Southern courthouses during the Civil War. New Kent County stands out in this community of archival destruction. Its courthouse was first incinerated nearly eighty years before the Civil War, then again in 1865.[9]

Consequently, no public records or family records survive of the slaves owned by John Dandridge, Martha Washington's father. The notion that Ann's enslaved mother was half-Cherokee is equally impervious to research, though it invites skepticism. The Cherokee lived in Virginia's southwestern tip, far from New Kent County. More plausible is another recounting of the Costin family tale that described Ann Dandridge's mother as "an Indian squaw of the Pamunkey tribe," since Pamunkey lands were closer to the Dandridge home. That version, however, is equally unsupported.[10]

Some facts focus the tale of Ann Dandridge. Martha was born in 1731. For a mixed-race half-sister to be her "playmate," Ann must have been born by at least 1736; otherwise, the age gap between the girls would have been too great. A woman born in 1736 would have been forty-four when she gave birth to Will in 1780, a late age for a birth mother, but not impossible.

But the woman who likely was Will Costin's mother had at least six children *after* Will was born; the last in 1801. By 1801, the hypothetical Ann Dandridge would have been well past sixty. That would take credulity into the basement and beat it with a rubber hose. Mary V. Thompson, Mount Vernon's research historian, plausibly speculates that the Costin family tale omits a generation: that Ann Dandridge gave birth to a daughter, and her daughter gave birth to Will Costin and his many siblings.[11]

---

9. The Library of Virginia in Richmond maintains a database for those attempting to research history in burned-record jurisdictions. These include Appomattox, Buchanan, Buckingham, Dinwiddie, Elizabeth City, Gloucester, Henrico, James City, King and Queen, Nansemond, New Kent, Prince George, and Warwick Counties, www.lva.virginia.gov/public/guides/burned_juris/. The 1787 fire in New Kent County was set by John Price Posey, a reprobate neighbor of Mount Vernon who had been a friend to Jack Custis, Martha Washington's son. In 1787, having served a month in jail for assaulting the county sheriff, Posey and two accomplices burned down the courthouse and county clerk's office. His retaliation proved ill-advised—he was hanged for the arsons. Malcolm Hart Harris, *Old New Kent County: Some Account of the Planters, Plantations, and places in New Kent County* (West Point, VA: Malcolm Hart Harris, 1977), 1:233.

10. Henry Wiencek, *An Imperfect God: George Washington, His Slaves, and the Creation of America* (New York: Farrar, Straus and Giroux, 2003), 286.

11. Mary V. Thompson, *'The Only Unavoidable Subject of Regret,'* 142-45.

This "Thompson correction" raises the question of the relationship among Martha, her hypothetical half-sister, and the half-sister's daughter (Martha's niece). If John Dandridge owned his daughter Ann, did he convey Ann to Martha? Did Martha then bring half-sister Ann and Ann's offspring into her marriages with Daniel Parke Custis and then with George Washington? Were Ann and her daughter enslaved or free? Mount Vernon's records describe no enslaved person by Ann's name of the age that Ann had to be.

Some historians have supposed that Martha would not have kept her half-sister in bondage, so that Ann and her descendants lived in a sort of half-free limbo, not governed by the overseer's lash but without resources to strike out on their own.[12] This supposition is not consistent with an island of hard fact that looms in this sea of uncertainty: the formal manumission (freeing) in 1802 of Will Costin and the woman (Nancy Holmes) who likely was his mother. That manumission also contradicts the family tale that Will was born free.[13]

MANUMISSIONS BY THOMAS AND ELIZA LAW

In his will, George Washington freed the slaves he owned, but he did not own the majority of Mount Vernon's, who derived from Martha's first husband (Daniel Parke Custis) and legally remained part of the Custis estate through Martha's life. As a widow exercising her dower rights, Martha possessed those slaves but did not own them—what the law called a "life estate" in that human property. Martha's life estate imposed a duty of preserving the estate's value for the benefit of Daniel Custis's heirs. When Martha's last surviving child, Jack, died in 1781 at age twenty-seven, Jack's four children became the Custis heirs. When Martha died twenty years later, the four grandchildren divided 160 Custis slaves among them.[14]

Will Costin and his relatives were assigned to the eldest granddaughter, Eliza, who had a reputation for being both smart and difficult. Even her portrait was intimidating. Eliza's English husband, Thomas Law, was easily the most interesting of the Custis in-laws. Son of an Anglican bishop and brother to two more, Law had another

12. Marie Jenkins Schwartz, *The Ties that Bound: Founding First Ladies and Slaves* (Chicago: University of Chicago Press, 2017), 64-65; Constance McLaughlin Green, *The Secret City: A History of Race Relations in the Nation's Capital* (Princeton: Princeton University Press, 1967), 26; Wiencek, *An Imperfect God*, 85.
13. Helen Hoban Rogers, Compiler, *Freedom & Slavery Documents in the District of Columbia* (Baltimore: Gateway Press, Inc., 2007), 1:75-76.
14. Erica Armstrong Dunbar, *Never Caught: The Washingtons' Relentless Pursuit of their Runaway Slave, Ona Judge* (New York: 37 Ink/Atria, 2017), 192.

brother who served in Parliament. A fourth became Lord Chief Justice of England. Thomas joined the East India Company to make his fortune in India, where he fathered three sons with an Indian woman he did not marry. After bringing his sons home, Law moved to America with two of the boys. In 1796, he married Eliza Custis, though he was twice her age, then rode the ups and downs of land development in Washington City.[15]

The Laws separated after only eight years together, and divorced in 1810. Eliza's aunt summarized the split: "She had a disposition completely opposite to his, and she wasn't sensible enough to put up with his peculiarities. The result is that they are both at fault, which is usually the case."[16]

Whatever their disagreements, Mr. and Mrs. Law evidently agreed that the Costin family should be free. As husband, Law controlled Eliza's property, including the enslaved people inherited from the Custis estate.[17] In late July 1802, a few months after acquiring Will Costin, Thomas Law signed manumission papers for "Negro Will," then twenty-two years old, and for three others in their early forties: "Negro Nancy Holmes," "Negro Paul," and "Negro Jenny." The records reflect no payments, though Law attested that they were "capable by labor" of supporting themselves. Their simultaneous emancipation suggests that Nancy Holmes and Costin were mother and son; indeed, the name "Nancy" derives from Ann, a link back to Ann Dandridge. Nancy Holmes' age in 1802 meant that she was born around 1760, several years after John Dandridge died, eliminating the possibility that Will's mother was herself half-sister to Martha Washington and confirming the Thompson correction.[18]

Those four emancipations in 1802 were only the beginning. Five years later, Thomas Law registered manumissions of eight more people named Costin: George (twenty-three years old); Margaret (nineteen); Louisa (seventeen); Caroline (fifteen); Jemima (twelve); Louisa (two);

15. Rosemarie Zagarri, "The Empire Comes home: Thomas Law's Mixed-Race Family in the Early American Republic," in Anupama Arora & Rajender Kaur, eds., *India in the American Imaginary, 1780s–1880s* (New York: Palgrave Macmillan, 2017).

16. Rosalie Stier Calvert to H.J. Stier, in Margaret Law Callcott, *Mistress of Riversdale: The Plantation Letters of Rosalie Stier Calvert* (Baltimore: Johns Hopkins University Press, 1991), 7.

17. William Waller Hening, *The statutes at large; being a collection of all the laws of Virginia, from the first session of the legislature, in the year 1619* (New York: R. & W. & G. Bartow, 1809-23), 2: 170 (codifying Virginia Act XII, 1662).

18. Rogers, *Freedom & Slavery Documents*, 1: 76; District of Columbia Deed Book, Liber H, No. 8, p. 382, National Archives.

Ann (four months); and Delphy (twenty-eight). Law simultaneously emancipated two minor children named Holmes. Boilerplate legal statements cloak whether any amounts were paid for those ten manumissions.[19]

Thus, by 1807, Thomas and Eliza Law had emancipated fourteen enslaved people, roughly one-third of the slaves Eliza inherited from the Custis estate. Delphy Costin was Will Costin's wife and mother to the infants Louisa and Ann. [20] Paul and Nancy Holmes, who had been freed in 1802, likely were parents of May and Eleanor Holmes, while Nancy likely also was mother to the Costins: Will, George, and the four teenaged girls.

Unanswered questions swirl around these manumissions. Thomas Law had the power to emancipate the Costins and Holmeses, but was he the moving force in doing so? As the father of mixed-race children, he likely empathized with mixed-race people who were related to his wife yet were trapped in chattel slavery. He showed devotion to his own mixed-race sons, educating one at Harvard, one at Yale, and bringing them into his business in Washington City.

But Eliza Law grew up near Mount Vernon and likely knew the various Costins, especially the middle-aged Nancy and Paul Holmes. In 1808, Eliza urged Thomas's son to help Will Costin recover funds he had lost, and noted that she had borrowed money from Will. Plainly she and Will shared a significant tie.[21] When the first four manumis-

15. Rosemarie Zagarri, "The Empire Comes home: Thomas Law's Mixed-Race Family in the Early American Republic," in Anupama Arora & Rajender Kaur, eds., *India in the American Imaginary, 1780s–1880s* (New York: Palgrave Macmillan, 2017).

16. Rosalie Stier Calvert to H.J. Stier, in Margaret Law Callcott, *Mistress of Riversdale: The Plantation Letters of Rosalie Stier Calvert* (Baltimore: Johns Hopkins University Press, 1991), 7.

17. William Waller Hening, *The statutes at large; being a collection of all the laws of Virginia, from the first session of the legislature, in the year 1619* (New York: R. & W. & G. Bartow, 1809-23), 2: 170 (codifying Virginia Act XII, 1662).

18. Rogers, *Freedom & Slavery Documents*, 1: 76; District of Columbia Deed Book, Liber H, No. 8, p. 382, National Archives.

19. Rogers, *Freedom & Slavery Documents*, 2:18, 45, 144.

20. Ibid., 2:145n200; Dorothy S. Provine, *District of Columbia Free Negro Register, 1821-1861* (Bowie, MD: Heritage Books, 1996), 51-52. The two infant Costin girls could not be legally emancipated, since they were not old enough to support themselves, which was a precondition for freedom. Nineteen years later, Louisa Costin attempted to repair this defect in her emancipation by acquiring a certificate of freedom based on a formal attestation that she was born free, although that attestation likely was false, since her mother (Delphy) was enslaved at the time of Louisa's birth.

21. Eliza Parke Custis to John Law, October 12, 1808, box Thomas Peter, MSSVII, Papers of John Law, Peter Collection, Fred W. Smith National Library at Mount Vernon.

sions occurred in 1802, Eliza and Thomas Law still lived together. Did she press for those emancipations? By 1807, Eliza had relinquished claims on the marital property, so Thomas may have had less need or inclination to consult with her on the later manumissions.[22]

A further unanswered question is whether the other Custis grandchildren played any role in the manumissions. After the death of Jack Custis, Eliza and a sister lived near Mount Vernon with their mother, while Martha and George Washington raised Jack's two younger children—Eleanor ("Nelly") Custis Lewis and George Washington Parke ("Wash") Custis—at Mount Vernon. All four, therefore, were exposed to the Costin-Holmes clan. Indeed, all four Custis grandchildren maintained connections with Will Costin through life.

WHAT ABOUT WILL COSTIN'S FATHER?

In this tale of echoing silences, also unknown is the identity of Will's father (or of the man who supplied his surname). The 1871 report recounted the family tale that the father was a white man from "a prominent family." An alternative version of the family story, unearthed years later, named Martha Washington's son, Jack Custis, as Will's father. That allegation is somewhat credible.

As a boy, Jack Custis disdained learning, an attitude that endlessly frustrated his stepfather Washington. Custis' tutor described Jack as "exceedingly indolent [and] surprisingly voluptuous. One would suppose nature had intended him for some Asiatic prince."[23] Custis's passion for the sister of a schoolmate led him into an early marriage. In 1779, when Will Costin was conceived, Jack Custis was married and living near Mount Vernon. With General Washington away fighting the British, Jack certainly visited his mother regularly; when she accompanied her husband at army encampments, Jack had free run of the property. A sensualist bred to privilege, with ready access to Mount Vernon, Custis could have been Will's father.

Were Jack Custis the father, that could account for the special privileges that the Costin clan enjoyed years later; after all, they were the largest group of Custis slaves to be freed. As demonstrated by Gordon-Reed's analysis of the Hemings/Jefferson connection, the unexplained emancipation of a group of enslaved people who were related to each other may reflect a blood connection between owner and enslaved.

---

22. Articles of Agreement between George Calvert & Thomas Peter with Thomas Law, August 10, 1804, in Peter Family Papers, Fred W. Smith National Library at Mount Vernon.
23. Jonathan Boucher to George Washington, December 18, 1770, in George Washington Papers, Founders Online.

Inconsistencies, however, persist. If the original family tale were true that Will's mother was Martha's half-sister, then Jack Custis coupled with his aunt. Although such episodes were not unknown, in 1779 Virginia it would have been deemed, at a minimum, ungenteel. Under the Thompson correction, which describes Will's mother as the daughter of Martha's half-sister, then Jack coupled with his cousin, an event common enough among Virginia's whites, though the enslaved tended to observe African taboos against such relations.

Supposing Jack to be Will's father threatens to splash onto Washington's reputation. If Martha and her grandchildren knew of this connection, then the master of Mount Vernon surely did, also. Under Virginia law, however, Washington could free Will Costin only by purchasing him from the Custis estate and then emancipating him. Such an action would have drawn attention to Costin and his possible connection to the Dandridges (and Jack Custis), attention that neither George nor Martha might not have welcomed. There could have been an understanding among Washington, Martha, and the grandchildren that Costin might not be freed shortly after Martha's death, which is what happened. All, alas, is conjecture.

As is the search for the source of the surname "Costin," which is common in Northampton County on Virginia's Eastern Shore, where the first Custis in the New World established Arlington Plantation in 1629. In the early nineteenth century, Arlington's farm manager was named William Costin, connecting the name to the Custis lands. Someone named Costin, in the service of the Custises, could have fathered a slave who then formed a slave marriage with Ann Dandridge's daughter, becoming father to Will (relieving Jack Custis of that historical burden) and his five siblings. Alternatively, some enslaved people adopted the surname of a steward or farm manager where they lived. A male slave owned by the Custis estate might have done so and then joined with Ann Dandridge's daughter.[24]

24. William Costin to G.W.P. Custis, October 2, 1807, April 9, 1814, and 1814, and James Anderson to G.W. P. Custis, March 18, 1806, in G.W.P. Custis Correspondence, 1806-1809, Virginia Historical Society. Because the farm manager at Arlington described himself as an older man, and since he resided far from Mount Vernon, that William Costin is not a plausible candidate to have been father of the Costin offspring. When Martha's grandson (G.W.P. "Wash" Custis) established his own residence on the Potomac River, he borrowed the name Arlington, which lives on in the name of the nearby Virginia town and Arlington National Cemetery on the Custis grounds.

Surviving correspondence cements the connection resembling intimacy between Will Costin and the Custis grandchildren. In the 1808 letter mentioned above, Eliza Law referred to Will's "faithful attachment to me" and sought financial help for him.[25]

Will was equally close to Nelly Custis Lewis. When Nelly's husband wrote in 1813 to request Will's services as a hack driver, Nelly added a postscript asking Will to drive her to Philadelphia. She invited Will's mother to join them on the journey, offering to "pay her in pork if she likes it." An 1816 letter from Nelly to Costin begins, "My friend Billy," and asks him to take an ailing friend to Baltimore. She made the request, she explained, "because I know you will be a nurse and friend to him." She signed with hopes that Will's family was well, adding, "I will ever be your friend" and that she had just paid $10 to her sister-in-law (wife to Wash Custis) for Will. A third, undated letter from Nelly asked Will to fetch items from her sister. These attestations of friendship, financial transactions, and the invitation for Will's mother to join a multi-day journey to Philadelphia, reflect both affection and reciprocal confidence.

An 1819 letter to Costin from George Calvert, uncle to the Custis grandchildren, sought help for Wash Custis's wife on a banking matter. Addressed to "Porter at Bank of Washington," the letter requested that Will ask certain gentlemen to satisfy "Mrs. Custis' note" at the bank. If they failed to do so, Calvert suggested that Will renew Mrs. Custis's note for another sixty days. The message shows the family's reliance on Will's competence, and that his bank duties included financial matters.[26]

A final consideration supports a blood relationship between Costin and the Dandridge/Custis family. His career involved handling large sums of money, working with paper records, and mixing with distinguished and prominent people. Will plainly had the skill and sophistication to perform those tasks, so he plainly received more education, greater opportunities, and more favorable treatment than other enslaved people at Mount Vernon.

THE CAREER OF WILL COSTIN

Costin began his work life in Washington as a hack driver, one of the few occupations open to free Blacks in the early days of Washington

25. Eliza Parke Custis to John Law, October 12, 1808, box Thomas Peter, MSSVII, Papers of John Law, Peter Collection, Fred W. Smith National Library at Mount Vernon.
26. Eleanor Lewis to William Costin, Washington, June 12, 1816; E.P. Lewis to Costin (no date); Lawrence Lewis to William Costin, October 6, 1813, & George Calvert to William Costin, April 1, 1819, Peter Family Papers, Fred W. Smith National Library at Mount Vernon.

City. He was nearly forty when he secured his position at the Bank of Washington, possibly with help from Thomas Law, a founding stockholder of that bank. Costin already had built a home for his family on A Street, in the shadow of the Capitol Building. His deposit accounts at the Bank of Washington reflect that he was a diligent saver and sometimes engaged in larger transactions that involved trading in building lots and houses (another activity of Thomas Law's). Such holdings would distinguish Costin within the community of free Blacks.[27]

Costin supported his fellow Black citizens in many ways. In addition to securing the 1807 manumission of his siblings, wife, and children, in 1820 he purchased a slave named Leanthe Brannan and emancipated her. Seven years later. Costin emancipated a woman named Oney, a "bright mulatto who is about thirty-five years old." In that same year, Costin also manumitted "a mulatto woman named Eliza Washington, aged about thirty, and her son Montgomery, aged about four years." Several years later he again filed manumission papers for Montgomery Parke, noting that the boy's mother had died. The names involved— Washington and Parke—hearken back to Mount Vernon. Added to the fourteen previous manumissions of his family members, Costin thus had a hand in gaining freedom for at least eighteen enslaved people.[28]

An advocate of education, Costin sent his children to school. Of his five daughters, three became teachers. When she was only nineteen,

27. Paul E. Sluby, Sr. and Stanton L. Wormley, Jr., *History of the Columbian Harmony Society and of Harmony Cemetery, Washington, D.C.* (Washington, DC: Printed for the Society, 2001), 3, 7; Charles E. Howe, "The Financial Institutions of Washington City in Its Early Days," *Records of the Columbia Historical Society*, 8:1 (1905), 18; PNC-Riggs Bank Records, Deposit and Trust Accounts, National Bank of Washington, MS 2213 RG 03 (George Washington University Library), Boxes 84, 86-92, 95-97; Green, *The Secret City*, 42-43. Two husbands of Custis granddaughters served as directors of local banks: Thomas Law was director of the Patriotic Bank; Thomas Peter held the same position at the Bank of Potomac. Two of Law's mixed-race sons served as directors of other local banks. Albert Culling Clark, *Greenleaf and Law in the Federal City* (Washington, DC: Press of W.F. Roberts, 1901); Harvey W. Crew, William R. Webb and John Woolridge, *Centennial History of the City of Washington, D.C.*, (Dayton, OH: United Brethren Publishing House, 1892).

28. Rogers, *Freedom & Slavery Documents*, 3: 10, 114, 196; Provine, *District of Columbia Free Negro Register*, 114. The Oney who was freed in 1827 was not Costin's sister-in-law, Oney Judge, a Custis slave who escaped from the presidential mansion in Philadelphia in 1796 and reached New Hampshire, where she married and had three children. In 1827, Oney Judge would have been at least fifty years old and was still in New Hampshire. The Oney emancipated in Washington City in 1827 was likely the daughter of a half-sister of Oney and Delphy Judge. Ibid., 139, 236.

William Costin. "A tribute to worth by his friends," c. 1842. (*Library of Congress*)

Louisa Parke Costin began a school in her father's home on A Street. After Louisa died young, her sister Martha took up the effort and continued the school for another six years. A third daughter, Catherine, taught at Union Seminary School, and served as head of the school's "female department." Will led an 1818 effort to reopen a school for free Black citizens, then served as the school's board president.[29]

Unhappy that his Methodist church imposed racial segregation, Costin led the establishment of Israel Bethel AME Church. He served as the first vice president of the Columbian Harmony Society, which formed in 1825 to create the first cemetery for Blacks in Washington City. According to Costin's bank records, he acted as agent for the Colored Female Benevolent Society for Mutual Relief, which evolved into the Columbia Female Benevolent Society. He also assisted with the Colored Female Roman Catholic Benevolent Society.[30]

In 1821, Costin boldly sued to invalidate new legislation requiring free Blacks in Washington City to post a bond and submit to annual registration. That he brought the lawsuit at all reflects real bravery. No slaveholding community embraced civil rights pioneers in the 1820s. Costin's lawsuit met with considerable success. Judge William Cranch (nephew of Abigail Adams) ruled that the statute could not apply to

29. *Special Report of the Commissioner of Education*, 202-03, 198; Russell, "The Operation of the Underground Railroad."
30. Sluby and Wormley, *History of the Columbian Harmony Society*, 8, 10, 80; PNC-Riggs Bank Records, Deposit and Trust Accounts, National Bank of Washington, MS 2213 RG 03 (George Washington University Library), Boxes 90 and 97.

free Blacks (like Costin) who resided in Washington City before the statute was enacted, which relieved them of a considerable burden. But Cranch also ruled that the provision applied to free Blacks arriving after its adoption.[31]

This litany of Costin's career explains the overflowing attendance by both whites and Blacks at his funeral. Costin's unique straddling of the racial divide also was visible during one of the national capital's worst episodes, a race riot in August 1835. Across two violent days, gangs of whites burned every school for Blacks except the one conducted in Costin's house. The mob respected Costin's position and his many connections with prominent whites. Yet after the disturbance ended, the former Mount Vernon slave insisted on testifying at trial on behalf of the Black youth accused of triggering the riot.

Commanding the respect of whites while standing up for an accused Black man was no easy accomplishment in Washington City in 1835. Perhaps no Black man but Will Costin could have done it.[32]

I am grateful for comments on a draft of this article from Gregory May, Mary V. Thompson, and Rosemarie Zagarri.

31. *Costin v. Corporation of Washington*, 2 Cranch 254 (October Term 1821).
32. Jefferson Morley, *Snow-Storm in August: Washington City, Francis Scott Key, and the Forgotten Race Riot of 1835* (New York: Nan A. Talese, 2012), 179, 183.

The Impeachment of Senator William Blount

⋇ ANDREW A. ZELLERS-FREDERICK ⋇

It is easy to suggest that William Blount made no significant contribution to the development of the United States. His achievements, although not negligible, were only on par at best, and far less than many of his more famous contemporaries. Blount served in the North Carolina militia during the American Revolution, but with little acclaim as a paymaster. From a prominent and influential southern colonial-era family, he was an unremarkable member of his state's House of Commons and later the state's Senate. He served as a delegate to the Confederation Congress, unsuccessfully seeking its presidency, and to the Constitutional Convention where his contributions were little better than negligible. As Territorial Governor of the Southwest and Superintendent of Indian Affairs, he performed adequately. As one of Tennessee's first federal senators, Blount finally achieved historical immortality, but for reasons he did not originally envision. He has the infamous distinction of being the first federal official, elected or appointed, to be impeached under the new republic's Constitution for "high crimes and misdemeanors." The trigger for the impeachment was a letter in Blount's own hand implicating him and his followers in a scheme to forcibly seize Spanish Florida and Louisiana for the British Crown.

This monumental first test of the Constitution's impeachment authority cannot be labeled a partisan political battle, as many charged, one of many that embroiled the nation at the end of the eighteenth and beginning of the nineteenth centuries. Although partisan politics did eventually engulf the affair, President John Adams and his administration ethically and morally followed the duties and dictates of their offices instead of sweeping the matter under the carpet. Their action was supported by the one individual who could be viewed as above biased party and private interests: former President Washington endorsed the government's pursuit of the affair, writing that, "It will be much re-gretted, *much*, if this business is not probed to the bottom."[1] Adams believed his actions were validated: "A conspiracy was fully proved, to dismember the empire, and carry off an immense portion of it to a for-eign dominion."[2]

Most historical interpretations stress that Blount, despite his wealth, political connections, and influential friends, was nothing more than a greedy land speculator who abused the power and prestige of his ap-pointed and elected offices. According to Buckner F. Melton, Jr., Blount displayed "a shrewdness and a degree of self-interest that would continue to rival his loyalty to the established political regime" with these traits growing "even stronger with time."[3] John C. Miller con-tends that Blount was originally "a Federalist who had become rich by using political office to further his business interests."[4] William H. Masterson echoes this belief that "his first army office, political place and power were to Blount the handmaidens of business power" and "he was a businessman in politics for business."[5] Arthur Preston Whitaker labels Blount "literally a land-jobber."[6] Andrew R. L. Cayton feels that "it was the pursuit of personal profit that gave" Blount "the direction for his life and "ordered the rest of his existence" with his "eyes always on the bottom line."[7] One biographical work makes a weak attempt to vindicate or excuse Blount from the conspiracy that bears his name. General Marcus J. Wright's 1884 work states that Blount was "defamed and traduced for a brief period in his life by the followers of a strong partisan administration."[8] The consensus among historians about

1. George Washington to the Secretary of War, Timothy Pickering, August 14, 1797 quoted in John C. Fitzpatrick, ed., *The Writings of George Washington from the Original Manuscript Sources 1745-1799*, 39 vols. (Washington: United States Government Printing Office, 1931-44), 36: 8.

2. John Adams in the *Review of the Propositions for Amending the Constitution submitted by Mr. Hillhouse to the Senate of the United States in 1808* quoted in Charles Francis Adams, *The Works of John Adams, Second President of the United States with a Life of the Author*, 10. vols. (Boston: Charles C. Little and James Brown, 1850-56), 2: 536.

3. Buckner F. Melton, Jr., *The First Impeachment: The Constitution's Framers and the Case of Senator William Blount* (Macon, GA: Mercer University Press, 1998), 63.

4. John C. Miller, *The Federalist Era 1789-1801* (New York: Harper & Brothers, 1960), 189.

5. William H. Masterson, *William Blount* (New York: Greenwood Press, 1969), 349.

6. Arthur Preston Whitaker, *The Mississippi Question 1795-1803: A Study in Trade, Politics, and Diplomacy* (Gloucester, MA: Peter Smith, 1962), 106-107.

7. Ronald Hoffman and Peter J. Albert, eds., *Launching the "Extended Republic": The Fed-eralist Era* (Charlottesville: University Press of Virginia, 1996). 157.

8. Marcus J. Wright, *Some Account of the Life and Services of William Blount* (Washington: E.J. Gray, 1884), 3.

Blount's continual quest of wealth is neatly summed up by the denouncing question asked by Abigail Adams: "When shall we cease to have Judases?"[9]

William Blount, a third-generation American and eldest of eight siblings, was born in 1749 on his influential family's Rosenfeld Plantation located near the Pamlico Sound region of North Carolina. The Blount family interests included cotton and tobacco farming with slave labor; the raising of cattle and hogs; the production and sale of maritime tar, pitch and turpentine; the mining of minerals, metals and additional ores; corn and the milling of other grains; saw mills and distilleries; and money lending. From his boyhood, Blount and his brothers "were accustomed to versatility of enterprise." As with many rural southern families, the Blounts were integrally linked economically, commercially, and socially with their relatives and they "acted in concert with a constant family interest."[10]

Blount's career of public service was almost continuous from 1777 until the end of his life in 1800. In 1780, as the fighting of the Revolution erupted in the Carolinas, he began a four-year stay as a member of his state's House of Commons and moved to the state's Senate for a two year-term in 1788. Blount had previously shown interest in political office in 1779, when he ran for the Assembly against Richard Dobbs Spraight, coincidentally later a fellow delegate to the 1787 Constitutional Convention; however, the election was declared illegal as both candidates strongly advocated dishonest voting.[11] Until finally securing his election to North Carolina's Lower House, Blount continued to occupy his time with business, militia matters and with his family's vast holdings, providing considerable statewide authority during a time of unchecked inflation. Blount even earned the resentment of his own cousin, Declaration of Independence signer Thomas Hart, who intimated that his relative was a usurer.[12] Blount was later appointed a delegate to the Confederation Congress in 1786 and 1787 and concurrently was a member of the Constitutional Convention.

9. Abigail Adams to Mary Smith Cranch, July 6, 1797 in Stewart Mitchell, ed., *New Letters of Abigail Adams 1788-1801* (Boston: Houghton Mifflin Company, 1947), 100.

10. Masterson, *William Blount*, 7.

11. Ibid, 40-41. The election reportedly was fierce and violent even by eighteenth century standards in North Carolina. Despite that both candidates countenanced illicit practices, the sheriff's decisions on eligibility matters were erratic and the ballot box (referred to as a "Tin Cannister without a Top") was unsealed and unguarded The result was that Spraight was declared the victor, but Blount formally protested; the committee on privileges and elections declared the entire election illegal and the House of Commons subsequently set it aside and neither party was re-elected in time to take his seat during that session.

12. Melton, *First Impeachment*, 63.

James Madison's sole comment on Blout indicates that he was most attuned to Blount's character: upon the completion of the Constitutional Convention, Madison wrote that Blount "declared that he would not sign, so as to pledge himself in support of the plan, but he was relieved by the form proposed and would without committing himself attest to the fact that the plan was the unanimous act of the States in the Convention."[13] Blount's evasive short answer speaks volumes on his ingrained trait of playing both sides of the fence for his own benefit.

On May 26, 1790, the area between Kentucky and the present states of Alabama and Mississippi, formerly claimed by North Carolina, was Congressionally designated the Territory of the United States South of the River Ohio. The Northwest Land Ordinance mandated that before statehood, a territory must be governed by five presidentially-appointed federal officials: a governor, a secretary and three judges. Blount, as the original "wheeling and dealing, land speculating, sharp-nosed manipulator, politician and financier" knew how to attain what he wanted, usually employing "the shortest route."[14] Blount seemingly grabbed the governorship (along with the title of Superintendent of Indian Affairs for the Southern Department) easily from President Washington by convincing a number of influential associates to intercede with the president on his behalf. Once his commission was confirmed, Blount fully utilized his authority to build a network of personal obligation and influence throughout the territory with officials including justices, sheriffs, constables, clerks, registrars, and every militia officer below the rank of general. He reportedly boasted that "no lawyer could plead in the Southwest Territory without a license from him."[15] The position evidently pleased the family and its vital land investments. To his brother, John Gray Blount, Blount openly admitted, "I thank you for your Congratulations on my Appointment and I rejoice at it myself for I think it of great Importance to our Western Speculations."[16] Blount's various appointments guaranteed him absolute control of his domain. He was also a "shrewd politician who knew all of the clever little devices for retaining the loyalty and support of his ap-

13. James Madison, *Notes of Debates in the Federal Convention of 1787* (New York: W.W. Norton & Company, 1966), 657.

14. Robert V. Remini, *Andrew Jackson and the Course of American Empire, 1767-1821*, 2 vols. (New York: Harper & Row, 1977), 1: 51.

15. Ibid.

16. William Blount to John Gray Blount, 26 June 1790 in Alice Barnwell Keith, ed., *The John Gray Blount Papers 1764-1795*, 2 vols. (Raleigh, NC: State Department of Archives and History, 1952-59), 2: 67.

pointees; and he knew particularly how to play upon the vanities of his superiors."[17]

Washington was no fool when it came to the intrigues of the Blount family and the western territories in general. The president correctly analyzed the regional political situation as delicate, and was "anxious to conciliate frontier leaders so that no new separatist movement" would split territories from the control of the Federal government.[18] Prior to ratification of the Constitution, James Wilkinson participated with many local veterans in the so-called 1788 "Spanish Conspiracy" with a goal of establishing an independent western republic allied with Spain, going so far as swearing allegiance to the Spanish Crown.[19] Washington, always the ultimate strategist, undoubtedly knew of Blount and his family's dubious business dealings and carefully planned his political movements. To counter the corruptive regional influence of Blount, Washington commissioned Wilkinson as a regular army brigadier general, countering Blount's power while concurrently maintaining Wilkinson under observation. Washington considered this as a long-term stratagem to solve or reduce his western problems by establishing "such a system of national policy as shall be mutually advantageous to all parts of the American republic."[20]

Although the Blount family used every opportunity to enrich themselves using Blount's position, Blount functioned in a strong manner to carry out the orders arriving from the capital in Philadelphia. As a demonstration of his executive authority, he issued a proclamation to the residents of the Southwest Territory:

> Whereas I have received certain information, that a number of *disorderly, ill disposed* persons, are about to collect themselves together, with an intention to go to the Upper Cherokee towns, on the Tennessee to destroy the same, and kill the inhabitants thereof, regardless of law, human and divine, and subversion of the peace of the Government.
>
> Now I, the said William Blount, Governor in and over the said territory, do hereby command and require the above described persons, and every one of them, immediately to desist from such their intention,

17. Remini, *Andrew Jackson*, 52.

18. James Thomas Flexner, *George Washington and the New Nation 1783-1793* (Boston: Little, Brown and Company, 1969), 267.

19. A.P. Whitaker, "Spanish Intrigues in the Old Southwest: An Episode 1788-89," *Mississippi Valley Historical Review*, Vol. 12, No. 2 (September 1925), 155-176; Melton, *First Impeachment*, 80-84.

20. George Washington to Harry Innes, March 2, 1789 in Fitzpatrick, *Writings of George Washington*, 30: 215.

and to disperse and retire peaceably, to their respected abodes, within one hour from the moment of promulgation of this proclamation.[21]

The Native American's Southwest military situation was never a cause for celebration by Blount or the federal government. Depending on inexperienced militias, combat with the Native American tribes had proven disastrous for the country. Military defeats made Blount's policies, in his dual role as Superintendent of Indian Affairs and Governor, precarious. By the time of his 1793 Proclamation, Blount, and thousands living in the territory, concluded that the federal government "was not in a position to be realistic about, even if it had accurately been informed of, actual conditions on the Southwestern frontier."[22] To Blount and other influential territorial individuals the "federal government in Philadelphia was a remote, impersonal operation that not only failed to assist the beleaguered westerners," but it also consistently "disgraced itself abroad by consenting to treaties that negated American commercial rights or land claims" with an ultimate result of "humiliating a proud and free people."[23] Blount's political alliances shifted to the expanding Republican Party under Thomas Jefferson, but his primary loyalties never wavered from his family and their quest for wealth. Captivated by accounts of gigantic sales of western land to European investors by major Eastern speculators, the Blounts felt compelled to re-affirm their efforts "to acquire fantastic amounts of acreage for the purpose of overseas disposal."[24]

The national government was able to successfully "turn the corner" in the Northwest by applying a newly rejuvenated military. By the mid-1790s, a well-organized and well-equipped Legion of the United States had crushed a Native American coalition. With the Northwest secured, the national government laid the foundations for law, order and rapid commercial development in the beginning of the nineteenth century. Unlike the Southwest, the investment of resources in the Northwest Territory had completely displayed not only the power of the national government, but also its "value." The cost was the ill-will and alienation of Blount and his constituents who felt alienated and left out.[25]

---

21. Henry Knox to Tobias Lear, February 28, 1793 with William Blount's January 28, 1793 Proclamation in Philander D. Chase, et al, *The Papers of George Washington –Presidential Series*, 12 vols. (Charlottesville: University of Virginia Press, 1989-2005), 12: 2n.
22. Masterson, *William Blount.*, 217.
23. Remini, *Andrew Jackson*, 80.
24. Ibid, 250.
25. Hoffman & Albert, *Extended Republic*, 171.

Countless stories of Southwest territorial schemes, intrigues and designs had started almost immediately following America's independence. While details varied from scheme to scheme, "the common theme was the aggrandizement of the Southwest, either at the expense of one of the contiguous powers (including the United States), or with the help of one of the contiguous powers, or both."[26] Frontiersmen, Eastern investors, and foreign opportunists saw this region as a place for riches and subsequent societal advancement. Blount was, in this respect, no different from many others. From the various plots, conspiracies and general discord in the region, European colonial powers stood to benefit with opportunities to expand or better secure their empires. This was especially true for the Spanish Crown, which was heavily involved in the region with their crucial settlement of New Orleans serving as a lynchpin on the strategic Mississippi River. Jefferson's views on this key settlement were, "There is on the globe one single spot the possessor of which is our natural and habitual enemy. It is New Orleans, through which three-eighths of our territory must pass to Market."[27] Many Americans worried that a Franco-Spanish alliance could result in Spain's ceding Louisiana to its partner. The exchange of declining Spanish reign for vibrant French authority filled with revolutionary fervor concerned Blount and the majority of residents in the Southwest: their trade, travel, and property rights, the foundations of their wealth and prosperity, were in grave jeopardy. Since the spring of 1796, Federalist leaders hypothesized that a secret clause had been inserted into the 1795 Peace of Basel which promised the cession of Louisiana to revolutionary France. Secretary of State Timothy Pickering commented,

> We have often heard that the French government contemplated repossession of Louisiana; and it has been conjectured that in their negotiations with Spain the cession of Louisiana & the Floridas may have been agreed on. You will see all the mischief to be apprehended in such an event. The Spaniards will certainly be more safe, quiet and useful neighbors. For her own sake Spain should absolutely refuse to make these cessions.[28]

26. Melton, *First Impeachment*, 80.

27. Thomas Jefferson to Robert Livingston, April 18, 1802 in Paul Leicester Ford, ed., *The Writings of Thomas Jefferson* (New York: G.P. Putnam's Sons, 1896), 143-47.

28. The Peace of Basel consisted of three peace treaties in which France made peace with Prussia and with Spain ending the War of the Pyrenees. The result was that revolutionary France emerged as a major European power; Timothy Pickering to Rufus King, February 15, 1797 quoted in Alexander DeConde, *Entangling Alliance: Politics & Diplomacy under George Washington* (Durham, NC: Duke University Press, 1958), 449.

As a result of regional and national reactions to these real and imagined geopolitical changes, Congress passed a deterrent, to prevent any hot-headed reactions that could have dramatic international repercussions, known as the Neutrality Act of 1794, stipulating that any person organizing a military expedition within the United States territory aimed at a foreign domination was guilty of a high misdemeanor.[29] This act, which carried a maximum penalty of three years imprisonment and a three thousand dollar fine, soon impacted the investigations of Blount.

The Blount Conspiracy originated with John Chisholm, a former American Loyalist who served as a British soldier; the nebulous plot centered on seizing the remains of Spain's decaying Southwest American Empire, with the support of the British government. This requested support was in the form of warships and military supplies; the project would be aided by Blount's sympathetic Native American allies. The reward for Great Britain's actions would be the transfer of the seized land's title to the British Crown. In late 1796 Chisholm, a confidant of Blount who detested the Spanish because of his imprisonment in Pensacola, approached British Minister Robert Liston in Philadelphia with his grand aspirations, primarily an assault on Spanish West Florida. Although Liston did not consent to endorse this ill-counseled venture, he did little or nothing to dissuade the "hotheaded" Chisholm.[30] By the time Blount entered the fray with his add-on project using the Native Americans, Liston had already informed his London superiors that over fifteen hundred whites, "principally British Subjects, attached to their Country and their Sovereign" were "ready to enter into a plan for the Recovery of the Floridas to Great Britain" but needed warships, supplies, and commissions.[31] Blount sounded out his regional cohorts with his grand plan which was "on a much larger Scale" than the one first proposed by Chisholm. Basically, there would be a three-pronged offensive on Spain's Southwest empire: the first thrust would utilize men "collected on the Frontiers of New York and Pensylvania" instructed to "attack New Madrid [in present-day Missouri], leave a Garrison in it, and proceed to the Head of the Red River and take possession of the Silver Mines;" the second attack, commanded personally by Blount, was to use men from Tennessee and Kentucky, "with those of the Natchez and Choctaws" to seize New Orleans; and the last, under Chisholm, consisting "of the Cherokees and

---

29. Melton, *First Impeachment*, 86.
30. Hoffman and Albert, *Extended Republic*, 160.
31. Robert Liston to Lord Grenville, January 25, 1797 in Frederick Jackson Turner, ed., "Documents on the Blount Conspiracy, 1793-1797," *American Historical Review*, Vol. 10, No. 3 (April 1905), 576-577.

the Creeks with the white men of Florida" would take Pensacola.[32] In return for its support, Britain was offered the seized territory and New Orleans would be declared a free port open for unrestricted use by interests such as those of Blount and his confederates.

It is ironic that Blount himself provided the crucial piece of incriminating evidence proving that there was truth to the conspiratorial rumors that spread throughout the Territory and the eastern United States. President Adams and the members of his administration heard these same tales. To verify information, a presidential summons was issued which ultimately deprived Blount of meeting personally with his frontier supporters; he made the ill-fated choice of committing his thoughts and instructions on his plan to paper. On April 21, 1797 he wrote a detailed letter to longtime friend and Indian interpreter James Carey at Col. James King's Iron Works in Tennessee. Blount confessed, "Among other things I wished to have seen you about, was the business Captain Chesholm mentioned to the British Minister last Winter in Philadelphia." He felt that "the plan then talked of will be attempted this fall; and if it is attempted, it will be in a much larger way than then talked of; and if the Indians act their part, I have no doubt but it will succeed." Blount provided his future prosecutors with the confession they required for "high crimes and misdemeanors" with his own ill-conceived words: "A man of consequence has gone to England about the business, and if he makes the arrangements as he expects, I shall myself have a hand in the business, and probably shall be at the head of the business on the part of the British." He admitted to Carey "that it was not yet certain that the plan will be attempted; yet, you will do well to keep things in a proper train of action, in case it should be attempted, and to do so will require all of your management," Carey ultimately did not heed Blount's cautious warning that "he must take care, in whatever you say to Rogers, or any body else, not to let the plan be discovered by Hawkins, Dinsmore, Byers, or any other person in the interest of the United States or Spain."[33]

Blount realized the seriousness of the incriminating letter, but felt that Carey could be completely trusted in both his loyalty and judgment.

32. Declaration of John D. Chisholm to Rufus King, November 29, 1797 in Turner, "Documents," 599-600.
33. William Blount to James Carey, April 21, 1797 in the Journal of the Senate, July 8, 1797 in Martin P. Claussen, ed., *The Journal of the Senate including the Journal of the Executive Proceedings of the Senate-Fifth Congress, First Session-John Adams Administration*, 2 Vols. (Wilmington, DE: Michael Glazier, Inc., 1977), 1: 105-108. Native American interpreter John Rogers, Former Congressman Benjamin Hawkins and the new Indian Superintendent, Silas Dinsmore, and Federal Government sutler/agent James Byers.

He advised Carey "to take care of yourself. I have now to tell you to take care of me too; for a discovery of the plan would prevent the success and much injure all the parties concerned."[34] Blount, always the schemer, believed he had a fall-back plan if his enterprise was unearthed. He felt that culpability, especially in regard to the use of and relations with the Native Americans, could be taken off of him and heaped "upon the late President, and as he is now out of office, it will be of no consequence how much the Indians blame him" for all of these actions.[35]

Blount's trust in Carey was poorly placed—Carey gave the letter to a government agent, who passed it up the chain of command. It reached Secretary of State Pickering in the middle of June, and then President Adams. News of the "extraordinary letter of Governor Blounts to Cary" quickly made the rounds throughout the government.[36]

In politics, his personal life and in all affairs, President Adams maintained a reputation of independent action. Concerning Blount, Adams took evils, such as political opportunism and factionalism, literally, and with him they amounted "to an obsession." Upon his inauguration to the presidency, Adams brought a long public career, "devoid of Political experience, a detestation of political parties—Federalist and Republican alike—and a deep suspicion of the great European powers."[37] These are the views that Adams brought to the table as the Blount Conspiracy quickly unfolded during the beginning of his administration.

Secretary of State Pickering investigated British involvement with Blount by quizzing the Minister Robert Liston. Liston, who by now had learned that the British Foreign Secretary Lord Grenville had declined any support, could truthfully deny his government's involvement by providing an official dispatch attesting to this fact—although he may have been vague as to what the British actually knew of the conspiracy and when they knew it.[38] Liston may have stretched the truth when he said that he had always been unsympathetic to the plot, but that the importance of the proposals made it impossible to reject them on his own authority.[39]

---

34. Ibid.
35. Ibid.
36. David Henley to George Washington, June 11, 1797 in Dorothy Twohig., et al., eds., *The Papers of George Washington-Retirement Series*, 4 Vols. (Charlottesville, VA: University Press of Virginia, 1998-99), 1: 179.
37. Stanley Elkins and Eric McKitrick, *The Age of Federalism* (New York: Oxford University Press, 1993), 534-539.
38. Melton, *First Impeachment*, 106.
39. Gerald H. Clarfield, *Timothy Pickering and American Diplomacy* (Columbia, MO: University of Missouri Press, 1969), 132.

Former President Washington was clearly angered and he urged that the appropriate action be taken:

> The interscepted letter, of which you were at the trouble to send me a copy, if genuine is really an abomination; disgraceful to the Author; and to be regretted, that among us, a man in high trust, and a responsible station, should be found, so debased in his principles as to write it ... I hope the original letter, if it carries the marks of genuineness, has been carefully preserved and forwarded to the proper departments, that the person guilty of such atrocious conduct may be held to public view in the light he ought to be considered by every honest man, & friend to his Ctry.[40]

Washington's letter undoubtedly portrayed the deep emotions of many Americans with the feelings of betrayal as Americans rather than as members of one particular political party or another.

The wheels of justice began to turn quickly throughout the remainder of June. Adams queried Attorney General Charles Lee for his official opinion on the Blount matter as the facts quickly began to solidify. Lee requested assistance from the United States attorney in Philadelphia, William Rawle, and prominent Federalist William Lewis. On June 22 they unanimously agreed that Blount's infamous letter was evidence of a crime—specifically, a misdemeanor—and that Blount was subject to impeachment for this offensive action.[41] The sword hung over the unaware Blount for nearly two weeks until his letter was presented to the President of the Senate, Thomas Jefferson, on July 3 and was read before the body with Blount absent. As the Senate chamber predictably exploded in an uproar, Blount entered and was treated to another reading of his document with Jefferson seemingly uncomfortably pressing if the senator was indeed the letter's author.[42] Blount admitted to writing a letter on or about that date to James Carey, but he stalled the proceedings by sayng he was unable to ascertain if the letter read to the Senate was a correct copy or not and requested a day, and a copy of the Senate's document, to check his personal files. With his request granted, Blount had some breathing space and departed the chamber. Simultaneously, downstairs in Philadelphia's Congress hall, the House of Representatives immediately formed a committee to investigate the entire matter. Initially the affair was kept confidential, but the patience of the Senate soon expired as Blount continued to stall

---

40. George Washington to David Henley, July 3, 1797 in Ibid, 229-230.
41. Melton, *First Impeachment*, 106.
42. Mitchell, *Abigail Adams*, 100.

and they formed their own investigating committee. When Blount was requested by Jefferson to appear before the Senate, it was discovered that he had fled Philadelphia.

For the next eighteen months, Blount and his actions consumed the Congress. Blount had quickly reconsidered his actions and returned to Philadelphia within a day to personally witness the first practical Congressional impeachment discussions. His primary issues settled on whether civil officers were subject to impeachment, and if so whether a senator was a civil officer. The dominant Federalists mainly took the Hamiltonian viewpoint that "all was granted except that which was denied" while the Republicans contended all to "be prohibited which was not expressly granted."[43] Whether Blount's reckless actions were private or public and if they were in any form related to duties as a federal senator required debate and scrutiny. Blount's attitude and his brief flight from justice clearly won the majority of condemnation from both sides of the aisle and the principal questions centered on: (1) how to deal with him; (2) why an investigation was in order; (3) who should conduct it; and (4) when should it take place.[44] By July 6, Blount's position was quickly failing as any attempts to delay the inevitable impeachment process had ended. During the investigative process, even with Blount going on the offensive with the hiring of two brilliant Philadelphia attorneys, the Senate had enough and decided, with a twenty-five to one vote, that Blount was unworthy to hold his seat. Blount's situation went from bad to worse as he was impeached, expelled, and continued to face the prospects of a senatorial trial. He also confronted a criminal action in a Federal District court in Pennsylvania. Matters for Blount continued to be bleak as a misdemeanor charge for disturbing the peace and tranquility of the United States was instituted and that charges could be made by the Attorney General that Blount had violated the Neutrality Act, which would elevate this case to federal circuit court. Blount decided to cut and run to his sanctuary of Tennessee.

Blount's flouting the national government's authority by fleeing to Tennessee, and refusing to return to Philadelphia, was a challenge to Congress. He demonstrated the vulnerability of the national government, causing it embarrassment throughout the world. The Senate's sergeant-at-arms reportedly could not get anyone in Knoxville to assist him in arresting Blount.[45] It is ironic that Blount triumphantly, in the eyes of his Southwestern supporters, managed to continually insult the

43. Melton, *First Impeachment*, 115.
44. Ibid.
45. Hoffman and Albert, *Extended Republic*, 182.

honor and dignity of the United States whose governance he sought to establish and promote in Tennessee.

Blount's deeds united, although briefly, many Congressmen of both parties.[46] They were furious with Blount's flight as it virtually rendered the government impotent. Blount's guilt was no longer a question for anyone; instead the question was "if the dignity of the government required him to be present for his trial in the Senate," as the very honor of the country and the legitimacy of the Constitution had been wounded.[47] Congressmen maintained that to prosecute Blount in absentia was to declare the government's defeat from the onset. On December 21, 1798, Congressman Robert Harper of South Carolina contended that Blount's reputation, "a man's dearest possession," and that of the United States were both in jeopardy. He declared, "Ought the public to be suffered to see the foolish spectacle of the House of Representatives going up to the Senate from day to day, to try a man laughing at them in the State of Tennessee, or the District of Maine?"[48] After much debate, the majority of the House of Representatives voted to continue with the impeachment. In the Senate, the special topic was if a senator was an officer to the government and, therefore, subject to impeachment for his actions, the same worry as to the stateliness of the national government that had repeatedly materialized within its members' debates. Senator James Bayard of Delaware asserted on January 3, 1799 that the subject of "impeachment . . . is not so much designed to punish an offender as to secure the State."[49]

Blount escaped further impeachment prosecution on a technicality that he was no longer an actively serving federal senator due to his expulsion. Although he had provided political fodder for both the Federalist and Republican Parties, the episode received a fraction of the political animosity, with its charges and counter-charges, that other individuals experienced. Secretary of the Treasury Oliver Wolcott felt that, "Had the Senator from Tennessee been a member of the federal party, much capital would doubtless been made out of his misconduct, as corroborating the standing charges of British influence. He was, however, a 'republican;' one whose vote had always been found, on party questions, among the opponents of the administration."[50]

46. The 5th United States Congress was comprised of ten Republicans and twenty-two Federalists in the Senate and forty-nine Republicans and fifty-seven Federalists in the House of Representatives.

47. Hoffman and Albert, *Extended Republic*, 82.

48. Robert Goodloe Harper in *Annals of Congress*, 5th Congress, 3rd Session, 2478.

49. James A. Bayard, *Annals of Congress.*, 5th Congress, 3rd Session, 2251.

50. George Gibbs, *Memoirs of the Administrations of Washington and John Adams, Edited from the Papers of Oliver Wolcott, Secretary of the Treasury*, 2 Vols. (New York: W. Van Norton, 1846), 2: 552.

The repercussions of Blount's exploits and the impeachment hearings did not fade upon his passing. Blount's name, like Aaron's Burr's or Benedict Arnold's, entered the American political lexicon as synonymous with words for illicit plots and intrigues. In the nineteenth century Thomas Paine, in a letter to Jefferson requesting logistical data prior to the acquisition of the Louisiana Territory, asked if New Jersey Congressman Jonathan Drayton was "an Agent for the British as Blount was said to be?"[51] Although Paine's comments were somewhat prejudicial, it is not an overstatement to say that the Anglo-American relationship during this period of covert operations was "close and respectful, if not always open and ingenuous," as British Prime Minister Pitt's government quickly renounced Robert Liston's only major American transgression.[52]

Although Blount's conspiracy was soon dwarfed by increasingly larger events. The majority of John Adams' administration was engrossed, to a degree unequaled in the majority of American presidencies, with a single ongoing problem: a crisis in foreign relationships. In his famous correspondence with Jefferson, Adams wondered about, "The escape of Governor Blount" and that there was "something in this Country too deep for me to sound." He had wondered, "Is a President of the United States to be Subject to a private Action of every Individual?"[53] Adams seemed always to believe that "Blount was able to escape with impunity." In reviewing propositions for amending the Constitution in 1808, he commented that it was "fully proven" that Blount had tried "to dismember the empire, and carry of an immense portion of it to a foreign domination." He bemoaned that for the legal process, "much time was consumed, and how much debate excited, before that important subject could be decided! and then the accused person, with all of the guilt upon his head" had avoided further prosecution.[54] Others in the government agreed with Adams that,

51. Thomas Paine to Thomas Jefferson, August 2, 1803 in Philip S. Foner, ed., *The Complete Writings of Thomas Paine*, 2 Vols. (New York: Citadel Press, 1969), 2: 1442. Congressman Drayton visited New Orleans in July of 1803 and consequently favored the United States purchase of the Louisiana Territory following his return to the capital. He was later indicted for participation in Burr's conspiracy.
52. Bradford Perkins, *The First Rapprochement: England and the United States 1795-1805* (Philadelphia: University of Pennsylvania Press, 1955), 99.
53. John Adams to Thomas Jefferson, May 1, 1812 in Lester J. Cappon, *The Adams-Jefferson Letters: The Complete Correspondence Between Thomas Jefferson and Abigail and John Adams* (Chapel Hill, NC: University of North Carolina Press, 1987). Almost always a highly moralistic and ethical individual, Adams furthered questioned whether this type of supposed responsibility would "introduce the Axiom that a President can do no wrong; or another equally curious that a President can do no right."
54. John Adams in Adams, *Works of John Adam*, 6: 536-537.

"This affair of Mr. Blount, has already been productive of very great injury to the United States." South Carolina Congressman Robert Goodloe Harper speculated that the Spanish had "been long apprised" of Blount's military attempts on their territory and "it furnished them with a reason or pretext at least, for delaying to deliver up their posts on the Mississippi" or to delay executing a treaty with the United States.[55]

The exposure of Blount's illegal plans did not lessen his lust for more land or power. Upon his return to Tennessee in 1798, he received almost a hero's welcome and was subsequently elected to the state's senate and to the Speakership, the state's second highest office. Blount may have achieved further political preferment within his home state, his and his family's vast fortune was substantially reduced. He died on March 21, 1800 at the age of fifty, reportedly of chills and a stroke. His impeachment proved that the new Federal Constitution could successfully function in a civilized manner (under Article Two Section 4) and that a nation could be effectively governed by laws even when threatened by potentially damaging crimes.

---

55. Robert Goodloe Harper, July 24, 1797 in Noble E. Cunningham, ed., *Circular Letters of Congressman to Their Constituents 1789-1829*, 3 Vols. (Chapel Hill, NC: University of North Carolina Press, 1978), 1: 103.

Instinctive Temporary Unity: Examining Public Opinion During the Whiskey Rebellion

JONATHAN CURRAN

The Whiskey Rebellion often falls into the background of the Federalist Era, overshadowed by the rise of a divisive two-party political system. This armed uprising in 1794, over taxation by the fledgling new government, threatened to destroy the new union within six years of the Constitution's ratification. Regardless of the outcome of the military confrontation, public support for the rebels' cause or indignation over President George Washington's response could have escalated into another revolution like the one that occurred in France. Yet this never materialized. Was the short life of this rebellion natural or artificial? Did public response to the excise differ by location or politics? How did the public react to Washington's response and why did the public respond in the way it did? An examination of press records indicates change in the general level of interest in the rebellion, but not of opinion, with the South far less interested than New England and the Middle States. Furthermore, the violently divergent opinions expressed in the press prior to open rebellion morphed abruptly into full support of the federal government and praise for both Congress and Washington in their handling of the crisis. This change arose primarily from existing opinions of Washington and the nation, aided by a lack of argumentation reaching the public sphere from the rebels.

Secretary of the Treasury Alexander Hamilton's initial imposition of a federal excise on whiskey in 1792 provoked predictable reactions across the United States divided roughly along partisan lines.[1] Feder-

---

1. "An Act Concerning the Duties on Spirits Distilled within the United States," May 8, 1792, *Readex*: Early American Imprints, Series I: Evans, 1639-1800, infoweb-newsbank-com.

alist newspapers reliably printed defenses of the excise as justified, with Philadelphia's *Gazette of the United States* on June 2 rationalizing that *"not one Member* of the Senate or representative body thought fit to move for the repeal of the law when the subject was reconsidered by Congress . . . This is never the case with a *bad* or *dangerous* law."[2] The Federalist-leaning *Columbian Centinel* republished this article in Boston on June 13.[3] One of the few contemporaneous views from the *Pittsburg Gazette*, the nearest newspaper to the burgeoning rebellion's locus to survive in a digitized archive, downplayed the opponents of the excise as an inconsequential, if vocal, minority.[4] Other papers, such as Boston's *Argus* and Baltimore's *Baltimore Evening Post*, presented both arguments in successive issues: *Argus* printed both an article mocking "Sydney and the Whiskey Drinkers"[5] and an article from "A REAL FEDERALIST"[6] subtly inciting rebellion over the excise, while the *Baltimore Evening Post* balanced an assertion that "to resist the Excise law, under the pretense of liberty, is inconsistent and absurd"[7] with calls to abolish the Senate as useless.[8] Thus, the Federalist-aligned papers generally, but not exclusively, supported the excise.

On the other political extreme, Democratic-Republican biased newspapers, which comprised a significantly larger market share in the 1790s than during the controversy over the ratification of the Constitution only a few years earlier, overwhelmingly came out against the excise. Ranging from the direct critiques of the *Independent Gazetteer* on January 14, 1792, to the multi-part attack by "Sydney" of Alexander Hamilton's policy published in *Dunlop's Daily Advertiser* beginning April 24, 1792, Pennsylvania formed the nucleus of publicly printed resistance.[9] Southern planters also resisted the excise: on March 10,

---

2. "Baltimore, May 29," *Gazette of the United States* (Philadelphia), June 2, 1792. In all cases, italics and capitalization reflect the original text, not authorial emphasis. Further URLs of newspaper articles have been redacted for ease of reading but can be found through the *Readex: America's Historical Newspapers* database at infoweb.newsbank.com.
3. "Maryland," *Columbian Centinel* (Boston), June 13, 1792.
4. "Pittsburgh; Gazette; Saturday; Law; Excise; Western Counties; Committee; Counties," *Gazette of the United States* (Philadelphia), September 8, 1792. While published—and thus possibly filtered—in the *Gazette of the United States* on September 8, 1792, it would appear that even papers local to the area were not unified in their opposition.
5. "To Sidney and the Whiskey-Drinkers," *Argus* (Boston), May 25, 1792.
6. "Legislative Acts/Legal Proceedings," *Argus* (Boston), November 6, 1792.
7. "Pennsylvania; Excise Law," *Baltimore Evening Post*, September 28, 1792.
8. "For the Baltimore Evening Post," *Baltimore Evening Post*, November 3, 1792.
9. "Legislative Acts/Legal Proceedings," *Independent Gazetteer* (Philadelphia), January 7, 1792. "Legislative Acts/Legal Proceedings," *Dunlop's American Daily Advertiser* (Philadelphia), March 19, 1792. "For the American Daily Advertiser. On the Secretary's Report on the Excise," *Dunlop's American Daily Advertiser* (Philadelphia), April 27, 1792. "For

1792, Philadelphia's *Independent Gazetteer* republished a letter from "An Independent Citizen" to the *North Carolina State Gazette* decrying the excise as only benefitting speculators.[10] The Philadelphia rhetoric spread to Connecticut, Massachusetts, and New York through the *American Mercury*, the *Boston Gazette*, the *Diary* and the *New-York Daily Gazette*.[11] The Philadelphia-based *National Gazette* published some lengthy articles by Hugh Henry Brackenridge (who would later become a vocal representative for the rebels and would write the only contemporaneous sympathetic historical account to survive), attacking the excise.[12] In fact, Brackenridge's August 18, 1792 article in the *National Gazette*, claiming the excise would reduce "the yeomanry of the United States . . . to the situation of slaves on the West-Indian estates,"[13] spread across New England and the Middle States within three weeks.[14] Despite the overwhelming bias in Democratic-Republican newspapers against the excise, the *National Gazette* still published a scathing response to "Sydney" which the Federalist *Gazette of the United States* republished on May 19, 1792.[15] At least some papers on each side regularly published views opposing their general bent. Similarly, while regional alignment directly related to the amount of coverage given to the issue, with the heaviest coverage in Pennsylvania followed by New England, the Middle States, and finally the South, regional alignment did not dictate the general opinion of the excise on whiskey.

the American Daily Advertiser. on the Secretary's Report on the Excise," *Supplement to Dunlap's American Daily Advertiser* (Philadelphia), April 28, 1792. "Legislative Acts/Legal Proceedings," *Dunlap's American Daily Advertiser* (Philadelphia), May 1, 1792. "Legislative Acts/Legal Proceedings," *Dunlap's American Daily Advertiser* (Philadelphia), May 8, 1792.

10. "From the (N. C.) State Gazette. Observations on the Assumption & Excise Acts," *Independent Gazetteer* (Philadelphia), March 10, 1792.

11. "From the National Gazette. Excise Law," *American Mercury* (Hartford, Connecticut), June 18, 1792. "From the National Gazette of May 7. Excise Law," *Boston Gazette*, June 11, 1792. "From the National Gazette. Excise Law," *The Diary or Loudon's Register* (New York), May 11, 1792. "Legislative Acts/Legal Proceedings," *New-York Daily Gazette*, May 4, 1792.

12. Steven R. Boyd, ed., "Hugh Henry Brackenridge, *Incidents of the Insurrection*," *The Whiskey Rebellion: Past and Present Perspectives*, ed. Steven R. Boyd (Westport: Greenwood Press, 1985), 61-62. Hugh Henry Brackenridge, "For the National Gazette," *National Gazette* (Philadelphia), February 9, 1792. Brackenridge, "For the National Gazette. Excise," *National Gazette* (Philadelphia), August 18, 1792.

13. Brackenridge, "For the National Gazette. Excise."

14. "From the National Gazette. Excise," *The Diary or Loudon's Register* (New York), August 23, 1792. "Excise," *Independent Gazetteer* (Philadelphia), August 25, 1792. "From the National Gazette. Excise," *Connecticut Courant*, August 27, 1792. "From the National Gazette. Excise," *Baltimore Evening Post*, August 31, 1792. "Excise," *Argus* (Boston), September 4, 1792.

15. "From the National Gazette. To Sidney and the Whiskey-Drinkers," *Gazette of the United States* (Philadelphia), May 19, 1792.

While 1793 brought a relative lull in press on the subject of the excise on whiskey, May 1794 brought the issue back into the public consciousness. Many newspapers of both political convictions resumed voicing their concerns over the excise and adding calls to action and direct attacks from both city and countryside.[16] While the *Philadelphia Gazette* fired the first proverbial shots on May 8, 1794, calling for "good citizens to resist, by every peaceable and constitutional method,"[17] by May 26 even the staunchly Federalist *Gazette of the United States* noted concerns that the excise was repressive because it did not affect the ruling class.[18] Both of these reached extensive audiences, particularly in Philadelphia and New York, with no rebuttals from supporters of the excise.[19] Those southern papers which reported on the subject noted concerns that those who failed to oppose the excise as federal overreach now might place themselves in a position to be unable to resist future governmental excesses.[20] On August 2, 1794, the same day that the nascent rebel movement marched through Pittsburg, Philadelphia's *General Advertiser* published a call to all citizens asserting it was "impossible to preserve liberty in a country where the public revenue is derived from *excise*."[21] This sentiment particularly resonated in Maryland, which had its own unrest over the excise brewing, although the *Washington Spy* also published a reasoned argument for the excise as well as a brief description of an "outrage upon the Collectors of the Revenue"

16. Roland M. Bauman, "Philadelphia's Manufacturers and the Excise Tax of 1794: The Forging of the Jeffersonian Coalition," *The Whiskey Rebellion: Past and Present Perspectives,* 135, 141-143.
17. "Advertisement," *Philadelphia Gazette,* May 7, 1794.
18. "For the Gazette of the United States," *Gazette of the United States* (Philadelphia), May 26, 1794. "For the Gazette of the United States. Excise," *Gazette of the United States* (Philadelphia), June 2, 1794.
19. "Excise," *Dunlap and Claypoole's American Daily Advertiser* (Philadelphia), May 8, 1794. "Excise:-Citizens Attend," *General Advertiser* (Philadelphia), May 8, 1794. "From the General Advertiser. Excise Citizens Attend," *American Minerva* (New York), May 9, 1794. "Excise—Citizens Attend!," *New-York Daily Gazette,* May 10, 1794. "Philadelphia, May 8," *The Diary or Loudon's Register* (New York), May 10, 1794. "Excise-Citizens Attend," *Columbian Gazetteer* (New York), May 12, 1794. "From the Gazette of the United States. Consideration on Excise," *American Minerva* (New York), May 30, 1794. "From the Gazette of the United States. Considerations on Excise," *New-York Daily Gazette,* May 30, 1794. "From the Gazette of the United States," *Columbian Gazetteer* (New York), June 2, 1794.
20. "From the American Daily Advertiser," *The South-Carolina State-Gazette, & Timothy & Mason's Daily Advertiser* (Charleston), May 28, 1794.
21. Thomas P. Slaughter, *The Whiskey Rebellion: Frontier Epilogue to the American Revolution* (New York: Oxford University Press, 1986), 187. "Excise. to the Citizens of the United States," *General Advertiser* (Philadelphia), August 2, 1794.

on August 6, 1794.[22] Pennsylvania's *Philadelphia Gazette* also mocked the whiskey distillers in an article widely republished north of Virginia.[23] The rising rhetoric culminated, almost anticlimactically, with a simple extract of a letter from Pittsburg published in Connecticut's *Litchfield Monitor* on August 6, 1794 detailing the attacks on the Inspector of Revenue, Gen. John Neville.[24]

The following day marked a significant shift both in federal policy and in the press debate: President Washington issued his proclamation ordering the rebels who had attacked Neville to "disperse and retire peaceably to their abodes."[25] This unified all divided rhetoric throughout the press to universal hostility towards the rebellious counties in Pennsylvania. The *Philadelphia Gazette* alleged that the rebels had intercepted supplies meant for Gen. Anthony Wayne's army gathering for a campaign on the frontier.[26] While casting the conflict as an East-West divide, the *American Minerva* claimed on August 20, 1794 that "the President may rely on the firm and unanimous support of the northern states," a sentiment echoed from Boston through Charleston.[27] Not to

22. "From the (Philadelphia) General Advertiser. Excise," *Baltimore Daily Intelligencer*, August 6, 1794. "From the Philadelphia, General Advertiser. Excise," *Washington Spy* (Hagers-Town, Maryland), August 13, 1794. "To the Printer of the Washington Spy," *Washington Spy* (Hagers-Town, Maryland), August 6, 1794.

23. "For the Philadelphia Gazette," *Philadelphia Gazette*, August 13, 1794. "Eulogy on Whiskey," *Kline's Carlisle Weekly Gazette* (Carlisle, Pennsylvania), August 20, 1794. "Eulogy on Whiskey," *Impartial Herald* (Newburyport, Massachusetts), August 23, 1794. "Eulogy on Whiskey. by Absolum Aimwell, Esq.," *Massachusetts Mercury* (Boston), August 26, 1794. "Eulogy on Whiskey," *American Minerva* (New York), August 27, 1794. "From the Philadelphia Gazette. Eulogy on Whiskey. by Absalom Aimwell, Esq.," *Virginia Chronicle, & General Advertiser* (Norfolk), September 1, 1794. "From the Philadelphia Gazette. Eulogium on Whiskey," *Windham Herald* (Windham, Connecticut), September 6, 1794. "Miscellany. an Eulogy on Whiskey," *Spooner's Vermont Journal* (Windsor, Vermont), September 8, 1794.

24. "Riot at Pittsburgh in Opposition to Excise, July 25. Extract of a Letter from Pittsburgh, Dated July 18, to a Mercantile House in This City," *Litchfield Monitor* (Litchfield, Connecticut), August 6, 1794. "Riot at Pittsburgh, in Opposition to Excise, July 25," *Vermont Gazette* (Bennington), August 15, 1794.

25. "Legislative Acts/Legal Proceedings," *Norwich Packet* (Norwich, Connecticut), August 21, 1794.

26. "Pittsburg; Major Kirkpatrick's; Major Craig," *Philadelphia Gazette* (Philadelphia), August 13, 1794. For General Wayne's activities, see "American Intelligence. Pittsburg, July 2," *Vermont Gazette* (Bennington), August 15, 1794.

27. "Remarks on Excise," *American Minerva* (New York), August 20, 1794. "Remarks on Excise," *Herald* (New York), August 21, 1794. "Remarks on Excise," *Columbian Centinel* (Boston), August 30, 1794. "Remarks on Excise," *New-York Daily Gazette*, September 12, 1794. "Remarks on Excise," *United States Chronicle* (Providence), September 11, 1794. "New-York, September 12. Remarks an Excise," *The City Gazette & Daily Advertiser* (Charleston, South Carolina), October 8, 1794.

be outdone, the Federalist *Gazette of the United States* printed a letter from a supposed Massachusetts farmer claiming possible foreign influence in the uprising by laying the violence at the feet of *"Jacobin Clubs."*[28] The *New-York Daily Gazette* took this one step further, implying that the rebels aimed for complete independence from the new nation while Boston's *American Apollo* and Newburyport's *Morning Star* used a lack of dissenting voices around Pittsburg as evidence of coercive influence by the rebels.[29] The *Salem Gazette* substantiated these reports with a letter from Fort Pitt indicating a local belief that secession was the aim of the insurgency, with political conformity to the rebellion enforced by threat of violence.[30] Stockbridge's *Western Star*, expressing the opinions of farmers in the far west of Massachusetts, undercut the rebels' motivations by pointing out that state excises had existed without complaint prior to the federal excise and asserting these complaints were a pretext, rather than reason, for action.[31] Almost overnight the phrases "Whiskey Insurrection" and "Pittsburg Insurrection" became the standard way for newspapers to refer to this conflict. The media in all quarters had rejected a group which many had previously favored, and even began to actively demonize the insurrectionists.

In the beginning of September 1794, during Washington's efforts at peaceful mediation, a softened tone entered the press, especially in New England. Newbury's *Morning Star* expressed concern on September 2 that whiskey being a potential staple food in western Pennsylvania explained the rebels' actions despite staunchly opposing the rebellion itself.[32] On the same day, New York's *Diary* printed speeches from the "six united nations of white Indians," republished a day later in Hagerstown's *Washington Spy*, providing the sole instance of reporting during the rebellion which outlined rebel rhetoric positively.[33] Yet even this

28. "From the Columbian Centinel," *Gazette of the United States* (Philadelphia), August 26, 1794.

29. "Philadelphia, August 12," *New-York Daily Gazette*, August 26, 1794. "Pittsburg; Commander; Chief," *Columbian Centinel* (Boston), August 20, 1794. "Philadelphia Aug. 9. Pittsburg Insurrection," *American Apollo* (Boston), August 21, 1794. "Philadelphia August 6. Pittsburg Insurrection," *Morning Star* (Newburyport, Massachusetts), August 26, 1794.

30. "United States of America. Pittsburg Insurrection. Baltimore, Aug. 16," *Salem Gazette* (Salem, Massachusetts), August 26, 1794. "Pittsburg, Insurrection, Baltimore, Aug. 16," *New-Hampshire Gazette* (Portsmouth), September 2, 1794.

31. "Pennsylvania; Previous; Excise; Pennsylvania; Congress," *Andrews's Western Star* (Stockbridge, Massachusetts), August 26, 1794.

32. "For the Morning Star. Messrs Robinson & Tucker," *Morning Star* (Newburyport, Massachusetts), September 2, 1794.

33. *The Diary or Loudon's Register* (New York), September 2, 1794. "Legislative Acts/Legal Proceedings," *Washington Spy* (Hagers-Town, Maryland), September 3, 1794.

was transient: the *Diary* published a far more widely distributed note from Trenton days later reestablishing the tone of scorn and enmity towards the insurrection while Connecticut's *Norwich Packet* labeled the insurrectionists as malcontents.[34] This tone turned even more to one of outrage, with the *Massachusetts Mercury* asserting the rebels had raised support through the Jacobin Clubs and accused them of attempting to dictate their will "to the GREAT MASS of the PEOPLE."[35] Newspapers publishing in Baltimore and South Carolina "for the benefit of country subscribers" characterized the rebellion as "the domestic tyranny of an ignorant banditti."[36] Within Pennsylvania itself, reactions to the new violence were mixed: the influence of the rebellion had spread east to Carlisle, where local officials permitted the raising of a whiskey-themed liberty pole, as reported by Elizabethtown's *New-Jersey Journal*, while a letter from Pittsburg published in the *American Apollo* noted that many who opposed the excise were startled by the violence and had no desire to actively support the insurrection.[37] The Democratic Society of Washington published an address in the *Virginia Chronicle* agreeing with the perceived oppression but condemning the actions of the rebellion, and New York's *Greenleaf Journal* concurred by emphasizing that only constitutional measures should have been taken. The rebels' base of potential political support had evaporated.[38] Even

34. "New-York. Saturday Evening, September 6," *The Diary or Loudon's Register* (New York), September 6, 1794. "Jersey Blue's Intended Answer to Captain Whiskey's Intended Speech to the Commissioners at Pittsburgh," *Kline's Carlisle Weekly Gazette* (Carlisle, Pennsylvania), September 10, 1794. "Jerseyblue's Intended Answer to Capt. Whiskey's Intended Speech to the Commissioners at Pittsburgh, If Their Session," *Columbian Gazetteer* (New York), September 11, 1794. "Jersey Blue, Intended Answer in Capt. Whiskey's Intended Speech to the Commissioners at Pittsburgh, If Their Session Continues till Sept. 14, 1794," *Middlesex Gazette* (Middletown, Connecticut), September 13, 1794. "Jersy Blue's Intended Answer to Captain Whiskey's Intended Speech to the Commissioners at Pittsburgh If Their Session," *American Apollo* (Boston), September 18, 1794. "Captain Whiskey," *Oracle of the Day* (Portsmouth, New Hampshire), September 30, 1794. "Secretary; Treasury; Malcontents; Pennsylvania; Southern; Excise," *Norwich Packet* (Norwich, Connecticut), September 4, 1794.

35. "Communications," *Massachusetts Mercury* (Boston), September 9, 1794. "Communicated for Insertion," *Massachusetts Mercury* (Boston), September 12, 1794.

36. "Insurrection of the Maryland and Whisky-Men," *The South-Carolina State-Gazette, & Timothy & Mason's Daily Advertiser* (Charleston), October 1, 1794.

37. "For the American Daily Advertiser. to the Public of the United States Letter IV," *Dunlap and Claypoole's American Daily Advertiser* (Philadelphia), September 2, 1794. "From the American Daily Advertiser. to the People of the United States. Letter IV," *Baltimore Daily Intelligencer*, September 8, 1794. "Pittsburg Insurrection! from the Gazette of the United States," *American Apollo* (Boston), September 11, 1794.

38. "Legislative Acts/Legal Proceedings," *Virginia Chronicle, & General Advertiser* (Norfolk), September 22, 1794. "New-York, Sept. 13," *Greenleaf's New York Journal and Patriotic Register* (New York), September 13, 1794.

outlets which lamented war as terrible, such as Vermont's *Farmer's Library*, showed no sympathies to the rebels.[39] Despite a brief period of greater neutrality in tone in the immediate aftermath of Washington's attempt to negotiate, the press increased both in volume of reporting and in anti-rebel sentiment throughout the nation.[40]

Washington's proclamation summoning the militias of Pennsylvania, Maryland, New Jersey, and Virginia on September 25, 1794 heralded the next shift in the press towards war correspondence with the united front of coverage continuing, particularly in New England. Newburyport's *Impartial Herald* noted on September 27 that troops were on the march to "quell the Insurrection at Pittsburg"[41] and Harford's *American Mercury* published hopes on October 13 that the volunteer militia "may soon return safely to their friends, with a good account of the Enemy.[42] The *Boston Mercury*, and later *New Bedford's Medley*, specifically labelled Washington's army as an anti-insurgent army in October; despite New England contributing no troops to the effort, it remained fully supportive of Washington in his exertion of federal control.[43] True to form, the *Gazette of the United States* confidently predicted the imminent demise of the rebellion.[44] Even Bostonian stargazers took the chance to express their condemnation of the insurrection, with the *Federal Orrery* decrying it as a "flaming meteor . . . composed of the *sulfur* of ANARCHY . . . revolving in the *eccentric path* of JACOBINISM" in a October 23 article republished in New York's *Diary* and echoed in the *Columbian Centinel*.[45] As previously seen, the first signs of any public opinion favoring the rebels were observed in Carlisle, with an officer in the New Jersey cavalry noting the tension between pro- and anti-

39. "Citizen; Commissioners; Excise; Alternative," *The Farmer's Library: Or, Vermont Political & Historical Register* (Rutland, Vermont), September 23, 1794.

40. "Western Insurrection," *Spooner's Vermont Journal* (Windsor, Vermont), September 1, 1794. "Inhabitants; City; Whiskey; Forest," *Gazette of the United States* (Philadelphia), October 11, 1794.

41. "Insurrection; Pittsburg; Carlisle; Sept; American; Danes; Swedes; British; Guernsey," *Impartial Herald* (Newburyport, Massachusetts), September 27, 1794.

42. "New-York; Mr. Jay; Pittsburgh Insurrection," *American Mercury* (Hartford, Connecticut), October 13, 1794.

43. "Boston, Tuesday, October 14, 1794," *Massachusetts Mercury* (Boston), October 14, 1794. "Anti Insurgent Army," *Medley or Newbedford Marine Journal* (New Bedford, Massachusetts), October 24, 1794.

44. "Inhabitants; City; Whiskey; Forest," *Gazette of the United States* (Philadelphia), October 11, 1794.

45. "Orrery-Observatory," *Federal Orrery* (Boston), October 23, 1794. "Insurrection at Pittsburgh," *The Diary or Loudon's Register* (New York), October 30, 1794. "For the Centinel. Worthy Consideration," *Columbian Centinel* (Boston), November 1, 1794.

rebel factions in the town.[46] Yet for all of this fury, the coverage of the conflict ended in much the same anticlimactic way as the rebellion itself: Charleston's *Columbian Herald* published a mere four lines noting that four ringleaders had been extradited to Philadelphia and jailed, and the Brookfield's *Worcester Intelligencer* published the December 30, 1794 proclamation of mass clemency by Henry Lee.[47] The press remained universally supportive of federal forces and largely indifferent to the fate of the rebels through the end of the conflict.

But what of public opinion after Washington quelled the rebellion? In every corner, regardless of political opinions, the papers published support of the President's actions and cast the rebels as part of an undesirable sect of foreign influence. After the departure of federal troops, "Rusticus" penned an ironic poem eulogizing the "Liberty Pole of Lewistown" while praising the virtues of "Law and Constitution" in the *Kline's Carlisle Weekly Gazette* on December 17, 1794.[48] Meanwhile, the Federalist *Gazette of the United States* returned to its party line, attempting to tie together the rebels with the Jacobins not only in politics but extremism, using the rebellion to increase support for Washington's anti-Jacobin policies in an article reprinted in the *Hartford Gazette*.[49] The *Columbian Centinel* and *Worcester Intelligencer* similarly listed the excise as one of "an infinity of *Bones*, which our first antifederalist, then jacobinial, and *now* anarchal *Bone-Pickers* have been mumbling about."[50] In response, the Democratic-Republicans continued to distance themselves ideologically from the insurrectionists, with the Democratic Society of the City of New York publishing a widely distributed statement in *Greenleaf's New York Journal* in which they "*condemned all unconstitutional opposition to the laws of our country*."[51] Worcester's *Mas-*

46. "The Insurgent Gentry. Trenton, Oct. 15," *Times, or, the Evening Entertainer* (Boston), November 1, 1794.
47. "Whiskey; Philadelphia," *Columbian Herald* (Charleston, South Carolina), November 12, 1794. "Legislative Acts/Legal Proceedings," *Worcester Intelligencer: Or, Brookfield Advertiser* (Brookfield, Massachusetts), December 30, 1794.
48. "Poetry," *Kline's Carlisle Weekly Gazette* (Carlisle, Pennsylvania), December 17, 1794.
49. "From the Gazette of the United States," *Hartford Gazette* (Hartford, Connecticut), December 22, 1794.
50. "From the Columbian Centinel. of Political Bones," *Worcester Intelligencer: Or, Brookfield Advertiser* (Brookfield, Massachusetts), January 20, 1795. "Jacobinial" is not capitalized in the original.
51. "Miscellany," *Greenleaf's New York Journal and Patriotic Register*, January 17, 1795. "Legislative Acts/Legal Proceedings," *Dunlap and Claypoole's American Daily Advertiser* (Philadelphia), January 20, 1795. "Legislative Acts/Legal Proceedings," *Independent Gazetteer* (Philadelphia), January 21, 1795. "Legislative Acts/Legal Proceedings," *Aurora General Advertiser* (Philadelphia), January 26, 1795. "From the New-York Journal, & C," *Federal Intelligencer* (Baltimore), January 26, 1795. "From the New-York Journal," *Herald* (New York), January 28, 1795.

sachusetts Spy wrote a political epitaph of the Third Congress, reprinted from Maine to North Carolina, praising Congress for, among other things, having "quelled an insurrection . . . without bloodshed; and to have Restored the confidence of the people in the Government of their choice."[52] This in no way meant the political issue of the excise had passed into irrelevance: quite the contrary, by July 4, 1795 bitter opposition was again being printed, this time in New Jersey, but without any support for violence or condemnation of the federal government's handling of the affair.[53] No public voices which have survived indicate widespread contemporaneous resistance to the exertion of federal power.

Having established the wide disparity in opinion throughout the nation, could the homogeneity of thought during the crisis have come from pro-government propaganda? While theoretically possible, the geographically decentralized nature of the articles from both sides of the political spectrum would have made deliberate manipulation of information difficult for the federal government. Information operations to sway public opinion were decidedly outside Washington's scope despite clear signs of meticulous planning in his campaign against the rebels.[54] Varying lag times from events or publishing from Philadelphia (the central hub of opinion and information surrounding the controversy) naturally arose from the time required for post riders to deliver Philadelphia papers to other regions for republishing. Philadelphia papers also incorporated other regions' perspectives in later editions of papers, albeit with a more significant lag, so the opinions from the seat of government did not inherently drive debate and opinion throughout

---

52. "Massachusetts. Boston, March 18," *Thomas's Massachusetts Spy: Or, The Worcester Gazette* (Worcester), March 25, 1795. "Legislative Acts/Legal Proceedings," *United States Chronicle* (Providence), March 26, 1795. "From the Columbian Centinel. Political Epitaph," *Gazette of the United States* (Philadelphia), March 27, 1795. "Poetry," *Eastern Herald* (Portland, Maine), March 30, 1795. "From the Columbian Centinel," *Andrews's Western Star* (Stockbridge, Massachusetts), March 31, 1795. "Massachusetts. Boston, March 25," *Worcester Intelligencer: Or, Brookfield Advertiser* (Brookfield, Massachusetts), March 31, 1795. "Legislative Acts/Legal Proceedings," *Connecticut Gazette* (New London), April 2, 1795. "Political Epitaph," *Impartial Herald* (Newburyport, Massachusetts), April 3, 1795. "Legislative Acts/Legal Proceedings," *The Philadelphia Gazette & Universal Daily Advertiser* (Philadelphia), April 4, 1795. "Poetry," *North-Carolina Journal* (Halifax, North Carolina), April 13, 1795.

53. "Legislative Acts/Legal Proceedings," *Jersey Chronicle* (Aberdeen, New Jersey), July 4, 1795.

54. Richard A. Ifft, "Treason in the Early Republic: The Federal Courts, Popular Protest, and Federalism During the Whiskey Rebellion," *The Whiskey Rebellion: Past and Present Perspectives*, 172.

the nation. Given the strong sentiment towards freedom of the press and resistance to any form of governmental control over printed materials, as well as the deep divides of partisan politics, any such attempts at control would more likely have ended in more bloodshed than did the excise on whiskey itself.[55]

If the union of opinion was spontaneous, rather than planned, why did publications fall into such uniform opinion? This was doubtless due in part to the unifying effect of Washington: as historian Alan Taylor notes, while both parties fought viciously because they believed the fate of the republic at stake, Washington provided a unifying figure respected by most, if not all.[56] Based on the number and location of articles published over those four years, as well as their content, national sentiment varied by region. Metropolitan areas generally published more reports and opinions on the rebellion while the southern states and rural areas printed far less about the issue until Washington's proclamation on August 7, 1794. Only after this proclamation did national opinion coalesce around a single perspective: Washington's opinion. The handling of information by the rebels themselves also contributed to this coalescence: during the rebellion little information and even less rhetoric emerged from rebel-held areas, as indicated by hand-bills which came through by post-rider.[57] Evidently little news except for successful pacification came to the other states from the formerly rebellious counties, as the *Charleston City Gazette* noted.[58] This precluded potentially winning support since Americans of all political persuasions were heavily invested in the preservation of their fledgling republic: once the rebels appeared willing to spark a civil war or even secede, they seemingly lost any base of public support.[59] Given the lack of serious challenge to the President's assessment, the country naturally rallied once again behind its figurehead, as even the Democratic-Republicans saw him as a beacon of hope.[60]

---

55. Indeed, when tried in the Alien and Sedition Acts, it helped to oust the Federalists from power. See Francis D. Cogliano, *Revolutionary America 1763-1815: A Political History*, 3rd ed. (New York: Routledge, 2017), 167-168.
56. Alan Taylor, *American Revolutions: A Continental History, 1750-1804* (New York: W. W. Norton & Company, Inc., 2016), 410-413.
57. "The following is the Copy of an Hand-Bill, Printed at Pittsburg. the Post-Rider Left That Place," *Daily Advertiser* (New York), August 11, 1794.
58. "Winchester, February 23," *City Gazette & Daily Advertiser* (Charleston, South Carolina), April 4, 1795.
59. Taylor, *American Revolutions*, 409-412.
60. Cogliano, *Revolutionary America 1763-1815*, 164.

Unsurprisingly, reactions to the excise fell largely along party, but not geographic, lines: Federalist papers generally favored the excise while Democratic-Republican papers generally railed against it despite some limited airing of contrary views. However, following Washington's proclamation, papers from both sides aligned in lockstep: while papers occasionally sympathized with the insurrectionists' concerns, all came out hotly against the rebellion, with its added implications of possible secession. Afterwards, there was similar universal praise for Washington and Congress for preserving the union, while Democratic-Republican societies and papers deliberately distanced themselves from the rebellion, decrying the influence of runaway Jacobinism. Importantly, rejection of the rebellion did not indicate that opposition to the excise had waned: such rhetoric returned with a vengeance in 1795. This unity likely occurred not due to any propaganda, but due to a confluence of Washington's influence, limited opinion from the rebels, and popular fear of losing the new republic to civil war. Much as Stephen Boyd noted in 1985, the historical community still knows far too little about the opinions of small farmers and frontiersmen to the rebellion, and this information may have disappeared from the historical record.[61] But what has remained in the form of newspaper articles paints a picture of remarkable unity in crisis despite stark political differences. Perhaps, then, the real story of the Whiskey Rebellion is neither the violent recalcitrance of frontier farmers nor the imposition of federal authority by threat of violence, but rather that the counter-revolutionary impulse pervaded society as a whole, not just Federalist elites in the seat of power.

---

61. Boyd, *The Whiskey Rebellion: Past and Present Perspectives*, 186.

"Good and Sufficient Testimony": The Development of the Revolutionary War Pension Plan

✦✦ MICHAEL BARBIERI ✦✦

One of the greatest sources of information on the American Revolution is the collection of pension applications submitted by American veterans of the war or their families. Over 80,000 files are available to researchers as part of the National Archives and Records Administration microfilm publication M804. Intent on finding some desired morsel of information, however, few researchers probing the collection give much thought to just how these files came into existence in the first place.

The idea of offering pensions to veterans did not originate in the Continental Congress. The British army offered pensions beginning in the late seventeenth century, and the system was well-established by the second half of the eighteenth century. Following England's example prior to the Revolution, the North American colonies provided some relief for soldiers injured while in the service. For example, in May, 1755, Virginia's governor Dinwiddie in a speech read before the House of Burgesses said, "The poor Men who suffered at the Meadows with Colonel Washington I recommend to your Favor, as they were disabled in the Service of their Country."[1] By June, the Burgesses had granted recompense to some of the petitioners.[2]

As fighting in the French and Indian War intensified, more attention came to be paid to the situation of the wounded. On January 10,

1. "The Meadows" refers to the Fort Necessity battle fought on July 3, 1754, between a force commanded by Washington and a larger force of French and Indians. Governor Dinwiddie to House of Burgesses, in H.R. McIlwaine and John Pendleton Kennedy, eds. *Journals of the House of Burgesses of Virginia: 1752-1755, 1756-1758* (Richmond, VA: The Colonial Press, E. Waddey Co. 1909), 231 (*JHB*).
2. *JHB*, 282, 293.

1757, in a portent of things to come in less than two decades, George Washington wrote to the British commander in chief, the Earl of Loudon:

> No Regular Provision is established for the maimed and Wounded, which is a discourageing Reflection and feelingly Complained of. The Soldiers very justly observe, that Bravery is often rewarded with a broken Leg, Arm, or an Incurable Wound, and when they are disabled and not fit for Service they are discharg'd, and reduced to the necessity of begging from Door to Door, or perishing thrô Indigence—It is true, no Instance of this kind has yet appeard—on the contrary, the Assembly have dealt generously by such unfortunate Soldiers who have met with this Fate—But then this is Curtesy—in no wise Compulsory, and a Man may suffer in the Interim of their Sittings.[3]

Compensation for disabled soldiers continued to be an intermittent consideration by the individual colonies up to the start of the Revolution.[4]

The transformation of the disagreement with England from a war of words to armed conflict brought a new approach to compensation for those disabled during service. The Continental Congress began looking at a centralized process and, in November 1775, the "Rules for the Regulation of the Navy of the United Colonies" included a section that set a dollar amount for those officers, marines, and sailors disabled or killed. If killed, the widow or children received the money.[5] Congress dealt with applications on an individual basis.

As weeks went by with the war expanding and hopes for a quick resolution fading, Congress saw the need for a more expansive plan to care for those disabled in combat not just in the navy, but in the land forces as well. Not all agreed with the idea, and Gen. Nathaniel Greene wondered why: "Is it not inhuman to suffer those that have fought nobly in the cause to be reduced to the necessity of geting a support by common Charity. Does this not millitate with the free and independant principles which we are indeavoring to support? Is it not equitable that the State who receives the benefit should be at the expence? ... I cannot see upon what principle any Colony can encourage the Inhabitants to engage in the Army when the state that employs them refuses a support

3. *The Papers of George Washington*, Colonial Series, vol. 4, *9 November 1756–24 October 1757*, ed. W. W. Abbot. (Charlottesville, VA: University Press of Virginia, 1984), 79–93.
4. *JHB: 1770–72*, 209–10, 234.
5. *Journals of the Continental Congress, 1774–1789*, ed. Worthington C. Ford et al. (Washington, D.C., 1904-37), 3:386-7 (*JCC*).

to the unfortunate."[6] In June, 1776, Congress finally appointed a committee of five to "consider what provision ought to be made for such as are wounded or disabled in the land or sea service, and report a plan for that purpose."[7]

The committee set to work and on August 26, 1776, Congress enacted the first national pension legislation.[8] It provided for half-pay to be distributed to officers and enlisted men of the army and navy who became disabled during their service and could no longer serve or earn a living as a result of the injury, and for men who were "wounded in any engagement . . . though not totally diabled." The pay would continue for the duration of the disability. The soldier submitted his petition to a person or board in his state of residence then decided how much to pay him providing it did not exceed the half-pay. The petitioner had to provide a certificate from his commanding officer and the surgeon who cared for him giving the nature of the wound and the engagement in which he received it. Getting Congress off the financial hook—for a while, at least—the legislation said that each state should make the payments "on account of the United States." The states would be reimbursed at some point in the future

The legislation had an interesting proviso: officers and soldiers eligible for a pension but capable of doing garrison or guard duty would become part of a corps of invalids. In like manner, disabled sailors would be given non-combatant duties.[9]

Over a year passed before Congress next addressed pensions. On January 5, 1778, a comprehensive motion regarding pensions—this time for uninjured soldiers—came to the floor for consideration.[10] Debate continued for another five months until a trimmed-down version finally passed on May 15 in which Congress resolved to grant half-pay for seven years to officers who remained in the service until the end of the war. The resolution limited the amount that general officers could receive to the same amount as a colonel. It also required that the officer had taken an oath of allegiance and lived in the United States (thereby eliminating the eligibility of the plethora of foreign officers serving in the American forces). Non-commissioned officers and private soldiers

6. Nathaniel Greene to John Adams, June 2, 1776, *The Adams Papers*, Papers of John Adams, vol. 4, *February–August 1776*, ed. Robert J. Taylor (Cambridge, MA: Harvard University Press, 1979), 4:227–31.
7. *JCC*, 5:469.
8. With no real power, Congress used the word "recommended" when directing the legislation at the states.
9. *JCC*, 5:702–5.
10. *Papers of the Continental Congress, 1774–1789*, roll 30, item 21, 177-9 (*PCC*).

who remained for the duration would receive a one-time reward of eighty dollars at the end of the war.[11]

The debate over pensions continued. A resolution on August 17, 1779, demonstrated the equivocation brought on by lack of funds, lack of centralized power, and the indecisiveness of the members of Congress. The act said that states should reward their soldiers, "either by granting to their officers half pay for life, and proper rewards to their soldiers; or in such other manner as may appear most expedient to the legislatures of the several states."[12] A second resolution regarding the widows of soldiers had a similar tone recommending that the states make such provision "as shall secure to them the sweets of that liberty" for which their husbands died.[13]

In the summer of 1780, Congress again took on the issue of support for the families of officers who died while in the service (the discussion did not include enlisted men). On August 24, the members voted that the provisions of the May 15, 1778, act (half-pay for seven years) would also apply to the unmarried widows of men who died—whether while in the service or after the war. Should the wife also die, the half-pay would go to any orphaned children.[14] Two months later, Congress increased the duration from seven years to life.[15]

Post-war support became a quite serious issue for Congress late in 1782. Men in the army kept track of the legislative action regarding post-war support and it became part of a letter of grievances submitted to Congress by a committee of officers:

> We are grieved to find that our brethren, who retired from service on half-pay, under the resolution of Congress in 1780, are not only destitute of any effectual provision, but are become the objects of obloquy. Their condition has a very discouraging aspect on us who must sooner or later retire, and from every consideration of justice, gratitude and policy, demands attention and redress.
>
> We regard the act of Congress respecting half-pay, as an honorable and just recompense for several years hard service, in which the health and fortunes of the officers have been worn down and exhausted. We see with chagrin the odious point of view in which the citizens of too many of the states endeavor to place the men entitled to it. We hope, for the honor of human nature, that there are none so hardened in the sin of ingratitude, as to deny the justice of the reward.

11. *JCC*, 11:502.
12. *JCC*, 18:958-9.
13. *PCC*, roll 30, item 21, 149.
14. *JCC*, 17:772-3.
15. *PCC*, roll 28, item 19, 6:307.

To correct this situation, the officers wrote that they would be will-ing to drop the half-pay-for-life provision in favor of full pay for a given number of years or a one-time lump-sum payment.[16]

The officers' letter did not materialize in a vacuum. It emerged as part of one of the darkest events for the army—the so-called "New-burgh Conspiracy" during which the possibility of wide-spread mutiny threatened the army. In March, Congress received from Washington a letter and several documents concerning the dangerous activity. He had successfully averted the serious problem and, in one of the letters, wrote down his feelings on the pension issue which echoed what he had writ-ten in 1757. Quoting the officers' letter, Washington wrote:

> if the officers of the army are to be the only sufferers by this revolu-tion; if retiring from the field they are to grow old in poverty, wretched-ness and contempt; if they are to wade through the vile mire of dependency, and owe the miserable remnant of that life to charity, which has hitherto been spent in honor,' then shall I have learned what ingratitude is, then shall I have realized a tale which will embitter every moment of my future life. But I am under no such apprehensions; a country rescued by their arms from impending ruin, will never leave unpaid the debt of gratitude.[17]

A committee took up the issue and returned a suggested resolution recommending full pay on March 22, 1783. Congress quickly passed a shortened version formalizing the proposal. Officers could accept a commutation of half-pay for life in favor of full pay for five years and added the alternative of issuing securities bearing annual interest of six percent.[18] The act helped soothe any left-over mutinous inclinations within the army.

The promise of peace and the imminent disbanding of the army in 1783 prompted even more attention to post-war support for the men. On April 23, a committee reported that the army expected three months' full pay when disbanded. Congress felt that "the expectations of the army are reasonable and very moderate and it is the ardent wish of Congress to make them as happy at the time of their retirement as possible." They resolved to grant all discharged soldiers, including en-listed men, their wish.[19]

In the eight years since the first efforts at a pension plan several pieces of legislation had been enacted, so Congress began work on cre-

16. *PCC*, roll 55, item 42, 6:63-5.
17. *PCC*, roll 171, item 152, 11:134-6.
18. *JCC*, 24:207-10.
19. *PCC*, roll 27, item 19, 4:391-3.

ating one document for administering the pension plan. It took two years but the resolution passed on June 7, 1785, with some changes. Proof of disability now could be shown through "good and sufficient testimony." Further, Congress created a tiered system of pay whereby less seriously disabled officers and men received a proportionately smaller amount. Lastly, each person receiving a pension had to annually take an oath before his county magistrate swearing to his disability.[20]

The formation of a new government under the Constitution led to Congress taking a new look at pensions. On September 29, 1789, President Washington signed into law a single paragraph sent to him by Congress. The new law announced that the federal government, instead of the states, would pay the pensioners directly. The rest of the existing legislation would remain in effect and be reviewed annually.[21]

Congress continued to tinker with the pension legislation. In March 1792 they passed an act saying that veterans not already receiving pensions should apply for them directly to the federal government rather than their home state. It also said that enlisted men could not transfer their pensions to others.[22] There was such restriction on officers.

Fourteen years passed before the next major alteration came along. Early in 1806, the House sent a bill to the Senate who, over the next three months, added several amendments. With little debate, the House accepted the Senate version on April 10, 1806. No other legislation since the original act in August of 1776 had as much impact on pensions as did this bill. The House version had been little more than an extension of the existing legislation but the Senate took a different tack once they received it. Most importantly, the amendments expanded the scope of the original laws to include veterans of state units as well as militia. Further, because the numerous modifications of the original wartime legislation had made applying for and administering pensions somewhat confusing, the new act voided all the previous legislation. Congress started anew.[23]

The next big step came in 1818. Prior to that time, a pension could be awarded solely on the basis of disability or death (with the exception of officers who served for the duration). The new act provided that ALL officers and enlisted men who served in the army or navy, disabled

20. *JCC*, 28:435-7.
21. *The Public Statutes at Large of the United States of America*, ed. Richard Peters, Esq. (Boston: Charles C. Little and James Brown, 1845-1866), 1:95 (*PSL*).
22. *PSL*, 2:243-5.
23. *PSL*, 2:376.

or not, would be eligible for a lifetime pension. Some important provisos appeared in the bill. First, an applicant had to prove he had served a total of at least nine months (which did not have to be consecutive). More importantly, he also had to show that he "by reason of his reduced circumstances in life, shall be, in need of assistance from his country for his support." Lastly, applicants had to relinquish any other pension claims they may have. Officers received twenty dollars per month and enlisted men eight.

The act also set out the administrative process. The applicant had to make a declaration under oath before a judge describing his service, and provide other evidence of his service and need. If the judge felt the claim to be proper, he forwarded it to the Secretary of War who reviewed the application and, if satisfactory, added the applicant to the pension list.[24]

Anyone who has worked with the pension files extensively knows that this 1818 legislation prompted a large number of applications. So many, in fact, that the overall expense of pension payments increased dramatically. The financial stress and charges of false claims of poverty caused Congress to create a corrective act in 1820. The new legislation required that each person who had been granted a pension under the 1818 act, and each new applicant, submit a certified account of his estate and income. The Secretary of War would review the accounts and strike from the pension list any who, in his opinion, did not need assistance. Any pensioner who had been placed on the list prior to 1818 and who had dropped that pension in order to receive the benefits of the latest act would have the earlier pension restored.[25] The new directive reduced the number of pensioners by several thousand.[26]

The requirement for a certified account created its own set of problems. Large numbers of pensioners dropped from the list appealed the decision for a variety of reasons. One of the more common reasons was erroneous assessment of property. Another was that life conditions and financial situation constantly change. The volume of appeals prompted the House to pass a bill addressing the situation in March, 1822. Disliking the bill, the Senate postponed debate indefinitely; the House developed a second bill in December. Again, members of the Senate tried

24. *PSL,* 3:410-11.
25. *PSL,* 3:569.
26. *Revolutionary War Pension and Bounty-Land-Warrant Application Files* (Washington: National Archives and Records Administration, 1974), 2. This is a very handy guide to the pension papers. It includes, among other things, a history of the collection and its administration, a list of the books in the collection files, and a listing of the range of files on each microfilm roll.

to kill the bill by offering several amendments.[27] An amended version passed the Senate but the House rejected one amendment. In two very close votes the Senate agreed and the bill became law.[28] The final version directed the Secretary of War to reinstate those who had been dropped but had subsequently proven their need for support provided that the applicant "has not disposed of or transferred his property, or any portion thereof, with a view to obtain a pension."[29]

Six years passed before the next major modification to the pension legislation. On May 15, 1828, Congress granted full pay for life to the surviving officers and enlisted men of the Continental Line who had served for the duration, but limited the amount to a maximum of a captain's pay. The act excluded enlisted men already on the pension list. Applicants did not have to provide proof of need, only their time in service.[30]

The final and most beneficial of the pension acts came nearly a half-century after the close of the war. Legislation enacted on June 7, 1832, expanded the 1828 provisions for full pay to more people by altering the time-in-service requirement to two years. Those who had served a shorter period but more than six months received pay on a graduated scale. This is the first act under the Constitution that allowed the pension to be paid to widows and children.[31]

Congress again addressed the situation of families of veterans in 1836. The act passed in August 1780 allowed the families of deceased officers to collect the veteran's benefits but only for seven years. Following the expiration of that proviso in 1794, it took a special act of Congress for a widow to collect any pension. On July 4, 1836, Congress passed legislation that provided a pension for post-1818 veterans but included a section that allowed the widow of any veteran eligible for a pension to apply for her husband's pension provided she had married the veteran prior to his leaving the service. Some of the most extensive applications resulted from this act as families tried to prove the veteran's service and the timing of the marriage.[32]

A handful of acts of Congress happened in next forty years. Legislation in 1838 granted pensions for five years to widows whose marriage had taken place before 1794.[33] Another in 1848 provided pensions for

27. *Senate Journal.* 17th Cong., 2d sess., February 21, 1823, 12:174-5.
28. Ibid., February 28, 1823, 12:221-2.
29. *PSL*, 3:782.
30. *PSL*, 4:269-70.
31. *PSL*, 4:529.
32. *PSL*, 5:127-8.
33. *PSL*, 5:303.

life for widows married before 1800.[34] Legislation in 1853 and 1855 removed any restrictions on the date of marriage.[35] The last legislation relating to widows of Revolutionary War veterans appeared on March 9, 1878, and stated that the widows of veterans who had served for at least fourteen days or had been in any engagement could apply for a pension for life.

There are hundreds of thousands of pages to explore in the M804 pension files. Even more would have been available but for fires in 1800 and 1814 that destroyed most of the early papers. Those that exist contain both historical and genealogical information applicable to the interests of a wide variety of researchers. There are also nearly seventy journals, diaries, and other record books in the files. In addition to the original documents, the files are arranged alphabetically on 2,670 rolls of microfilm available for viewing at several NARA reading rooms across the country. They are also available and searchable on-line at the fee-based Fold3 website.

It takes patience to work with the pension files. They contain many pages that will not be of value to you but you will often not know that until you read them. Your nerves—and your eyes—will be tested trying to decipher the several styles of handwriting that appear in each file—even on a single page. You will be frustrated by the frequent lack of detail and occasional alterations discrepancies that reveal the effects of time on human memory. In spite of that, the information—even only bits and pieces—that you do recover will make it worth your while. As a bonus, reading the pension files will bring you quite close to the people of a different time. It's time travel. Give it a try.

34. *PSL*, 9:265.
35. *PSL*, 10:154, 616.

AUTHOR BIOGRAPHIES

Mark R. Anderson

Mark R. Anderson is an independent historian and retired US Air Force officer. He earned his BA in history from Purdue University and an MA in military studies from American Military University. He is the author of *The Battle for the Fourteenth Colony: America's War of Liberation in Canada, 1774-1776, The Invasion of Canada by the Americans, 1775-1776: As Told through Jean-Baptiste Badeaux's Three Rivers Journal and New York Captain William Goforth's Letters, Down the Warpath to the Cedars: Indians' First Battles in the Revolution*, and contributed to *The 10 Key Campaigns of the American Revolution*.

Jordan Baker

Jordan Baker holds a BA and MA in History from North Carolina State University. A lover of all things historical, he concentrates his research and writing, and maintains his own blog, https://eastindiabloggingco.com, on the history of the Atlantic World.

Michael Barbieri

A life-long Vermonter, Mike has spent over forty years researching and interpreting the Revolution with a concentration on the northern theater. He has taught history at high school and college levels and has given innumerable presentations on the eighteenth century. In 1974, Mike helped form Whitcomb's Rangers and subsequently based his master's thesis on the original unit. He worked for a number of years at the Lake Champlain Maritime Museum and, now semi-retired, is active supporting the Hubbardton and Mount Independence state historic sites and transcribing documents for Fort Ticonderoga.

Bill Bleyer

Bill Bleyer is the author of *George Washington's Long Island Spy Ring: A History and Tour Guide*. He is coauthor, with Harrison Hunt, of *Long Island and the Civil War* and author of *Sagamore Hill: Theodore Roosevelt's Summer White House, Fire Island Lighthouse: Long Island's Welcoming Beacon*, and *Long Island and the Sea: A Maritime History*. A prize-winning staff writer for *Newsday* for thirty-three years, Bleyer has been an adjunct professor at Webb Institute, the naval architecture college in Glen Cove, New York, and Hofstra University.

Joseph Lee Boyle

Joseph Lee Boyle attended Towson State, University of South Carolina, and Saint Joseph's University. He worked for the National Park Service for thirty-two years, retiring as historian at Valley Forge. His first book was *From Redcoat to Rebel: The Thomas Sullivan Journal*, and he has published two volumes of the Ephraim Blaine papers, and two volumes of the Samuel Hodgdon papers. Taken from newspaper accounts, he has also compiled two volumes of deserters during the American Revolution, and is working on a third. His eight volumes of documents written from Valley Forge has been published by Heritage Books.

Todd W. Braisted

Todd Braisted is an author and researcher of Loyalist military studies. Since 1979, Braisted has amassed and transcribed over 40,000 pages of Loyalist and related material from archives and private collections around the world. He is author of *Grand Forage 1778: The Battleground Around New York City* and has been a guest historian on episodes of "Who Do You Think You Are?" (CBC) and "History Detectives" (PBS). He is the creator of royalprovincial.com, the largest website dedicated to Loyalist military studies. Braisted is a Fellow in the Company of Military Historians and member of the State of New Jersey American Revolution 250th Advisory Commission.

Jonathan Curran

Jonathan Curran is a native of Massachusetts, U.S. Army infantry officer, and graduate student at George Washington University. He received his under-graduate degree at the United States Military Academy and took an eight-year sabbatical from academia before returning in preparation for a teaching assignment at his alma mater. He specializes in military history and enjoys examining smaller and lesser studied conflicts.

Robert S. Davis

Robert S. Davis is senior professor of History at Wallace State College, Hanceville, Alabama. His many publications include several articles and books on the American Revolution in Georgia and South Carolina, including for the online *Journal of the American Revolution* and *Southern Campaigns of the American Revolution*.

John DeLee

John DeLee developed a fascination with history while growing up in south Mississippi, where he enjoyed early American and frontier history focusing on the role of the US Army in those theaters. He holds a BS in American History from the United States Military Academy, and is currently pursuing graduate studies, focusing upon the development of American Indian policy. After traveling around the country and the world with the military, John enjoys exposing his friends and family to local history, exploring the outdoors, and settling into his "permanent" home.

Douglas J. Dorney, Jr.

Douglas R. Dorney, Jr. is an independent researcher with a particular interest in the southern states during the Revolutionary War. He is currently researching pension applications from South Carolina and Virginia to add to his demographic studies of other southern states. His article on the first invasion of North Carolina in 1780 was recently published in the *Journal of the Society for Army Historical Research*. He is a licensed architect specializing in higher education, science, and technology projects. He holds degrees in architecture from the University of North Carolina at Charlotte and lives in Chapel Hill, North Carolina, with his wife and two sons.

Gary Ecelbarger

Gary Ecelbarger has written seven books, co-written three others and is also the author of two dozen essays, journal and magazine articles about past events and personalities in American history. He claims ten direct-line ancestors who served as Patriot soldiers in the American Revolution. Born and raised in Western New York, ten miles upriver from Niagara Falls, Ecelbarger obtained his MS at the University of Wisconsin-Madison and has lived in Virginia for over twenty-five years with his wife and three children. He is currently writing a single-year campaign biography of George Washington.

John Ferling

John Ferling taught American history for forty years, mostly at the University of West Georgia. He is the author of numerous books on Colonial America, the American Revolution, and the Early Republic. His books include biographies of George Washington and John Adams, *Almost a Miracle*, a history of the War of Independence, and *Whirlwind*, a history of the American Revolution. His most recent book is *Winning Independence: The Decisive Years of the Revolutionary War, 1778-1781*.

Brian Gerring

Brian Gerring is a retired US Army soldier who served his final twenty-five years in the Army's Special Forces, which included multiple combat deployments to Afghanistan and Iraq. He has worked with and trained military personnel worldwide. He gained his interest in all things related to the military as a young boy during America's Bicentennial celebration, during which his family was involved in Revolutionary War re-enacting. He holds a BS degree in Strategic Studies and Defense and a MA degree in Military History from Norwich University.

Don N. Hagist

Don N. Hagist is managing editor of *Journal of the American Revolution* and an independent researcher specializing in the British army in the American Revolution. His books include *Noble Volunteers: The British Soldiers Who Fought The American Revolution*; *The Revolution's Last Men: the Soldiers Behind the Photographs*; *British Soldiers, American War*; *Wives, Slaves, and Servant Girls*;

A British Soldier's Story: Roger Lamb's Narrative of the American Revolution, and *General Orders: Rhode Island.*

MICHAEL C. HARRIS

Michael C. Harris is a graduate of the University of Mary Washington and the American Military University. He has worked for the National Park Service in Fredericksburg, Virginia, Fort Mott State Park in New Jersey, and the Pennsylvania Historical and Museum Commission at Brandywine Battlefield. He has conducted tours and staff rides of many of the east coast battlefields. Michael is certified in secondary education and currently teaches in the Philadelphia region. He is the author of two books on the Philadelphia Campaign: *Brandywine: A Military History of the Battles that Lost Philadelphia but Saved America, September 11, 1777* and *Germantown: A Military History of the Battle for Philadelphia, October 4, 1777.*

GEORGE KOTLIK

George Kotlik studied British colonial North American history at Oxford University. His interests include Loyalists, the eighteenth-century North American frontier, the Great War for the Empire, the Imperial Crisis, and the American Revolutionary War.

ARTHUR S. LEFKOWITZ

Arthur S. Lefkowitz is an independent historian whose books tackle offbeat but interested subjects that present a research challenge. His most recent book is *Colonel Hamilton and Colonel Burr: The Revolutionary War Lives of Alexander Hamilton and Aaron Burr.* His other books are *The Long Retreat: The Calamitous Defense of New Jersey 1776; The American Turtle Submarine; George Washington's Indispensable Men: The 32 Aides-de-Camp Who Helped Win American Independence; Benedict Arnold's Army; Eyewitness Images from the American Revolution; and Benedict Arnold in the Company of Heroes.* Arthur has an BA degree from New York University and an MBA degree from Long Island University.

MIKE MATHENY

Mike Matheny is an Adjutant General (Human Resources) officer in the U.S. Army and currently an instructor at the United States Military Academy where he teaches American History. He holds a MA degree in history from the University of Maryland and a BA degree in history from James Madison University.

CHRISTIAN McBURNEY

Christian McBurney resides in the Washington, D.C. area and is an independent historian. He is the author of *George Washington's Nemesis: The Outrageous Treason and Unfair Court Martial of General Charles Lee during the Revolutionary War; The Rhode Island Campaign: The First French and American Operation of the Revolutionary War; Kidnapping the Enemy: The Special Operations to Capture Generals Charles Lee & Richard Prescott*, and *Abductions in the*

American Revolution: Attempts to Kidnap George Washington, Benedict Arnold, and Other Military and Civilian Leaders. He is also the founder, publisher, and editor of the *Review of Rhode Island History*, at www.smallstatebighistory.com.

JUSTIN MCHENRY

Justin McHenry is the University Archivist at American Public University Systems. He received his undergraduate degree from Shepherd University and his master's degree in history from West Virginia University. He has written and published on a variety of historical topics. Of particular interest has been the Medical Department during the American Revolution and the characters involved in running it. He lives in West Virginia with his wife and two daughters.

RAND MIRANTE

Previously a lawyer with McGraw-Hill, Rand Mirante is a fundraiser for Princeton University; he graduated from Princeton and Harvard Law School. For a number of years, he taught Treason: From Henry V to John Walker Lindh in Princeton's Writing Program, which included treatments of Benedict Arnold by John Marshall and Mercy Otis Warren. He has written *Medusa's Head*, a biography of the regicide Joseph Fouché, Napoleon's sinister and chameleonic police minister. Rand has given talks on the 1776-77 campaign to alumni, federal judges, and Washington's descendants, and has lectured on a variety of topics ranging from the fall of New France to the Berlin Airlift on "Princeton Journeys" trips on the St. Lawrence, Danube, and Elbe Rivers and to Normandy.

DAVID PRICE

David Price is the author of *John Haslet's World: An Ardent Patriot, the Delaware Blues, and the Spirit of 1776: The Road To Assunpink Creek: Liberty's Desperate Hour and the Ten Crucial Days of the American Revolution*, and *Rescuing The Revolution: Unsung Patriot Heroes and the Ten Crucial Days of America's War for Independence*. His Revolutionary War blog "Speaking of Which" is featured at dpauthor.com. A historical interpreter at Washington Crossing Historic Park in Pennsylvania and Princeton Battlefield State Park in New Jersey, David is a contributing author to "An American Revolution Diary: Reliving Ten Crucial Days of 1776-77" on the Princeton Battlefield Society's website and the recipient of a Sons of the American Revolution Certificate of Appreciation. His work has been recommended by the American Revolution Podcast, the Princeton Battlefield Society, and Ten Crucial Days.org.

JOHN U. REES

John U. Rees, a lifelong resident of Bucks County, Pennsylvania, has been writing about common soldiers' experiences in the War for American Independence for over 30 years, on subjects ranging from battle studies, army food, and the soldier's burden, to army wagons and watercraft, campaign shelters, Continental Army conscription, and women with the army. He has authored over 150 articles, and one book, *They Were Good Soldiers: African Americans*

Serving in the Continental Army, 1775-1783. An online compendium of articles on African Americans in the Revolutionary era is available at http://tinyurl.com/jureesarticles.

JOHN A. RUDDIMAN

John Ruddiman is an Associate Professor of History at Wake Forest University. His 2014 book, *Becoming Men of Some Consequence: Youth and Military Service in the Revolutionary War*, explores the lives and choices of young men in the Continental army. His current research explores the place of slavery in soldiers' travel writing during the War of American Independence and the diverse relationships among American and European soldiers and enslaved people. Across these projects, his work as a historian of Revolutionary America explores how people built their lives, reshaped their communities, and constructed meaning for themselves and for posterity.

JAMES M. SMITH

James M. Smith graduated with BS degree from Virginia Commonwealth University and lives in King William County, Virginia. It is his hope to write a political, not military, history of the revolution—the history that John Jay asked Charles Thomson, the secretary to the Continental Congress, to write, but which never got written—telling the story from the point of view of the Loyalists as well as the Patriots. He believes it is important to understand that the American Revolution was as much a civil war as it was a revolution.

SCOTT M. SMITH

After a thirty year career on Wall Street, Scott retired in 2014 to pursue a lifelong passion to write. His cybersecurity novel, *Darkness is Coming*, won Distinguished Favorite in the Thriller category in the NYC Big Book Award competition. In 2017, he began researching the life and times of Nathan Hale, the official hero of his adopted home state of Connecticut. The effort resulted in a biographical novel, entitled *But One Life*, as well as whetted Scott's appetite to further explore this period in American history.

DAVID O. STEWART

David O. Stewart, formerly a lawyer, writes books of history and historical fiction, including most recently *The New Land*, which recounts the experience of the Louisbourg expedition of 1758 through the eyes of German immigrants to America, and *George Washington: The Political Rise of America's Founding Father*. His other works are *The Summer of 1787: The Men Who Invented the Constitution*, winner of the Washington Writing Award as Best Book of 2007, *Impeached: The Trial of President Andrew Johnson; American Emperor: Aaron Burr's Challenge to Jefferson's America*, and *Madison's Gift: Five Partnerships That Built America*. He has twice won the History Prize of the Society of the Cincinnati, The George Washington Memorial Award of the George Washington Masonic National Memorial Association, and the William H. Prescott Award of the National Society of Colonial Dames of America.

Gregory J. W. Urwin

Gregory J. W. Urwin, a recent past president of the Society for Military History, is a professor of history at Temple University. He earned his PhD at the University of Notre Dame, and has published nine books and many articles, essays, and reviews. He is now researching a social history of Lord Charles Cornwallis' 1781 Virginia campaign. Urwin is a Fellow of the Company of Military Historians, Senior Fellow at the Foreign Policy Research Institute's Center for the Study of America and the West, Academic Fellow of the Foundation for Defense of Democracies, and general editor for the Campaigns and Commanders Series from University of Oklahoma Press.

Richard J. Werther

Richard J. Werther is a retired CPA and history enthusiast living in Novi, Michigan. He studied business management at Bucknell University in Lewisburg, Pennsylvania.

Jason Yonce

Jason Yonce graduated from Pittsburg State University where he completed his thesis work under the direction of Dr. Chris Childers. His interests include the later careers of the constitutional framers, constitutional history, and post-Reconstruction southern politicians. He lives in Virginia Beach, Virginia.

Andrew A. Zellers-Frederick

Andrew A. Zellers-Frederick earned a BA in History from Temple University, an MA in History from La Salle University, and a Historic Preservation Certificate from Bucks County Community College. He has served with the National Park Service at Independence and Colonial National Historical Parks; and as the executive director of Historic RittenhouseTown, the Masonic Library & Museum of Pennsylvania, the Woodlands Trust, and the Northampton County Historical & Genealogical Museum. Also, he was the Director of the Historic Jamestowne Fund for The Colonial Williamsburg Foundation.

INDEX